Beggar
Your Neighbours

Beggar Your Neighbours

Apartheid Power in Southern Africa

JOSEPH HANLON

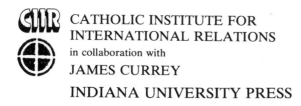

CATHOLIC INSTITUTE FOR
INTERNATIONAL RELATIONS
in collaboration with
JAMES CURREY
INDIANA UNIVERSITY PRESS

Catholic Institute for International Relations (CIIR)
22 Coleman Fields, Islington, London N1 7AF

James Currey Ltd.
54b Thornhill Square, Islington, London N1 1BE

Indiana University Press
Bloomington, Indiana 47405

© CIIR 1986
First published in 1986

British Library Cataloguing in Publication Data
Beggar Your Neighbours
Hanlon, Joseph

1. South Africa — Foreign relations — Africa, Southern
2. Southern — Foreign relations — South Africa
1. Title
327'.0968   DT771.A356

ISBN Cased 0-85255-307-2 (James Currey)
     Paper 0-85255-305-6 (James Currey)
     Cased 0-946848-36-X (CIIR)
     Paper 0-946848-27-0 (CIIR)

Set at CIIR and Russell Press, Bertrand Russell House,
Gamble Street, Forest Road West, Nottingham NG7 4ET

Printed in England by Villiers Publications,
26a Shepherds Hill, London N6

Contents

List of Maps

Acknowledgements

This book would have been impossible without the help of more than a hundred people who provided information, introductions, leads, suggestions, advice, guidance, and hospitality. People opened their houses and files to us. Confidential documents found their way into our hands. Colleagues read early drafts and commented on them and debated with us. Many of those who helped did so on condition that they would not be identified. It would be invidious to identify some of those who were so important to this project and not others, so we would simply like to thank all those who helped and say that we hope they feel it was worth their effort.

The author and publishers would like to acknowledge the kindness of Penguin Books in allowing them to make use of maps prepared for *Apartheid's Second Front* by Joseph Hanlon (Penguin 1986). That book is a useful introduction to the subjects treated here.

Author and Contributors

Dr Joseph Hanlon was correspondent in Mozambique for the BBC, the *Guardian* and various financial magazines from 1979 to 1984. His previous books include *Mozambique: The Revolution Under Fire* (Zed Books, London, 2nd ed. 1985), *SADCC: Progress, Projects and Prospects* (Economist Intelligence Unit, London, 1985) and *Apartheid's Second Front* (Penguin, London 1986).

Dr John Daniel spent 11 years at the University of Swaziland where he was Associate Professor of Political Science and Director of the Social Science Research Unit. He was forced to leave in 1985, and became a Research Fellow at the Free University of Amsterdam.

Teresa Smart was a teacher and researcher in southern Africa from 1980 until 1985 and is now coordinator of mathematics at Islington Sixth Form Centre, London.

Paul Spray has worked as an economist in Botswana and Lesotho, and is now a staff member of the Catholic Institute for International Relations.

Colin Stoneman is an economist and is Leverhulme Research Fellow at the Centre for Southern African Studies at York University. He is the editor of *Zimbabwe's Inheritance* (Macmillan, 1981) and the forthcoming *Zimbabwe's Prospects*.

Currencies

1985 exchange rates

		US$1	UK£1
Angola	Kwanza (Kw)	30.2	39.0
Botswana	Pula (P)	1.75	2.26
Lesotho	Maloti* (M)	1.92	2.52
Malawi	Kwacha (K)	1.78	2.34
Mozambique	Metical (Mt)	43	56
Swaziland	Emalangeni* (E)	1.92	2.52
Zambia	Kwacha (K)	2.36	3.04
Zimbabwe	Dollar (Z$)	1.56	2.00

*The forms quoted are plurals, these being the basis of the abbreviations. The singular forms are *loti* and *lilangeni*.

Abbreviations

Acronyms are explained on first occurrence and in the index.

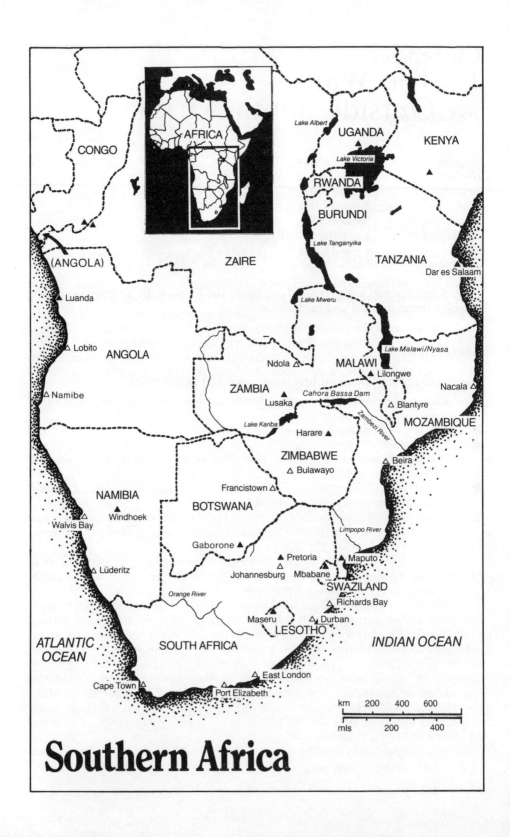

Southern Africa

1. The War Outside South Africa

In October 1985, the Australian Foreign Minister explained his goverment's policy towards South Africa: 'We want to bring it to its senses, and we want to do so before the violence in South Africa spreads beyond its borders.'[1]

One of the main purposes of this book is to demonstrate that this widely-shared perception is dangerously wrong. For years Pretoria has been waging a war in defence of apartheid well beyond its borders, with severe consequences for its neighbours. The occupation of Namibia, declared illegal by the United Nations twenty years ago, is clear for all to see. But elsewhere, because the South African offensive is largely covert, aggression against the neighbouring states is far more widespread than has been appreciated in the West. Since 1980, in the eight majority ruled states of the region, South Africa has:

- invaded three capitals (Lesotho, Botswana, Mozambique) and four other countries (Angola, Swaziland, Zimbabwe, and Zambia);
- tried to assassinate two prime ministers (Lesotho and Zimbabwe);
- backed dissident groups that have brought chaos to two countries (Angola and Mozambique) and less serious disorder in two others (Lesotho and Zimbabwe);
- disrupted the oil supplies of six countries (Angola, Botswana, Lesotho, Malawi, Mozambique, and Zimbabwe); and
- attacked the railways providing the normal import and export routes of seven countries (Angola, Botswana, Malawi, Mozambique, Swaziland, Zambia, Zimbabwe).

More than 100,000 people have been killed, most of them starved to death in Mozambique because South African-backed rebel activity prevented drought relief. Famine was used as a weapon of war.

More than one million people have been displaced. The largest single group is Angolans fleeing various South African invasions. But all the majority-ruled states have had to care for refugees of South African attacks and destabilisation.

In purely financial terms, the cost is immense. It was detailed by the Southern African Development Coordination Conference (SADCC), the economic organisation of the majority-ruled states of the region, in a memorandum reproduced as Appendix 1. Over the five-year period 1980 to 1984 South Africa cost the region $10,000 million — more than all the foreign aid these states received in the same period. The biggest single component ($3bn) was direct additional military expenditure.

But most of the $10bn was the cost of South Africa's attacks on the economies of the neighbouring states — direct war damage ($1.6bn); higher transport and

1

energy costs due to disruption ($1bn); losses of production, exports, and other revenue ($1.8bn); and lost and deferred economic development ($2 bn). Thus the price of destabilisation is not simply seen in the dead and displaced, and in the enlarged military budgets. It is also seen in lost development and reduced living standards. Furthermore they reinforce each other. Military action creates economic havoc. Economic havoc lowers morale amongst defence forces, and fosters dissatisfaction and a sense of hopelessness. The ordinary people of the region are suffering so that minority rule can continue in South Africa.

Deliberate strategy

These actions are part of a coherent South African strategy to use the neighbouring states in the defence of apartheid. The neighbours are wanted as a barrier against guerrillas — and thus, it is naively hoped, against insurrection inside South Africa. But Pretoria also wants to use them both as hostages to head off international sanctions, and as a useful export market in the region for South African industry (strategically important in its efforts to become self-sufficient in the face of sanctions). In addition, disruption and poverty in the neighbouring states is used for propaganda at home and abroad, as 'proof' that black majority rule does not work. Finally, cross-border military activity justifies the growing power of military leaders in the South African government.

As will be seen in the following chapters, these goals are in part conflicting. Furthermore, inside South Africa there are different assessments of the neighbours in military, diplomatic, and business circles. This leads to disagreements within South Africa and to contradictory actions against the neighbours, which sometimes seem to have no obvious pattern.

Economic power

The military attacks catch press headlines, but outside Angola and Mozambique South Africa's economic power in the region is in some ways more critical. South Africa dominates the economies of the three smallest states (Botswana, Lesotho and Swaziland). It is the main trading partner for Zimbabwe and Malawi and the main source of imports to Zambia. Zimbabwe is the most industrialised of the region's majority-ruled states and is pivotal in any independent economic development — yet South African corporations have a very large stake. The Anglo American Corporation of South Africa is everywhere, even involved with diamond mining in Angola. There are 275,000 legal migrant workers from the region in South Africa; half are from Lesotho and they provide the country's main source of income, while nearly 60,000 come from Mozambique. Finally, South Africa dominates transport. Its ports and railways handle most imports and exports for Lesotho and Botswana, half for Zambia, Zimbabwe, and Swaziland, and increasing amounts for Malawi; a single South African company controls most forwarding of imports and exports, even those passing through Mozambique. The dependence of the region is summarised in Tables 1-3 of the Statistical Annex.

This gives South Africa immense power over its neighbours. The government and university academics talk openly of 'economic levers' which can be used to force neighbouring states to be amenable. While the West has yet to make up its mind about sanctions against South Africa, South Africa has already imposed sanctions against its neighbours, and demonstrated their effectiveness.[2] All of the majority-ruled states that have transport links with South Africa have been subject to embargoes, border closures, and rail and port delays. Sometimes these are imposed as punishment for an anti-South African statement in a public forum like the UN or OAU, but more often it is an attempt to extract political concessions, such as the signing of non-aggression pacts. This economic power is also used, often by private companies rather than the government, to undermine efforts by governments to delink from South Africa. But the most important role of economic power is to create dependence, which in turn allows South Africa and its allies to say that sanctions against South Africa would rebound on the neighbours.

Often economic and military power work in tandem. For example, Zimbabwean imports and exports are forced to go through South Africa both by South African commandos and South African-backed sabotage of the railways in Mozambique, and by South African shipping agencies and South African Railways, which make it difficult to send cargo through Mozambique.

The neighbouring states are also of direct economic importance to South Africa. They are firstly a useful source of foreign exchange. The region imports goods worth around $2,400 million from South Africa — and sends only $400 million in the other direction.[3] Even after other payments are taken into account, South Africa has a balance of payments surplus with the region of at least $1,500 million a year. What this means is that foreign exchange earned by the majority-ruled states in exports to Europe, the United States and Japan (often under special agreements for least developed countries) becomes available for South Africa. It is a valuable amount, some 10% of South Africa's total export earnings.

South Africa's exports to the region are largely manufactures and services, and as such also play a more specific role. South Africa is a newly industrialised country, like India or Brazil; furthermore, that industrialisation is seen as an essential step toward self-sufficiency in arms and other production in the face of likely sanctions. The internal market is small, and in normal economic conditions most South African manufactured goods are not competitive on the world market. Thus the neighbouring states are not simply a source of revenue to South Africa — they are also a vital and captive market for its small, protected, monopolised manufacturing industry.

Another way of putting this is that what white South Africa is defending is not merely a set of racial taboos but an economic system. This system concentrates wealth inside South Africa, and also allows South Africa to benefit from the whole region. 'Apartheid' in this book is shorthand for that whole system.

This brings South Africa directly into conflict with regional attempts to delink and develop more independently. It is important to distinguish between economic dependence on South Africa, much of which is inherited from the colonial era, and actual economic sabotage. But the dependence itself is intrinsically dangerous to the neighbouring states. It provides the 'economic levers' — pressure points for destabilisation and the ties that mean sanctions will hurt the neighbours. On a more subtle, day-to-day level, these ties are also self-reinforcing. It is not that South African companies or their agents take deliberate political decisions to sabotage — though there have been instances of that. Rather, perfectly logical business decisions by South African companies often in practice work against the interests of the neighbouring states and in the interests of apartheid.

The majority-ruled states of the region have recognised this. With the independence of Zimbabwe in 1980, they formed SADCC 'to liberate our economies from their dependence on the Republic of South Africa, to overcome the imposed economic fragmentation, and to co-ordinate our efforts toward regional and national economic development'. This marked a psychological turning point in the region — the majority-ruled states were working together and there was a genuine opportunity for coordinated development that reduced dependence. The founding of SADCC came just after P.W. Botha became Prime Minister of South Africa, espousing a 'total strategy' to defeat a 'total Marxist onslaught' against apartheid. SADCC and the neighbouring states became one of South Africa's main targets, and regional relationships changed dramatically. Hence 1980 is taken as the main starting point of this book.

This study thus has four objectives:

● to document military and economic destabilisation since 1980;
● to show how this is related to the goals of various interest groups in South Africa, principally the retention of apartheid;
● to demonstrate that continued economic dependence on South Africa is seen in Pretoria as essential to the defence of apartheid, and thus to look at dependence and how it is maintained; and
● to consider attempts by the majority-ruled states to reduce dependence.

This book is therefore about power — the economic, military, political, and social power of South Africa in eight neighbouring states. It details the vast power South Africa actually wields and shows how it is used. It looks at attempts to delink from South Africa and to reduce that power. An important subsidiary issue is to consider how forces inside and outside the eight states support or oppose that process of delinking, and to·ask sometimes embarrassing questions about how groups in the various states contribute to their own dependence on South Africa. With such a picture clearly in view, it is possible to explain the sometimes contradictory actions taken by the neighbouring states as well as to look at the best ways to support them.

The eight states in the study are Angola, Botswana, Lesotho, Malawi, Mozambique, Swaziland, Zambia, and Zimbabwe. Together with Tanzania they form the Southern African Development Coordination Conference (SADCC). Angola, Botswana, Mozambique, Zambia, Zimbabwe, and Tanzania form the Front Line states. Tanzania has not been included in this study. Except for Angola control of its diamond marketing, there seems little evidence of South African power there.

Namibia is also excluded, for the opposite reason to Tanzania. South African power there is overwhelming and overt. Namibia is an illegally occupied territory and so, *de facto*, a colony; the issue there is fundamentally different from South African attempts to impose neo-colonial rule on the other states in the region.[4] When Namibia becomes independent, however, it will face the same problems as the eight countries in this study. Indeed, South Africa is today creating in Namibia the kind of divided political structure and dependent economy that will be weak and easily destabilised after independence.[5]

This book is not about South Africa but because of it. The war against the eight neighbours is a direct result of apartheid and of the liberation struggle in South Africa. That struggle remains the central one in the region and the ending of apartheid is the only way to bring peace to the neighbouring states. It is the subject of much research and writing by many people more qualified to look at South

Africa itself. Thus we look at South Africa only in the context of its relationships to its neighbours.

The neighbouring states are the Front Line. They are bearing the brunt of an even more devastating war than has yet been waged inside South Africa. Support for them and a deeper understanding of their dilemma is essential to the campaign for the liberation of South Africa and Namibia.

2. The Total Strategy to Defend Apartheid

The mid-1970s shook the confidence of white South Africa. Mozambique and Angola became independent in 1975, breaking the 'cordon sanitaire' of white-ruled colonies that had protected South Africa until then. The following year the South African Defence Force (SADF) had to leave Angola with its collective tail between its legs. The invasion of Angola killed Prime Minister B.J. Vorster's *détente* initiative, in which he was trying to gain support from conservative African governments. The Soweto uprising began in June 1976, followed by the first guerrilla actions of the long dormant African National Congress (ANC). Then Jimmy Carter, newly elected president of the United States, abandoned Henry Kissinger's famed 'tilt' toward white rule; instead he pushed for changes in apartheid and a settlement in Namibia. The police killed Steve Biko in September 1977, causing an international outcry. In November 1977 the UN Security Council imposed a mandatory arms embargo. The crisis of confidence was capped by 'Muldergate', also known as the Information scandal, which showed corruption and, even worse, massive incompetence, at the top.[1]

There was an economic crisis too. The early 1970s saw a wave of strikes, particularly in Duban. The economy was in decline from 1974 up to 1978, and there was a substantial outflow of foreign capital following the Soweto uprising and the Biko murder.[2]

White hegemony seemed under siege. The response, as so often in such cases, was to turn to the military. P.W. Botha, who had been Defence Minister since 1966, became Prime Minister in 1978 and tried to forge a kind of national unity government to defend white rule. Attacks on neighbouring states emerged as part of the wider strategy of this government, and of the interest groups pressing on it.

Facing the 'total onslaught'

The new government argued that white South Africa faced a 'total onslaught' from beyond its borders, and that it must respond with a 'total national strategy'. This was to be a 'comprehensive plan to utilise all the means available to the state according to an integrated pattern,' according to the 1977 Defence White Paper, which first articulated the concept. There was never complete agreement as to what the phrases 'total onslaught' and 'total strategy' meant, which may be why the terms themselves have dropped from currency. But the concepts were widely accepted and understood; they have shaped foreign policy since 1978, and continue to do so.[3]

The total onslaught was seen as a specifically communist plot to overthrow white rule in South Africa. In 1978, P.W. Botha explained that 'South Africa enjoys a high priority in the onslaught by Moscow.'

> The ultimate aim of the Soviet Union and its allies is to overthrow the present body politic in the Republic of South Africa and to replace it with a Marxist-oriented form of government to further the objectives of the USSR. Therefore all possible methods and means are used to attain this objective. This includes instigating social and labour unrest, civilian resistance, terrorist attacks against the infrastructure of South Africa, and the intimidation of black leaders and members of the security forces. This onslaught is supported by a worldwide propaganda campaign and the involvement of various front organisations, such as trade unions and even certain church organisations and leaders.

Initially, Mozambique and Angola were the main examples of the communist thrust; Frelimo and the MPLA had won liberation wars with socialist bloc support, while Cuba had come to the aid of Angola to repel a South African invasion. But the victory of Robert Mugabe and ZANU in Zimbabwe, the return to action of the ANC, and the opening of Eastern bloc embassies in Lesotho added them to the demonology. Louis Nel, in a speech in November 1982, stressed that southern Africa had been selected as an important target for Soviet overt and clandestine activities. And he pointed out that

> The Kremlin has actively supported the southern African Marxist-Leninist revolutionary movements in their quest for power in Angola, Mozambique, and Zimbabwe. The Kremlin is currently backing SWAPO, the South African ANC and the South African Communist Party who operate against SWA/Namibia and the Republic of South Africa, respectively.[4]

Nel was later appointed Deputy Foreign Minister, and in 1985 admitted links with the anti-government MNR in Mozambique (see Chapters 6 and 12).

There is, however, not always total agreement as to who is part of the onslaught. The 1982 Defence White Paper called Zambia a 'Marxist satellite', while Nel in his speech seemed to count Zambia's President Kenneth Kaunda as what he termed a 'black moderate'.

Despite the minor disagreements, the South African government has consistently held to its overall view that its problems are caused by the Marxist total onslaught. Justifying the commando raid on Gaborone, Botswana, on 14 June 1985, the government radio stressed that Botswana and Lesotho were 'friendly towards the Soviet Union' and that they provided the access routes to 'the terrorists [who] are behind the current unrest in some of South Africa's black cities and towns'. Agents of the Soviet Union were acting 'internally by instigating discontent among the country's black people through the exploitation of real and trumped-up grievances, and externally by orchestrating a worldwide isolation campaign against South Africa. Behind the meticulously planned and executed campaign is the Soviet KGB', which is also organising 'a cleverly planned disinvestment campaign'.[5]

The concept of total onslaught equates the 'red peril' with the 'black peril', and defence of apartheid with defence of Western Christian values. This formulation of the problem has two important advantages for white South Africa. On the one hand, all criticisms of apartheid can be dismissed as communist-inspired. On the other hand, it allows South Africa to demand that the West support it as a bastion against communism, despite any distaste for apartheid; when the West attacks apartheid it only aids Moscow.

This line occurs repeatedly, and it is not only the province of the military or the right wing. Foreign Minister Pik Botha warned in 1979 that 'like creeping lava and suffocating gas ... the menacing hegemony of Russia is spreading over this planet'. In his 1982 speech, Louis Nel argued that the West must respond to 'Moscow's global strategy' and that 'the West will have to be quite explicit in including South Africa within its defence perimeter,' while accepting the continuation of apartheid. Defence Minister Magnus Malan warned that in attacking apartheid, 'the Western powers make themselves available as handymen of the communists and they are indirectly contributing to the destruction of capitalism and the establishment of world communism'.

The State Security Council

One of the most important aspects of the total onslaught is precisely that it is *total*. As well as military action, the onslaught takes political, diplomatic, and economic forms and even makes use of sport and culture. This justifies bringing all aspects of foreign and domestic policy under the purview of the military.

The 1977 Defence White Paper explained that the 'total strategy should encompass the state, the private sector, diplomacy, commerce, industry, and organisations like Armscor [and] the Council for Scientific Research'. Defence Minister Magnus Malan talks of the 'four power bases' of the state as political/diplomatic, economic, social/psychological, and security. These must be coordinated by a new 'national security management system', with the State Security Council (SSC) at its heart.

The SSC takes the key decisions in South Africa, and thus it holds the real power. Its decisions are sometimes referred later to the cabinet or parliament for ratification, but they are now subsidiary bodies. The SSC is like a corporation board of directors or the Politburo of a communist country. P.W. Botha is often described as an 'organisation man' and the SSC acts in a technocratic and managerial way.

The SSC is dominated by the military, although it also includes the key political figures. It is unusual in also including several top civil servants. The Prime Minister is chairman and the SSC includes the Ministers of Defence, Foreign Affairs, Justice, Law & Order, Finance, and Manpower. Also members of the SSC are six top bureaucrats: the heads of the National Intelligence Service (formerly BOSS), Military Intelligence, the Police, and Defence Force, and the directors-general of Foreign Affairs and Justice. Other ministers and officials are co-opted. Before his retirement in 1983, the general manager of South African Railways, Dr J.G.H. Loubser, was frequently a co-opted member, showing the political importance of transport. (It was Loubser who coined the phrase 'transport diplomacy').

A particularly powerful figure is the head of the SSC secretariat, who controls agendas, the preparation of papers, and so on. Until 1985, the head of the secretariat was General A.J. van Deventer, who had been head of the retreat from Angola in 1976;[6] he had previously been head of the Security Planning Branch, which provides the bulk of the secretariat, thus increasing the military-security aspect of the SSC. When A.J. van Deventer retired, he was replaced by the head of military intelligence, General P.W. van der Westhuizen, who had been in charge of surrogate armies in the neighbouring states.

The constitutional changes introduced in 1983 further increased the power of

P.W. Botha and the SSC. New 'Indian' and 'coloured' chambers were created and the old white parliament had its power reduced. P.W. Botha was made State President with substantially increased power; furthermore, the cumbersome nature of the three-chamber parliament increases the power of the SSC. Thus the 1983 changes effectively completed the transformation to a managerial style of government in which the military play a central role.

Interest groups

One of the most important aspects of the 'total strategy' was its attempt to bridge some of the sharp tribal and class divisions within the ruling white elite. At various times, particularly in 1979 and 1984, the government did seem to be having some success in building a white consensus. At other times, it was at least able to channel the conflicts into the SSC and other official organs for resolution. For the most part, however, the total strategy has singularly failed to unify white South Africa to defend its own control. Three overlapping groups with different interests are important to this study, and will be discussed below in more detail: big business, the National Party (NP), and the military.

The business community plays a central role in continued white control of South Africa, although it has largely been excluded from formal political power. The South African economy is highly monopolised, in two different senses. First of all production of many key commodities (ranging from beer to fertiliser) is controlled by one firm or by a small cartel. Second, the entire economy is dominated by a handful of conglomerates. On paper, there seem to be hundreds of large companies operating in South Africa, but in fact most are either direct subsidiaries of (or are at least controlled by) one of the groups. Thus this handful of conglomerates are usually referred to as 'monopoly groups'.

The largest, the Anglo American group, controls companies which together account for 56% of the total value of the Johannesburg Stock Exchange, and is a major transnational. In the group are the Anglo American Corporation of South Africa, De Beers (which controls world diamond marketing), and Minorco (one of the largest foreign investors in the United States). Thus the key figures in Anglo, particularly retired chairman Harry Oppenheimer and the present chairman Gavin Relly, are voices to be reckoned with. Six other monopoly groups control another 24% of the value of the Johannesburg Stock Exchange.

There are two major divisions within the business community, English versus Afrikaner and big versus small. Historically, the mining companies such as Anglo were English. But now Afrikaners are playing an increasing economic role — three of the six smaller monopoly groups are Afrikaner — so the first split is decreasing in importance. But the growing monopolisation and the deepening recession are worsening the second split. Over the past decade, the monopoly groups have taken control of many medium size firms — often in the face of some resistance. In 1983 Anglo even took control of one of the other monopoly groups, South African Breweries. In the depression of the early 1980s the monopoly groups found themselves with substantial cash (and little to invest in), while they were increasingly investing in Europe and the US, so they were able to ride out the depression; smaller firms were much harder hit and many went bankrupt. Thus big and small business had very different attitudes on economic issues.

On regional policy there are also disagreements within the business community. As we will show later, the neighbouring states provide the most important market for South African manufactured goods, and thus a key export market for both large and small business. Several of the monopoly groups have significant investments in the neighbouring states, and we will also argue in this book that they sometimes use their economic power in 'political' ways, for example joining government actions against neighbouring states and trying to extract changes in governments or government policy there. Although they are anxious to continue exporting to them, the monopoly groups are not generally interested in further investment in the neighbouring states, preferring the safer fields of Europe and the US, and some have been disinvesting. They could afford a wait-and-see policy. Medium-sized firms were much more seriously hit by the depression of the mid-1980s. They looked to the neighbouring states both as a potential market, and (as they were being squeezed out of South Africa by the monopoly groups) as a possible place for investment. They could no longer afford to wait, and opposed anything that would delay immediate profits.

The second important group is the largely Afrikaner National Party (NP), which came to power in 1948 and has governed ever since. During that period of more than 35 years, it has wrested control of government and the military from the English-speakers, while institutionalising and reinforcing apartheid. Through the use of government contracts, bank accounts, and the like it was able to boost Afrikaner business.

The resulting expansion, as well as changing economic conditions in general, led to political divisions. A central issue was the two-fold need of business to draw non-whites more directly into the economy. First, it was essential to expand beyond an increasingly saturated white market. Second was the changing demand for labour, toward a better paid, more highly skilled, permanent black workforce and away from the pool of interchangeable, poorly paid, unskilled hands organised under various internal and international migrant systems. The traditional apartheid system had been the foundation stone of rapid capitalist accumulation, but an increasingly technologically advanced and capital-intensive industry required some modifications and modernisations of the apartheid system. Also, business had a more international outlook, and was sensitive to threats of sanctions.

This led to divisions within the NP, and to the formation of opposition parties. Within the NP there are the 'verligtes' (the so-called 'enlightened'), who want some reforms in the apartheid structure in order to maintain white rule, and the 'verkramptes' or reactionaries, whose position depends on total suppression of blacks and who thus oppose any change.

The very success of Afrikaner businessmen, promoted by the NP, and the tentative moves by the NP to form some alliance with business and make some changes in apartheid regulations, have seen the NP leave some of its traditional supporters behind. White farmers, small businessmen, and skilled workers are correctly concerned that regulations that have given them a privileged position are being abandoned at the behest of big business. The Conservative Party was formed as a split from the NP in 1982, and is the third largest party in parliament. The far right Herstigte Nasionale Party was formed in 1969, but only won its first seat in a 1985 by-election. Although the NP still commands a large majority in parliament, it is losing ground as its slow reform policy is attacked by both the far right and the liberals.

To some extent, the opposition Progressive Federal Party (PFP) is the party of liberal capital. The former Anglo head, Harry Oppenheimer, effectively created the Progressive Party, a predecessor to the PFP, and he remains the most important source of PFP funding; several Anglo directors have been Progressive or PFP MPs. The PFP does not support one-person one-vote, but it does want to abolish apartheid structures and form some sort of multiracial coalition incorporating a group of relatively well-off urban blacks, such as small businessmen, teachers and skilled workers. In the 1981 election the PFP was the main opposition to the NP, but gained only 18% of the vote, so it hardly represents a serious electoral challenge.

The third group is the military itself, particularly the South African Defence Force (SADF). It is predominantly Afrikaner and the key institution supporting white minority rule. Despite its close links to the NP, it seems clear that, as Philip Frankel argues, it is

> grossly simplistic and reductionistic to relegate the SADF to the role of a 'knee-jerk' agent of the White state, not only because the South African state is composed of a diversity of fragments each seeking to carve out its segmental and institutional interests within the transcending racial framework, but also because the military is one of the most powerful of these fragments by virtue of its dual responsiblity for external and internal state control.[7]

In general terms, the military leadership in the early 1980s took a softer line inside, and a harder line outside, than previous governments — pressing for some reforms inside, while being much more aggressive against the neighbouring states. But the SADF is itself politically divided. On internal issues, it reflects the *verligte-verkrampte* and NP-CP splits of Afrikanerdom as a whole. Furthermore, the conflict over restructuring apartheid and the inclusion of non-whites in previously white areas has a direct reflection in the military: is it safe to arm non-whites to defend white rule?

On regional issues, there are also divisions. The most important one is between those who want what might be called 'forward' and 'laager' strategies. Proponents of the 'forward' line, who were clearly dominant in the early 1980s, argued for fighting the war in neighbouring states as much as possible in order to push back the ANC and create a 'cordon of instability'. Those who supported a 'laager' or defensive strategy argued that the forward strategy would only suck the SADF ever more deeply into foreign wars, and would involve the South African government supporting proxy armies and perhaps puppet governments in an increasing number of African states. These divisions are seen clearly over Namibia: some senior officers see their prestige tied to a decisive victory over SWAPO, and the Angola border as the line of defence; others feel that the war in Namibia has become an expensive waste and that victory is impossible anyway, so it makes more sense to consolidate behind South Africa's shorter and more defensible natural borders.

In part the choice between these strategies relates to the belief in the total Marxist onslaught. Not all the top leaders blindly accept this dogma, although it must be more widely accepted at lower levels since it plays a role in training and indoctrination. For example, there seem to be sharp divisions as to whether it is safe to deal with Mozambique's Marxist president, Samora Machel, or whether efforts should be made to overthrow him.

Finally, there are disagreements between police and security. After the Muldergate scandal, BOSS (which was a branch of the security police) was downgraded and the leading role was taken by military intelligence which, for example, runs the surrogate armies like UNITA and the MNR. On the other hand, Police Commissioner Johan Coetzee plays an important role in policy-making; he is said to have been a key figure within the SSC supporting the signing of the Nkomati non-aggression pact with Mozambique (against military opposition). Traditionally the police have been concerned with internal security and the SADF with external. This would naturally lead the police to support a laager strategy (which would give them a bigger role), while many in the SADF would argue for a forward strategy, in part because the SADF needs raids into neighbouring states to justify its existence and large budgets. However, since late 1984 the army has been in the townships along with the police to control the uprisings.

Changes

The total strategy required four critical and interrelated changes. These were, in part, intended to support the three interest groups and bring them closer together; this they partly did, although they also widened the splits within those groups. These four changes were: streamlining apartheid, strengthening the military, supporting business and bringing it into partnership, and creating a new regional policy (the main focus of this book).

Apartheid needed to be streamlined. In the late 1970s the military recognised more than many NP leaders the need to try to co-opt some of the non-white population, for example with the two new parliaments, and to try to head off future Soweto-style uprisings. Petty apartheid regulations needed to be abolished to satisfy international critics. And changes were required to satisfy the changing needs of business.

Second, the total strategy required a massive strengthening of the military. The military budget had already increased sevenfold between P.W. Botha's appointment as Defence Minister in 1966 and his becoming Prime Minister in 1978; it nearly doubled again in the next five years.[8] Armscor (the Armaments Development and Manufacturing Corporation) was set up in 1968 and is among the 25 largest corporations in the country. It has been critical in thwarting the arms embargo; only one-quarter of South African arms are not now produced locally, compared to more than half in the mid-1970s.

The other two changes are increased links with business, and a different regional policy, and must be considered in more detail.

Business partnership

Big business, especially the English-speaking mining houses, traditionally had a cool and distant relationship with the NP. Former Prime Minister B.J. Vorster believed that the 'business of business is business' and that politics should be left to the government. But in the new total strategy the economy was one of the four power bases which had to be included. Furthermore, much of the total onslaught was said to be economic, while the ideological basis of the total strategy was defence of capitalism.

In his speeches, P.W. Botha stressed his commitment to free enterprise and to a new partnership between government and capital. This reached a peak at a conference in the Carlton Hotel in Johannesburg in November 1979, when the entire cabinet met with South Africa's top business leaders. Anglo Chairman

Harry Oppenheimer said the meeting 'marks the beginning of a new relationship between state and private business in South Africa'. Business leaders made clear their demands for some changes to apartheid regulations, particularly with respect to labour mobility and training, and the government promised some reform.

The role of the government in the economy is closer to that in socialist countries than capitalist ones. Many of the largest corporations are parastatals, including SATS (transport), Iscor (iron and steel), Sasol (oil from coal), and Escom (electricity). The private sector is tightly regulated. But, as part of the reform package, the government sold off some state companies, like Safmarine and Sasol; state controls and state regulated cartels were reduced; and exchange controls were temporarily weakened.

As we will see, the 'new relationship' never really got off the ground. Tensions between business and government increased in 1982 and 1983. The Nkomati accord marked a 'new new relationship', but that, too, collapsed the next year. Nevertheless, even if the political marriage was never consummated, the Botha government did build an increasingly close practical relationship with business.

P.W. Botha had close links with industry during his tenure as Defence Minister. He talked of 'uniting business leaders behind the South African Defence Force' (SADF) and tried to forge a local military-industrial complex. Soon after his appointment as Defence Minister, he established the Defence Advisory Council; in 1980 it included top executives from all the biggest businesses, including Anglo (Relly, later to become chairman), Barlow (chairman Mike Rosholt), Sanlam (F.J. du Plessis, soon to become chairman), Old Mutual (chairman J.G. van der Horst), SA Breweries (managing director Dick Goss), Gencor, Volkskas, Tongaat, Anglovaal, Standard Bank, and Nedbank.

Armscor, although a parastatal, has a board of directors chosen largely from the private sector. In 1979 Barlow Rand seconded John Maree to be Armscor executive vice-chairman. Armscor policy is to maximise the use of the private sector; in 1978 it used 800 subcontractors, but four years later the figure was 3000.

At the same time, however, the private sector is being militarised by the total strategy. For example, the National Key Points Act of 1980 allows the Minister of Defence to designate a 'key point', such as a factory, for which the owner must establish a militia and undertake other security precautions. More than 600 have been designated. There has also been strong SADF pressure for making more goods locally if they have military significance, such as diesel engines and lorry gearboxes. Such goods are protected by high tariffs, which provides an opportunity for business to expand, but also increases inefficiencies and has led to some complaints. (See Chapter 9).

The Constellation of States

The 1977 Defence White Paper also saw an important regional component to the total strategy. It identified the need 'to maintain a solid military balance relative to neighbouring states and other states in southern Africa'. And it called for 'economic action' and 'action in relation to transport services, distribution and telecommunications' to promote 'political and economic collaboration among the states of southern Africa'.

This proposed collaboration was later formalised as a Constellation of States (Consas) involving South Africa, various client and pseudo states, and several of the independent states of the region. As well as South Africa itself, Consas was to include the bantustans (the so-called 'independent' homelands), and the two states on which internal settlements had been imposed in 1978 — Zimbabwe-Rhodesia under Bishop Abel Muzorewa and Namibia under the Democratic Turnhalle Alliance. It was assumed that the three members of the customs union, (Botswana, Lesotho, and Swaziland) would join, along with Malawi, the only independent state to maintain diplomatic relations with Pretoria. Zaire and Zambia were seen as other possible members.

In various speeches during 1979, P.W. Botha and Pik Botha (Foreign Minister) spelt out the basis for the constellation.[9] Most importantly, it was seen as an integral part of the total strategy. It involved international recognition of apartheid, of the 'independence' of the bantustans, and of the legitimacy of the internal settlements in Namibia and Zimbabwe. Although Consas was to be basically an economic organisation, members would also be expected to sign non-aggression pacts with South Africa, and there was a hope that this might even lead to a multilateral Consas defence pact. Pik Botha saw the countries in the region developing 'a common approach in the security field, the economic field, and the political field'.

The Bothas believed that, on two grounds, the neighbouring states would be forced to participate in Consas. First, they thought that the 'moderate' states of the region agreed that they all faced a common 'marxist threat' and could not rely on the West for support. Second, they assumed that the economic pull of South Africa was inexorably sucking the neighbouring states into closer and more formal relations with Pretoria, and that this would overwhelm any scruples about apartheid.

A Development Bank of Southern Africa was to be an integral part of Consas, and it was formally established in 1983 — with only South Africa and the bantustans as members. This was to give some new money to the neighbouring states as a carrot for participating in Consas. But there was also talk of including customs union revenue as a way of forcing Botswana, Lesotho, and Swaziland to join.

Business was to be an integral part of Consas, and the proposal was formally launched by P.W. Botha at the Carlton Conference with 300 business executives in November 1979. For business, Consas was to be the main gain from the total strategy, because it offered dominance over a much larger market. On the other hand, the government saw business as an advance guard which would build bridges across ideological divides, thus increasing the centripetal pull towards South Africa. Initially business responded favourably; Harry Oppenheimer told the meeting that the concept of Consas 'attracts us all, and businessmen will want to help'. The Association of Chambers of Commerce even promoted the notion of 'business diplomacy' and the view that business executives acted as 'ambassadors of prosperity'.[10]

New crises

The total strategy was a response to the crisis of the mid-1970s. It was modified in response to the much worse crisis of the 1980s. But the underlying thinking has not changed. White South Africa is still seen to face a total Marxist onslaught which requires an integrated response involving all aspects of South African life. When government policy is criticised, for example by the press and academics, the total strategy is often the understood frame of reference — and the complaint is often of policy being too military and not 'total' enough. Regionally, the idea of Consas and even the phrase 'Constellation of States' recur in speeches by government ministers and business leaders.

The argumént of this chapter is that, in analysing South African actions in the region, it is useful to keep in mind three main concepts — total onslaught, total strategy, and Consas — and three main actors — business, National Party, and military. Their exact form may change, but their presence does not.

The first big defeats for the total strategy occurred in 1980, as part of a dramatic restructuring of regional politics which is discussed in the next chapter. But this only served to reinforce the fear of the total onslaught; every defeat for the total strategy was more evidence of the Marxist threat.

3. SADCC, the ANC and Constructive Engagement

South Africa's regional plans faced drastic setbacks in 1980. The Zimbabwe war finally ended with the agreement at Lancaster House on 17 December 1979. Zanu (PF) won a landslide victory at the British-supervised elections on 4 March 1980 — to the shock of both Britain and South Africa. Bishop Muzorewa, on whom South Africa had staked its regional policy, was humiliated. Zimbabwe's independence came on 17 April but on 1 April the majority ruled states had already agreed to set up SADCC (the Southern African Development Coordination Conference), dashing Pretoria's dreams of Consas.

Internally, white South Africa found itself facing unexpected problems. Because of the international oil boycott, South Africa had imported all its petroleum from Iran. After the Shah was overthrown, that ended. In late 1979 and early 1980 South Africa nearly ran out of oil.[1] Then on 1 June 1980 the ANC hit South Africa's oil industry in an unprecedented four-part raid. Bombs damaged two Sasol oil-from-coal plants and a refinery.[2] They caused substantial damage, and the guerrillas eluded what the SADF itself had called 'the most effective Commando in the land', which was guarding the site.[3]

White South Africa was suddenly under pressure, both inside and out, and its defences were inadequate. But the lifeline came in November 1980, when Ronald Reagan was elected President of the United States. This chapter looks at the three actors who came on the scene in 1980: SADCC, the ANC, and President Reagan.

SADCC

Zimbabwe is key to any regional economic grouping. Sitting astride all the main roads and railways, it is the heart of the region; during the sanctions and border closures of the UDI period, it was the missing link which prevented the other majority ruled states from cooperating with each other. It is also the most industrialised state (other than South Africa itself). Both the South Africans and the Front Line states expected their favoured party to win, and drew up plans for economic associations to include Zimbabwe. For South Africa it was Consas, and for the Front Line states it was the Southern African Development Coordination Conference (SADCC).[4] At the founding meeting on 1 April 1980 in Lusaka, all nine majority ruled states joined SADCC: the then six Front Line states of Angola, Botswana, Mozambique, Tanzania, Zambia, and Zimbabwe, plus Lesotho, Malawi, and Swaziland.[5] South Africa was dumbfounded; it had been sure that at least Malawi and Swaziland would join Consas. But even the most

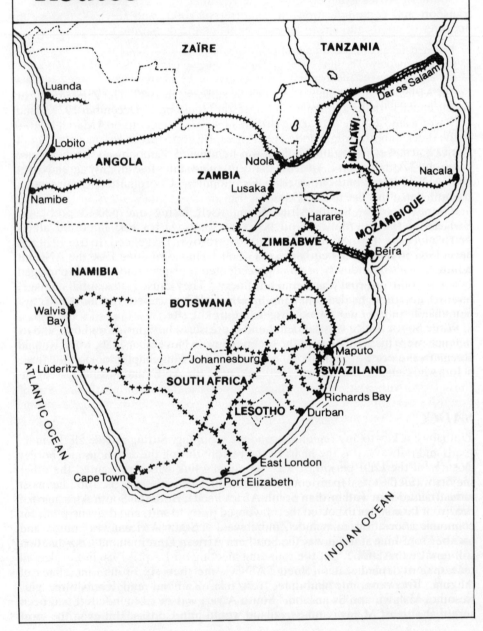

Rail and Pipeline Routes

Legend:
+++++ SADCC railways
◆◆◆◆◆ South African railways
▨▨▨▨ Pipeline
----- International boundaries

ZAÏRE

TANZANIA

Luanda

Dar es Salaam

Lobito

ANGOLA

Ndola

MALAWI

Nacala

Namibe

ZAMBIA

Lusaka

MOZAMBIQUE

Harare

ZIMBABWE

NAMIBIA

Beira

Walvis Bay

BOTSWANA

ATLANTIC OCEAN

Lüderitz

Johannesburg

Maputo

SWAZILAND

SOUTH AFRICA

Richards Bay

LESOTHO

Durban

East London

Cape Town

Port Elizabeth

INDIAN OCEAN

conservative neighbours showed that they thought apartheid a worse evil than socialism.

The goal of SADCC is 'to liberate our economies from their dependence on the Republic of South Africa, to overcome the imposed economic fragmentation, and to coordinate our efforts toward regional and national economic development', according to the Lusaka Declaration.[6] The declaration stressed that 'economic liberation is as vital as political freedom'.

'Southern Africa is dependent on the Republic of South Africa as a focus of transport and communication, an exporter of goods and services, and as an importer of goods and cheap labour', explains the declaration.

> This dependence is not a natural phenomenon, nor is it simply the result of a free market economy. The nine states and one occupied territory of Southern Africa were, in varying degrees, deliberately incorporated — by metropolitan powers, colonial rulers, and large corporations — into the colonial and sub-colonial structures centring on the Republic of South Africa. The development of national economies as balanced units, let alone the welfare of the people of southern Africa, played no part in the economic integration strategy.

SADCC defined its strategy as working together to 'gear national development to provide goods and services presently coming from the Republic of South Africa and weave a fabric of regional cooperation and development'. The declaration continued that the 'key to this strategy is transport and communications'. Thus the first priority was to rehabilitate and upgrade existing transport links, particularly ports and railways in Mozambique, Tanzania, and Angola which serve the entire SADCC region. Efforts were also made to integrate telecommunications and to provide earth stations for satellite links which would reduce the need to use South Africa.

The second priority was agriculture and food security. One key area was research into drought-resistant peasant crops, which had been tackled in Asia but not Africa. Another was animal disease control. A third was to reduce the impact of the droughts which regularly hit the zone, with policies ranging from increased regional food storage to irrigation. Soon after the founding of SADCC, the region was hit by the worst drought of the century, and agriculture came to the forefront.

Industrial development, energy, and training were the next areas to be considered, with a stress on reducing imports and preventing duplication of expensive development projects. More recently cooperation in mining, tourism, and trade has been discussed.

SADCC's approach

Inevitably SADCC is dependent on international aid for its projects, and there is a annual conference with foreign partners each year. SADCC has asked for help for nearly $5000m worth of projects, about three-quarters in transport and communications. By early 1986, more than $1100m had been committed and another $1150m was under discussion — a remarkable international response to a still new organisation.

Despite its dependence on foreign aid, however, SADCC is determined to call the tune. 'Our economic plans have to be conceived and prepared by ourselves. No one knows our needs and our priorities better than ourselves. We must not accept the habit of plans made outside the region', Mozambique's President

Samora Machel told the Lusaka summit in April 1980. This has provoked conflict with some donors who insist on trying to tell SADCC what to do, but the nine have held out and still determine their own priorities.

In three important ways SADCC is different from other international organisations. First, it decentralises power and thus does not have a magnificent marble headquarters with hundreds of staff. In many respects, SADCC learned the lessons of past failures, particularly the East African Community. Thus it has only a tiny secretariat (in Botswana) which serves a purely coordinating function. There are no SADCC institutions like shipping lines. Even agreed SADCC development projects are negotiated between the donor and the member state in which the project actually takes place. And each member state is responsible for coordinating a particular subject area: Transport & Communications (Mozambique), Industry (Tanzania), Energy (Angola), Agriculture & Food Security (Zimbabwe), Animal Disease and Agricultural Research (Botswana), Fisheries (Malawi), Training (Swaziland), Mining (Zambia), and Tourism (Lesotho). For the larger areas like transport, energy, and agriculture, the responsible member state has established a technical unit, usually set up with foreign help.

Second, SADCC works on the basis of small steps which are agreed to be of mutual benefit, rather than grand regional strategies requiring interminable negotiation. The key to SADCC strategy is to avoid conflict and look instead for areas of agreement. So far it has found sufficient areas of mutual benefit to avoid the need to tackle areas of conflict and controversy. Despite membership of the Front Line states and a political commitment to cooperate, there is a long history of jealousies and minor conflicts, for example over colonially defined borders and about supporting different liberation movements. Furthermore, the effective removal of UDI Rhodesia from the region meant that for more than a decade the newly independent countries had relatively little day-to-day contact with each other. And South Africa has exploited these regional divisions for its own ends.

SADCC aimed for a slow and steady building of confidence, and the development of an entirely new habit of cooperation. This led its founders to take a step-by-step approach. For example, member states are very jealous about energy self-sufficiency (and South Africa has exploited this, see Chapter 16), so that it would take a decade or more to negotiate a regional electricity grid. Instead, SADCC opted for initial small links across borders, which will slowly build up a *de facto* regional grid (probably in less time than it would have taken to negotiate one into existence). A central feature has been to build up working links at technical and managerial levels, so that in addition to meetings of energy ministers, there are also meetings of the heads of electricity parastatals and of electricity technicians. Over time, they come to trust their neighbours and think more in a regional context, which leads to cooperation over bigger projects in later stages.

The third difference is that SADCC is not a free trade zone, but rather is aiming for planned and widely spread regional development. Clearly, trade is essential, but it is not an end in itself. Rather it must be a means to increased development, and that requires balanced trade rather than free trade. The reason for this is that free trade zones always direct new industry to the most developed member; in SADCC that is Zimbabwe. So some degree of planning and cooperation is necessary to ensure that industry develops in other countries as well as Zimbabwe.

SADCC is a threat to Pretoria precisely because the SADCC states could provide each other with the goods and services currently obtained from South Africa. Transport is the most obvious one — imports and exports should go through SADCC ports and not South African ones. But SADCC is also the main export market for South African chemicals, plastics, and machinery, and is important for other goods as well; many of these are easily produced and the SADCC market often justifies local production. Thus if SADCC is successful in reducing dependence, it sharply decreases South Africa's profits and its economic leverage.

SADCC is also a political threat, particularly because it was much more successful and drew much more foreign support than even its most ardent promoters expected. It soon won an impressive level of cooperation, and establish an internationally credible programme. Its first annual donors conference in Maputo in November 1980 attracted pledges of $800m, and a political commitment from much of Europe.

Most SADCC states are also members of the/ Preferential Trade Area for Eastern and Southern Africa (PTA), and the others are likely to join soon. This came into being on 1 July 1984 after more than a decade of planning by the UN Economic Commission for Africa. It is open to the SADCC states, the Indian Ocean states, and east African states as far north as Djibouti and Ethiopia. The PTA aims to increase trade by reducing barriers, in particular through lower tariffs and through the use of a payment clearing house which could eventually allow member states to pay for PTA goods in local currency.

Because of the preference of many SADCC leaders for balanced as distinct from free trade, there have been conflicts between SADCC and the PTA. Nevertheless, Zimbabwe and Zambia are active members of both groupings, and the PTA and SADCC must eventually come to terms with each other. In any case, the payments clearing house will work only if trade is effectively balanced, because if countries buy more from PTA members than they export to them, they must pay in hard currency (which they do not have).

Whatever its political problems with SADCC, the PTA also accelerates delinking from South Africa. This occurs first because it does increase trade between member states, in some cases of goods previously bought from South Africa. Equally important in the long term is a PTA rule that to qualify for tariff reductions, exporting firms must be mainly locally owned and managed; this could force some South African companies to relinquish majority control of subsidiaries in the neighbouring states, particularly in Zimbabwe (see Chapter 16).

The African National Congress

The African National Congress (ANC) is not a new actor like SADCC, but its return to centre stage in 1980 followed a long period in the wings. Founded in 1912, it is the oldest of the anti-apartheid organisations. Its mass campaigns in the 1950s won widespread support and its president, Chief Luthuli, won the Nobel Peace Prize in 1960. But after the Sharpeville massacre of 21 March 1960, both the ANC and the Pan-Africanist Congress (PAC) were banned, which prevented them from conducting any form of legal and non-violent protest against apartheid. In 1961, both chose the armed struggle as the only option left. But effective police work broke the underground organisations of both groups, leaving them largely exile bodies.

Through the 1960s internal resistance was limited. But the 1970s saw a wave of strikes and the growth of the new black consciousness movement. This was given an important psychological boost by the independence of Mozambique and Angola in 1975, which was widely celebrated in South Africa. In 1976 the Soweto uprising provoked a crackdown and a wave of refugees, many of whom joined the ANC. This provided a vital injection of new blood, and the ANC began sabotage actions inside South Africa again. But it was the 1 June 1980 Sasol raid, more than any other, that marked the return to battle.

In the rhetoric of the total strategy, the ANC seemed to be everywhere and was blamed for any form of disturbance. It was seen as an agent of Moscow, through the South African Communist Party, which is allied to the ANC. South African ministers, including Magnus Malan, have also accused the ANC of having close links with the Palestine Liberation Organisation (PLO); this is used to justify South African links with Israel and the use of Israeli-style tactics.

ANC guerrillas and political cadres began infiltrating into South Africa from the neighbouring states in the late 1970s. Some entered from Mozambique via Swaziland, while others were helped by ZAPU guerrillas fighting in southern Rhodesia. This provided the excuse for what became a South African military obsession — that if the ANC could be expelled from the neighbouring states, then the unrest inside would end.

The South African leadership intentionally confused a number of issues. It alleged that neighbouring states had ANC 'bases', when in fact they only allowed transit and the only major ANC camps were far away from South Africa, in Tanzania and Angola.[7] This was used in particular to justify raids on the neighbouring states. Another confusion was between ANC political cadres and guerrillas. The Organisation of African Unity and SADCC both recognise the ANC and several states in the region allowed the ANC to open offices and have official or semi-official representatives. Several of these representatives have been assassinated, even though they have no military role. Finally, the South African government has intentionally confused ordinary refugees, some of whom may have sympathy with the ANC, with ANC guerrillas. There is a steady flow of refugees into the neighbouring states, particularly Lesotho and Botswana, and South Africa accuses them of harbouring guerrillas when they are merely giving sanctuary to refugees.

Undoubtedly the ANC is a major force now in the struggle against apartheid, and it has contributed to the insurrection now under way. But the South African government has regularly exaggerated its role, and also the role of the guerillas infiltrated from outside. The base for the present uprising is inside the South African townships, not in the neighbouring states. Rioting in the townships would not stop even if the ANC were pushed back across the Mediterranean.

The South African government's stress on ANC 'bases' in neighbouring states seems to serve three purposes. First, at least some in South Africa really do believe that the ANC and communism and not apartheid are the cause of the troubles, and thus there necessarily must be bases in neighbouring states. Second, even those who do not believe it find it useful propaganda for their white constituents. Third, it provides an excuse for attacking the neighbouring states, and thus a way of applying pressure on them. The purpose of such pressure varies, but includes both political goals such as cracking down on anti-apartheid statements by refugees and even the government, as well as economic goals such as trying to prevent SADCC-inspired delinking. (This is discussed further in Chapter 7).

Whatever the reasons, the South African military is openly trying to emulate Israel. Just as Israel is trying to push the PLO out of all neighbouring states and attack it even farther afield, so South Africa is trying to push the ANC out of all states in the region. This has become a cornerstone of regional policy.

Constructive engagement

The creation of SADCC and the return to battle of the ANC were both defeats for the total strategy. But it gained support later in 1980 with the election of Ronald Reagan as President of the United States.

The arrival of Jimmy Carter as US president in 1976 had made white South Africa apoplectic. Sanctions against South Africa suddenly became a serious possibility. In August 1977 B.J. Vorster declared that the result of the new US pressure on South Africa 'would be exactly the same as if it were subverted by the Marxists'. By March 1979 Foreign Minister Pik Botha was talking of taking 'a neutral position in the struggle between East and West' — a remark that sat strangely with his continuing anti-communist rhetoric. He accused Western powers of preventing South Africa from bringing 'salvation' to the neighbouring states. And he diagnosed a 'paralysis in the mind of the West to acknowledge the importance of South Africa'. The new British Prime Minister, Margaret Thatcher, was the only healthy exception.

Relief arrived for the embattled white laager with the election of Ronald Reagan in November 1980. Anti-communism replaced human rights as the main issue in US foreign policy. Whereas Carter had accepted the OAU line of isolating Pretoria, the Reagan policy was 'constructive engagement'. The US tried to push South Africa to mend its ways by being friendly to it and convincing it of the merits of change, rather than by being antagonistic and imposing sanctions.

Chester Crocker was named Under-Secretary of State for African Affairs, and he largely determined US policy on the region. He summarised his position best in a speech in August 1981.[8] 'We are concerned about the influence of the Soviet Union and its surrogates in Africa,' he said, and pointed to the US need for South African minerals — exactly the points white South Africa had been making.

Crocker repeatedly stressed his opposition to apartheid, which he called 'South Africa's domestic colonialism'.[9] But he has also argued that 'you cannot get government changes in the right direction unless you have a white majority for change'.[10] Change, he argued, was already taking place, albeit slowly. 'South Africa's government is a reformist government',[11] and the military leaders are Gaullist 'modernising patriots'[12]. He made clear his opposition to 'denationalisation of South Africa's blacks' in the bantustans, and stressed that the 'disenfranchisement of blacks must end'. But he also implied that one-person one-vote was not required. Furthermore, it was not for the US to set a timetable for change; 'we don't think it is effective diplomacy to give deadlines and threats to foreign sovereign governments. ... It is not for outsiders to determine benchmarks'.[13]

To encourage South African 'trust', the Reagan administration relaxed some of the Carter bans on military exports to South Africa, and backed a 1982 IMF loan to Pretoria. In exchange for reform inside and a settlement in Namibia, the US offered readmittance to the Western anti-communist fold. US Secretary of State Haig even suggested that NATO's military 'shield' could be extended to cover South Africa.

The United States also introduced the concept of 'linkage' — that South Africa should leave Namibia only if the Cuban troops withdrew from Angola. It apparently came about when Deputy Secretary of State William Clark and Crocker were in Cape Town for talks in June 1981. Seeing Pretoria's reluctance to settle in Namibia, Clark offered to get the Cubans out of Angola if they would compromise on Namibia.[14] No doubt he also hoped that this would make it easier to bring pressure on Angola to get the Cubans out, which was a major US goal. In a key memo, Crocker argued that 'African leaders would have no basis for resisting the Namibia-Angola linkage, once they are made to realise that they can only get a Namibia settlement through us'.[15]

Crocker did stress to the South Africans that their aggressive policies were only increasing Soviet and Cuban involvement in the neighbouring states, but it was an argument that worked both ways — if South African destabilisation did increase the socialist military presence in the region, then the US would be forced to provide more help to South Africa as a counter. On Angola itself, Crocker argued for the repeal of the Clark amendment which barred US support for UNITA, and met with UNITA leaders. He stressed that he did not want to see a total UNITA victory. However, 'we believe very strongly that there is not in fact any prospect for a military solution or a military victory by either side,' and thus that there must be a 'political reconciliation'. Effectively, the US wants UNITA included in the government.

US foreign policy is riddled with contradictions. Sanctions are right for Nicaragua or Poland, but not South Africa. The MPLA should be pressed to include UNITA in the government, but no pressure should be put on white South Africa to include the ANC in government. It was hardly surprising that constructive engagement and linkage pleased Pretoria. One Johannesburg newspaper correspondent talked of 'South Africa's new ally, Mr Ronald Reagan'.[16]

Crocker's position on South Africa and Angola has remained remarkably consistent, despite its singular failure to meet what he defined as its two main goals: 'Independence for Namibia and the Cubans out of the region'.[17] On SADCC and Mozambique, however, vociferous protests and quiet diplomacy by the majority-ruled states have caused US policy to shift somewhat. This has been most marked with respect to Mozambique. In 1981 the US seemed to link Mozambique with Angola as 'Soviet satellites'. But the 1984 Nkomati non-aggression pact between Mozambique and South Africa was seen as one of the few triumphs of constructive engagement; it would bring Mozambique closer to South Africa and involved US backing for the Machel government. By 1985 Crocker was arguing that 'UNITA is very different' from the Mozambique National Resistance (MNR or Renamo). The MNR has

> a history of involvement with the government of Portugal, with the government of Ian Smith, with the government of South Africa, with foreign ex-colonial or neocolonial interests, if you will, which seek a policy of revenge, of seeking to reverse the nationalist victory that took place in 1975. That's a very strange and elaborate combination of interests and relationships there, which makes us ask some pretty basic questions about what the Resistance stands for.

And he went out of his way to stress that, in contrast to Angola, the US is not pushing the Mozambicans to negotiate with the MNR. Indeed, he implied that he does see a possibility of military victory for Frelimo. 'It is not our view that backing Renamo represents a path to any accomplishment on Mozambique. ... Renamo guerrillas do not, in our view, represent the forces of democracy and Christianity'.[18]

On SADCC there has also been a shift, although not as clear-cut or public. In 1980 Crocker called SADCC 'the triumph of ideological economics, ... the region's own folly'. Instead he argued for the continuation of the present 'natural' economic linkages because South Africa's economic dominance was the 'basis for the survival and economic development of [the region's] highly vulnerable economies'.[19] By 1983 the line had shifted somewhat. Lawrence Eagleburger, US Under Secretary of State for Political Affairs, stressed that 'we are supporting the regional efforts in transport and food security of SADCC, while also quietly urging South Africa and its neighbours to maintain pragmatic trade and customs agreements based on mutual benefit'.[20] This, of course, contradicts the main goal of SADCC, but it did mean that the US increased its support for SADCC projects. By 1985 it had still not abandoned its views that 'pragmatic' trade links with South Africa should continue, but it put $5m into the Beira port and railway line in Mozambique, which are vital for delinking.

In part US policy on SADCC is genuinely schizophrenic. On the other hand, there is an undertone of efforts to divide the SADCC states — in this instance the US is supporting projects in Mozambique while assisting UNITA to overthrow the government of another SADCC state.

Changing world views

Reagan's election and constructive engagement did offset some of the impact of Zimbabwe's independence, and especially of the founding of SADCC, by changing the international political climate. The US and the EEC have always wanted to safeguard their interests in the region and reduce the influence of the Eastern bloc. In the late 1970s, liberal anti-communism seemed in the ascendency. The initial thinking was that SADCC was a way of drawing Marxist Mozambique and Angola (and eventually Zimbabwe) into a Western-oriented body which would provide new openings to the private sector and reduce Eastern bloc influence. The Carter administration actively supported this view and encouraged the EEC to make the running. This was clearly seen by the socialist bloc itself, which tended to avoid SADCC despite attempts by Mozambique to bring it in.

The climate shifted with the elections of Margaret Thatcher and Ronald Reagan. They did not support this subtlety of approach, and took a hard line both on choosing between East and West, and on the need to protect existing interests in South Africa itself. At the time of the November 1980 SADCC meeting in Maputo, Reagan had been elected but had not taken office, so at the conference the Carter-appointed US delegation gave SADCC fulsome support. The only negative view came from the British delegation, headed by Thatcher's Overseas Development Minister, Neil Marten. In private meetings they stressed that while the UK supported SADCC regional cooperation, Britain was opposed to SADCC's reducing dependence on South Africa. As we have seen, the new US government also took this line. At later SADCC conferences, both Britain and the US tried to stop SADCC from denouncing South African destabilisation.

West Germany was also initially hostile to SADCC, and in particular tried to challenge the SADCC policy that it, not the donors, should set priorities.[21] Both

Britain and West Germany have funded SADCC projects, but in the early years only very grudgingly.

The changing mood also created splits in the EEC. Some officials tried to direct EEC support to those projects which did not reduce dependence on South Africa. At the same time they backed those which increased South African links, particularly Lesotho's Highland Water Scheme. Privately they reminded South Africa that it benefited indirectly from EEC aid programmes, as money was often spent in South Africa despite restrictions (which were in any case sometimes quietly waived), and tried to find ways in which South Africa might be involved, at least through the back door, in SADCC projects. On the other side, liberal EEC officials argued that the eventual accession of Mozambique and Angola to the Lomé Convention was partly due to the role the EEC had played in SADCC, and thus proof that their approach had been correct. They also pointed to SADCC's opening to the private sector in industry and energy. And they reminded South Africa that destabilisation which damaged European-assisted development would inevitably harm its case in the EEC.

With the end of the liberal consensus, a clear division opened between Western governments. The US, Britain, and West Germany, the three states with the heaviest investment and trade links with South Africa, were hostile to sanctions, and SADCC's emphasis on delinking. They tried to channel new investment through South Africa. However, those without traditional links to South Africa — particularly the Scandinavian states, Netherlands, Belgium, Italy, and Canada — looked at the SADCC states both as a new source of raw materials and a market. They saw that the regional energy and mineral potential put SADCC in a special position, both as a supplier and a market for machinery and consumer goods. They also saw that delinking from South Africa would reduce the competition and make it easier for them to gain access to the SADCC states. Accordingly they have actively backed SADCC and invested in the member states.

4. Destabilisation: 1981-83

With apartheid under pressure both inside and outside South Africa, Pretoria lashed out. On 30 January 1981, just ten days after Reagan took office, South African commandos hit the capital of Mozambique. In the suburb of Matola, they attacked three houses, killing 13 ANC members and a Portuguese electricity technician. It was South Africa's first official cross-border raid, outside the war in Angola.

The total strategy called for a mix of diplomatic, military, and economic actions. Diplomatic activity did continue, particularly with Swaziland, as well as with Zambia and Lesotho. Similarly, South Africa was already militarily embroiled in several of the neighbouring states. Nevertheless, January 1981 marked a drastic change in the balance. The soft line of trying to co-opt the neighbours into Consas was replaced by the hard line of active destabilisation.

The Matola raid was probably testing the water. The US raised no objections. Indeed there were unconfirmed reports that Washington had approved it in advance. In March a high-ranking intelligence delegation led by Piet van der Westhuizen went to the US for talks with the Pentagon and other high US officials; van der Westhuizen was head of military intelligence and thus the man responsible for surrogate armies like the MNR and LLA.

After that, the State Security Council (SSC) obviously saw 'constructive engagement' as a licence to attack the neighbours. High officials, including Police Minister Louis le Grange, warned that the Maputo raid would be repeated elsewhere. During 1981 all of the neighbouring states were attacked (the incidents are detailed in Chapters 10-19):

- In Angola, incursions and bombing raids were stepped up, particularly after June. In August the SADF launched a full-scale motorised invasion, named Operation Protea. On 30 November 1981 commandos attacked the oil refinery in the capital, Luanda.
- In Zimbabwe, the ANC representative was assassinated on 30 July 1981. Commandos blew up an ammunition dump on 16 August and nearly assassinated Prime Minister Robert Mugabe on 18 December.
- In Mozambique, South African troops came over the border again on 17 March 1981, retreating after a clash with Mozambican soldiers. Commandos returned and blew up two key bridges linking the port of Beira to Zimbabwe on 29 October, and marker buoys in Beira port on 13 November.
- In Lesotho there was a series of bomb explosions in the capital and elsewhere.
- In Swaziland, a South African refugee was kidnapped by the South African security services in February 1981; two ANC men were killed in December.

● In Zambia, South African troops occupied the south-western corner of the country, mining roads and confiscating a ferry boat.
● In Botswana, there was a series of border incidents and incursions by South African troops.
● And in the Seychelles (not a subject of this book), there was an unsuccessful South African-organised coup on 25 November 1981.

Cross-border raids continued in 1982 and 1983. The most appalling occurred on 9 December 1982, when South African commandos hit Maseru, Lesotho, and killed 42 people. On the same day they attacked the fuel storage depot in the port of Beira, Mozambique, which serves Zimbabwe and Malawi, doing $20m worth of damage. Others included an attack on Thornhill air base in Zimbabwe on 25 July 1982, an air force raid on Maputo which killed six people on 23 May 1983, and the Operation Askari invasion of Angola in December 1983. There was even a raid in London, where the ANC office was bombed on 14 March 1982.

South Africa's main actions were not the spectacular raids. The neighbours suffered a wide-ranging economic and military assault which is commonly called 'destabilisation'. Military action was largely through surrogate armies: UNITA in Angola, MNR in Mozambique, LLA in Lesotho, and the so-called 'super-ZAPU' in Zimbabwe. UNITA and the MNR had been nearly moribund, but were revitalised with massive new South African support, and became active in large parts of Angola and Mozambique respectively. The LLA and 'super-ZAPU' were entirely new South African creations.

At the same time economic sanctions were imposed against Zimbabwe and Mozambique, and lesser actions taken against other states. In March 1981 South Africa announced that it intended to cancel a bilateral trade agreement which gave some Zimbabwean goods preferential access to South Africa.[1] At the same time, it severely disrupted rail traffic to and in Zimbabwe, costing Z$5m per week in lost exports at the worst period. A *de facto* embargo was imposed on Mozambique, leading to a rapid decline in South African traffic through the port and minor disinvestment.

Economic and military action were closely linked. The four surrogate armies all focused on economic targets, particularly transport links. Roads and railways were mined; trains, lorries, buses, and cars attacked. The key was to prevent goods flowing through Mozambican and Angolan ports; in 1980 the Benguela railway in Angola had been reopened, but with South Africa active it soon came under UNITA attack and was closed again. In Mozambique the MNR first hit the oil pipeline and railway from Beira to Zimbabwe; when Zimbabwean troops came in to guard them, South Africa turned its attention to other lines. By 1983 it had effectively closed the railways from Zimbabwe to Maputo and from Malawi to Beira.

SADCC was both a practical and a symbolic target. In the month before the second annual conference (in Malawi in November 1981), South Africa hit two key rail bridges near Beira and marker buoys in Beira port — which serves Malawi. In the two months before the third annual meeting (in Lesotho in January 1983), South Africa attacked the host city and also blew up an oil storage depot in Beira port. Rehabilitation of the depot was already listed as a SADCC project. And South Africa and the LLA hit other economic targets in Maseru the day before the conference started.

The theory of destabilisation

Destabilisation involves a mix of military and economic weapons, perhaps reflecting its roots in the total strategy. And the mix is different for each country: Angola faced a purely military assault, Mozambique a combination of military and economic, and Zimbabwe and Lesotho primarily economic backed up with some military intervention. Even Malawi came under military pressure (the intentional cutting of Malawi's railway links inside Mozambique). Inevitably, this reflected the power that South Africa had over its neighbours — it had a significant economic hold over Zimbabwe and Lesotho, less economic power in Mozambique, and very little in Angola. In a few cases, notably Swaziland, South Africa was also prepared to dangle significant political and economic inducements. But in most cases there was a lot of stick and very little carrot.

Deon Geldenhuys, who became an associate professor of political science at Rand Afrikaans University in 1982, was a major theoretician of destabilisation, both explaining the concept and showing how it could be done.[2] In a key paper in September 1982 he set out to establish South Africa's right to destabilise its neighbours, and to elaborate the methods. Since it reflects apartheid thinking on the subject, this paper is worth quoting at length. First, Professor Geldenhuys argues that

> The destabiliser's primary objective is an avowedly political one. Essentially, he wishes to promote (or force) profound political changes in the target state. They may or may not involve structural changes — in effect toppling the regime in power — but certainly would involve major changes in the target's behaviour. ... At the very least, the destabiliser demands a fundamental shift or reorientation in the target state's policy vis-à-vis the destabiliser.

Next, he argues that the neighbours are trying to promote such fundamental changes in South Africa, namely ending apartheid and ending South African control of Namibia. Furthermore,

> The provision of sanctuary to SWAPO and the ANC, together with the presence of Cuban and other communist forces in neighbouring states, represents attempts to destabilise the Republic [of South Africa]. Similarly, black states' political and moral support for the so-called liberation movements, and their clamour for sanctions against South Africa and for its international isolation, are part of a concerted campaign to destabilise the country.

Thus he concludes that it would 'be naive to expect [South Africa] to renounce the destabilisation option for at least as long as black states remain committed to destabilise it'. A key point of this formulation is that South Africa is justified in destabilising its neighbours even if they never directly interfere in South Africa's internal affairs, but only oppose apartheid, call for sanctions at the UN, and have military help from socialist states.

Geldenhuys goes on to stress that since the aim is a fundamental shift in the opponent's policies, 'the destabiliser is not interested in actions which the target state would consider to be mere irritants or annoyances, or actions causing the target state strictly limited discomfort or injury'. He also warns that 'destabilisation activities ... usually take a covert form, with the destabiliser taking care to cover his tracks to and from the scene of the crime.' With these points in mind, he gives a prescription for South Africa to destabilise its neighbours.

South Africa must 'be guided by the target state's political, economic, and military vulnerabilities'. Thus he first suggests manipulation of food supplies in an attempt 'to cause serious hardship to the population, who would in turn direct their frustration and fury at the target's regime'. (This was done in Mozambique, and more than 100,000 people starved to death in the resulting famine.) Next he suggests continued support to 'disaffected groups in the target state'.[3] This would include 'providing arms and equipment; recruiting and arming mercenaries; [and] sending out military personnel as advisers, or as combatants blended into the local forces, or as a force in its own right'. (This was already being done for the four surrogate armies.) Finally, he stresses that, 'psychological means are crucially important in a destabilisation campaign' and notes that it is necessary 'to provide the rebels with their own radio station, whether situated in the destabilising or the target state'. (This was done for Zimbabwe, Mozambique, and Angola).

Destabilisation is as much economic as military. Geldenhuys first made his mark with a seminal study on 'the ways in which the Republic could use its economic relationships in southern Africa for non-economic purposes'.[4] It was commissioned by the Institute for Strategic Studies of the University of Pretoria (ISSUP), and published in January 1981 — the month of the Matola raid. In Geldenhuys' own words, ISSUP is 'a policy-oriented academic research institution, leaning heavily towards the Defence Force'.[5] ISSUP was one of the recipients of secret government money exposed in the 'Muldergate' information scandal. As Geldenhuys commented in the article, 'the fact that a study of this nature is commissioned ... is in itself significant'.

In his study, Geldenhuys proposed thirteen ways in which South Africa could regulate and manipulate the flow of goods and people between the black states and South Africa. All but three were tried in the following years:[6]

- 'Limiting or prohibiting the use of South Africa's railways and harbour facilities ... e.g. by manipulating the availability of railway trucks or berthing facilities in harbours, or harsher measures such as imposing surcharges on goods transported, or officially announcing restrictions on the amount of goods that may be exported via South Africa.' (This was done particularly to Zimbabwe, but also to Botswana, Lesotho, and Zambia.)
- 'Limiting or banning the importation of labour from black states.' (This was done to Zimbabwe, and threats were made against Lesotho and Mozambique.)
- 'Regulating the access to and movement through South Africa of nationals from black states ... e.g., by deliberate delays at border posts. Interruption of postal and telecommunications services provided to black states may also be considered.' (Lesotho and Swaziland suffered public border closures. The other three bordering countries, Zimbabwe, Botswana, and Mozambique, have also seen disruptions of cross-border traffic.)
- 'Placing curbs on imports of goods from black states through the imposition of tariffs or quotas.' (Zimbabwe)
- 'Regulating the export of goods to black states,' especially 'food and oil, but machinery, spares, and various other goods could also be added. ... Restrictions on the availability of loans and credit could also be added.' (Lesotho, Botswana, Zimbabwe, Zambia, Mozambique, and Malawi)
- 'Curtailing or terminating the provision of technical expertise', particularly with respect to harbours and railways, but also possibly medical and veterinary services. (Zimbabwe railways)
- 'Regulating investment by both South African public and private sectors in the black states.' Either curtailing investment as a 'disincentive lever' or

channelling it through the Development Bank of Southern African as 'an incentive lever'. (Disinvestment took place in Mozambique, Lesotho, Swaziland, Botswana, and Zimbabwe, although the South African government role is not clear.)

● 'Regulating the supply of South African-generated electricity to neighbouring states.' (Lesotho and Mozambique)

● 'Regulating the flow of South African tourists to neighbouring countries.' (Lesotho and Swaziland through border closures aimed at tourists, and Zimbabwe to a lesser degree by propaganda and other means.)

● 'Suspending the Customs Union Agreement ... or violating its provisions.' (Botswana, Lesotho, and Swaziland)

For these techniques to work, 'South Africa should endeavour to keep black states as economically dependent as possible, thereby circumscribing their freedom of economic, political, and also military action vis-à-vis South Africa'. Thus it is essential that 'black southern African states would retain substantial economic ties with South Africa despite their efforts to reduce their economic dependence on the Republic (through the so-called counter-constellation)' — that is, SADCC — and that 'the relationship would largely remain one of dependence (on South Africa) rather than becoming a symmetric one of mutual dependence or interdependence'.

Geldenhuys admits there may be certain repercussions. Most serious, such actions might further erode 'South Africa's already poor international standing', but he admits the widespread view 'that South Africa has not much more to lose internationally and could therefore act with virtual impunity'. More seriously, however, if South Africa were seen to be imposing sanctions against the neighbours, 'this will certainly bring grist to the mill of those persistently demanding tougher economic measures against South Africa'. Another possible problem is that the 'instability' created by destabilisation might create 'new opportunities for Soviet involvement' and 'provide a useful cover for exile movements'. Finally, Mozambique could cut off the supply of Cahora Bassa electricity.[7] It is unclear how much influence Professor Geldenhuys has. It seems likely that his ISSUP paper was used in deciding how to employ 'economic levers'. In other cases, he seems simply a well-placed reporter. What is important, however, is, first, that he did reflect the thinking of some parts of the government and military at the time and, second, that his work was published in the open literature. At a time when most Western countries still accepted South African denials that it was destabilising its neighbours, its handbook of destabilisation was available for all to read.

Justification

In early 1981, with Consas a failure, the previous policy of building friendly links through economic power was obviously in tatters. At the same time, strikes, unrest, and ANC sabotage actions were increasing within South Africa itself. There were probably few in the apartheid elite who would have disagreed that destabilisation seemed the only answer.

Destabilisation had a variety of goals, which are outlined in more detail in Chapter 7. The two most important goals were unspoken (except by academics like Geldenhuys). The first was to reassert economic and political hegemony, to use pressure to bring the neighbouring states back into line. Pretoria wanted to force the neighbours into continued economic relations with South Africa (thus breaking SADCC) and into some public acceptance of apartheid, or at least reduced criticism. There were repeated demands that neighbouring states sign non-aggression pacts, really more a political than a military demand. Some in the military hoped to be able to force the neighbouring states to reduce their links with the socialist bloc.

The second goal was simply to create chaos in the neighbouring states, especially those which could not be forced into line. It was an attempt to replace the old *cordon sanitaire* with what was sometimes described as a 'cordon of instability'. The neighbours were to be too concerned with their own survival to provide any threat to apartheid.

In contrast to the other two, a third goal was repeatedly stated, and indeed was the public justification for destabilisation. It was to prevent the neighbouring states from harbouring ANC and SWAPO 'terrorists' and to destroy the 'terrorists' in their lairs. The SADF magazine *Paratus* (January 1982) published an article called 'The case for cross-border operations in southern Africa', by Dr M. Hough, the director of ISSUP (Institute of Strategic Studies of the University of Pretoria). He argued the importance of pre-emptive strikes 'in order to, at least temporarily, delay or destroy an insurgent's military capacity'. He also pointed to the usefulness of cross-border raids in 'boosting public morale' and in building a 'stronger bargaining position during negotiations'. Finally, he stressed that 'cross-border operations could serve both as a warning to the governments of states harbouring insurgents as well as to the insurgent leaders that further operations will be carried out if terrorism does not cease'.

Dr Hough cited Rhodesian raids into Mozambique and Zambia, and Israeli raids into Jordan and Lebanon, as successful precedents. The Israeli connection proved increasingly important, as a source of both equipment and ideas. In several instances, South Africa followed the Israeli example of massive raids into neighbouring states in retaliation for ANC actions. For example, the 23 May 1983 raid on Maputo came just three days after an ANC car bomb exploded outside the South African Air Force headquarters in Pretoria.

Pretoria also took up the idea of using surrogates in the way Israel used the Lebanese Christian militias. UNITA was built up as a barrier to SWAPO infiltration, and there was even talk of creating a UNITA-controlled buffer state in southern Angola. The LLA in Lesotho actually attacked ANC targets, and the so-called 'super-ZAPU' in Zimbabwe was partly intended to block ANC infiltration.

Hawks, doves and qualms

But there were doubts; to some people in the apartheid leadership the military seemed to be simply thrashing about like a wounded elephant. The goals were not clear, and thus there was no real measure of success or failure. The idea of a cordon of instability also conflicted with the regional interests of business.

The 1981 sanctions against Zimbabwe were a first area of disagreement. Dr J.G.H. Loubser, South African Railways General Manager and a co-opted member of the SSC, was reportedly unhappy about the use of his trains to throttle Zimbabwe. Some in the business community, particularly Anglo executives, also thought that they could work with Mugabe. And the first negative reactions from the US came over this issue; Chester Crocker told Pretoria that it was making a mistake, and that sanctions only reduced its power and influence in Zimbabwe. Finally, in late 1981 and early 1982, South Africa backed down on economic sanctions; the railway boycotts were ended and the trade agreement renewed instead of cancelled. Military pressure was maintained, however.[8]

In 1982 talk of divisions and of 'hawks' and 'doves' began to emerge. The hawks promoted destabilisation to keep neighbouring states weak and dependent, and even advocated overthrowing neighbouring governments. The doves put more stress on gains to be made from economic links, and were more concerned with South Africa's foreign image. They argued that the threat of destabilisation was sufficient, and South Africa could use economic power to gain security; actual destabilisation ran the risk of bringing international sanctions down on South Africa's head without producing any direct benefit. As presented, the hawks were largely associated with the more reactionary elements in the military, while the doves were often associated with the Foreign Ministry; some commentators talked of an open split between defence and foreign ministries. In practice there seems to have been a continuum, with hawkish and dovish elements in both foreign and defence.

For many 'doves', the Maseru raid went too far, and in early 1983 dissent broke into the open. Geldenhuys and other academic advisers complained in the press about military dominance of South African foreign policy. They reminded the military about its own oft-stated view that action must be only 20% military and 80% political. The more sophisticated approach of the total strategy, with its mix of military, diplomatic, and economic, had been replaced by the search for 'military quick-fix solutions'. The powerful role of the SSC and the military weight in it were finally discussed in the media.[9]

For the first time there was also open acceptance by the English-language press that South Africa was supporting the MNR and UNITA and was destabilising its neighbours (although this was still denied by government). A Johannesburg *Star* leader (25 April) was headlined simply 'Destabilisation — a shortsighted policy'. And it warned that 'far from curbing Soviet influences in Africa, [destabilisation] is more likely to bring about further calls for Russian aid and intervention'. John Barratt, director general of the SA Institute of International Affairs, warned that destabilisation was creating such regional instability that it was putting off businessmen from investing in South Africa itself.[10]

On top of this came a growing view that destabilisation was not working — chaos was being created in the neighbouring states to no obvious benefit to South Africa. Military credibility was further dented by the 23 May 1983 air raid on Maputo. Defence Minister General Magnus Malan said that the planes had destroyed six ANC bases and a missile battery and killed 41 ANC 'terrorists'; foreign journalists (including myself) were free to tour the area and found that the targets were in fact a jam factory and ordinary surburban houses, and our reports were widely published in South Africa.

The main defection, however, was of business. Business leaders were slow to abandon P.W. Botha because he was in such sharp contrast to Vorster, who had treated them with contempt. Instead P.W. had courted them, and for the first time, they were rubbing shoulders with political leaders. Yet it was clear that the government was mismanaging the economy, and it had failed to fulfil its two promises as part of the total strategy package: Consas and internal reform. Consas was an obvious failure, and the promised changes to the race laws were not forthcoming.

P.W. Botha was scheduled to have another meeting with business executives in October 1981, but he cancelled it in anger when the press reported that the executives were planning to press him on sensitive issues like labour, black housing, education, and influx control. P.W. Botha then hosted a conference at the Good Hope centre in Cape Town, intended to be a re-run of the 1979 Carlton Conference which had been the peak of building the business-military alliance needed by the total strategy. But at the Good Hope meeting the business leaders vented their dissatisfaction at the slow pace of political reform.

Meanwhile, there had been a minor economic boom in 1980 and 1981. But this soon wore off, and South Africa had to go to the IMF for money in 1982. Real GDP fell 1% in 1982 and a massive 13% in the first half of 1983. The number of bankruptcies began to rise, and smaller businesses were hit hardest. The monopoly groups were reasonably able to ride out the depression and seemed more concerned with internal issues and reforms of apartheid. Indeed, there are several cases where the monopoly groups seem to have supported destabilisation. But medium-sized firms were being badly squeezed by the depression. They saw the neighbouring states as a possible area of expansion and profit, and were not pleased at the effect of destabilisation, which seemed to be only to reduce trade with South Africa, while SADCC was moving from strength to strength.

The issues were somewhat different for the various SADCC states. For South Africa, unlike the United States, there was little commercial interest in Angola, for example, while Lesotho seemed so closely tied that business had little fear of losing out there. Medium-sized business was particularly interested in Mozambique (which seemed virgin territory) and Zimbabwe. Some of the monopoly groups (particularly Anglo) seemed willing to deal with Robert Mugabe, but none showed any great interest in Mozambique.

But the general concern of the business community was clearly expressed in an outspoken attack on 29 March 1983 from W.B. Holtes, chief executive of the South African Foreign Trade Organisation (SAFTO), which represents smaller exporters.[11] Appropriately, he chose ISSUP for his speech. Holtes was explicitly critical of the unpublicised embargo on Maputo, which had by then halved South African cargo through the port, declaring that South Africa should 'utilise to a maximum extent neighbouring countries' facilities such as Maputo harbour'. Not to do so would only encourage delinking and push SADCC to build new facilities to avoid using South Africa. He continued that South Africa must 'go out of its way to create markets for SADCC products in the Republic'. It was, he declared 'short term folly to expect South Africa's current domination in these sectors ... to continue *ad infinitum* without any backlash'. And he concluded that 'South Africa's ability to further grow as a major supplier to SADCC countries may in years to come be dependent on sincere efforts in developing a more balanced two-way trade pattern.'

By all accounts, the SSC was deeply divided throughout 1982-83. In December 1982 the Foreign Ministry had opened talks with both Mozambique and Angola, despite the strongest objections by the military. The 23 May 1983 air raid on Maputo took place just days after the second meeting with the Mozambicans; not surprisingly, Frelimo was very angry and cut off further talks, which may have been what the military wanted. Meanwhile, the Pretoria government was coming under stronger international pressure, and the role of the United States became increasingly important. In late 1982 the CIA head William Casey had met with P.W. Botha, Pik Botha, Malan, and senior army chiefs to argue that it was possible to build a new *cordon sanitaire*. This would involve the expulsion of the ANC from neighbouring states in exchange for an end to destabilisation, and a deal in Namibia and Angola based on linkage (Cubans to withdraw in exchange for a settlement in Namibia).[12] The military remained unconvinced; support for the MNR escalated and some high military officials wanted to overthrow Machel.[13]

The Maseru raid embarrassed the Reagan administration, because it showed that constructive engagement was not producing results; the US voted in favour of a UN Security Council resolution condemning the raid. In 1982 Mozambique had begun courting the US, and asking for pressure on South Africa. The first mark of an improved relationship was a statement by the US State Department in early 1983 that South Africa was providing the 'bulk' of the support to the MNR. By early 1983 the South African press was reporting the US pressure.[14] Meanwhile, Chester Crocker was stressing to South Africa the Reagan administration's belief that it was possible to, as the press described it, 'pluck Mozambique from the Soviet orbit'. And he made clear that the US 'did not want anything to happen that would push Mozambique back to the Communists — such as a repeat of the Matola raid in 1981'.[15] Malan's answer was to do just that, and bomb Maputo in May.

At a SADCC heads of state meeting in Maputo on 13 July 1983, eight of the nine heads (only Banda was missing) admitted that 'South Africa can invade and occupy sovereign states, blow up vital installations, and massacre populations at no apparent cost to its relations with its main allies'. In a statement pointed directly at the West, they continued that 'some of the friends of South Africa who provide the racist regime with the capital, technology, management skills, and deadly weapons necessary to carry out such a policy also seek to improve their relations with SADCC'. The best way to do so would be to 'use their influence to check the aggression being waged against SADCC member states'.

A turning point came in October 1983 when President Machel visited western Europe to appeal for help, and to stress his openness to Western private investment. This was taken as public evidence of Mozambique's 'turn to the West', and led to discreet European pressure on both South Africa and the US. There was also pressure on Machel, however, to improve relations with South Africa; in Britain, for example, Machel was told in no uncertain terms that British investment would naturally go to Mozambique through South Africa. Foreign Minister Pik Botha followed Machel around Europe, and was told that South Africa had to be seen to negotiate with Machel. This strengthened Pik Botha's hand, while the military suffered a further loss of credibility when its December 1983 invasion of Angola ran up against unexpectedly strong opposition, causing unacceptably high losses of men and machinery.

President Reagan faced a re-election campaign in 1984, and southern Africa was hoped to be an area in which he could show political success. Thus the US wanted action on Namibia, Angola, and Mozambique. By late 1983, Crocker was arguing increasingly strongly to South Africa that its military actions had succeeded and that it was time to reap the harvest — that major economic and political gains could be achieved if South Africa negotiated.

5. South Africa as a Regional Power

Suddenly Pretoria went to the conference table. On 16 February 1984 it signed the Lusaka agreement with Angola, under which it promised to withdraw its troops. And on 16 March, with an unexpected circus of pomp and publicity, P.W. Botha and Samora Machel signed the Nkomati Accord 'on non-aggression and good neighbourliness'. In May there were even talks between South Africa and SWAPO in Lusaka.

The signings followed the 2 November 1983 referendum, in which white voters agreed to the establishment of 'coloured' and 'Indian' parliaments, the reduction in power of their own white parliament, and the elevation of P.W. Botha to a new and more powerful post of State President. The new constitution approved at the referendum was the final step in consolidating power in the new quasi-military government controlled by the State Security Council. It was billed, however, as the first step to dismantling apartheid. But, as the *Economist*'s political editor commented, 'No government which has recently introduced a racially classified parliament, segregated local government, and a segregated welfare state can seriously expect the world to believe it is intent on dismantling apartheid.'[1]

In his biography P.W. Botha said that the referendum was the high point of his domestic policy. And he argued that it created the climate which promoted the Nkomati accord, the high point of his foreign policy.[2]

These two high points were crowned by an official visit to western Europe from 29 May to 9 June 1984. He went to Britain at the invitation of Prime Minister Margaret Thatcher, the first such invitation to a South African Prime Minister in 23 years. Accompanied by Foreign Minister Pik Botha, P.W. also visited Portugal, West Germany, Belgium, Switzerland, France and the Vatican. Suddenly P.W. Botha was *persona grata* in polite company. The press noted that such a visit would have been impossible six months before, and that it was due to the diplomatic thaw created by Nkomati. The route to the West truly did go through southern Africa, as P.W. and Vorster before him had believed. According to P.W. Botha, Nkomati showed that 'we could undertake our diplomacy with self-confidence born of strength — economic and military strength — and make standing room for ourselves in southern Africa'.

The tour marked the crest of a wave which broke soon after. Within weeks of his return, the Lusaka agreement had publicly broken down and top South African ministers were colluding in the resupply of the MNR in violation of the Nkomati accord. Internally, in elections in August, 'coloureds' and 'Indians' overwhelmingly rejected the new constitution, and unrest broke out in the townships (and continues at the time of writing, more than a year later). ANC activity inside South Africa and SWAPO action in Namibia continued despite the accords. The small economic recovery which started in late 1983 ended by mid-1984; the rand began to collapse and interest rates jumped to 32% for overdrafts.

This showed just how fragile the position of the government was. It also became clear that even if there had been agreement within the State Security Council on *signing* the Nkomati and Lusaka accords, there was no consensus on *abiding* by them. This is discussed in detail in the next chapter, while this chapter looks at the brief period in the first half of 1984 when white South Africa was riding high.

This period was important because it saw the coming together of a large part of the white elite. For the first time since 1979, business actively supported the government. Business gave overwhelming support to the new constitution,[3] and also to the Nkomati Accord. Change at home and abroad seemed to promise peace at home and in the region, and an end to South Africa's pariah status.

The Lusaka agreement and talks with SWAPO were important to the overall picture of South Africa as peacemaker, but less useful because neither would sign a formal agreement. Nkomati was the key to the whole process. Mozambique signed the non-aggression pact that South Africa had been demanding for the previous decade — the diplomatic victory that it had long sought. Militarily, it was also seen as a fatal blow to the ANC. Economically, Mozambique was seen as moving into Pretoria's orbit and there was renewed talk of Consas. SADCC, it was hoped, had received a mortal wound.

Lusaka

The first diplomatic success was an agreement signed in Lusaka on 16 February 1984. South Africa agreed to withdraw its troops from Cunene Province by the end of March. Neither SWAPO nor UNITA were supposed to move into the zone, and a Joint Monitoring Commission composed of both South African and Angolan military was to supervise the withdrawal. The agreement was never published but by all accounts it was extremely limited in extent (some further details are given in Chapter 13). After an unexpectedly bruising confrontation, both sides wanted to withdraw their troops from the zone, and that was all they agreed. The Lusaka accord was not the formal non-aggression pact that South Africa wanted, while by excluding Kuando Kubango province it did not deal with South African support for UNITA, as Angola had hoped. In the first instance, South Africa did withdraw its troops, albeit more slowly than expected. Then in April it suddenly stopped the withdrawal, continuing to occupy a 40 km wide strip along the border. This was not formally announced until July, four weeks after Pik and P.W. Botha had returned from Europe (and will be discussed further in the next chapter).

Carried on by the momentum of Lusaka and Nkomati, South Africa also held direct talks with Lesotho in the period just before the Bothas went to Europe, but these did not produce results. South Africa put Lesotho under very heavy pressure and almost succeeded in forcing it to sign a non-aggression pact, but in the end the Prime Minister, Leabua Jonathan, balked.

And in May 1984 there were talks in Lusaka about Namibia involving South Africa, Zambia, SWAPO, and the South African sponsored internal parties; SWAPO and South Africa met again in the Cape Verde Islands in July. According to diplomatic sources, South Africa hoped that with SWAPO's access routes through Angola temporarily cut off, it might be willing to agree to a settlement in

Namibia not based on UN Security Council resolution 435 (which calls for UN supervised elections). But this was a vain hope, and neither meeting succeeded. But the May meeting was good for South Africa's image, coming just before the European tour.

Nkomati

As P.W. Botha recognised, the 16 March Nkomati non-aggression pact was the crucial event. Under it, Mozambique agreed to stop supporting the ANC and expel all but official refugees and a ten-strong diplomatic mission. All but the ANC mission left soon after. Mozambique had never allowed ANC bases, but it had permitted transit; guerrillas and political cadres had passed from Mozambique into Swaziland and then South Africa, and returned to Mozambique the same way. Under Nkomati, this, too, was stopped. Clearly it hurt the ANC, but not as badly as forecast.[4] For its part, South Africa pledged to stop supporting the MNR. It did close down the MNR radio station (but, it turned out later, actually stepped up other support — see the next chapter).

The United States, which had used all its influence in Pretoria and Maputo to secure the accord, saw it as central to the future of the whole of southern Africa, and as a justification of the policy of constructive engagement. Chester Crocker claimed that with the Nkomati accord 'the illusion that armed struggle will solve South Africa's problems had been dealt a body blow. It could even be an irreversible body blow'. White South Africa was ecstatic. The *Sunday Times* called it the success of a 'Bismarckian thump-and-talk strategy', and of 'diplomacy backed by unchallengeable military superiority'.[5]

Nkomati was 'the true fruits of destabilisation', wrote columnist Brian Pottinger:[6]

> Military force, economic muscle, and diplomatic pressure were part of a long-term strategy worked out in a rational assessment of the best way to defend South African interests. That being so, military 'destabilisation' of neighbouring states becomes something not antithetical to South Africa's foreign policy interests but complementary. [7]

Consas returns

P.W. Botha stressed that 'the Nkomati Accord was the result of a process which began years ago in accordance with our philosophy of total strategy'.[8] In the philosophy, business has a crucial role, and Nkomati was seen as the next step in reincorporating the business community.

Mozambique had wanted the Nkomati talks to be purely about security (which, technically, the accord was) but South Africa forced the inclusion of economic issues. So there were three parallel economic commissions which met while the security talks were going on: general economic, Cahora Bassa, and tourism.[9]

Most of South Africa's top business people attended the signing. In his speech at the ceremony P.W. Botha specifically referred to the 'constellation of states' (Consas). The vision of 1979 was revived. The head of the Associated Chambers of Commerce (Assocom) said that 'we stand closer to the Prime Minister's constellation of states goal than ever before'.[10]

The business community saw four somewhat different but overlapping advantages in Nkomati. First, it was a direct blow to SADCC. Second, some businessmen saw Mozambique as an important, potential market. Third, taken with the Lusaka agreement, the non-aggression pact with Swaziland, and the SWAPO talks, it seemed to improve the chances for peace and South African hegemony in the region. And fourth, it substantially improved South Africa's world image, and seemed likely to increase the flow of foreign capital. This mix was stressed by John Maree of Barlow Rand, who attended the signing. He called Nkomati 'a tremendous breakthrough' that would lead to 'improved capital flow, a better market, and a stronger rand'.[11]

Nkomati was seen as a welcome blow to SADCC as well as the ANC. The *Financial Mail* (27 April) predicted that Nkomati would kill SADCC, and called for 'a nine-nation Rand monetary area consisting of Angola, Zimbabwe, Zambia, Namibia, Mozambique, South Africa, Swaziland, Botswana, and Lesotho'. Others argued for co-opting SADCC. In a speech in Malawi, Anglo chairman Gavin Relly lauded Consas; he called on the SADCC states to 'not place too much emphasis on diminishing their links with South Africa, for that flies in the face of economic reality', and rather accept the so-called independent bantustans and become 'associated in some way with Consas'.[12]

Like the first introduction of Consas at the Carlton Conference in 1979, the Nkomati signing was a highly publicised bringing together of business executives. Suddenly Consas seemed real again, and many were enthusiastic. There was a veritable flock of business executives flying into Maputo in the following weeks. Sam Motseunyane of the National African Federated Chambers of Commerce (Nafcoc) urged his members to 'join the stampede to establish relations with Mozambique'.[13] However, serious interest in Mozambique soon proved to be restricted to small or medium-sized business, and particuarly to concerns based in regions near the border with Mozambique. Johnny Henn, a wealthy farmer and the mayor of the small border town of Komatipoort (where Nkomati was signed), organised a Lowveld Liaison Committee which negotiated small-scale tourism and farming agreements. A majority of members of delegations organised by Assocom and other groups were small business operators.[14] The regional implications were also stressed. Assocom predicted a 'dramatic rise' in trade with all of Africa, and announced 'business safaris' to go 'as far as the equator'.

What soon became clear, however, was that most of the interest in Mozambique and in other African states came from those who wished to sell goods and services. There was little interest in investment. Because of all the hyperbole by South African politicians and businessmen about how the dynamic South African economy could save the neighbouring states, there was an assumption in some quarters in both South Africa and Mozambique that the government would put up seed money and that this would be followed by investment. This confidence was soon shattered. South Africa did not have the money to back up the economic links proposed as part of Nkomati. P.W. Botha stressed that South Africa could not play 'Father Christmas' to Mozambique, and that he was depending on private capital.[15] Unfortunately, that was not available due to the recession — particularly ironic after years of public statements about how South Africa would be the engine of development for the entire region.

The only monopoly group to invest was Old Mutual. It owned Rennies (now Renfreight), which spent R10m in Maputo port. Rennies was already one of the main shipping agencies in the port, and would quickly earn back the cost of the new cranes. Nevertheless, its newly appointed chief executive stuck his neck out and said that he felt Rennies was 'contributing to the price that private enterprise must pay to ensure southern African stability. What is more, we are prepared to put some money up front'. He proved to be the only one.[16]

Far from investing in Mozambique, South Africa hoped that Nkomati would bring capital to South Africa. This would come in two ways. First, it was hoped that Nkomati would improve South Africa's international image enough to generate new loans and investment, and second it was hoped that Nkomati would reassert the role of Johannesburg as regional financial centre and thus bring in money for use in the neighbouring states.

In the early 1980s, South Africa's credit rating fell and international banks lent to it for shorter and shorter periods and at higher interest rates. In the first half of 1984, credit terms for South Africa eased substantially — interest rates were only slightly higher than for European countries, while loans were made for five or even eight years, which would have been unthinkable a year before. The government and parastatals borrowed significant amounts of new money. There was wide agreement that it was Nkomati that made this possible. P.W. Botha visited Switzerland in June 1984 specifically to talk to bankers there.

Pik Botha called on Western countries to 'help Mozambique' with investment routed through South Africa. It was a point that Margaret Thatcher had made to Samora Machel more than a year earlier — that British investment should go through South Africa. And when the Mozambican Chamber of Commerce sent a delegation to the United States, it found the same thing; that the Americans 'will try anything to ensure that their initial investments go through South Africa and Portugal'.[17]

This was exactly what South Africa wanted; not only would it reinforce its position as the centre of the region, but it also would provide South Africa itself with increasingly scarce capital. It was even suggested that since South Africa did not have the money to spend in Mozambique, Western countries should provide the funds to South Africa for use in Mozambique. SAFTO head W.B. Holtes also expressed the hope that after Nkomati, transnational companies would use South Africa as their base for selling to the region. In the event, this too proved a chimera; business gained relatively little from Nkomati.

Regional power

Based on Nkomati and its newfound political acceptability, South Africa declared itself a 'regional power'. Pik Botha explained that this meant that 'no problems in southern Africa can be resolved unless the legitimate interests of this regional power, South Africa, are taken into account'.[18] He went further and asserted South Africa's right to demand the withdrawal of the Cubans from Angola: 'They must go, fair or not, that's it. We are a regional power. It is our region.'[19] It was to be a kind of Monroe Doctrine for southern Africa; at other times Pretoria talked of establishing the same kind of hegemony over southern Africa that the USSR has over eastern Europe.

P.W. Botha elaborated on this in an important speech on 31 August 1984.[20] He named the US and USSR as having legitimate interests in the region, and accepted that regional states could have links with the Soviet Union. He said that South Africa 'would not exert itself against any of the justifiable global interests of the superpowers, including those in the southern African context, and they in turn would not endanger South Africa's essential regional interests'. In a dramatic bit of sabre-rattling, he warned the superpowers 'that in a confrontation situation in the region, the RSA enjoys certain advantages over even their massive capabilities, not least of which being the incontrovertible geographical fact of physical proximity'.

He then cited a number of South Africa's essential interests, three of which are significant:

● The superpowers have no right to force 'adjustment' of South Africa's 'value system and social structure' — that is, they cannot press for changes in apartheid or the bantustan system.
● South Africa reserves the right to intervene in neighbouring states to prevent 'political instability' or if the benefit 'of superpower assistance fails to materialise'.
● The superpowers must be careful as to how they support SADCC. In a direct reference to the Lusaka Declaration issued at the founding of SADCC, he said that 'there have been frequent calls for the states in southern Africa to seek their economic "liberation" from South Africa'. In fact, development in southern Africa cannot 'be achieved without South Africa's active participation'.

He also turned to Botswana, Lesotho, and Zimbabwe, all of whom had resisted South African pressure to sign non-aggression pacts before his European tour. 'I sincerely hope that those states in the region who still refuse to normalise their relations with South Africa will soon realise that they have chosen an impossible path.'

Even the press was swept along on the tide of euphoria. Simon Jenkins, political editor of the *Economist*, wrote in the Anglo house magazine *Optima* (31 Jul 84):

> The army has thrown overboard the apologetics of the foreign affairs department. Pretoria has stopped pleading with the world to love South Africa despite apartheid. Instead, it has gone on the regional offensive, bluntly assuming that the enemy must at least shake your hand if your gun is in his back.
>
> Those emperors of suasion — notably UN resolutions — have no clothes. South Africa has for a decade been victim of a bluff: that world opinion mattered and better behaviour by South Africa would win it round. The past two years have seen that bluff called and the black states of southern Africa forced (with the help from several successive years of drought) to treat with their newly assertive regional superpower. . . . If there is any revolutionary danger, it is of South African counter-revolution rolling northwards.

Yet world opinion does matter; much of Nkomati and South Africa's stress on its status as a regional power is an effort to extract concessions from the neighbours and the West. The most explicit example of this was the continuing effort to break the arms embargo. There were a variety of attempts to use Nkomati as an excuse to acquire arms. Pressure was put on Crocker to weaken the arms embargo in exchange for South Africa's signature to Nkomati. And Pretoria made false claims that Mozambique had agreed to South Africa's guarding the Cahora Bassa power line and that this would require it to purchase helicopters and other embargoed equipment.

The other aspect was repeated efforts to push neighbouring states to allow in South African troops. In Mozambique this involved, in addition to the totally dishonest statement that its troops would guard the Cahora Bassa line, attempts to have its soldiers (or even private South African security guards) protect the railway to Maputo. At a press conference, Pik Botha suggested that 'apart from monitoring a ceasefire [between Frelimo and the MNR], South African forces might be used in an emergency role to tackle socio-economic problems. This might include civic action programmes to help with agriculture, medical care, schooling, and technical training.'[21] Pretoria was particularly anxious, as part of its claims to be a regional power, that its troops were seen to have a right to be present in neighbouring states. But Frelimo wouldn't have it.

The conjurer makes dark clouds disappear

Pretoria rode the wave of self-confidence and international approval through two crises which previously would have been much more traumatic. First, in the weeks after the election black unrest grew. On 3 September 1984 troops moved into the townships, apparently for the first time. But the response of liberal whites was unexpected, and far from the hysteria that greeted the Soweto uprising eight years before. This time, there was a view that there was an acceptable level of violence, and that sending in the troops was reasonable and a mark that under P.W. Botha, whites were in control and not panicking. A South African journalist explained to me in November 1984: 'Before, we suffered from the perfect paranoia of guilt. We never understood why 20 million people didn't rise up against us and strike us into the ground. Now we really do believe we are king.'

A similar conjuring trick dealt, initially, with Mozambican protests about Nkomati violations. Pretoria professed clean hands, and blamed the 'Portuguese connection' and a few dissidents in South African military intelligence. Further they argued that the MNR was now an independent force. In August and September they arranged 'proximity talks' between the MNR and Frelimo, in which they shuttled back and forth between the 'two sides' to try to arrange a settlement. The outcome was the curious 3 October Pretoria declaration, signed by the MNR, Frelimo, and South Africa, which said that there ought to be a cease-fire. In effect, Frelimo had been tricked into giving formal recognition to the MNR while Pretoria was able to present itself as a 'peacemaker' — the regional power mediating between two sides in a civil war.

David Austin, emeritus professor of the University of Manchester, accurately reflected white thinking when he wrote late in 1984:

> It is certainly worth recalling how shaken White South Africa was at the end of the 1970s. ...The change of fortune is remarkable. In 1980 South Africa appeared under siege ... The comparison was with Vietnam. ... No one draws such parallels today. The image presented by Pretoria is very different. It is that of an aggressive, anti-communist, dominant power. Success has heightened the rhetoric: South Africa is a regional superpower, southern Africa is a subcontinent. The position of White South Africa is no longer that of Israel, a beleaguered state, but of the United States in, say, the Caribbean; a protective power that keeps at bay external forces.[22]

6. Pricking the Balloon

Within a few months, white South Africa's new-found euphoria and arrogance had collapsed like a pricked balloon. Its claims to be a 'regional power' proved to be all hot air. It could not control its own townships. Its economy was in crisis, with the rand collapsing and foreign banks and transnational corporations disinvesting. The cracks between business and government widened into a yawning chasm. And far from being the region's peacemaker, Pretoria was shown to be violating its peace agreements with Mozambique and Angola.

Wars continue

The period from March to October 1984 was particularly confusing in the region. On the one hand, South Africa seemed to be trying to live up to its image as peacemaker. In Angola, it did pull back its troops. In Mozambique, it did reduce supplies to the MNR and cut off the MNR radio. In Lesotho and Zimbabwe, South African-sponsored dissident actions were halted. And yet in Mozambique and Angola the war increased, despite the Nkomati and Lusaka Accords. What happened in that period can only be disentangled retrospectively.

In Mozambique, it is now clear from captured documents and from interviews with captured MNR men that, in the two months before Nkomati, South Africa gave the MNR six months' supplies. Furthermore, they organised an offensive against the capital, Maputo, to begin about the time of the signing, and sent a training team to Zambezia province in the centre of the country to organise an offensive there. The resupply was not completed by the 16 March signing, but by the end of the month the South African presence and the level of resupply had been substantially reduced. In Angola, the withdrawal proceeded, but very slowly. This permitted Pik and P.W. Botha to go to Europe and proclaim themselves as regional peacemakers.

Once they returned to Pretoria, changes began. On 2 July the South African Foreign Ministry announced that it was halting the withdrawal from Angola (which had in fact stopped in May). Suddenly there was a spate of South African raids in Angola: ANC member Jeanette Schoon was assassinated on 28 June, an oil pipeline was blown up in Cabinda on 12 July, and two boats were sunk by frogmen in Luanda harbour on 29 July.

Support for UNITA was not covered by the Lusaka accord, and this continued. In May Jonas Savimbi had met separately with Chester Crocker and Pik Botha;[1] in mid-1984 Defence Minister General Magnus Malan visited him at his bush headquarters of Jamba, just over the border from Namibia, to give him a personal pledge of continued support.[2] Savimbi was an invited guest at P.W. Botha's inauguration as State President in September. Air drops of supplies and men supported a UNITA push into northern Angola.

In Mozambique, there was no public announcement, and the position was more complex. Documents captured from the main MNR base, Banana House in the foothills of the Gorongosa mountain, show that radio communication had been maintained (in violation of a specific clause of the Nkomati accord).[3] They contain a copy of a message from the MNR to the South Africans dated 16 June 1984. 'We no longer have the war material to go on squeezing Machel,' it said, and 'we want to remind our friends of the pledge they gave us of keeping up support to us clandestinely.' The reply two days later from the contact man, Col. Charles van Niekerk, said that 'the political climate here, and internationally, is still bad for continuing to supply Renamo'. ('Renamo' is another acronym for the MNR.) Consequently, the MNR should 'use as little war material as possible. Avoid combat with the Mozambique armed forces, giving more attention to destroying the economy,' Col. van Niekerk advised.

On 20 July, Col. van Niekerk radioed that the position had changed. The MNR leadership travelled by submarine to South Africa, and on 12, 13 and 16 August the MNR met with Pik Botha, Magnus Malan, and the head of Military Intelligence, van der Westhuizen. (In between those meetings, the South Africans met with a Mozambican delegation which complained about continued South African support for the MNR.) Further supplies were agreed, but it was decided that private aircraft should be used, and that the Banana House airstrip should be improved to allow them to land rather than drop the supplies by parachute. Major supply drops were made on 21 and 31 August, including material for the landing strip. But there were obviously still problems because the MNR leadership returned to Pretoria for further talks on 1 September. This time they met with Pik Botha, Magnus Malan, and armed forces chief of staff General Constand Viljoen. It was agreed that supplies should be called 'humanitarian aid'; after that, there were several supply flights per week.

Some effort was made to cover up and reroute further supplies. Increasingly they were flown via Swaziland, Malawi, and the Comoros. More use was made of Portuguese businessmen in Portugal and in South Africa. For example, Frama Inter-trading was given a Dakota by the SADF to make supply flights to the MNR;[4] the company is owned by Portuguese South Africans with close links to UNITA (it exports UNITA's timber, for example; see Chapters 12 and 15). Contacts were established with right-wing politicians in Portugal and West Germany, and with reactionary groups in Portugal and the United States to coordinate supplies. South Africa orchestrated a campaign to try to show that the MNR was independent and that it had new sources of supply; indeed, much of the information about the Portuguese and Comoros links came initially from South Africa, almost surely from security sources anxious to play down their own links. Nevertheless, the main centre for supply and command remained South Africa.

The timing of these events is important. There was obviously a change in policy, and some decisions by the State Security Council, during June and July 1984. It seems likely that the leadership felt that it had been highly successful, and could extract further concessions from Angola and Mozambique.

According to the South African Foreign Ministry, the withdrawal from Angola had been halted 'pending a response from Luanda on key issues'. It was never officially said what those issues were, but an orchestrated series of press reports provided a long list of South African demands:

● An agreement that the Joint Monitoring Commission would remain in existence on the Angola-Namibia border, and would have a US presence. Angola had specifically rejected this at the Lusaka talks.
● An agreement on the Ruacana power station, which Angola had also refused at Lusaka.
● Angolan government talks with UNITA.
● That the Angola government further restrain SWAPO, or put pressure on it to negotiate a settlement not involving UN Security Council resolution 435. (The announcement of the ending of the withdrawal came at a key time in South African efforts to force a Namibia settlement. It was just before Pik Botha offered SWAPO a ceasefire not linked to resolution 435, and three weeks before a meeting between SWAPO and South Africa.)
● A closure of ANC facilities in Angola.
● Withdrawal of some or all Cuban troops.

There was a similar series of press reports with respect to Mozambique, setting out a variety of demands:

● Mozambique should negotiate directly with the MNR.
● References to Marxism should be deleted from the constitution, and there should be multi-party elections.
● Former Portuguese-appointed clan chiefs should have returned to them the power they had in colonial times. (In a few areas, such deposed chiefs supported the MNR.)
● The MNR should be included in government. One article suggested that 'such cabinet posts as Finance, Agriculture, Defence, and Transport would go a long way towards satisfying Renamo's political ambitions'.[5]
● Portuguese who left at independence and abandoned businesses and other property should be allowed to return and reclaim that property.
● Mozambique should be further opened to South African and other foreign investment.
● Mozambique should link itself more closely with the South African economy, for example by joining the Development Bank of Southern Africa and the Rand Zone.
● South African troops should be allowed into Mozambique. They would protect vital installations such as the Cahora Bassa power line, defend MNR men who return under the government amnesty, or even, in the words of Pik Botha, engage in 'civic action programmes to help with agriculture, medical care, schooling, and technical training'. Mozambique should support a waiver to the arms embargo to provide them with equipment.

It is unclear if any of these were formally presented to the Angolan and Mozambican governments. What seems more likely is that the State Security Council decided to delay further implementation of the Lusaka and Nkomati Accords in an effort to test the water. It wanted to see what further concessions it might gain, and a wide range of suggestions was floated. The SSC may also have wanted to see what the response would be at home and abroad to not implementing Nkomati and Lusaka.

An important restriction on South African action seems to have been the US elections due in November 1984. Apartheid had become an election issue, and there was a hope by the Reagan administration that it could present some diplomatic victory as a result of constructive engagement. The importance of the election is noted several times in the Gorongosa documents, which mention in one place 'pressure from the USA' for South Africa to organise Mozambique-MNR talks 'before November', and in another place the US demand to 'ensure that the Mozambican question be settled' by mid-October. Chester Crocker was unhappy about South African support for the MNR, who he argued 'did not represent the people of Mozambique', according to the documents.[6]

In the event, there were three-way talks between Mozambique, South Africa, and the MNR in Pretoria on 3 October, leading to the nearly vacuous Pretoria Declaration saying that there ought to be a cease-fire but not providing any way to reach one.[7] This seemed to satisfy the conditions that the US had laid down, and had the useful side effect of allowing South Africa to appear as mediator between Frelimo and the MNR, rather than as a party in negotiations with Mozambique. The growing unrest inside South Africa also drew both national and international attention away from destabilisation, giving the military a freer hand. By this time, South African support for the MNR was increasing substantially, with more supply drops and a wider range of weapons. The Gorongosa documents, for example, talk for the first time of 'material for urban guerrilla warfare' including 'time bombs and timing devices'.

By November and Reagan's re-election, South African support for UNITA and the MNR had increased substantially. About this time, Zimbabwe reported the first new incursions by South African trained 'super-Zapu' since early in the year. In 1985, the LLA again became active in Lesotho. The short period of 'peace' had really only lasted through the first half of 1984. South African ministers continued to deny and ridicule claims both of violations of the Nkomati Accord and of support for UNITA, but their denials looked increasingly threadbare (see Chapters 12 and 13). At first, it seemed that Frelimo believed Pretoria's claim to have clean hands. But by December 1984, Maputo was openly objecting. In January 1985, press reports blamed Pretoria for the escalating war. In February President Machel said 'South Africa is not complying with the Nkomati accord'. On 8 March, just a week before the first anniversary of the signing, the heads of the Front Line states issued a statement saying that South Africa had 'refused to honour the Nkomati accord'.

In Angola, Pretoria's mask of non-involvement was rudely pulled off with the capture of a South African commando on 21 May 1985. He was part of a team trying to attack the Gulf Oil installation in Cabinda and give the credit to UNITA, in a carbon copy of the raid on the Beira, Mozambique, oil tanks on 9 December 1982. Then a much improved Angolan army and air force launched a major offensive against UNITA. South African troops and air cover were sent in to defend the UNITA forward command post at Mavinga, and South Africa admitted that one of its people was killed in action with UNITA. Finally Defence Minister Malan was forced to admit that South Africa was still aiding UNITA; indeed, he declared that it would not allow UNITA to be defeated.

In Mozambique, the tide was turned by substantially increased military help from Zimbabwe, agreed at a 12 June 1985 meeting in Harare of Robert Mugabe, Samora Machel, and Julius Nyerere.[8] Most important was a joint Mozambican-Zimbabwean effort to capture the MNR's main base at Banana House. In the captured base, they found substantial evidence of continued South African support and control, ranging from a recent South Africa newspaper to a log book and other documents which listed radio, air, and ship contact with South Africa (and which are the source of the earlier quotes). Finally in September 1985, Pik Botha called a press conference to admit the violations.

A mark of the return to the military hard line was the South African commando raid on the capital of Botswana, Gaborone. The raid, on 14 June 1985, killed a dozen people. It was just before the ANC conference in Zambia and two days before the ninth anniversary of the Soweto uprising, but it was also an Israeli-style retaliation for grenade attacks on two 'coloured' MPs in Cape Town, one of whom had recently been appointed a deputy minister. And on 2 July the ANC office in Lusaka was attacked — the first attack in the Zambian capital since the end of the Rhodesian war. The hardliners reached a new peak in January 1986, when an economic tourniquet, following a commando raid, encouraged a coup in Lesotho. At the same time, there were explicit threats of attacks on Botswana and Zimbabwe, after ANC landmines exploded in South Africa near their borders, and the SSC criticised even Swaziland for not curtailing ANC activities.

Splits or confusion?

It became clear that South Africa had no plans to abide by either the Nkomati or Lusaka accords. No-one had expected them to stick to the letter of either agreement, but the extent of the violations came as a shock to many people since Pretoria had entered into the agreements with such publicity and had accepted such kudos.

Much was made in late 1984 of splits, either within the military (between the supporters of 'laager' and 'forward' strategies) or between 'hawks' and 'doves'. The argument was that not even apartheid South Africa would try an international confidence trick of that audacity, and thus the violations must be the work of some group acting against the instructions of P.W. Botha. Privately, Pretoria pushed this line, and Mozambique seemed to believe it.[9] It is now clear that such divisions did exist; at one point the Gorongosa documents say that General Viljoen 'recommended that we [the MNR] not be fooled by the schemes of Pick Botha as he is a traitor'(sic).[10]

Although sharp policy divisions do exist, it seems likely that the dispute was only over the degree to which Nkomati should be violated (and not over whether to abide by it or not). It is clear that the violations had high-level support; MNR officials met regularly with Magnus Malan, Pik Botha, and others, and one of the regular visitors to the MNR base at Gorongosa was Louis Nel, Deputy Foreign Minister.

How could the South African government agree to sign the Nkomati and Lusaka accords, and then so blithely ignore them? It seems most likely that it agreed to sign the accords without taking any decisions as to what was to happen afterwards. Until May 1984 there seems to have been at least a climate of opinion that the accords should be partly followed, but this changed in June after the return of the Bothas from Europe. Perhaps a new policy was agreed, but it seems more likely that the military was simply given a freer hand. To understand how this is possible, it is useful to look at the SSC itself, and also at the reasons for the signing of Nkomati in the first place.

P.W. Botha describes the SSC as a 'team'. Yet the members of that 'team' represent sectional interests, and often serve as delegates for their ministries or agencies. As head of the 'team', does P.W. Botha act as captain and provide the lead, or is he simply a referee? It has been argued that P.W. Botha 'preferred to mediate rather than lead'. Not all observers would agree. What seems agreed, however, is that the SSC works by consensus. Together, this means that decisions are likely to 'be stated in broad, vague terms to cover disagreements that might otherwise exist'.[11]

Before Nkomati there were apparently three competing views on what to do to Mozambique: the active military solution of overthrowing the government; continue as before supporting the MNR, as part of a policy of creating the 'cordon of instability' where the neighbouring states were too busy with their own troubles to threaten South Africa; or return to the more balanced line of the total strategy, put more stress on diplomatic and economic levers and sign a non-aggression pact. The first was never generally acceptable, so the SSC seems to have chosen a 'broad, vague' position somewhere between the other two options.

It also seems highly likely that the SSC did not take any decisions as to what was to happen after Nkomati was signed, in part because of the common (and false) assumption that Mozambique would violate the accord. Next, as Robert Davies argues,

> It is also quite possible that a tacit understanding might have been reached that certain issues would not be raised for explicit discussion on the SSC. If this were the case it would have to be regarded as nothing more or less than the deliberate creation of a convenient loophole to enable ministers to disclaim knowledge [of further actions in Mozambique].[12]

This might occur particularly if the divisions were so wide as to make consensus impossible within the SSC. Rather than force a vote, which would mean that there would be winners and losers, P.W. Botha might feel it better not to raise the matter at all. This leaves the various interest groups free to conduct their own policy, and also to negotiate with each other outside the SSC.[13]

Finally, in the months after the signing of Nkomati and Lusaka, the SSC will have been much more concerned, first with P.W.'s foreign trip and then with the rising domestic troubles; action in Mozambique and Angola probably had a low place on any agenda. Until June 1984 there was some consensus that South Africa should be seen to abide by the accords, probably to protect P.W. Botha on his trip; this had fallen away by July. Some decision was taken then to allow or encourage more pressure on the neighbours, although probably with no clear goal in mind. It was either an explicit decision to loosen the rein on the military or, more likely, an agreement not to discuss the matter, which would have the same effect. Once the SSC declined to give clear instructions, the backers of the MNR were free to do what they wanted. While the final verdict must be left to historians, it seems that the SSC went into Nkomati not so much intending to violate it, but simply with no commitment and no plans as to how to abide by it.

Contending forces

The SSC only signed Nkomati in the first place because of an unusual conjunction of forces. By late 1983 the government was coming under heavy pressure on two fronts. First, there was a growing international demand for action on Namibia and, to a lesser extent, a reduction in destabilisation. This came particularly from the USA, which was trying to win Mozambique away from the Marxists; Chester Crocker claimed later that 'we helped to "godfather"' the Nkomati process.[14] But also the Soviet Union had monitored the build-up for the Operation Askari invasion and, in September 1983, bluntly warned South Africa that its invading forces should not attack Cuban defensive positions south of Luanda.[15] Second, the economic crisis which had caused real GNP falls in 1982 and the first half of 1983 was bringing the government under pressure from business, which saw a regional settlement as one way to reduce the defence budget and create the necessary room for the free market reforms promised by P.W. Botha at the Carlton Conference.

A critical third factor was that the military had lost credibility, particularly by its bungled air raid on Matola and its Operation Askari invasion of Angola which met unexpected military resistance as well as the Soviet warning. Destabilisation was not bringing home the bacon, and there was a growing feeling that Pik Botha and his Foreign Ministry should have a chance to do better. This also weakened those within the military who were advocating a 'forward' policy of fighting in neighbouring states, and strengthen those who supported a 'laager' or defensive strategy.

By late 1984, the settlement constituency was substantially weakened, while the war constituency remained strong. There was less and less reason for the SSC to abide by the agreement. First, the crucial gains had been won simply by signing Nkomati: the ANC had left Maputo and South Africa had won diplomatic credibility and international acceptance as a 'regional power'. Given Frelimo's clear commitment to Nkomati, it was unlikely to readmit the ANC, and thus there was little need to abide conscientiously by the accord. Second, US pressure was largely linked to the approaching presidential election; after mid-October the US was simply less important.

Third, business interest in Mozambique was on the wane. The smaller businessmen who flew to Maputo hoping to sell convenience foods and consumer luxuries found an economy too devasted by destabilisation to be a market. As Graham Perry of Standard Bank pointed out, many businessmen had been 'too optimistic' about possible sales to Mozambique.[16] Larger firms which had hoped to benefit from foreign capital flowing into Mozambique via Johannesburg lost interest when it became apparent that the flow would be at best a trickle.

Fourth, and perhaps most important, was the growing township unrest within South Africa itself. Serious rioting broke out in September 1984, and has continued ever since. This automatically strengthened the hand of the military and those who wanted to strike out at neighbouring states in Israeli-style retaliation. But it also occupied both national and international attention; no one noticed what went on in the neighbouring states any more. The diplomatic gains of Nkomati were lost on the streets of the townships.

Finally, the military (and the 'forward' strategists within the military) regained some of its prestige. The hawks were seen to have got away with their fraud — destabilisation had increased despite Nkomati and with virtually no protest. Suddenly there was widespread support for using the MNR to extract further concessions — and the bizarre sight of South Africa not knowing what new concessions it wanted, because there were no clear goals.

Military and business views

There remain serious differences within the SSC, within the military, between the military and business, and even within the business community. Nearly a year before Nkomati, Simon Jenkins had warned that although talks were already going on between Mozambique and South Africa, 'it is unlikely that the SADF will honour its side of this bargain, though it may temporarily halt cross-border assistance'. This was exactly what happened. Jenkins, political editor of the *Economist* and sympathetic to the *verligtes*, has good contacts inside South Africa and had clearly been informed. And within South Africa, the right opposed the accord. 'No peace possible with the communists,' headlined *Die Afrikaner* (25 Apr 1984), adding that the Marxists had merely made a tactical retreat, and many in the military agreed.

Yet military perceptions of the politics of the region often bear little relation to reality, or to Foreign Ministry thinking. (Which is not to say that South Africa has not sometimes been tactically brilliant in its confrontation with its neighbours.) For example, the Ministry of Defence in its 1982 White Paper called Zambia a 'Marxist satellite', along with Zimbabwe, Mozambique, and Angola. And the military totally failed to appreciate the popularity of Robert Mugabe, or to understand why big business is happy to deal with someone they dismiss as a Marxist lackey. Likewise on 15 June, the day after the Gaborone raid, South African state radio warned of a plot by the 'Soviet KGB' to bring 'South Africa to its knees' and thus prevent the 'political and constitutional reform process'. All this is because the Soviets want to grab South African minerals away from the West. As agents of the plot, the radio listed a combination of countries so diverse as to be fantastic: Angola, Tanzania, Botswana, Lesotho, and Libya.

A similar misperception may partly be behind continued support for the MNR. Major General J. Roux of military intelligence (which controls the MNR) told a Federated Chambers of Industries seminar that the MNR had at least 60% to 80% popular support in Mozambique. 'We are not just saying this — we're very sure of our facts.'[17] Very few observers, and certainly not Chester Crocker, would agree with that.

Although few in the business community would support the right wing of the military, there was still substantial disagreement within the business world. After Nkomati, Mozambique joined the IMF and World Bank, and also published a private investment code. So big business, some South African politicians, and some people in the US hoped to extract further concessions to private business and to draw Mozambique into Consas or the Rand Zone and away from SADCC. At the Nkomati signing itself, Harry Oppenheimer had stressed that 'it is a bit early to talk of economic involvement in Mozambique'. US financier David Rockefeller met with Samora Machel for seven hours, but he concluded that 'Mozambique has a long way to go before foreign investors are going to find it an attractive place to put their money'. He called on Mozambique, and the other Front Line states, to tie their currencies to the Rand. And he suggested they join South Africa's Southern African Development Bank, although he admitted it would need some political modification such as two different subsidiaries for the Front Line states and the bantustans.[18]

But some foreign firms felt that Frelimo had made adequate concessions and they wanted the war to stop; Lonrho and Italian parastatals are two examples. Similarly smaller (non-Portuguese) South African business was badly hit by the recession and just wanted improved security so they could go to Maputo. The monopoly groups, and particularly Anglo, which has close links with big business in Portugal, were prepared to wait. As Robert Davies explains, the monopolies 'are not affected by the recession to the same degree or in the same way' as smaller companies.

> While profit rates have clearly fallen, the recession, at a time of rapid concentration of capital, has seen the real value of assets controlled by the small number of major monopolies which dominate South African capitalism rocketing. For the monopolies the 'opening up' of Mozambique can never have the same significance as for smaller capitals. ... They can afford to wait and see how things develop.

Finally, big business is now much more interested in Europe and America; the rest of Africa was once important to them, but outside South Africa itself, Africa is now just a minor sideshow. Undoubtedly the market is important for exports, but the big firms are less desperate to expand their exports than the smaller ones. A business journalist summed it up this way: 'Business wants stability in the region, particularly on the borders. It also wants non-Marxist governments in the region, but won't fight to get it. Neither will it oppose destabilisation — if it doesn't cost too much.'

One widely canvassed suggestion, which still remains a serious possibility, is to settle the war in southern Mozambique but continue it in the north. This would have the advantage of bringing peace to the zone near Maputo, where South Africa's main economic interests lie. At the same time, the MNR would remain, either to extract further concessions from Frelimo or eventually to split Mozambique (like Korea or Germany), with a right-wing northern half.

After the stayaway

The real split between government and business was over internal issues, although it has important regional repercussions. The crisis was triggered by a two-day general strike, or 'stayaway', in the industrial belt around Johannesburg on 5 and 6 November, 1984. It was the first time that community groups, emboldened by their success over the August elections, had worked together with trade unions. The London *Financial Times* (7 Nov 1984) estimated that the stayaway was 70% successful, and business was shocked. But business leaders were even more upset by the arrest of the union leaders, disrupting delicate negotiations then under way; on 14 November the three major business associations (including a key Afrikaner group) publicly criticised the arrests. This, in turn, angered the government, and it marked the end of any attempts to resurrect a business-government alliance. Two months later, the three were joined by other business organisations in issuing a reform manifesto; together they represented employers of 80% of the nation's workforce, and their statement was described as 'a fundamental repudiation of government policies'.[19]

There is no dispute over the continued aim of maintaining some form of white dominance, albeit with limited non-white participation. Gavin Relly, chairman of Anglo and one of the most important, as well as one of the most 'liberal', businessmen stressed that he saw majority rule as unrealistic and unacceptable, and that 'immediate universal suffrage ... would have a devastating effect on the country'.[20] Nevertheless, extremely wide gaps had opened up between business and government as to how to maintain white hegemony. One mark of how the corporations were trying to distance themselves from the government was the offer of business organisations to 'mediate' between the government and South African blacks.[21] Relly and other business executives called for talks with 'leaders with black credibility'. In this group they included Chief Buthelezi and the leaders of the bantustans, perfectly acceptable to P.W. Botha, as well as ANC leaders

Nelson Mandela and Oliver Tambo, who clearly are not.

Relly finally led a delegation to meet the ANC in the Luangwa game park in Zambia on 13 September 1985. P.W. Botha accused the businessmen of disloyalty, and of 'showing signs of weakness to the enemies of South Africa'. He told the businessmen that the ANC leaders were nearly all communists, and that his intelligence services could have told them all they needed to know. Finally he called on white South Africans to stand together against the 'forces of darkness calling on foreign aid to destroy our fatherland'.[22]

Relly's role is a crucial mark of the split. When the outspoken Harry Oppenheimer retired, Relly had been chosen as Anglo chairman precisely because he was more conservative and acceptable to government. In recent years he personally helped to organise sanctions busting oil deliveries. He has acted as an informal diplomat, carrying messages for the government; as Anglo head in Zambia he built good relations with Kenneth Kaunda, and he helped to organise the 1975 Victoria Falls Bridge meeting between Kaunda and Vorster. So it was an ironic reversal that, at Relly's request, Kaunda helped to set up the ANC meeting.

Business gave its thumbs-down when South Africa's most important business magazine, the conservative *Financial Mail*, on 6 September 1985 ran a leading article headlined simply 'Leave Now'. P.W. Botha, it said, had 'nothing more to offer and should therefore pay the appropriate penalty'. He 'is hopelessly out of his depth and should, forthwith, go into well-earned retirement'. As South African commentator Stanley Uys pointed out, 'capitalism in South Africa has now entered the fight for its survival. It faces the risk that, unless it can distance itself from apartheid, it will go down the drain with it'.[23]

Burning townships and economic collapse

The sudden crisis of confidence resulted from the linked problems of continued black unrest and the withdrawal of foreign capital. The well organised and highly successful boycott of the 'Indian' and 'coloured' elections in August 1984 set in train a series of uprisings in black areas. One of the first to explode was Sharpeville, known throughout the world for the 1960 massacre there.[24] The uprisings spread all over the country. Far from a sign of strength that would curb the problem, sending in the troops and imposing a state of emergency only inflamed black protest. Furthermore, the Nkomati Accord had totally failed to curb the ANC. The number of incidents in the six months after Nkomati was the same as in the period one year before; ANC demands and ANC banners became a feature of the protests. No wonder Relly felt that he had to open talks with the ANC.

Meanwhile, the economy went into a tailspin. The rand, which had been worth more than $1 in 1983, fell below $0.80 in 1984 and below $0.35 in 1985. After a small recovery, GDP began falling again in the second quarter of 1984. Interest rates topped 25% (up to 32% for an overdraft). South Africa imposed an extra 10% import duty and reintroduced exchange controls. Bankruptcies and unemployment soared, which increased black discontent, which increased the repression, which further damaged international financial confidence.

A key factor had been the falling price of gold, from more than $600 an ounce in 1980 down to $300 in 1985. Yet government expenditure had risen more than 20% per year since 1980, well above the rate of inflation; this was mainly for defence, but also for the triplication of facilities required by apartheid and the new constitution.[25] Business executives saw an export-led recovery as the only possibility.[26] Nkomati and peace in the region offered business a new respectability in the West, and thus the chance of at least maintaining markets there. Respectability also might ward off sanctions.

Africa itself, and especially the neighbouring states, are the main destination for manufactured exports. Ron Mitchell, Johannesburg-based vice president of the US Citibank, pointed out that 'Africa remains one of the major markets for South African goods. ... It is vital to keep all our doors wide open and even expand our position there'.[27] Yet, until the rand collapsed, exports to Africa, and particularly the SADCC states, were falling due to competition from cheaper suppliers such as Brazil, as well as security and financial problems.

Peace in Mozambique would improve the position of South African business throughout the region. And despite the disappointment of the initial excessive expectations, there were still contracts to be won. Their main interests were near Maputo — just where South Africa stepped up the war after Nkomati. In June 1984 the MNR spokesman in Lisbon had warned that foreign businessmen, particularly South African, 'will not be permitted to pass'. In July two South African businessmen driving to Maputo were attacked by the MNR but escaped. The same month two technicians employed by the South African construction firm Murray and Roberts were kidnapped on the way to work in Maputo port for Rennies (owned by Old Mutual of South Africa); they were robbed and released. But in January 1985 two Britons living in South Africa were murdered by the MNR on the main road just four kilometres from the border post; the killers then escaped back into South Africa. In July 1985, two men working for a South African company repairing a sugar mill were kidnapped by the MNR, and only released two months later. The pressure was kept up with repeated attacks on the rail and power lines from South Africa to Maputo during 1985 and 1986.

All this made South African companies very nervous. Proposals by South African companies for involvement in gas, sugar, and irrigated farming were all held in abeyance until the 'security situation' improved. Inevitably, continued MNR raids frightened off any US or British investment (except from Lonrho) that might have come via South Africa.

At the end of 1984, the *Financial Mail* warned that 'if the security situation does not improve within the next six months, Nkomati will be out the window and all these opportunities ... in the way of exports and imports ... will be lost. And Africa will never trust us again.' And, in a comment clearly aimed at the military, it went on to argue that 'it is in no one's interest that the MNR takes over the government. ... With them in power and Frelimo in opposition, Mozambique will be in greater chaos than before. And we will be the first to feel it.'[28]

Meanwhile, there had been a steady disinvestment. In the eight years after the 1976 Soweto uprising, more than R1000m in long term capital had left South Africa. Probably another R1000m left in the following year (mid-84 to mid-85). A steady stream of companies had taken advantage of the relaxation of exchange control to disinvest; precisely because of the recession the South African monopoly groups had surplus funds and were happy to buy out the foreign interests, but it still represented a vital capital outflow. Since 1980, 30 US firms had left South Africa while only 11 new ones arrived. Associated British Foods (UK) and Jardine Mathieson (Hong Kong) were among those to withdraw. A number of firms thought it politic to reduce to a minority interest, including Standard Bank (UK), Barclays Bank (UK), Ford (US), and Asea (Sweden).

At the same time, foreign banks stopped lending long term money; South Africa could only obtain short and medium term funds. Banks were sensitive to the political and security position inside the country. Bankers who had become nervous after 1981, but were reassured by the IMF loan and then Nkomati, were soon nervous again. Several important US banks, faced with political pressure at home and increased concern about the risk of South African loans, due both to unrest in the townships and the deteriorating economy, halted or restricted lending to Pretoria. By mid-1985, South Africa had $22bn in foreign debts, of which an unusually high proportion, $12bn, was due in six months or less. It was fundamentally a political rather than an economic problem — because of South Africa's growing international unacceptability the banks first cut the length of time for which they were prepared to lend, and then refused to renew short term debt. On 27 August 1985, Finance Minister Barend du Plessis admitted South Africa could not pay, and announced a repayments freeze. Mighty South Africa had defaulted.

Chester Crocker noted that disinvestment was already taking 'place in the private market place as a result of decisions taken by private firms and their management'. The US government didn't need to impose sanctions; indeed, he hoped the US could help to curb the 'pullout of Western financial business interests'.[29]

Anglo's Gavin Relly warned that, 'more by accident than design', international banking was doing just what those who advocate sanctions want. 'Though few politicians yet seem to perceive it, that prospect is already sufficiently close as to render irrelevant and academic the motions calling for sanctions in so many legislatures around the world.'[30]

7. What does South Africa Want in the Region

The SADF told anti-government rebels in Mozambique to cut the Cahora Bassa electricity line, and the result was a power shortage in South Africa. The South African government cut the rail service to Zimbabwe in the face of opposition by its own railway officials and when big business was looking for improved relations with Prime Minister Robert Mugabe.

These are just two examples which show the disagreement inside South Africa about how to deal with the neighbours. The military (and the various groups within it), other parts of the government, the National Party, and big, medium and small business all have different interests and different demands. There are fundamental policy and perceptual divisions, for example over how to deal with socialist leaders. Some high military officials argue that it is never safe to talk with Marxists. On the other hand, many argue that it is possible to have business dealings with Mozambique which are beneficial to South Africa.

Also, attitudes change. Consider the way that the Africa Institute, Pretoria, has shifted its views on SADCC. G.M.E. Leistner, director of the Institute, in 1981 held out 'little prospect for the success of SADCC'. He concluded that 'the exclusion of South Africa will be as meaningful as *Hamlet* without the prince'. Two years later, when it was clear SADCC was succeeding, Leistner's chairman, P. Smit, saw SADCC as a threat. He warned that 'Western support for SADCC ... undoubtedly encourages South Africa's neighbours to adopt a much less conciliatory attitude towards this country than would be the case otherwise.' Two years further on, in 1985, Leistner had reversed his position, and wrote that 'informed opinion in South Africa generally views SADCC favourably'. His reason was a new hope that SADCC could be co-opted and was merely 'a step towards a regional grouping that will ultimately include South Africa as well'.[1] His strong statement in fact recognises that there are still many in South Africa who see SADCC as a threat, and who hoped that the Nkomati Accord really was the death of SADCC.

With such a range of views, it is hardly surprising that there is disagreement as to whether it is in Pretoria's best interests to support or attack SADCC. Or that South Africa sometimes has no policy at all, as was apparently the case with Mozambique from late 1984.

Regional Hegemony

Despite such sharp divisions, there is no disagreement about the basic goal of maintaining white dominance. From that, it is possible to outline a few agreed strategic goals, and then to produce a list of tactical objectives. It is important to try to do this, in order to explain what sometimes seems odd behaviour. For example, Pretoria often seems to put undue stress on a token issue, like demanding that a bantustan representative attend a meeting, insisting on ministerial level meetings over minor issues, or pressing for South African troops to be involved in disaster relief in neighbouring states. Sometimes the demands are simply the limit of agreement, sometimes the goal of a particular interest group, and sometimes they are symbolically important.

What South Africa would really like is sympathetic, non-socialist neighbours who would accept apartheid, support South Africa in world forums, and remain economically dependent on it. Since this is impossible, the main goal of the South African government is to have regional economic, military, and political hegemony. If it cannot gain its dominance by any other means, South Africa adopts the alternative objective of causing instability and chaos in unsympathetic, Marxist states.

The overriding goal of regional dominance (at whichever level) can be divided into three parts, relating to security, international relations (primarily with developed northern states), and regional issues. Each of these has economic and military/diplomatic components. We look at each in turn.

Security

In the early 1970s, the *cordon sanitaire* of white-ruled states provided the first line of defence. Now that has disappeared, and just those victories in Zimbabwe, Mozambique, and Angola showed that safe rear bases do speed the revolution. Thus the South African government feels it must build a new barrier — a ring of states which do not aid the attempt to overthrow apartheid. Either the neighbours will act on their own, voluntarily or under duress, or South Africa will create a 'cordon of instability' which prevents the neighbours from acting against it.

South Africa has developed close links with Israel; many SADF officers are openly enthusiastic about Israel's way of fighting the PLO, and South Africa is taking an increasingly Israeli view of regional security issues. In regional terms, that means the ANC must be kept as far away as possible — forcing neighbouring states to expel all South African refugees, making pre-emptive strikes against the ANC wherever possible, setting up surrogate forces equivalent to the Christian militias in Lebanon, and even having a military presence.

South Africa's massive economic power in the region gives it an important regional leverage that Israel does not have. As Deon Geldenhuys comments,

> If the black states succeeded in loosening their economic ties with South Africa to a meaningful degree and in developing a reasonable military capability, the fear is that they would become more assertive, even provocative, in their relations with South Africa — such as by providing sanctuary for the ANC because they would no longer be as vulnerable to South African economic and military pressure.[2]

In one key respect the Israeli experience is not relevant. In South Africa a white minority is trying to control a much larger black majority. This will eventually end, no matter what the SADF does in the neighbouring states. To assume that the armed wing of the ANC is responsible for the ferment inside South Africa is palpably absurd; the cause is apartheid. At best, pushing the ANC out of the neighbouring states may buy a small amount of time for apartheid.

The South African government's fear of the ANC is surely legitimate, but for the wrong reasons. The South African military acts as if the ANC is like the MNR or UNITA — a puppet organisation that can be turned on and off (by Moscow or Maputo) relatively at will. Just as the security problems in Mozambique would be much easier to end if South Africa stopped its support for the MNR, so the South African military seems to believe that if only it could prevent the neighbouring states from helping the ANC then the uprisings inside South Africa would end.

The ANC is a threat to the South African government precisely because that is not true. It is the oldest anti-apartheid organisation, and more than 60 years later it still has the greatest credibility inside and outside South Africa. With the election of the Nationalist government, the ANC led the struggle against the tightening of apartheid, particularly the mass anti-pass campaigns of the 1950s. It drew strong support from all races and varied groups, including the churches. The ANC turned to armed struggle only after it was banned in 1960, but its military wing Umkhonto we Sizwe became really effective only after the ANC was joined by young people radicalised by the government's brutal repression of students in Soweto in 1976.

In the early 1980s Umkhonto's sabotage actions, particularly the raids on the Sasol oil-from-coal plant and the Koeberg nuclear power station, gave an important psychological boost to the anti-apartheid struggle. The 1955 Freedom Charter adopted and promoted by the ANC formed the basis for the growing demands. The Charter is important because of its explicitly non-racial character; it declares that 'all national groups have equal rights'. The demand for the release from prison of ANC leader Nelson Mandela was widely taken up, both internally and internationally. Opinion polls show the ANC to have the widest support of any organisation in South Africa.

Nevertheless, by 1984 the struggle was very broadly based, involving many trade unions and literally hundreds of community groups, many of which had grown out of the campaigns against the new constitution and the 'coloured' and 'Indian' elections. Two new umbrella organisations, the United Democratic Front and the smaller National Forum, played an increasingly important role. The exiled ANC leadership had to run to keep up with the rapidly expanding uprising inside South Africa.

Thus the position has been reached where the struggle is so broadly and deeply based inside South Africa that it will continue whatever happens to the ANC's regional position. Likewise, whatever happens in the region, the ANC is widely recognised as the leading anti-apartheid organisation. So the white government is right to fear the ANC, but can do little about its effect, no matter what military action is taken against the neighbouring states.

International

André Beaufre, the French general who originated the concept of the 'total strategy', and whose writing so influenced the Botha government, stressed that in the sort of 'indirect war' being fought in the region, the outcome is almost always determined by the level and commitment of external assistance.[3] South Africa's white leadership recognises that apartheid makes it a pariah and it can no longer hope for international acceptance. Instead, the goal now is to maintain *international tolerance*; apartheid's rulers can live with policies like 'constructive engagement', which criticise apartheid but do nothing concrete to attack it.

International tolerance is essential to ward off sanctions, and to ensure the continued flow of investment, new technology, and military hardware.

Prime Minister John Vorster often argued that the road to the West led through Africa; this is still the view in Pretoria, so much of South Africa's diplomatic and military energy is invested in the neighbouring states. One thing has changed, however. Vorster had hoped to build bridges through *détente* and a softly-softly approach; that has clearly failed and P.W. Botha puts much greater stress on brute force.

Two aspects of his bid for international tolerance affect the neighbouring states. First is that apartheid is often defended on the overtly racist grounds that blacks cannot govern themselves; either their countries are a shambles or they are beholden to South Africa. To use this argument, the South African government wants turmoil or subservience outside its borders. Second, and probably most complex, is South Africa's claim to be a regional power, with the implication that the West has no right to interfere in its internal affairs (e.g. apartheid), while Pretoria does have a right to interfere in the affairs of its neighbours. In part, it needs overall regional hegemony to justify its claim. But various specific demands, listed below, are also intended to support its claim to regional power status.

With its efforts to gain international tolerance meeting only mixed success, white South Africa also needs to cushion the impact of more direct actions against it. Thus it wants to turn its neighbours into a *buffer against sanctions*. This would be largely through increased dependence on South Africa for food, fuel, and other goods and services, especially transport. For this SADCC is crucial, and must be destroyed or co-opted. Pretoria wants its neighbours to oppose sanctions openly. Where that is not possible, it at least wants to be able to point to the economic dependence and say that sanctions will hurt the neighbours; privately Pretoria and its allies say that the neighbours 'really' are against sanctions but cannot say so for fear of offending their OAU colleagues.

This leads to a particularly vicious circle. By blowing up railways and a variety of other actions, South Africa forces the neighbours to be dependent on it. This permits South Africa to argue that because the neighbours are dependent, they will be hurt by sanctions. Thus destabilisation creates the dependence which allows South Africa to argue against using sanctions to end destabilisation.

Regional market

South Africa likes to portray the neighbouring states as tiny, weak, and unimportant. G.M.E. Leistner claims that economic links between South Africa and its neighbours 'would be almost like talking of the Anglo American Corporation joining forces with the grocery shop next door'. The corollary is that the neighbouring states are of no economic importance to South Africa, but that the benevolent white giant might be willing to help the poor benighted blacks to develop — so long as they know their place.

On the surface, the statistics seem to support this. South Africa has only half the population of the SADCC states combined, yet it has more than triple their GDP and four times their exports. This disguises the fact that South Africa remains a Third World country, largely dependent on mineral exports. Its industry is similar to that in other newly industrialised countries such as India or Brazil. Its main export market for manufactured goods, as well as for services, is the neighbouring states. For example, half of South African exports of machinery, plastics, and chemicals go to the SADCC states.[4]

South Africa has an annual $1.5 bn balance of payments surplus with the SADCC states, net after all trade, transport fees, and customs union and migrant miner remittances are considered. This is hardly a small item.

Thus a small but significant portion of South Africa's non-mining GDP and non-mining employment is dependent on exports to the SADCC states. Furthermore, those states had more buoyant economies than South Africa and estimates suggest that the SADCC states account for as much as 20% of the *increase* in South African manufacturing GDP during the 1970s.[5] Roughly 5% of the non-coal traffic through South Africa's ports is for the SADCC states. Thus the neighbouring states are an important factor in the South African economy, which it cannot lightly afford to lose.

Yet in a genuinely free world market, the neighbouring states would buy much less from South Africa. For many manufactured goods, South Africa is a high-cost producer.[6] In part, this is because industry has developed behind a high wall of protective tariffs and is thus relatively inefficient. Also, the arms and oil boycotts have forced South Africa to push for self-sufficiency at substantial cost. Thus under military pressure many goods have a very high local content, and items like diesel engines and lorry gearboxes are made locally at a much higher price than they are available on the world market. The expensive Sasol oil-from-coal plant pushes up fuel costs, and thus prices. And so on. Thus when neighbouring states buy from South Africa, they are often paying high prices to support an inefficient and increasingly militarised industry. And often paying for the expansion and modernisation of South African industry instead of their own.

Thus the neighbourhood market is both militarily and economically important for South Africa. Since its goods are often uncompetitive on the world market, it must use other means to maintain that market. These range from extended credit terms, to military pressure, and are discussed throughout this book.

TACTICAL AIMS

Within this strategic framework of goals relating to the neighbouring states, it is possible to pinpoint a series of specific aims pursued by South Africa in the early 1980s:

Economic

1. *Continue and expand exports.* Sales to the neighbours are central to South Africa's economic growth and to continued dependence. This would involve both export incentives and various forms of manipulation and pressure.
2. *Maintain transport dependence*, ensuring that most regional cargoes continue to flow through South African ports and railways. This would maintain the most important economic leverage while sabotaging SADCC.
3. South Africa to *remain the economic focal point* for the region. In particular, new investment should be channelled through Johannesburg, and technical support for new projects should come from there.

4. *Encourage transnational corporations*, especially those based in South Africa or with regional centres there, as a way of increasing South African control and combating socialism.

5. *Ensure water and electricity supplies.* The two biggest economic constraints on South Africa are the absence of oil and the shortage of water. These are linked, because coal can replace oil in many ways, but using coal to produce either oil or electricity consumes massive amounts of water. Thus South Africa wants to ensure the supply of electricity from Cahora Bassa in Mozambique and Ruacana in Angola, wants to build the Highland Water Scheme in Lesotho, and is even looking for ways to tap water from the Zambezi River. South Africa would also like to use other regional energy supplies; access to Angolan oil seems unlikely, but Pretoria wants to exploit the Kudu gasfield off Namibia.

6. *Support large projects* in neighbouring states which link them closely to South Africa, like the Lesotho Highland Water Scheme, the Swaziland northern rail link, and proposals to produce soda ash in Botswana and ammonia in Mozambique. In all cases the neighbouring states supply goods or services which they could, in principle, cut off. Thus such projects seem to involve 'mutual dependence' and give the host states more power than traditional one-way links in which the neighbouring states simply buy goods and services from South Africa. In practice, this is not the case. South Africa is demanding cast iron, sanctions-proof guarantees against any cutting off of supply. And such projects are so much more important to the smaller economy of the host state than to South Africa, that Pretoria retains and increases its leverage.

7. *Open new areas to South African tourists.* This provides another economic lever, as tourists can be stopped quickly and easily, for example by border closures. It also provides access for agents. And it gives some tangible benefit to the white middle class.

Political and military

8. *No South African refugees in neighbouring states.* In part, this is simply the desire to force the ANC out of the region. It does not distinguish between those who are simply ANC members, those who are political militants, and those who are members of Umkhonto we Sizwe. That, in turn, partly reflects a real attempt to ignore the political role of the ANC. But it also recognises the inability of both the SADF and the neighbouring states to prevent guerrillas crossing the border, and thus argues that the only way to keep Umkhonto out is by keeping all South African refugees out of neighbouring states. Finally, demanding the expulsion of refugees has a political purpose. Refugees who successfully live and work just over the border serve as models of an alternative for South Africa itself and as living proof of the nonsense of apartheid.

9. *Non-aggression pacts.* South Africa has been trying to promote non-aggression pacts with its neighbours since 1970 (when only a few were independent). Such pacts were signed initially only by the bantustans, but the issue took on a new urgency in the 1980s when Pretoria saw them as a way to force the ANC out while also forcing recognition of it as a regional power. It was able to pressure Swaziland into signing secretly in 1982 and Mozambique

into signing publicly in 1984. However the failure of South Africa to abide by Nkomati means that any further non-aggression pacts would require the most extreme pressure.

10. *Put pressure on the ANC to 'renounce violence'* and then negotiate with the government. This is clearly a vain hope, because the ANC would never agree no matter what the neighbouring states said. Nevertheless this has been raised in various talks and press statements. As Nelson Mandela declared in February 1984, when he refused to renounce violence in exchange for a release from prison, the ANC will renounce violence only when the South African government also renounces violence — and agrees to dismantle apartheid. In any case, the lead is clearly in the townships; if the ANC renounced 'violence' it might alienate the township residents from the ANC, but it would not convince them to end their rebellion.

11. *Recognition of the bantustans*, initially indirectly and at a technical rather than diplomatic level, for example through the talks relating to the customs union, water, transport, police, or the Swazi land deal. The bantustans were the cornerstone of apartheid, and of the South African policy of eventually removing South African citizenship from all 'Africans'. Yet no independent state was willing to agree with South Africa's unilateral announcements that four of the bantustans were 'independent' states. Thus South Africa hoped to force some of the neighbouring states into recognising the 'independent' bantustans, at least tacitly, and hoped that this in turn would permit some of the more conservative United Nations members to follow suit, leading eventually to full international recognition of the bantustans — and of apartheid itself. Because it was such a central point, it was strongly resisted despite very heavy South African pressure in the early 1980s. By 1985, however, the growing realisation inside South Africa that the bantustan policy was a failure led this to become a less important demand; more stress was placed on the next two objectives.

12. *Tacit diplomatic recognition.* South Africa accepts that it can no longer hope for full embassies, like the one in Malawi. But recognition as a regional power demands some further diplomatic links with neighbours. One form is the opening of *new trade missions*, as happened in 1985 in Swaziland, and which serve as quasi diplomatic missions while recognising the limitations imposed by OAU membership. The other demand is for *high-level contact*, preferably meetings between State President P.W. Botha and leaders of neighbouring states. If that is not acceptable, South Africa often demands ministerial level meetings to resolve technical issues, for example over security or railways.

13. *Allow in South African troops.* This is seen as important recognition of South Africa's claim to be a regional policeman (and thus a regional power). The Foreign Ministry suggested that South African soldiers be involved in a non-military role in development assistance or flood relief, or in a military role to guard the railway or power line in Mozambique, or even to protect MNR men returning to Mozambique under its amnesty. So far this has been limited to Malawi (military links) and Swaziland (military assistance for cyclone relief in 1985, and more general police links). There are some conflicts within the South African government on this, however. There are no disputes about the SADF role in Malawi or Swaziland, or about social action in Mozambique. But the SADF probably would not have agreed to guard installations inside Mozambique against MNR attack, even though the Foreign Ministry was

pressing Mozambique to allow this.

14. *To be seen as a source of aid.* Emergency aid would include drought and cyclone relief, as well as repair of damage done by South African backed dissident groups (like the MNR in Mozambique). Longer term assistance would be through the Southern African Development Bank. These are often linked to other demands, for example the presence of South African troops or recognition of the bantustans (who are members of the bank).

15. *Publicly oppose sanctions.* One of South Africa's most insistent demands has been that black states should not only not support calls for sanctions, but should at least demur, and preferably publicly oppose them.

16. *Curb anti-apartheid rhetoric.* In 1981 Deon Geldenhuys saw as an important South African objective that

    Black states in southern Africa [should] display some moderation in expressing their customary criticism of the republic's domestic policy and in suggesting solutions. ... it simply cannot be expected of OAU member states to refrain from denouncing apartheid; at issue is the manner in which it is done.[7]

Disagreements

It is essential to keep in mind, however, the disagreements between the military, the foreign ministry (or between hawks and doves), monopoly groups, and smaller businesses. The confusion over troops in Mozambique has already been noted. Similarly, business would broadly support the encouragement of foreign transnational corporations using Johannesburg as a base, so long as it was in partnership with local firms and the foreign partner brought in capital and technology; they would be opposed if it meant direct competition. Nevertheless, there is probably a general acceptance of these aims.

The disagreement comes over priorities — which aims are most important — and over how to push for them. There are two broad areas of conflict: over the use of military power, and over the use of economic levers for political ends. Destabilisation is often intended to weaken the neighbouring states economically, but that makes them less able to buy South African goods. Thus business executives may support *in principle* the goal of wanting the neighbouring states to sign non-aggression pacts (aim 9), but many will be unhappy about extensive destabilisation to reach that goal; to them the desire to increase exports (aim 1) will be much more important. To take another example, SADF-promoted MNR attacks on the Cahora Bassa power line and railway to Maputo clearly conflict with some of the other aims in this list (such as 5)

There is also sharp disagreement, even within the business community, about when to use the economic levers for political and military ends. As in the debate in the West about imposing sanctions against South Africa, so in South Africa in the debate about imposing sanctions against the neighbours, there is a basic conflict: sanctions may bring about a desired political change, but they also cut off a source of profit.

Finally, it is important to note that the South African goverment is *not* making all 16 demands at all times to all eight countries in this study. Some are simply not relevant: there are few economic links with Angola to expand; there are no big projects waiting in Zambia; there are no pressure points that could be used to force Zimbabwe to recognise the bantustans; Malawi does not allow in many

South African refugees and has no links with the ANC, and so on. Similarly, there are different priorities at different times, based both on changes inside South Africa and on what is possible in the neighbouring states. Thus the pressure on Mozambique to give more space to transnational corporations and recognise South Africa as the economic focus (aims 4 and 5) came only after Mozambique had signed a non-aggression pact (aim 9).

With these obvious caveats, however, this list of 16 aims generally reflects the specific goals of South African regional policy since 1980, the period of this study. These aims recur throughout the individual country chapters and provide some limited guidance to the actions of various South African groups.

8. Ties that Bind

South African economic power in the region is expressed through a variety of channels. These range from institutions through organisations to the movement of people and goods. Some channels are closely linked to others, while many are only loosely connected. A number of these channels will appear in several later chapters discussing individual countries, where their impact on that country will be discussed. But it is important also to look at them in a more general South African context, which is the subject of this and the following chapter.

In this chapter we look first at the most important private and parastatal economic links, dealing specifically with the major corporations that control the South African economy and looking at the key areas of transport and trade. Next we look at energy and water, both of which are in short supply and subject to conflict and manipulation. Finally, we look at people — migrant workers going to South Africa.

The next chapter is devoted to the Southern African Customs Union and the Rand Zone, which dominate the relations between South Africa and Botswana, Lesotho, and Swaziland.

THE CORPORATIONS

Seven giant corporations control nearly all South African business. Following a spate of takeovers, the seven giants control the companies that account for 80% of the entire value of Johannesburg Stock Exchange shares. The Anglo American Corporation of South Africa alone controls 56%. It is followed by Sanlam (9.4%), Barlow Rand (7.4%), Anglovaal (3.2%), Rembrandt (2.1%), Liberty insurance (1.1%), and Old Mutual insurance (0.8%). But the seven giants are themselves intertwined. Barlow is only semi-autonomous, with Old Mutual owning 24.1%, Anglo 13.4%, and Sanlam 3.9%; all appoint directors to Barlow. In addition, Anglo owns 4.5% of Anglovaal, and has shares in subsidiaries of Sanlam and Rembrandt. Old Mutual owns 5.4% of Rembrandt. Sanlam owns 18% of Anglovaal and 8% of Rembrandt. Anglovaal, Old Mutual, and Sanlam all have shares in Anglo or its subsidiaries.[1] Sanlam and Rembrandt represent Afrikaner capital, the others English.

Anglo American Corporation of South Africa

As well as dominating South Africa, Anglo is one of the world's giant corporations, and is an important foreign investor in the US (through its

Bermuda-based Minorco subsidiary).[2] Regionally, it has substantial interests in Botswana, Zambia and Zimbabwe. Its roots are in gold and diamond mining, and it still owns two-thirds of all South African mining capital. An Anglo company, De Beers, dominates non-USSR diamond mining and marketing; in southern Africa there are De Beers group diamond mines in South Africa, Namibia and Botswana, and De Beers has a strong interest in the mines in Angola and Tanzania. Because of its mining interests, it is also important in the metals, engineering, and chemicals industries.

The disinvestment of Associated British Foods in May 1983 set off a chain reaction which further concentrated ownership. Anglo paid R337m to ABF for its controlling share of Premier Milling, the largest food and feed company in South Africa.[3] Because of existing shareholdings, the Premier takeover gave Anglo control of South African Breweries, until then the ninth largest of the monopoly groups.[4]

Anglo has always been a very political company. It has been closely associated with the opposition Progressive and then Progressive Federal parties. Anglo chairman Gavin Relly led the team which met the ANC in 1985. Nevertheless, after meeting the ANC Relly made strong statements in support of P.W. Botha. Anglo has also been important in organising fuel supplies in the face of the oil embargo, after the fall of the Shah cut supplies from Iran, and has steadily been buying interests in foreign oil companies and oil fields. Anglo, through Freight Services, also played a central role in Rhodesian sanctions busting, particularly over oil.

Anglo heads have the standing of world statesman. Harry Oppenheimer has met nearly all the neighbouring heads of state. (He is Anglo's largest shareholder, although he has retired as chairman of Anglo.) He had a well publicised meeting with Robert Mugabe soon after Zimbabwe's independence in 1980, and Anglo pushed for a normalisation of South African relationships with the new government. Oppenheimer met secretly with Samora Machel in London in November 1983, but that meeting was less successful. Anglo has close business connections with the millionaire Portuguese backers of the MNR, and Machel hoped that Oppenheimer would use his influence in both South Africa and Portugal to reduce support for the MNR. Anglo was reported at one time to support Jonas Savimbi and UNITA.[5]

Old Mutual

Officially South African Mutual, but still normally called by its former name of Old Mutual, this is the largest life assurance company in South Africa — and in Botswana, Lesotho, Swaziland, Malawi and Zimbabwe. It did not normally acquire controlling interests in companies, but this is now changing.

In 1984 Old Mutual dramatically took control of South Africa's, and the region's, international shipping. This is detailed below (pp 70-71). One side effect of the deals was also to make it a major force in regional tourism through Sun International, which controls casinos and hotels in Swaziland, Lesotho, Botswana, and Mauritius, as well as in South Africa's bantustans.[6]

Sanlam

Of the other monopoly groups, Sanlam is most important regionally. Sanlam is the second largest life assurance company, just behind Old Mutual, and has been a major force in the growth of Afrikaner capital; it has close links with the *verligte* wing of the National Party. Its most important holdings in the region are Gencor, South Africa's second largest mining house; Sentrachem, the fertiliser and chemicals group that includes Fedmis; the Kirsh wholesale and retail group, including Metro; and the Murray & Roberts construction group.

Banks

Two British banks, Barclays and Standard, control the banks which have more than two-thirds of the assets of all banks operating in South Africa. In 1985 both Standard (UK) and Barclays (UK) reduced their shareholding in their South African subsidiaries to less than half (41.9% and 40% respectively). This allows the British parent companies to say that they cannot dictate to the South African subsidiary, but in fact they retain significant control. Anglo owns 14% of Barclays (RSA) and a smaller share of Standard.

Both banks are active in the neighbouring states. In recent years they have broken official ties between the South African bank and the subsidiaries in SADCC, except for the two Rand Zone members, Lesotho and Swaziland, but informal links remain close, with exchanges of staff and other contacts. Shortly after the founding of SADCC with its goal of reducing dependence on South Africa, the managing director of Barclays Zambia, Mark Tress, praised Zambia for its 'pragmatic' choice to increase trade with South Africa. Despite the SADCC goals, he stressed that 'any southern African economic bloc should logically include South Africa'.[7]

British firms

Measured in terms of numbers of employees, the two banks are the largest British companies in South Africa. The two next largest in the early 1980s, Associated British Foods and Metal Box, have both disinvested. Next in line is Lonrho, which is an important producer of gold, platinum, and coal in South Africa; a new gold mine is being developed jointly with Anglo. Lonrho is active in several of the neighbouring states — Zimbabwe, Zambia, Malawi, and Mozambique. Normally its interests are controlled locally and then from London, but it also encourages South African links. It controls its Zimbabwe gold mines and some of its Mozambique interests from South Africa. Like Harry Oppenheimer, Lonrho chief executive Tiny Rowland believes in personal diplomacy, and he meets with Kenneth Kaunda and Samora Machel. His earlier backing of Joshua Nkomo rather than Robert Mugabe somewhat limited his personal role in Zimbabwe, but Lonrho is now expanding rapidly there. Lonrho openly backs Jonas Savimbi and UNITA in Angola (see Chapters 12 and 13).

Although Lonrho is active in most of the SADCC states and presents itself as a supporter of those states, some of its officials are open supporters of South African government policy. For example, in a particularly brazen letter to SADCC officials, one Lonrho executive suggested that SADCC should support investment in 'the Republic of Bophuthatswana', one of the bantustans. And Lonrho officials in South Africa are trying to encourage South African firms to invest in Mozambique.[8]

TRANSPORT

One-third of the international cargo for the neighbouring states is carried by South African Railways; if only the inland states are considered, this rises to nearly half (Statistical Annex, Table 4). Thus transport is highly political — South Africa's control of transport is a significant economic lever, and it is not surprising that SADCC gave such high priority to reducing transport dependence. The former General Manager of South African Railways, J.G.H. Loubser, coined the phrase 'transport diplomacy', and his role was sufficiently important for him to be co-opted on to the State Security Council. Under his guidance, neighbouring railways built up dependencies in other ways; for example, there are typically more than 5000 SAR wagons on neighbouring railway lines, and more than 50 locomotives (mostly steam) leased to neighbouring railways. These provide important levers; locomotives can be withdrawn (and were from Zimbabwe in 1981), while SAR demands, not unreasonably, that cargo in its wagons go to South African ports rather than Mozambique or Tanzania.

South African Transport Services (SATS) is the parent parastatal corporation that includes the railways, harbours, airline, and some road haulage. It is the third largest company in South Africa, after Anglo and Sanlam. For SATS, the transit traffic provides roughly 5% of non-coal port and railway traffic (half of South African port traffic is coal). This is not essential, but it is very useful; SATS reportedly earned R177m (then $200m) in 1979/80 and R213m ($240m) in 1980/81 from carrying the goods of neighbouring states.[9] This is particularly important because South Africa over-invested heavily in its ports in the 1970s, spending more than R2000m on containerisation alone. Thus it has substantial over-capacity, particularly at East London. As traffic has fallen sharply with the economic depression, cargo from the neighbouring states has become even more important.

The other important company is Safren, formed in 1984 by Old Mutual after two acquisitions. In 1983 the then Hong Kong-based Jardine Matheson disinvested from South Africa, selling its 74% share in Rennies to Old Mutual. Then in 1984, the government sold to Old Mutual its controlling stake in the national shipping line, Safmarine, which in turn had a 60% interest in Manica Freight Services (the other 40% was held by Anglo). Manica and Rennies are freight forwarding agencies which together controlled 90% of South African forwarding and clearing, and the vast majority of forwarding in the neighbouring states (including Mozambique, but not Angola). Manica and Rennies were merged to form Renfreight. Safren is the holding company for Renfreight, Safmarine, and Sun International.

Safmarine carries an estimated 38% of all trade to and from South Africa. In addition, Safmarine is the dominant partner in the shipping cartels, called 'conferences', that serve South Africa (and Maputo and Beira).[10] Under government rulings these conferences carry a high proportion of South African cargo. Forwarding agencies organise transport, handling the paperwork, arranging the ships and trains, and shepherding the cargo through the ports; in principle, they simply take instructions from the clients, but in practice the clients leave the main choices to the agent. Thus forwarding agents have substantial power. With Renfreight and Safmarine both owned by Safren, it is not surprising that there is immense pressure to use South African ports and conference shipping lines. It might be cheaper (and sometimes quicker) for the shippers to use a Mozambican port or Dar es Salaam, but Safren earns more by routing traffic through South Africa.

Together, SATS and Safren have a stranglehold over regional transport. As the depression has deepened in South Africa, they have worked together to cut rates and attract traffic away from SADCC ports (see Chapter 15). SATS and Safren are a formidable enemy of SADCC; in the event of sanctions they could control the lifelines of several states.

TRADE

South Africa is a relatively open economy, highly dependent on trade. Imports and exports are each roughly one-third of GDP. Table 5 in the Statistical Annex gives some key features. Its mineral, gold, and diamond exports go all over the world. But its agricultural and manufactured exports find a less ready market, because it is a relatively high cost and underdeveloped producer. Africa is the main market for South African manufactured goods, which tend not to be competitive in Europe and North America. Estimates of this lack of competitiveness are provided in the next chapter.

To compete with goods from other countries, South Africa resorts to a variety of export incentives which have become a sore point in the neighbouring countries (other than Botswana, Lesotho and Swaziland, who are members of the Customs Union). In some cases, South Africa is undercutting European prices or providing longer credit terms because of its various export subsidies. Trade between the SADCC states is particularly badly hit by South Africa's long credit terms.

Although South Africa is a member of the GATT (General Agreement on Tariffs and Trade), it has never signed the GATT Subsidies Code, under which signatories agree to restrict export incentives to prevent unfair competition. One reason South Africa cannot sign, as the South African Industry, Commerce, and Tourism Minister, Dawie de Villiers, admitted, is that South African incentives violate the code.[11] Many of these incentives are secret, and because of growing international complaints South African exporters and government officials are reluctant to talk about subsidies. The South African Foreign Trade Organisation (SAFTO) even refuses to show its 'Exporters' Manual' to the press.

The most important incentive is a tax deduction scheme, under which exporters are allowed to reduce their taxable income by amounts which include: (1) 10% of the total value added of exports, (2) 50% of the duty that would have been paid if inputs had been imported instead of being locally produced, and (3) up to 200% of expenditure in 'maintaining and developing export markets'.

The second of these tax credits is an effort to let South African industry have it both ways — protect it against competing imports while subsidising exports. Recognising that protective tariffs have made South African industry inefficient, and thus many locally manufactured goods are far more expensive than equivalent items available elsewhere in the world, this incentive gives a credit for the imputed extra cost of locally made inputs. When protective tariffs run to 100% or higher, exporters claim as much as half the cost of manufactured inputs, significantly lowering their export costs.

The third of these credits effectively makes overseas sales trips free, while SADCC exporters have to beg for foreign exchange for each air ticket. Few other countries have such a generous subsidy for trade promotion.

Nor are tax credits the only subsidies. Food exports, particularly, are directly subsidised. For example the Meat Board loses R370 to R690 per tonne of meat exported.[12] In 1985, following good rains and a food self-reliance campaign, Swaziland harvested a bumper maize crop — but thousands of tonnes rotted in silos because it was more expensive than subsidised South African maize, and because the country's only mill (which is South African owned) temporarily closed down rather than give preference to Swazi maize.[13] Finally, there are a number of special incentives for firms to move to the bantustans, including huge transport and wage subsidies.

Three factors are causing South Africa to rethink its subsidy system. The first is pressure from US firms claiming unfair competition. In 1984, after the US threatened to ban the import of subsidised steel, Iscor (the state-owned Iron and Steel Corporation) phased out its seven-year-old steel export subsidy scheme under which local consumers paid extra for their steel so Iscor could export at below cost. Iscor also had to impose a 'voluntary' ceiling on exports to the US.

The second factor is that some people in both business and government feel it would be useful, particularly in terms of US trade, to sign the GATT Subsidies Code. Attempts are therefore being made to remove the subsidies which most obviously violate the code. But trade experts argue that South African exports will never be competitive without subsidies, so that new, more hidden ones will have to be introduced.

The third factor is the recession, which has hit South African industry particularly hard. Tax credits come at the end of the year, and then only if the firm makes a profit. With the current squeeze, companies need cash in hand. So tax incentives will probably be replaced by some system of direct payment. South Africa can therefore be expected to make significant changes in its export incentive system. The changes are unlikely to reduce subsidies in real terms, however and may actually increase them.

In 1985 the competitive position of South African exports temporarily improved, ironically as a result of the political and economic crisis in South Africa, which caused the value of the rand to fall precipitously against other major currencies. This has had a serious effect on the production and exports of goods from neighbouring countries. As the rand falls, imports from South Africa become cheaper. In itself, that might appear an economic gain for Botswana and Swaziland, who import primarily from South Africa, but whose exports go to the outside world and therefore earn hard foreign exchange.[14] However, cheaper South African goods weaken the competitive position of local producers, both in their home markets and even more in exporting to the region. For example, Botswana's previously rapidly-growing manufacturing sector has suffered severe reverses since mid-1984: at the end of 1985 over half its export-oriented garment firms had closed or were in danger of closing. The same problem of increased South African competition has affected Zimbabwe and Malawi, and Zambia (at least until its dramatic devaluation by over two-thirds in late 1985). South Africa was taking only 40% of Zimbabwe's manufactured exports in 1985, compared with 75% in 1983, according to the CZI (Confederation of Zimbabwean Industries). One Zimbabwean exporter commented: 'It is now very difficult for our manufacturers to hold on to the South African market, with only very few exceptions. Most firms have already been pricing their goods on a marginal-cost basis, and can scarcely drop their prices more without trading at a loss'.[15]

A parallel phenomenon exists in transport rates. The rand has fallen sharply relative to both the Mozambican metical and the Tanzanian shilling, cutting or in extreme cases reversing the cost advantage of SADCC transport routes.

In the long run, South Africa's underlying high costs are likely to reassert themselves, because its inflation will be higher than that of its Western (if not regional) competitors. The rising level of internal struggle against apartheid may also disrupt South African production and transport routes. In the meantime, the sharp fall in the value of the rand, and the increased need of South African firms to capture export markets as their domestic demand stagnates, has severe short term implications for the region. It is yet another of the costs to the region of the continued survival of apartheid.

In addition to direct trade with the neighbouring states, South Africa uses its links with the neighbours in various ways to boost its secret trade with other countries. Because of trade embargoes, there are a number of overtly fraudulent tactics used by South Africa, usually involving relabelling. In the Middle East, which has a strong South African embargo, some goods like matches and jelly have been sold with 'Made in Swaziland' labels, even though such goods are not manufactured there. South African beef has also been relabelled.

Another trick is for agents to change shipping invoices at Maputo port, especially on goods destined for Asia. South African grain has been redocumented as Mozambican, and goods from Zimbabwe and Zambia sent via Durban have been marked as sent via Maputo.[16]

As sanctions are imposed against South Africa, this kind of trick will become increasingly important. One additional reason that South Africa would like to keep SADCC traffic passing through its ports is that this provides an opportunity to add in South African cargo. For example, if Zimbabwean chrome is exported via South Africa, it is easier to add in South African chrome to the shipment and say it is all Zimbabwean. The new rail link through northern Swaziland due to open in early 1986 offers another opportunity for this. South African products can be sent to Swaziland, be relabelled and reinvoiced there, and then be exported through Durban or Maputo as Swazi goods.

ENERGY AND WATER

Water and energy supplies are not uniformly distributed throughout the region, creating a significant interdependence.

Oil

Angola is the only SADCC state to produce oil; all the other member states meet all their oil needs by imports. (Mozambique may have exploitable quantities and exploration is under way.) Zambia and Mozambique have refineries and import crude oil — Zambia via a pipeline from Dar es Salaam. The other states import refined petroleum products. Zimbabwe imports diesel and petrol through a pipeline from Beira and other products by rail through and from South Africa (The statistics do not distinguish, although it appears that little is now bought from

South Africa; most is imported via Maputo and railed to Zimbabwe, but via South Africa). Zambia and Mozambique have imported small amounts of diesel from South Africa; until 1981 Mozambique sold heavy fuel oil to South Africa. Malawi buys most of its fuel from South Africa; the BLS states (Botswana, Lesotho and Swaziland) buy all their oil products from South Africa. Thus Pretoria has a significant control over the region's fuel supply.

South Africa has been the object of a voluntary international oil embargo. It obtained 90% of its oil from Iran until February 1979, soon after the fall of the Shah. Since then it has bought on the free market. At first however, this was difficult. In 1979 South Africa nearly ran out of oil, and it became embroiled in various now well-publicised shady deals. It paid hundreds of millions of dollars in commissions and became enmeshed in frauds like the sinking of the oil tanker Salem in 1979, which cost South Africa $26m. Up to two years' supply of oil is now stored inside the country. Sasol oil-from-coal plants now produce about one-third of South Africa's oil needs, and that percentage will increase as additional plants are built, but the cost of coal conversion is much above the normal world market price of oil. Substitution of coal and electricity for oil has taken place wherever possible, and is not likely to be extended any further.

Various estimates have been made of the cost of the oil embargo to South Africa. In 1984, the parliamentary opposition leader, Frederik van Zyl Slabbert, alleged that the government had paid at least R385m (then $300m) too much for crude oil purchases in recent years.[17] But the Shipping Research Bureau in Amsterdam estimates that the total *extra* costs of Sasol, stockpiling, higher prices, and payments to middlemen are at least $1850m per year.[18] That means South Africa is paying an effective 40% surcharge for its oil. Some of that is passed on to neighbouring states through a variety of surcharges; if the BLS states paid a proportionate share, it would cost them $25m per year.[19] Finally, because of the way it is calculated, importing oil through South Africa actually reduces customs union revenue.[20] So the BLS states pay through the nose for the privilege of consuming South African fuel.

Regional oil consumption and production is estimated to be (in thousands of barrels per day):[21]

	Consumption	*Production*
South Africa	450	150
Angola	10	150
Botswana	3	0
Lesotho	1	0
Malawi	3	0
Mozambique	11	0
Swaziland	2	0
Zambia	17	0
Zimbabwe	18	0

South Africa also uses its control of oil politically, causing shortages in neighbouring countries when it wants to make political points. After several incidents, Botswana in 1980 decided to set up a four-month strategic reserve, but for more than a year South Africa simply refused to supply extra fuel for it to be formed. Pretoria stressed its power by delaying fuel supplies in January 1981, causing a severe petrol shortage.

Obviously it would be cheaper and easier for the BLS states to import fuel directly. Lesotho tried, and in 1982 Algeria sent to Maputo for refining enough crude to give Lesotho a four month reserve. South African Railways simply refused to transport it, and after 18 months Lesotho gave up and sold it on the spot market.[22] Botswana made provisional arrangements for the supply of crude from the Middle East to be refined at Durban and railed to Botswana, but Pretoria made it clear that this would not be acceptable. In principle, Botswana and Swaziland could import refined oil directly, because they have direct rail links to Maputo that do not pass through South Africa. But South African raids on oil storage facilities in Lesotho, Mozambique and Angola are a reminder of how far South Africa is prepared to go to maintain its fuel monopoly.

Electricity

The region has massive hydro-electric generating potential, and also huge coal reserves, so the main energy source will always be electricity. The biggest hydro resources are the Zambezi river in Mozambique, Zimbabwe, and Zambia, plus several rivers in Angola. In the late 1960s Portugal and South Africa started on two massive projects to send electricity from Mozambique and Angola to South Africa. The Cahora Bassa dam, which began generating in 1979, is contracted to supply 10% of South Africa's demand; since 1981 it has been largely cut off by the MNR. In Angola the SADF occupied the Ruacana dam on the Namibia border for five years to ensure that it supplied power; a repeated South African demand is that Angola come to some agreement over the dam, like the one South Africa has with Mozambique over the Cahora Bassa.

In the other direction, South Africa supplies all the electricity to Lesotho and most to Swaziland. It also supplies some power for Botswana (temporarily while a new power station is built), for Maputo, Mozambique (ostensibly from Mozambique's small share of Cahora Bassa power) and Beit Bridge, Zimbabwe.

Water

One of South Africa's major problems is shortage of water, particularly in the Transvaal. Coal-fired power stations and Sasol plants are both massive consumers of water — both required because South Africa's increasing isolation makes it difficult to buy oil and electricity. Rapidly expanding irrigation schemes also consume water, while afforestation (needed to meet timber and paper demands) reduces run off, and thus cuts the amount of water available for other uses. Massive and complex systems have been built to transfer water to rivers flowing past power stations. Mozambique and Swaziland complain that South Africa is already drawing more water than international norms permit from the rivers that flow into them. Lesotho, however, is a possible source of water, and the Highland Water Scheme is now under discussion (see Chapter 11). There has also been sporadic discussion about South Africa's drawing water from the Okavango in Botswana; this would be more expensive than the Highland Water Scheme and seems to be raised largely as part of the bargaining with Lesotho.

South Africa's interconnected shortages of oil, electricity, and water mean that these are considered issues of vital national interest in Pretoria. Thus they are highly political in a regional sense as well, having a place in the total strategy and in overall South African demands. At the same time, despite its own shortages,

Pretoria is anxious to supply the neighbouring states because of the economic leverage it gives.

MIGRANT WORKERS

South Africa may be rich in minerals, but those minerals have been wrested from the soil by men from the neighbouring states. For much of this century, the South African mining industry was based on cheap migrant labour from the neighbouring colonies. A formal recruiting system was established, and the governments of the colonies received roughly half of the miners' wages (which were then passed to the miner in local currency when he returned at the end of his contract). This became a vital source of foreign exchange and was continued by most of the neighbouring states after independence.

The proportion of foreign miners has shifted substantially during the century. In 1905, fully 85% of miners were foreign. The proportion stayed at around 60% from 1908 through 1929, fell slowly to 42% in 1942, then rose steadily to 80% in 1974 — the highest proportion of foreign miners since early in the century. These changes reflected both the steady increase in the number of miners, and quite rapid shifts in the number of South African workers — there were 215,000 South African miners in 1942, and only 86,000 in 1971.

Until 1970, the largest group of foreign miners was always Mozambicans — their numbers regularly exceeded 100,000 and they were often more numerous than South Africans. Then, in the early 1970s, Malawians also exceeded 100,000 — a clear mark of the improved relations between Malawi and South Africa at that time. The number of Malawians fell dramatically in 1975, when Life President Banda banned recruiting. This was ostensibly because Malawian miners had been killed in a plane crash, but was widely ascribed to the need for more plantation labour in Malawi. And in 1976, after Mozambican independence, the Chamber of Mines cut back recruitment of Mozambican labour.[23] Numbers fell to below 45,000, in direct violation of the labour agreement between Mozambique and South Africa, which sets a minimum of 60,000. The only other sudden change was the decision in 1981 to end the recruitment of Zimbabwean miners.

In the decade after 1975 there were two important changes in recruitment. First, increasing pressure for jobs from within South Africa (especially in the bantustans) led to increasing internal recruitment. The percentage of foreign workers fell from 75% in 1974 to 57% in 1976 and under 40% in 1984. Second, the increasing mechanisation of the mines increased the demand for skilled workers. Whereas the mines had been built on a relatively rapid turnover of poorly paid workers, now they needed a more stable workforce of skilled workers. Combined with the first change, this has meant that skilled miners from the neighbouring states have been encouraged to return for further contracts, but that new unskilled miners tend to be recruited from South Africa.

Another important change took place in the early 1970s. Mine wages had changed little in real terms in 30 years, then suddenly jumped. The average wage per shift went from R0.81 in 1973 to R1.78 in 1975 and R3 in 1976.[24] This was forced by a wave of strikes in 1973, particularly in Durban, but also in the mines themselves. And it was made possible by the increased productivity allowed by mechanisation and by the rising price of gold. Thus the earnings of the miners themselves, and of the sending states, soared in the late 1970s. Until then miners had been a useful source of income; now they were a major source of revenue.

In the period since 1978 the number of miners from each sending state (except Zimbabwe) has remained roughly steady, and it has been estimated that this will continue at least into the early 1990s, unless there is political interference.[25] But the South African government has repeatedly threatened to use mine labour for political ends. When Mozambique signed a non-aggression pact and Lesotho refused, South Africa privately threatened to transfer some of Lesotho's quota to Mozambique. Government ministers have publicly threatened to expel migrants and cut off recruiting if sanctions are imposed.

The mining houses have said they oppose any mass expulsion of miners, in part because the remaining international migrants are so highly skilled and cannot easily be replaced. This points to short-term profits and protection — the skilled men earn increasingly high wages and are unlikely to be displaced. But it also points to long-term problems. New miners are being recruited from inside South Africa rather than from the neighbouring states, and as the highly skilled, highly paid men retire in the 1990s they will not be replaced by men from their home countries. Thus the 1990s are likely to see a sharp fall in both jobs and income.

The trap

The sale of labour has caught several of the neighbouring states in a deep trap. Before independence it was easy for the colonial power to simply rent out workers. No jobs or facilities were created for them. Indeed, in Lesotho and southern Mozambique, mine work became an essential part of the reproduction process. Nearly all men worked at least two mine contracts, which was the only way they could earn the money to pay the bride price, build a house, and buy agricultural implements. That is still true in Lesotho, but less so in Mozambique. Nevertheless, in southern Mozambique today most vehicles carry South African registrations — they were brought home by miners, and form the basis of petty trading in many areas.

Thus many of the most skilled workers have no place in the home economy, and they look to South Africa and not their home country as the source of money. Any reduction in dependence on South Africa requires that jobs be found for these miners — and for those who will not be able to go to the mines. And in sharp contrast to the position of two decades ago, mining is relatively well paid, at least in comparison to agricultural work in Mozambique or Lesotho.

In addition to miners, there are also migrants in other areas — agriculture, domestic service, manufacturing, and construction. In the late 1960s more than one-third of all migrants were outside the mines, but they have been steadily replaced by South African workers, so that by 1984 only 16% of migrants were not miners. The second largest group after miners has always been agricultural workers. Lesotho and Botswana have been hardest hit by the drop; although the number of their miners has not changed much since 1977, the number of non-miners has been cut sharply.

Five countries still send significant numbers of legal migrants to South Africa. Lesotho is most dependent on migrant income. More than half of all its workers are in South Africa, and their remittances are 40% of GDP. Mozambique is next most dependent, with mine remittances earning more than any single export crop. Migrants are only 5% of the wage labour force, but Mozambique would be hard-pressed to find them jobs. For Botswana and Swaziland, migrant labour is a source of employment which would be hard to replace in the short term, but the remittances are less essential. Of those countries sending migrants, Malawi could probably stop with the least internal damage. Finally, Zimbabwe has stopped sending migrants and there are none in the mines, although there are still more than 7000 working on farms and in industry.

It is curiously difficult to obtain consistent figures for the number of migrant workers in South Africa. Not all governments in the region publish figures, while different South African government departments give different figures. In part this is due to the relatively short contracts (typically 12-16 months) and thus high turnover, which leads to considerable variation. There also seems to be an attempt to label some South Africans as migrants. These figures, from the South African Yearbooks, seem to correspond reasonably closely to the numbers given by the countries themselves, where such figures are available:

Number of Workers	1974	1980	1984
Angola	108	291	48
Botswana	33 357	23 200	26 433
Lesotho	134 667	140 746	138 443
Malawi	137 676	32 319	29 268
Mozambique	139 993	56 424	60 407
Swaziland	9 984	19 853	16 823
Zambia	703	918	1 274
Zimbabwe	5 961	10 377	7 492
Total	462 449	284 128	280 188

It is even harder to obtain accurate figures for mine remittances. There are certain difficulties as to how they should be calculated and most states do not publish complete figures. Lesotho actually produces two sets of figures, one for actual remittance and deferred pay withheld by the mining houses and sent to Lesotho (the figure most commonly reported, if at all, by other states), and a second estimating the total earnings transferred to Lesotho. Theo Malan of the Africa Institute of South Africa produced the estimates below, which seem reasonable.[26] Malan's figure for Lesotho, for example, is midway between the two government figures.

Remittances (in million rand)	1980	1983
Angola	—	
Botswana	32.0	47.6
Lesotho	153.3	280.6
Malawi	30.7	51.3
Mozambique	66.6	116.8
Swaziland	13.2	32.1
Zambia	0.6	1.0
Zimbabwe	15.4	8.7
Total	311.9	538.2

There are also large numbers of illegal migrant workers, particularly in agriculture and domestic service. Although the South African government has claimed numbers in excess of one million, this seems to include large numbers from the bantustans. The number of illegals from the neighbouring states is probably no higher than the number of legal workers — about 300,000.[27] This group probably brings relatively little money back to its home countries, and it seems likely that if the Pretoria government could identify many of these workers it would have expelled them long ago. Nevertheless, if South Africa did carry out its threat to expel illegals, the neighbouring states would surely have to find more than 100,000 jobs — not an easy task.

Unpicking the web

The neighbouring states are woven into a complex web of economic relationships with South Africa, involving migrant labour, transport, and trade. Some relationships seem beneficial, but most have high hidden costs including lost development opportunities and higher prices.

The problem for the neighbouring states is that these ties provide South Africa with highly effective economic leverage. And the inevitable fear for the neighbouring states individually is that if they cut off or even reduce one of these links, then the whole network will unravel, as South Africa responds and retaliates. Furthermore, as the attacks on transport links and fuel supplies make clear, Pretoria will not give up its economic power easily.

9. No Free Lunch
The Southern African Customs Union

The Swazi Plaza in Mbabane is always a busy place. Bustling shops are full both with shoppers and with a wide variety of goods — a decreasingly common sight in Africa today. A closer look shows that the main shops are OK Bazaars, Sale House, Jet, Select-a-Shoe, Edworks, and so on — all South African. To find Swazi-owned shops you have to go to the more out-of-the-way corners where the chemist, a small sports shop, and the odd food take-away are located. Inside the shops, virtually all the goods are South African. Indeed, Swazi Plaza is managed and partly owned by a South African firm. And out in the car parks, you discover all the cars are made in South Africa. Swazi Plaza is similar to the shopping precinct in any big South African town. The scene is repeated in the capitals of Botswana and Lesotho.

The reason is that Botswana, Lesotho, and Swaziland (the so-called 'BLS states') are members, with South Africa, of the Southern African Customs Union (SACU), which allows the free movement of goods throughout the four states. Consequently, whatever is available in South Africa is also on sale in the BLS states. More than any other single factor, SACU has led to the integration of BLS into the South African economy.

The main benefit of SACU to BLS is cash in hand without the expense and trouble of collecting it. As well as being a free trade zone, the SACU involves a central customs pool.[1] South Africa collects customs duties for the four states and then distributes the money to BLS — R314m in 1982/83. At virtually no direct cost to themselves, these three states gain more than half their total government revenue from the SACU (and thus from South Africa's tax collection structures). In practice, South Africa unilaterally determines all customs rates, and operates the system to maximise the market for its producers behind substantial protective barriers.

Origin and operation

The customs union was never intended to benefit the BLS states. It was set up in 1910 as a way of linking the then three British protectorates to the newly formed Union of South Africa, and defined that the three protectorates should get exactly 1.31% of total customs revenue. By the time they came to independence (in 1966 and 1968) the three accounted for 4% of SACU imports, so they were clearly getting short shrift. They demanded a renegotiation, and in 1969 the four signed a new agreement.[2] The new formula is complicated, but has three essential parts:
1) The calculation for each of the BLS states is based on its total imports, both

from South Africa and from outside the SACU. This means that BLS earn customs revenues on goods imported from South Africa even though no money goes into the SACU pool for these items — in other words, South Africa pays extra to BLS out of its share of the pool.

2) The figure of imports for two years previously is used as a basis for initial payments, supposedly to allow for accurate calculations. But since the value of imports has risen every year, this means the customs revenue on the increase is delayed two years, and that money is meanwhile held by South Africa. Botswana estimated that by 1980 the value of these arrears was over R60m, nearly equal to the R83m that Botswana received from the pool that year.[3] This is listed in Botswana's accounts as an interest-free loan to South Africa !

3) Finally, the figure (now based on actual import share) is multiplied by 1.42 to give the BLS states an 'extra' 42%. This effectively comes out of South Africa's share. No-one seems to know where this number came from,[4] but it is intended to compensate for the effect of protective tariffs (discussed later) as well as for the payment lag.

Unquestionably, the SACU provides for a real and significant cash transfer each year from South Africa to BLS. The BLS governments collect from SACU roughly 18% of the value of their imports, which is in the normal range for African countries. But does this provide sufficient compensation? Several studies suggest not. For example, Botswana calculated the amount of duty it would have collected itself in 1979 had it not been a member of SACU but charged SACU tariff rates on all imports.[5] Botswana found that because it imported higher duty items, it would have collected R65m, compared to the R66m it received from the SACU, meaning that its real rate of compensation for the negative effects of SACU was not 42% but more like 1%. Similar calculations have been done for Swaziland.

Problems

A major problem with the SACU is the total lack of fiscal control by the BLS. South Africa not only sets the rates of duties, but even the kinds of duty. For example, it initially had a selective sales duty on luxury goods. In 1978 it unilaterally replaced this with a general sales tax (GST). Whereas selective sales duties had gone into the SACU pool, GST does not, resulting in a direct loss of income to the BLS states. BLS could, and eventually did, impose their own sales taxes. However, they are politically unpopular because (if applied on all goods) they are regressive, imposing an unnecessarily heavy burden on the lower paid, compared to sales duty on luxury items. Furthermore, a genuine GST requires almost as complex a collection mechanism as a full-blown customs collection system — which SACU is supposed to make unnecessary for the BLS countries. But once South Africa decided on a general sales tax, there was little BLS could do. Indeed, some South African firms set uniform prices within the SACU, including the 6% South African GST rate: if BLS did not impose a tax, the firms simply pocketed the 6%.[6] Even with a sales tax, BLS lose, because people from BLS frequently take shopping trips to South Africa and miners often buy goods in South Africa before returning home; BLS gain no GST revenue on such items.

A similar problem occurred with a 15% import surcharge — a blanket duty on all imports — imposed by South Africa in 1977 because of a balance of payments deficit, in an attempt to discourage imports by making them more expensive. It was then cut to 12.5%, to 7%, and then abolished, only to be reimposed again in

1982 at 10%, abolished in 1983, and imposed yet again in 1985. All this is without consultation with BLS, and has a yo-yo effect on BLS economies. When the regional economy is doing badly, South Africa imposes a surcharge, which immediately makes BLS imports more expensive and thus raises their cost of living, purely to solve a South African economic problem. And the additional revenue earned through SACU surcharges stays with South Africa for two years, helping it rather than BLS through the financial crisis.

For BLS, customs tariffs are primarily a way to collect a significant proportion of government income. In stark contrast, customs tariffs are only a tiny portion of South African government revenue, and South Africa sees them mainly as a means of protecting new local industry in order to promote industrial development. Inevitably, then, there is a conflict of interest.

South Africa imposes high import duties on those items which it produces. These can be quite specific. For example, to protect its textile industry, made-up clothing has an average tariff of 30%, with the unique exception of 'suits and overalls used by overhead transmission linesmen', which happen not to be made in South Africa. Often the government will impose a protective tariff when a firm wishes to begin production of a new product. Even when imports are permitted, South Africa notoriously operates a 'paper tariff' on unwanted imports, by subjecting them to tedious and elaborate documentary checks while storage and interest costs accumulate and the goods deteriorate.

Protective tariffs raise the prices of goods, and sometimes lower the quality as well. This has happened particularly with vehicles, where there are also local content requirements.[7] Sometimes this is linked to military demands and the threat of sanctions. For example, the military persuaded the government to produce diesel engines, which vehicle-makers must use despite their being of inferior quality and one-third more expensive than imported ones.[8] Similarly, lorry gearboxes are now protected by a R700 duty per unit, but the manufacturer (Astas, owned by Gencor) is asking for that to be increased because imported gearboxes are still cheaper. Furthermore, lorries with the locally made engine and gearbox use 15% more fuel.[9]

A Lesotho study compared the prices of commodities bought from South Africa but also available on the world market, and discovered that South African ex-factory prices were on average 37% higher than world prices.[10] Even when transport costs were taken into account, they estimated that because of protective tariffs, Lesotho paid 23% more than the cost of buying on the world market. Lesotho's revenue from the SACU is equivalent to 18% of the value of imports, even with the compensation factor of 1.42%. Thus, in principle, if Lesotho were to leave the SACU and import goods from the world market, it could charge a 23% average import duty which would raise substantially more revenue without increasing the cost of living.

SACU and industrial location

BLS are by far the smallest states in the region — even together they have a population of barely three million, less than half that of Malawi or Zambia. In economic terms, their combined domestic production is smaller than that of any of the other states in the region except Malawi. It is argued that they are so tiny that they can never be self-sufficient; few industries are viable for such a small market. Thus one 'benefit' sometimes claimed for the SACU is that BLS gain from being part of a larger economy. BLS pay a high price, in terms of increased cost of living, for high SACU tariffs (or, more accurately, for the high prices charged by South Africa's cartelised, protected manufacturers). But South Africa is a good example of local industry successfully developing behind a wall of high protective tariffs. Membership of SACU should allow BLS to develop larger industries to see to the whole market, and thus share in the region's industrial development.

In fact, this has not happened. A Ford Foundation study of Lesotho looked at the trade creating effects of the SACU, and found that in 1976 Lesotho gained only R1m from exports to South Africa, while the apartheid state gained R66m from selling products to Lesotho that the latter would have bought elsewhere if it had not been a member of the SACU.[11]

Indeed, a consultant to the Botswana Ministry of Finance came to the surprising conclusion that

(although) the combined gross domestic product of the three BLS countries is barely 3% of RSA's GDP, yet in 1979 almost 7% of RSA's manufacturing value added and employment (about 100,000 workers) and 5% of RSA value added and employment in other non-mining sectors (more than 200,000 workers) can be attributed to the level of BLS imports from RSA.

Even more important, he found that 'during the 1970s the BLS market for RSA exports was much more dynamic than the rest of the RSA economy'. Thus about 23% of the growth in South Africa's manufacturing in the 1970s (involving 67,000 new jobs) was due to BLS imports.[12] BLS sales to South Africa in that period created only a tiny fraction of that number of jobs at home.

One reason for this is that South Africa is, for most goods, a highly cartelised, not a free, market. A new, small producer in a BLS country finds it extremely hard to win a share of the South African market, and even harder to keep that share in the face of concentrated, destructive competition. Sometimes a BLS firm — or more commonly a BLS branch of a South African firm — can negotiate a small quota in the South African market (as well as freedom from competition at home). But this does nothing to reduce costs to the BLS consumer, and tends to break down.

Swaziland seemed an exception. It did develop manufacturing industries selling fertilisers, zips, cutlery, and other goods into South Africa. Exports to South Africa increased fourfold in just five years from 1978. But with the recession in South Africa and changing South African policies, this collapsed completely in 1983-84, and Swaziland found itself no better off in its manufacturing exports than Botswana or Lesotho (see Chapter 10).

It is not surprising that BLS have failed to gain a proportionate share of the new industry. Long before they became independent, the Witwatersrand (with Johannesburg at its centre) had become the industrial heart of southern Africa. When BLS became independent, they remained peripheral, and gained little new industry. Even South African government officials accept this as a natural result of the free trade zone aspects of the SACU. 'A concentration of economic activities has always been characteristic of the economic process of growth within the mainly free market system,' commented the Director of Economic Programming in the Office of the Economic Adviser to Prime Minister P. W. Botha.[13]

Equally important is that BLS economies have mainly external linkages and few internal ones. In a closed economy with mainly internal linkages, there is a high 'multiplier' effect of new investments, because supplies and raw materials come from within the economy — thus a single new investment in a factory or road has multiple effects because it stimulates other linked developments. This is an important way in which growth is stimulated in an economy, and the linkages thus developed should form the basis for sustained growth. But in BLS all expenditures have a very high import content: in all three, imports are more than 90% of GDP. This means that most supplies — and, for larger projects, even the building contractors — come from South Africa. Thus BLS government expenditure helps the South African economy to grow, while new firms tend to be isolated from the rest of the local economy.

Industry will only move to the SACU periphery with special incentives. BLS are trying to encourage new industry with subsidies, and by stressing that BLS industry has the unique advantage of access to South African as well as black African, US, and EEC markets. To non-South African transnationals, BLS stress the added advantage of being able to sell into South Africa without the stigma of operating in it. Despite increasingly aggressive promotion, success remains limited, with job gains still numbered in the hundreds rather than thousands.

One reason has been concerted efforts by the South African government to block BLS industrialisation, in direct violation of the spirit, if not the letter, of the SACU. Pretoria prevented a Japanese car manufacturer from opening a motor assembly plant in Lesotho in 1971.[14] Taiwanese investors built a textile mill in Swaziland to use imported cloth. Workers were hired and production was about to start when South Africa imposed a duty on imported fabric, making the mill non-viable.[15] Production never started, and the machinery was just left to rust. Similarly South Africa delayed and eventually forced the closure of a fertiliser plant in Swaziland.

In another case, Swaziland Packaging made bags from imported hessian. South Africa suddenly imposed a 30% import duty on hessian, pushing up the price of hessian bags from R0.80 to R1.05. This followed an application by the giant Fibre Spinners and Weavers, which made woven polypropylene bags in South Africa with local fibre. They only cost R0.72 each, but hessian bags last longer and are easier to stack, so buyers preferred the hessian bags. But when hessian cost one-and-half-times as much as polypropylene, many users switched.[16]

Meanwhile, the South African government has increasingly been trying to direct industry to the bantustans. It faces the same problems as BLS in trying to move firms to the periphery. It has resorted to a mix of pressure and offering massive subsidies for firms that move to bantustans. These vary somewhat from one bantustan to another, but typically include 95% of the wage bill for seven years, 80% of the rent on premises for ten years (all buildings are provided), 37% of interest on other capital investments for ten years, and 40% of interest on housing. In addition, there is a rail transport cost rebate of up to 60% (in direct violation of SACU rules, which ban such rebates) and a 10% tender preference on goods bought by the South African government. These incentives cannot be matched by BLS, and all have lost firms to the bantustans, thus losing more industrial jobs than they have gained through the SACU.

In addition to high import duties, South Africa also uses quotas as a way of restricting imports and protecting its industry.[17] Quotas are not part of SACU, so BLS should be able to use South African quotas to their own advantage. Not only can they import goods for internal consumption independent of South African quotas; they can also import raw materials or semi-finished goods for further processing and sale in South Africa so long as the value added in BLS is more than 25%.

However, South Africa manipulates the SACU rules to ensure that this opportunity is not taken up. For example, a South African firm opened a plant in Botswana to recycle imported second-hand jute bags for the South African market. In 1984 it was forced to close, with a loss of more than 50 jobs, because South Africa claimed the bags did not have the required 25% local content. Within days it was announced that it would reopen just over the border in the Bophuthatswana bantustan — aided by a South African government grant of R600,000.[18]

Television is an even better example.[19] In 1971, when the South African government announced that it would finally begin television broadcasting five years later, it set out to ensure that all TV sets were made locally, preferably in or near the bantustans. To prevent oversupply, only six companies were licensed to build sets — and at least one had close links with the ruling National Party. There was no legislation permitting such an action, but the government made clear that it would simply prevent other firms from importing key components. No production was planned for BLS, but it provided a clear industrialisation opportunity, with interest both from BLS and from foreign firms which were not in the privileged six. TV set assembly was begun in both Swaziland and Lesotho, but both firms are now closed. South Africa eventually allowed the Finnish firm Salora to produce sets in Swaziland, if it agreed to limit TV production to 60% of capacity and assemble other electronic products using South African components.[20] The Lesotho plant closed quickly because South Africa refused to allow it certain customs duty rebates given to the other firms. The Swazi plant was eventually bought by one of the other six firms, which closed it in 1984 to reduce TV set competition, and moved the non-TV production to a bantustan.

When BLS renegotiated the SACU agreement in 1969, they were admittedly very naive, assuming that they were largely talking about money. At the time this was understandable, given that the old agreement was grossly exploitative in straight revenue terms. One delegation admitted: 'During the course of negotiations of the 1969 agreement the BLS countries were not aware of the intricate administrative controls and voluntary arrangements existing in South Africa, nor had they been mentioned by the South African negotiators.' But they soon discovered that BLS did not benefit 'from the voluntary compliance with the arrangements which had been made primarily for the benefit of South African industries'.[21]

Finally, the customs union does allow BLS to protect new industries serving the local market by imposing prohibitive duties for up to eight years on goods from other SACU members. There are a few industries which are viable for these tiny markets, but BLS has had only limited success using this protection. In part this is because the nature of the high duty means that the new industry must be able to satisfy the local demand, and it cannot be used to protect new firms that can initially only supply a small portion of local demand. Infant industry protection has so far only been attempted for beer and milling; a Botswana attempt to introduce a German firm having failed, South African Breweries (SAB) now has a *de facto* monopoly in the SACU, so the protection is now only a method by which SAB divides up the market.

Various protection arrangements do exist for food and agricultural products. In 1979, when the price of flour rose and South Africa decided to subsidise the price of bread, Botswana was able to keep out the cheap bread and thus prevent unfair competition with its bakeries. Botswana and Lesotho both use licensing systems to restrict the importation of eggs, chickens, fruit, and vegetables to allow first preference to local producers.

Bantustan recognition?

Ten years after their independence, BLS were more sophisticated about the workings of the customs union, and realised that they were paying a high price for the seemingly free revenue. BLS pressed for renegotiation of the SACU agreement; eventually, South African civil servants accepted BLS arguments. At the SACU commission meeting in Pretoria on 28 October 1981, a new formula was agreed under which the two-year time-lag in payments would be ended, which with other adjustments would lead to a 10% increase in payments. In addition, BLS would receive about R200m to pay off past arrears. Unexpectedly, however, the South African government rejected the new formula at a SACU meeting in Mbabane the following year. No official reason was given.

However, Prime Minister P.W. Botha, in a speech to bantustan leaders that year, said, 'We see the Customs Union not in isolation as a revenue sharing arrangement, but as part of a comprehensive regional strategy'.[22] Privately, Pretoria has made clear that any renegotiation of SACU would require some form of BLS recognition of the bantustans. BLS consistently refuse to deal with the bantustans and so they have never been permitted to attend SACU meetings. But when South Africa talks about the SACU, it now includes the bantustans (and, less clearly, Namibia). Former Finance Minister Owen Horwood talked about Transkei, Bophuthatswana, Venda, and Ciskei having 'de facto membership' of the SACU. South Africa transfers to these four bantustans and Namibia payments from its SACU share of just slightly more than BLS receive. More recently South Africa has suggested that SACU payments should go through its new Southern African Development Bank, whose only other members so far are the bantustans.[23] Botswana, in particular, has staunchly resisted any meeting which includes the bantustans; as any change in SACU rules must be unanimous (and South Africa has used its veto often), the opposition of the BLS states prevents any direct inclusion of the bantustans.

So South Africa tries to use the SACU to force recognition of the bantustans in other ways. For example, there are anti-poaching provisions in the SACU agreement. But when BLS complain to Pretoria about industries moving to the bantustans because of the massive South African government subsidies, they are told that it is nothing to do with South Africa and that BLS must talk to the 'independent homelands' — and that this would not be a problem if the bantustans were officially members of SACU.

The cost of staying in

More than 85% of BLS imports come from South Africa while less than 25% of BLS exports go there, giving South Africa a R1400m per year trade surplus with BLS. This is a massive boon to South African industry and agriculture, which is hardly compensated for by R400m in SACU payments and miners' remittances. For BLS the customs union simply means money: for South Africa it means protectionism, markets, and industrial dominance of the region. Even the World Bank, hardly the most radical of organisations on this sort of subject, concluded that if Lesotho were to secede from the SACU it 'would gain under optimistic or intermediate assumptions'.[24]

The Ford Foundation is another respected body not given to starry-eyed nationalist economics. Its Lesotho study was one of the most detailed ever done of SACU membership, and its summary is sweeping:

> To the superficial observer, Lesotho's membership of SACU appears inevitable and beneficial; inevitable because of the close integration of the Lesotho economy with that of South Africa and because of the Lesotho government's dependence on customs union revenues, beneficial because of the apparent fiscal transfer in the revenue sharing arrangements. A more careful analysis points to very different conclusions: the protection of South African industry imposes a massive net burden on the Lesotho consuming economy; the revenue sharing formula, apart from creating the most acute form of dependence on Pretoria, has ... contributed to the distortion of government spending patterns and a skewing of the distribution of income; above all the open product market has suppressed the development of a local manufacturing capacity even for basic needs products, and has generated a psychology of consumerism and dependence on South African goods.[25]

The outcome of the study is radical: 'The conclusions of this discussion may be stated quite simply: membership of SACU is impeding economic development in Lesotho and has exacerbated dependence. ... Lesotho should accordingly take active steps towards disengagement from the customs union.'

The prerequisites for withdrawal

Given these manifest advantages of withdrawal, it appears surprising that it has been seriously considered only by Botswana, and then more as a defensive measure than a national initiative.

One reason is the simple administrative weakness of the present BLS Customs and Excise services, particularly serious given the long and porous boundaries of all three BLS states. Governments are perhaps reluctant to undertake the considerable task of training and establishing new administrations.

Secondly, there are no large, independent import houses in the BLS states, of the sort that are essential if cheaper goods are to be found from outside South Africa. BLS firms are either members of South African groups, or small local enterprises. They have either no interest in ordering or no capacity to order other than from South African catalogues and quotations. Furthermore, some government ministers and officials have direct interests in this existing commercial structure, with its South African links. Until it is clear that a BLS country really wishes to increase imports from non-South African sources, and will resist South African pressures, worldwide import export houses are unlikely to open branches. A joint venture with the state, or with a parastatal development corporation, might be attractive to some trading houses (including Zimbabwean ones), as it would guarantee a local ally. But while this approach has been canvassed, to date no action has resulted.

Finally, South Africa would probably retaliate, so that shifting away from South African imports probably requires shifting away from South African transport routes. South Africa could be expected to insist on complex transit traffic procedures, inspect and reinspect all documents and shipments, and create 'technical problems' when handling imports to BLS. Therefore, while withdrawal from SACU would have substantial potential for gain, there would be considerable changes required to reap that potential. Unfortunately, the costs are short-term, whilst the gains are largely further off and harder to calculate with any certainty.

The rand

As well as being members of a customs union with South Africa, BLS are also linked to South Africa through the rand. When BLS became independent, they simply used the South African rand as currency and had no central banks of their own. In 1976, with rising diamond and copper-nickel exports to back it up, Botswana set up its own currency (the pula) and withdrew from the Rand Monetary Area. Since then, Lesotho and Swaziland have established their own currencies (loti and lilangeni, respectively) and central banks, but remained in the rand zone. This means

$$1 \text{ loti} = 1 \text{ lilangeni} = 1 \text{ rand.}$$

The rand is legal tender and circulates in parallel with the new local currencies in both countries. Both countries must keep sizable rand deposits with the South African Reserve Bank to back up their own notes, although they also receive some compensation for rands in circulation. Interest rates and other monetary policies are largely set by South Africa. South Africa abolished exchange controls in 1983 and reintroduced them in 1985 with no concern for the effect on the neighbouring states.

The main commercial banks in Swaziland and Lesotho are also closely linked to South Africa. Nevertheless setting up national banks and currencies has had some effect. Lesotho, for example, requires the commercial banks to keep in Lesotho assets representing 85% of liabilities, and miners' deferred payments must be deposited in Lesotho banks. On balance, however, there remain substantial deposits in banks in South Africa which increase the funds available for investment there rather than in Swaziland and Lesotho.

There would seem to be some advantages in Lesotho and Swaziland following Botswana and withdrawing from the Rand Monetary Area. In particular, Lesotho and Swaziland would be better off holding their assets in dollars instead of rand — the collapse of the rand effectively halved the value of that portion of their foreign reserves held in rand, in less than two years.[26]

There are two drawbacks, however. The first is that because of the customs union BLS are integrated into the South African economy and thus inherit its inflation and devaluations simply through the prices of goods. So even an independent currency is, in reality, closely allied to the rand.

Second, Lesotho and to a lesser extent Swaziland do not have the firm economic base that Botswana had when it left the Rand Monetary Area, and thus there are certain advantages to having a currency tied to a larger economy — even one as weak as South Africa. Thus the merits and demerits of rand zone membership for Lesotho and Swaziland seem more finely balanced than those of SACU membership. The Ford study of Lesotho did not pronounce on this issue, in contrast to its strong recommendation that Lesotho should withdraw from the customs union, but it did say that an independent currency was possible.[27] Swaziland has been more active as a result of the 1985 fall in the value of the rand, announcing its intention to delink the lilangeni from the rand in the February 1986 budget speech.

10. Swaziland

WITH JOHN DANIEL

'Ambush! Rail Link Now Shut' shouted the newspaper headline that greeted delegates arriving for the SADCC annual conference in Mbabane on 30 January 1985.[1] In an explicit show of power, South African-backed MNR rebels in Mozambique had attacked a Swazi train on the main line to Maputo port. The attack had been carried out just over the border in Mozambique.[2]

The point was not lost on the Swazis, who had resisted strong South African pressure not to host the SADCC conference. Prime Minister Prince Bhekimpi Dlamini scrapped the prepared text of his opening statement of welcome to SADCC. Speaking impromptu, he declared that however important SADCC was, 'the Kingdom of Swaziland will always consider first that the needs of the Swazi nationals are properly met.' This means 'that the Kingdom of Swaziland has no choice but to cooperate' with South Africa. The Prime Minister noted the 'criticisms showered' on Swaziland because of her South African links, but declared: 'Today I want to make it clear that there is nothing wrong with our policy.'[3]

The SADCC conference showed the path Swaziland has chosen to walk. The meeting was held in Swaziland's main hotel, the Royal Swazi Sun. At past conferences, SADCC has completely taken over the main hotels. In this case, the hotel proprietors refused. The hotel is run by Sun International, owned by South African Old Mutual. Not only did they refuse to give the conference organisers enough rooms, but they simultaneously booked into the Sun a South African professional golf tournament. So some SADCC delegates were forced to stay in small hotels far from the conference centre, while others had to rub shoulders with South African golfers who had rooms at the conference hotel.

Swaziland may have hosted the SADCC conference, but it balanced it by that same month becoming the first African state since Malawi in 1967 to allow South Africa to open a diplomatic mission. Technically it is just a trade mission, but Swaziland already buys 83% of its imports from South Africa. 'Trade will look after itself,' notes the mission's head Sam Sterban, who says it is 'virtually an embassy in everything but name'.[4] He is a career diplomat, not a trade expert, and he has diplomatic status (and was thus invited by Swaziland with all other recognised diplomats to the official SADCC reception). Even he argues his main role is not trade, but rather aid, consular, and security functions. For 1985, South Africa planned a R12m aid programme, he said.

Swaziland is surrounded by South Africa except for a short border with Mozambique. Nowhere in Swaziland is more than 60 kilometres from South Africa. With only 630,000 people and an area of just 17,364 square kilometres (similar in area to Wales), it is the second smallest country in Africa.[5] This is why it must, according to Bhekimpi, come to terms with South Africa.

The government is essentially aristocratic; power rests with the 'Swazi Nation' composed of a traditional monarchy, a council of elders, and an appointed supreme council known as the Liqoqo. This small elite is nationalistic and very conservative, maintaining its power by a mix of tradition and patronage (which has led to increasing corruption in recent years). King Sobhuza II ruled for 61 years and held considerable personal power until his death on 21 August 1982. Since then there has been a bitter internecine battle for power (which remains unsettled at the time of writing).

Swaziland remained a distinct geographical entity through the nineteenth century by skilfully playing off the English, Boers and Zulus. However, after the Anglo-Boer War, Britain took over the administration of Swaziland, as a 'protectorate'. The territory, and thus present-day Swaziland, was much smaller than that controlled by the 19th century Swazi kings. To make matters worse, the British carved what was left of Swaziland into three zones, and removed two-thirds of the land from Swazi ownership. The expropriated areas contained all the best riverine land and all the known mineral deposits. Regaining ownership and occupation of this land — both inside and outside present day Swaziland — has been the dominant issue in 20th century Swazi politics, closely linked to security issues and to economic development.

Inside the country, foreign-owned land has been steadily purchased, partly with British aid. From only one third in 1914, the Swazi Nation had 45% of the land by independence in 1968, and 57% by 1985. Since independence the main vehicle for this has been the Tibiyo TakaNgwane fund — the Swazi National Development Fund. It, not the government, receives mining royalties and invests them in development projects as well as land. It was set up by the king, and is not subject to public scrutiny.[6]

A few Swazis, particularly prominent politicians like Sishayi Nxumalo, the late R.V. Dlamini and ombudsman Robert Mabila, have become large landowners. Others have moved into businesses such as bars and bus companies. But the Tibiyo fund has become the main focus of Swazi capital accumulation. As well as buying back foreign-owned land, it has taken a minority share in almost every major foreign development. It usually owns 25% to 40% and leaves management with the foreign partner; it has often bought back foreign-owned land only to give it over to foreign-managed plantations. Thus the small Swazi economic elite has built its power initially as part of the monarchy and more recently as junior partner to foreign (increasingly South African) capital.[7]

In terms of international politics, Swaziland is one of the more conservative states in the region. It has diplomatic missions from Israel and Taiwan, and has always been nervous about the Marxist government in Mozambique.[8] Thus Swaziland has been sympathetic to the anti-communist rhetoric from South Africa, while expressing opposition to apartheid.

Swaziland often seemed to be walking a tightrope, swinging first to one side and then to the other, but trying never to fall. In the early days it balanced between Boer and English, later between South Africa and Britain. In the past decade the changing geopolitical relationships of the region have led Swaziland to try to balance its links with its newly independent neighbours against those with South Africa, and it has seemed to shift back and forth. King Sobhuza was very skilled at this, and applied the same techniques inside Swaziland, favouring first one group and then another, playing one off against another, and somehow always keeping on the high wire.[9]

South African economic power increased in Swaziland through the 1970s. But the independence of Mozambique and then Zimbabwe gave King Sobhuza an opportunity to move away from South Africa, while the unrest and crackdowns of 1976-78 inside South Africa gave him increased motivation to support anti-apartheid forces.

Pretoria's objectives

Swazi support for the ANC and SADCC threatened the white rulers of South Africa politically, economically, and militarily. So, in the period after 1980, South Africa set out to regain its dominance in Swaziland, as well as Malawi, the two conservative states it saw as natural allies. Thus its main goal was to win Swaziland back into the fold, in the most general sense.

There also seem to have been five specific goals, which will be discussed in more detail in the rest of this chapter. The most important was to expel the ANC and plug the security gap, through a non-aggression pact. The other four relate to Pretoria's perception of the Swazi government as sufficiently conservative to support South Africa on certain key issues. Thus Pretoria wanted (1) recognition of the bantustan policy (reflected in an offer to transfer South African land to Swaziland), (2) some further diplomatic recognition (gained eventually through a trade mission), (3) opposition to sanctions against South Africa, and (4) acquiescence in South African actions against Mozambique, for example, by providing rear bases in Swaziland for the MNR.

These South African objectives have been played out in a number of fields. This chapter looks first at three of them — land, transport and security — and then at the wider issue of South African economic power. Relations with South Africa are intertwined with Swaziland's complex internal political developments, and these inter-relationships are examined in the final section.

The land deal

Swaziland was offered the most dramatic deal in the region: transfer of land from South Africa. By receiving part of KwaZulu south of Mozambique, Swaziland would gain a link to the sea; in addition it would acquire all of KaNgwane, a bantustan stretched along a thin strip to the north and west of Swaziland which is South Africa's 'homeland' for 'ethnic Swazis'. The proposals would have increased Swaziland's area by a third — but more than doubled its population, a mark of the overcrowding of the bantustans.[10] The offer dovetailed with the issue at the centre of Swazi politics: recovery of lost land. Swaziland has long claimed parts of South Africa, and many Swazis supported the deal as redressing the colonial appropriation of land and people.

The proposals were however widely condemned, not least because they would have deprived 750,000 South Africans of their citizenship and turned them into Swazis without their approval. They were said to be ethnic Swazis, but 400,000 of them did not even live in the areas proposed for transfer. Thus the deal would have given the bantustan system a form of international legitimation and reinforced the apartheid tenet that blacks are not South Africans. Black Africa also saw it as breaking the OAU policy on maintaining old colonial boundaries.

Inside Swaziland, some pointed out that the country could never provide jobs for twice as many people, and thus the deal would ensure Swaziland's permanent dependence on South Africa for jobs and money. For Pretoria, the more significant opposition came from the bantustans affected. In particular, it could ill afford to antagonise, or show up as powerless, the leader of the KwaZulu administration Chief Buthelezi, whose public position as a black 'moderate' became increasingly important as South Africa's own internal crisis deepened.

Negotiations over the land deal began seriously in 1981. In February 1982, Swaziland signed a secret security pact (see below). That achieved, South Africa's interest in the land deal waned. The negotiations dragged on, but with less and less prospect of coming to fruition, until Pretoria effectively withdrew them in 1984.

Transport battleground

International transport is particularly vital to Swaziland because it is such a small and open economy — exports and imports are 60% and 80% of GDP respectively. Early in the century, South Africa refused to link Swaziland to South African Railways unless Swaziland actually joined the Union of South Africa. Swaziland refused and no railway was built.[11] Finally, in 1964 the first railway was opened — to send iron ore from north-west Swaziland to the seaport of Lourenço Marques (now Maputo), but it was operated by the Portuguese staff of Mozambican railways.

After Mozambican independence in 1975, the Swazis became worried about the new Marxist government in Mozambique, so a railway to the South African ports of Richards Bay and Durban was opened in 1978. For a while Swazi Railways was run with the assistance of the Canadian International Development Agency. Then in the late 1970s, with the opening of the southern link, South African Railways (now SATS — South African Transport Services) took over the assistance programme, so that 'officials seconded by the SAR for service in Swaziland form a large section of the top management of Swaziland Railways.'[12] The present chief executive officer, Danie Slabbert, served more than 40 years with SATS; his previous post was as head of Durban and Richards Bay harbours — the alternatives for Swaziland if it does not use Maputo. Slabbert succeeded a seconded SATS official, Fanie Botha.

Road transport is more important to Swaziland and is also dominated by South Africa — 90% of imports come from South Africa by road; perhaps 10% of exports go out that way as well. Most goods between Swaziland and South Africa are carried by SATS lorries,[13] largely because of restrictions imposed by Pretoria, such as the requirement that goods only be taken by road as far as a rail head. South Africa issues few licences to non-South African operators.

Thus imports generally come by road, while exports go by rail. The iron mine is now closed, but sugar, coal, wood pulp, and some citrus is railed directly to Maputo. The southern link was never commercially successful because Richards Bay is twice as far as Maputo; the only regular export via Richards Bay is some citrus, although SATS has tried to encourage this by sometimes making wagons for citrus available only to Richards Bay and not to Maputo.[14] Asbestos is sent out of the country to South Africa on a cableway, then railed to Maputo. Tinned pineapple is taken by lorry to South Africa and then by rail to Durban.

Swazi railway links with Mozambique were further weakened when Swaziland agreed to a South African plan for a new 120km railway. Construction began in 1984, and was completed in early 1986. It runs from Komatipoort in the eastern Transvaal south to Swazi Railways, tying in to the southern link to Richards Bay. For South Africa the scheme has obvious economic advantages, cutting 250km from the existing route around the bulge of Swaziland and thus providing a short-cut through Swaziland for minerals from the eastern Transvaal being exported via Richards Bay. The new route also has gentler gradients and will ease congestion on the Johannesburg to Durban line. Initially it will be used for 2m tonnes per year of phosphates and other cargo that at present is sent the long way to Richards Bay.

But it will have a direct impact on SADCC, and especially on the port of Maputo. As the then General Manager of South African Railways admitted, 'Such a connection will make it possible to divert traffic coming from northern Transvaal over this route to Richards Bay and Durban. Mozambique is fully aware that we may at any time now be diverting this traffic from Maputo.'[15] Furthermore, the diversion of traffic opens spare capacity to carry traffic to Durban from Zimbabwe and Zambia which, in line with SADCC's aims, should flow through Maputo and Beira. But South Africa can keep this traffic moving south by rate cutting, or by using the MNR to attack competing rail lines (see Chapters 12 and 14).

The scheme offered South Africa other indirect benefits. Pretoria probably had to pay for the line,[16] but most of that capital was spent in South Africa, as the main contractor is South Africa's Murray and Roberts (Sanlam) and the rails come from Iscor (the South African parastatal iron and steel corporation). Even so, Swazi Railways sees the project as a 'lifesaver' because it finally puts to use the loss-making southern link, and hopefully ends the railway's chronic deficit. So, as in the case of Lesotho's Highland Water Scheme (see Chapter 11), South Africa is promoting a project which broadens a neighbour's economic base, but at the price of increased long-term dependence on South Africa.

Concurrently with the launching of this project, and in an illustration of the contradictory path pursued by Swaziland, work began on a SADCC project to improve links between Mozambique and Swaziland. This involved the paving of the mountainous dirt road linking the two states. It is funded by Sweden and the African Development Bank and the contract necessarily went to a non-South African contractor. As there was no Swazi-based contractor without South African links, the tender was finally won by Mota from Portugal. However on the ground Swaziland's paradoxical position was again illustrated when both Mota and Murray & Roberts located their construction camps in the same village, and the two groups of workers shared the same restaurants, bars, and shops.

Water is also a serious problem for Swaziland. It has more irrigable land than water to irrigate with, and most of its rivers rise in the Transvaal. Water consumption in the Transvaal has increased dramatically because of the building of power stations and Sasol oil-from-coal plants. For example, the Heyshope Dam on the Assegaai River, built to supply water to Sasol 3, takes enough water out of the Usutu River (Swaziland's largest) to irrigate 3000 hectares. South Africa took the water with little regard for the downstream countries, Swaziland and Mozambique, which were finally forced to join three-way water negotiations with South Africa in 1982.[17] The obvious worry is South Africa's ability to regulate the short-term flow of water into Swaziland in rivers which it has dammed upstream. An even more immediate potential for destabilisation is Swaziland's dependence on South Africa for half its electricity.

Cross-border raids

Security is another area where the Swazis walk a narrow line. There has been close cooperation between the Swazi and South African police since before independence, with South Africa providing equipment and training.[18] More recently South Africa provided new police cars.[19] South African police have repeatedly entered Swaziland. Israel, too, has provided assistance.[20]

South Africa's main concern has been the ANC, which received some protection from King Sobhuza II as some of his close relatives had been involved in its founding. By the late 1970s ANC members were crossing Swaziland on their way in and out of South Africa. ANC activity was increasing sharply inside South Africa, and Swaziland had become an important conduit both for guerrillas and for political cadres moving to and from Mozambique. Pretoria began raids into Swaziland.

The most bizarre incident occurred in February 1981, with the kidnapping of a South African refugee teacher, Joe Pillay, from St Joseph's mission near Manzini. Some of Pillay's kidnappers were caught because one dropped a passport. They were arrested and charged, and much to the embarrassment of both Swaziland and South Africa, they turned out to be members of the Mozambique National Resistance (see below and Chapter 12). South Africa demanded a deal. The Ministry of Justice ordered the state prosecutor not to oppose bail, so bail was granted and the MNR men all absconded. Shortly after, Pillay was dumped over the border and back into Swaziland. With the failure of the kidnapping, South Africa switched to more permanent methods. On 8 December 1981, two ANC men were killed in their car in Swaziland, ambushed close to the border. Under pressure from South Africa, several ANC men were arrested by the Swazi police, and strict travel bans were imposed.

The carrot and stick were clearer than ever before. Just when South African security was pressing Swaziland hardest, the South African foreign ministry began apparently serious negotiations on the land deal. On 17 February 1982, just six months before his death, King Sobhuza agreed to a secret security pact with South Africa. The pact is much broader than that signed by Mozambique two years later, and requires the two parties not to allow 'any act which involves a threat or use of force against each other's territory'. It also calls for action 'individually and collectively... as may be deemed necessary or expedient to eliminate this evil', leading to the suggestion that South Africa now has the right to intervene unilaterally in Swaziland. Soon after the signing, the ANC's representative in Swaziland, Stanley Mabizela, was forced to leave the country. Shortly afterwards, on 4 June, his deputy Petros Nzima was assassinated by a car bomb, along with Petros' wife Jabu.

It was not just South African security forces that moved against the ANC. The Swazi police always had close links with South Africa, but King Sobhuza had imposed limitations on their actions against the ANC. The two years following his death saw a sharp increase in anti-ANC actions. In December 1982 there was a round up of ANC men; some were expelled to Mozambique. This followed the South African raid into Maseru, when South Africa privately warned Swaziland that it would turn the country into another Lebanon if the Swazis did not tighten up on the ANC. A year later, in December 1983, a team described by observers as 'whites with foreign sounding accents' raided a flat in Manzini and machine-gunned the two occupants.[21] One was an ANC man, Zwelahkhe Nyanda; the other was a Swazi but the Swazi government made no protest.

Two weeks after Mozambique and South Africa signed the Nkomati Accord of 16 March 1984, Swaziland and South Africa announced that they had signed the secret security agreement two years before. South Africa stepped up its pressure on Swaziland to crack down on the ANC, both those who had lived in Swaziland for a long time, and those who had crossed over from Mozambique just before Nkomati. Clearly Swaziland did not act fast enough. South Africa effectively closed the borders during two important holiday weekends in April, hurting the Swazi tourist trade.[22] South African security policemen were sent to put pressure on the Swazis.[23] Three ANC men and two Swazi policemen were killed in gun battles. Four ANC men were handed over to the South Africans in a staged kidnapping, intended to make it look as though the ANC had abducted some of its own people from prison. Several of the ANC members were badly beaten in prison. Eventually all the ANC detainees were expelled.[24]

Swaziland's openness to South African security forces was demonstrated by the widely publicised assistance of South African soldiers, army lorries, and helicopters in the relief efforts in February 1984, after a serious cyclone. The new trade commission will also have security links, as Commissioner Sterban made clear: 'The policies of both countries are reflected in the relations between the two police forces. ... I think this is only to be expected between police forces of any neighbouring countries that have a similar policy.'[25]

Nevertheless, Pretoria kept up the pressure. In December 1985 the State Security Council named Swaziland amongst neighbouring states who had not adequately curtailed the ANC, and on Christmas Eve a SADF patrol crossed into Swaziland, according to the Swazi protest, in search of ANC guerrillas.

Swaziland and the MNR

The final security link between South Africa and Swaziland is the Mozambique National Resistance (MNR — see Chapter 12). South Africa recruited for the MNR among Mozambicans in Swaziland, many of whom are there illegally. This activity has enjoyed varying levels of tolerance on the part of the Swazis, depending on their relationships with the Mozambicans.

The MNR was directly involved in the kidnapping from Swaziland of Joe Pillay. A leader of the raid was Amaro Silva, who worked for the South Africans in at least five countries. He was a well-paid Mozambican school teacher who had crossed over to South Africa in 1978 and turned himself in to the police. They sent him to Rhodesia, where he was trained and put into the MNR. He was caught on a sabotage mission inside Mozambique in 1980, but escaped the following year and returned to South Africa. This time he was sent to kidnap Pillay. Next he went on anti-SWAPO missions in Namibia. Finally he returned to Mozambique with the MNR, was caught again, and was executed in June 1982.[26]

After the signing of Nkomati, South Africa actually set up MNR bases in the Swazi mountains near the Mozambique border.[27] In April 1984, when the Swazi police and army were trying to root out the ANC, they fought with the MNR by mistake at least twice.[28] From these bases, the MNR made raids into Mozambique. Unfortunately for the Swazis, these raids included attacks on Swazi trains going to Maputo. For example, attacks in May, July, and September 1984 caused a backlog of sugar to build up in Swaziland.[29]

In February 1985 Mozambique protested to Swaziland. The response came on

27 February when the Prime Minister, Prince Bhekimpi, told a meeting of businessmen that he knew some of them had been helping 'illegal refugees' with food and money. Some kept arms caches on their premises and even helped to ferry insurgents with their arms to neighbouring countries.[30] It was a direct reference to Portuguese businessmen helping the MNR, and it was the first time this had been publicly mentioned. Bhekimpi told the businessmen that this could not be tolerated. But the speech was never followed up by any kind of action, and the support continued.

South African economic dominance

Although British capital was predominant before independence, this has changed. There has been increasing Swazi ownership of land and minority holdings in companies, but the economy is now effectively dominated by South Africa. Swaziland is a member of the South African Customs Union and the rand zone (see Chapter 9). Customs Union revenue accounts for two-thirds of the government budget. In addition, 14,000 men, about 15% of the wage labour force, work legally in South Africa and probably a similar number work illegally.

Wholesaling and retailing are controlled by South African firms, which tend to import and distribute South African goods. Kirsh Industries, linked to Sanlam, operates the largest wholesaler (Metro) and the two largest shopping centres.[31] The largest supermarket is OK Bazaars, a subsidiary of South African Breweries (SAB), itself controlled by Anglo American. Another important wholesaler is Frasers, of South Africa. Swaziland News Agency — the only distributor of newspapers and magazines — was recently sold by the South African CNA (Anglo) to Edesa (Economic Development for Equatorial and Southern Africa), a Swiss-registered firm linked to South Africa's Rembrandt.[32] Edesa also owns Swazi Printing and Publishing and the largest crafts marketing outlet, Mantenga. The government, in its Fourth National Development Plan, noted that

> The linkages to external markets ... have been further strengthened by recent public investment decisions. Thirty-five percent of the National Industrial Development Corporation's investments over the past five years have gone into buildings for wholesale/retail service enterprises of which the parent companies are South African based.[33]

In the tourist sector, two-thirds of visitors are from South Africa. Sun International (Old Mutual) controls both of Swaziland's casinos; two-thirds of visitors stay in the four luxury hotels run by Sun.

Mining has become monopolised by South Africa. The first mine, Havelock Asbestos, had been operated since 1938 by a British firm, Turner & Newall, but was taken over in 1985 by Gencor, Sanlam's mining subsidiary. Gencor has also taken over Swaziland's only coal mine from Anglo. Diamond mining was started in 1984 by Trans-Hex, part of South Africa's Rembrandt group, and initially sold through the (De Beers) Central Selling Organisation.[34] Anglo American led the consortium which sold Swazi iron ore to Japan from 1964 to 1980, leaving Swaziland with nothing but a hole and a railway to Maputo.

Agriculture, dominated by the plantation sector, remains largely British. Swaziland is Africa's second largest sugar producer (after South Africa) and sugar is its largest export. There are three large estates, all owned or managed by British firms: Lonrho (which used South African government export credits for its most recent expansion),[35] Commonwealth Development Corporation (CDC), and Tate & Lyle. Timber and wood pulp come next, and there are several large plantations. The biggest, Usutu, is British, owned by CDC and Courtaulds. CDC also owns the third largest plantation, Shiselweni. Mondi (Anglo American) owns Peak Timbers, the second largest, while Uniply (Barlow Rand) in 1984 bought Swaziland Plantations, the fourth largest. Citrus plantations are owned by CDC and a Danish firm. Pineapples are produced by Swaziland Fruit Canners, which was 89% owned by Nestle and trading under the Libby label, but in 1984 was sold to a South African firm, Zululand Fruit Producers. Cotton is an increasingly important crop, grown mainly by larger expatriate farmers on estates; the only cotton gin is South African.

Agro-industries dominate the manufacturing sector — sugar, timber (pulp and saw mills), and pineapple canning. Next comes Langa Brick, recently built by London Brick and CDC (both British).[36] Swaziland Brewers, the sole brewer of beer, is owned by South African Breweries, which also bought the main soft drinks bottler in 1984. The main producer of packaging materials, particularly for citrus, is Neopack, owned by Barlow Rand. Maize milling is controlled by Kirsh (Sanlam), which is also building a new spinning mill with CDC and African Development Bank money.[37] The Swazi National Development Fund, Tibiyo, owns significant shares in virtually all the big projects.[38]

Ownership is not the only issue, however. The British dominated Langa Brick largely sells to South Africa through a marketing arrangement with Corobrick, the near monopoly producer there. All citrus is marketed through the South African Co-operative Citrus Exchange. Cotton prices are set by South Africa.[39] Equally important is the continuing role of South Africans in the economy. The Fourth National Development Plan notes that 'the management of almost all medium to large scale enterprises continues to be almost exclusively non-Swazi.' Most are South Africans.[40] In 1981 the parliamentary subcommittee on localisation criticised the 'historical tendency' of private companies to give preference to foreigners over equally trained Swazis.[41]

The expansion of South African business into Swaziland reflected a variety of factors. On one hand, TNCs from outside the region lost interest; Swaziland is very small and their interests there were relatively tiny, while rising oil prices and the long distances to Europe made some exports less profitable. On the other hand, South African firms had surplus capital and were anxious, because of exchange controls, to expand within the rand zone. Thus there was some replacement of British capital by South African. In addition, South African wholesale and retail chains were expanding in this period, and the BLS states provided obvious areas to move into because of their membership of the customs union.

This increased dependence on South Africa has, as we note below, generated some disquiet in Swaziland. As with SADCC as a whole, it seems intrinsically dangerous to be so dependent on one other country — especially one with a racist, unstable, and potentially hostile government. Although there are examples of economic sabotage by South African firms and the government (more for economic than political reasons), the main problem is that the total dominance of South African goods and companies weaves a thickening web which eventually integrates Swaziland into the South African economy and separates it from the majority ruled states of the region. And that, as we have noted, provides South Africa with immense leverage.

Looking both ways

Like Botswana and Lesotho, Swaziland has tried to use its position in both the SACU and the Lomé convention as a way of attracting industry.[42] They argue that new industry can have the advantages of South Africa without the disadvantages. On the one hand SACU membership means duty-free entry to the South African market, plus access to South African services and inputs. On the other hand, there is not the political stigma of being in South Africa; it is possible to export to African and Arab states which ban South African goods, while Lomé and other preference schemes give access to EEC and US markets not available to firms in South Africa.

At least two firms are exporting in both directions. The South African owned Swazi Pine exports furniture made with Swazi wood to both the EEC and South Africa. And Bata Shoes is moving an entire factory to Swaziland from Pinetown, near Durban in South Africa, for sales to both black Africa and South Africa. Bata officials privately talk of concern with political and security problems in South Africa and say they are anxious to broaden their base in the region and avoid the clashes inevitable in the apartheid state. But it remains unclear if this is the full story or if the move is more simply a response to the growth of South African trade unions and an attempt to find a more docile, less-unionised work force. Bata is already active in several majority ruled states in the region; its other South African factories will continue to operate.

First world markets remain the most important for Swazi industry. Swaziland's main export — sugar — as well as beef, pine furniture, and tinned pineapple are dependent on access to EEC and US markets.[43] Sugar is still under British control, but South African companies dominate the other areas. This gives South Africa access to markets not normally available to it.

Sometimes the use made of this access is questionable. As well as canning Swazi pineapples and exporting them to the EEC, Zululand Fruit Producers now processes in Swaziland pineapples grown on its farms in South Africa. In this way, it is able to ensure that EEC local content requirements are met. Swaziland never has enough cattle to meet its EEC beef quota, and it is suspected that this quota is sometimes improperly filled with cattle from South Africa.[44] And some products, ranging from matches to jelly, have shown up in the Middle East with 'Made in Swaziland' labels — even though no firm in Swaziland makes such items.[45]

Another slightly odd EEC — South African link is that under the Stabex system, the EEC compensates Swaziland for losses in earnings from cotton exports to South Africa, due to drought or prices depressed by South Africa. South Africa manipulates and the EEC compensates.

On the other hand, Swaziland did use its access to the South African market so that for a time it seemed to be a small customs union success story — in sharp contrast to Botswana and Lesotho. A variety of new industries opened, and the share of exports going to South Africa nearly doubled in five years, from 20% in 1977 to 37% in 1982. Most important, these were largely manufactured goods like television sets and fertiliser (which moved up in importance to replace pulp and wood as the second most important export). Firms like Langa Brick and the Japanese zip fastener company YKK produce mainly for the South African market. But now the boom has evaporated, like a phantasm that was never there. South African policy created the boom in the first place; changes in that policy, combined with the recession, destroyed it. There was a direct loss of 1500 jobs —

one-eighth of the manufacturing workforce. Another 600 workplaces already announced were not created.

The main reason was the series of incentives introduced in South Africa in 1982 to attract industry to the bantustans. It succeeded. In the next three years, four firms moved from Swaziland to bantustans, while others closed down in the face of bantustan competition. Swazi Carpets had only opened in 1981 with 183 workers making 'oriental' rugs for the South African market; two years later it moved to the Transkei. After 10 years in Swaziland, the Taiwanese-owned Swazi Metalware moved to Bophuthatswana, putting 130 women out of work. The firm's general manager said that it was purely because of the incentives offered. Other firms made copper products and clothing.[46] In 1983 Kirsh industries abandoned a far advanced plan to build a textile mill that would have provided 1000 jobs, and decided to locate it in King William's Town — a 'decentralisation point' adjoining the Ciskei bantustan which enjoys similar subsidies.[47] Ten years earlier the threat of South African protectionist measures had stopped a Taiwanese firm opening a textile mill in Swaziland.

The most dramatic closure was that of Swaziland Chemical Industries (SCI), owned by two South Africans. SCI opened in 1975 and produced ammonium nitrate for fertilisers and explosives, using ammonium imported initially from Iran via Maputo. It also blended other imported fertiliser components.

At the time SCI was started, the South African market was comfortably monopolised, with government support, by two firms, Triomf and Fedmis (Sentrachem). They used their monopoly position to produce high cost fertiliser. On the other hand, SCI could use customs union (SACU) rules to import raw materials much more cheaply. From the start, the South African government, the fertiliser board, and the fertiliser producers association all tried to break SCI. First, Triomf and Fedmis cut their wholesale prices in Swaziland to well below those in South Africa, so their Swazi distributor (Kirsh) could undercut SCI. Then SCI was denied potash import subsidies given to South African firms, while South Africa tried to raise tariffs (naturally without consultation, as South Africa sets duty rates for the entire SACU). And South African Railways refused to carry SCI fertiliser to South Africa.

Finally SCI agreed with the South African manufacturers to buy more raw materials from them and import fewer from outside the SACU, and concluded a marketing agreement with them. Nevertheless in 1980 and 1982 South Africa imposed further duties that seemed aimed at SCI. Then, as part of a more general policy of free enterprise and under pressure from its powerful farming lobby, the South African government changed tack dramatically, and cut all import duties on fertiliser. SCI's advantage was ended, as it had to compete with imported fertiliser. The South African fertiliser producers were large enough to weather the storm. For SCI, the final blow came with the opening of two new fertiliser plants by Triomf and Sasol at a time when drought was depressing demand, causing a fertiliser glut.

SCI closed in 1984, throwing 300 people out of work. The previous year, it had accounted for 13% of Swaziland's exports, making it second after sugar and ahead of wood pulp and pineapples. It had debts of more than R60m, half to Standard and Barclays banks.

Tourism was also hit by bantustan competition. From a 1975 peak of 132,000, visitors fell steadily to 72,000 in 1983. Consistently, nearly two-thirds are South Africans. Sun City in Bophuthatswana, also operated by Sun International (which now controls the main Swazi hotels), and other bantustan attractions have drawn away the visitors who came for gambling, blue movies, and interrracial sex. In response, Swaziland has exploited the sports and entertainment boycotts of South Africa by hosting big name entertainers like reggae star Peter Tosh and Liverpool Football Club to attract integrated audiences across the border. Swaziland is a member of SARTOC, the South African-dominated regional tourism promotion organisation, but membership has brought few visible benefits.

Faltering attempts to delink

In the late 1970s and up to 1982, Swaziland made an attempt to reduce its links with South Africa and align its foreign and domestic policies more with those of the Front Line states. This occurred at a time when the regional power balance appeared to be shifting away from South Africa, while socialist states were emerging in the region. It also coincided with the premiership of Prince Mabandla Dlamini (22 November 1979 to 18 March 1983), who was distinctly more wary of South African links than either his predecessor or his successor.

Most importantly, Swaziland joined SADCC and rejected South African overtures to join Consas. Politically, Mabandla improved relations with Mozambique, and President Samora Machel of Mozambique visited Swaziland in February 1980. Shortly afterwards Swaziland detained a number of MNR men and threw out several people who had been recruiting Mozambicans working in Swaziland to send to MNR training camps in South Africa.[48] The following year, on 6 April 1981, Mabandla hosted a meeting of Machel, Botswana President Quett Masire, and Lesotho Prime Minister Leabua Jonathan. The meeting, probably unique in Swazi history, issued a communique sharply critical of 'attempts by South Africa to destabilise her neighbouring black-ruled states'.[49] Mabandla also strongly opposed the land deal with South Africa. Although publicly supporting it, in fact he worked against it in private.[50]

Relations with the ANC improved as well. Soon after Mozambican independence, King Sobhuza met with ANC President Oliver Tambo; an agreement was reached to allow the ANC a low-key diplomatic presence with a recognised official representative. From then on, the ANC had more freedom and a blind eye was usually turned to the infiltration of guerrillas into South Africa.

Swaziland also edged away from South Africa on the economic front. In February 1982, the Prime Minister's office issued an 'Economic Review' which stated: 'There is a declared policy by the Government of Swaziland to lessen dependence on the Republic of South Africa.'[51] The parliamentary subcommittee on localisation also criticised the role of South Africans in the economy.

Two major projects were begun in this period. The most important was an E40m hydroelectricity generating station which doubled Swazi capacity (40 million emalangeni is equal to R40 million). Swaziland is linked to the South African grid and the proportion of imported electricity was rising steadily, from less than half in 1977 to more than three-quarters in 1982; the new scheme brings it down to half again. Swazi-generated electricity will be more expensive than that bought from South Africa, but the government successfully arranged funding from West Germany, the African Development Bank, and other international agencies because of its desire to reduce dependerce on South Africa.

The other project was an E3m earth station for satellite telecommunication links. Until it was completed, all Swazi international telex and telephone traffic passed through South Africa. which charged such high rates that the new station was immediately profitable. In addition, as Deputy Finance Minister John Masson reminded parliament, 'there are security problems' with traffic going through South Africa. For example, in 1980 South Africa simply banned Swazi calls to some other African states.[52]

Two other actions in this period had anti-Pretoria overtones, even though this was not their primary focus. In 1981 Swaziland blocked the attempt by two British firms, CDC and Courtaulds, to sell the largest forest in Swaziland to a South African company. They had agreed to sell the Usutu forest and pulp mill to Mondi (Anglo) for R110m.[53] Although Anglo planned R40m in new investment, it intended to continue exporting pulp, whereas Swaziland had hoped to see paper production or some other industry there which processed the pulp. (SADCC, for example, has proposed a toilet roll factory — largely to export to South Africa.) However, a more important consideration may have been Anglo's unwillingness to give the Swazi development fund Tibiyo a 40% share in Usutu; Tibiyo had been involved with Natie Kirsh in an earlier offer to CDC and Courtaulds involving much less money.[54]

The second action was in 1980, when Swaziland used the threat of cholera in neighbouring South Africa to ban the import of fruit and vegetables. Although initially a health measure, the ban was continued until early 1984 in an attempt to stimulate local production by creating a protected market for fruit and vegetables,[55] and to force the South African owned wholesale and retail traders to establish Swazi sources of supply.

Reasserting dominance

These Swazi moves were paralleled elsewhere, so that by the early 1980s South Africa faced a challenge to its dominance throughout the region, symbolised by the creation of SADCC. In response Pretoria became more interventionist, using both carrot and stick methods to reassert its position.

Towards Swaziland it was mostly carrot. The number of Swazi miners in South Africa, which had fallen steadily from a peak of 21,000 in 1976 to half that in 1981, began to rise again. The north-south railway was agreed, ensuring that South African cargoes would push Swazi Railways back into profitable operations. Soon after, South Africa gave Swaziland a veiled R50m gift. It occurred when Swaziland claimed that it was owed R118m as its customs union share for 1982/83, compared to just half that in the year before. South African officials said the figure was much too high, but the South African cabinet 'noted the error' in the Swazi figure and accepted it anyway — the money was paid. The most important offer of all was the land deal, for which serious negotiations began in this period. At the same time, some pressure was applied, in the form of raids into Swaziland to attack ANC personnel.

Just when South Africa seemed most magnanimous, it won its biggest victory — on 17 February 1982 Swaziland secretly signed the security agreement. Swaziland then slipped back into the South African orbit. Within a year of the signing, Prince Mabandla was dismissed. And South African largesse ended as quickly as it had begun two years before.

Conflicting forces

South Africa's renewed ascendancy was not due simply to Pretoria's carrots and sticks. Equally important were the intense internal conflicts which plagued the country after Sobhuza's death in 1982. This factional conflict has been largely confined to the palace and royal family, and has been over control of the royal family itself, the state machinery, and royalty's riches held by the Tibiyo fund. Swaziland retains what is virtually a feudal system, with an all-powerful monarch and a group of powerful princes and elders, known as the 'Swazi Nation'. There is a government with the normal ministries, but ministers are appointed by the monarch. The elected parliament was abolished in 1973 and reinstated only in a very restricted form in 1978, with all candidates selected or approved by the monarchy. Thus the government is really an administrative body for policies set by the Swazi Nation.

Tibiyo's conservative stance is shown in its royal charter, which requires that while Tibiyo raise the standard of living of the Swazi people, it must also preserve 'the customs and traditional institutions of the Swazi people so as to prevent the rapid disillusionment and instability which has followed from their rapid breakdown in other parts of the world'. But its power increasingly comes from its links with foreign (primarily South African) capital.

Despite its subordination to the monarchy, there developed within government a group of technocrats with a somewhat different outlook. Tibiyo tends to ignore or oppose government; there is little contact and considerable competition between Tibiyo and government development agencies, like the National Industrial Development Corporation. Tibiyo, unlike the government agencies, has substantial money; Tibiyo stresses capital-intensive projects while the government agencies try to promote more labour-intensive job-creating projects. This has been particularly true in the case of sugar, which has been expanded at high capital cost to produce more than double the guaranteed US and EEC market. The rest must be sold on the world market, usually at a substantial loss. In a 1982 report, the office of Prime Minister Mabandla openly criticised Tibiyo for pushing Swaziland into a monocrop economy and for using water and capital that could better have been used for other projects. 'The expansion of sugar production over the last few years may not have been in the best interests of the country.' It added that when the biggest need is to create jobs, 'additional estate agriculture based on the intensive use of capital at the expense of labour is inappropriate for Swaziland'.[56]

King Sobhuza II kept the various tendencies in balance, but in the late 1970s he allowed technocrats on the outer fringes of the royal group to gain some power. This seemed to reflect his discontent with those who had ruled until then. In part, it was a response to changing regional relationships and the realisation that South Africa was no longer the only regional ally. More important, however, was a reaction against the corruption of many in senior positions in both the state and the Swazi Nation. The King's new stance was most clearly seen in his appointment in November 1979 of Prince Mabandla Dlamini as Prime Minister. He was not closely related to the King and had been an obscure plant manager (and was thus part of the technocratic rather than the royalist group, despite being a prince) but he had a reputation for honesty and gained in popularity when he quickly established a Corruption Commission. Prince Mabandla also tried to shift the locus of power away from the Swazi Nation and more to the government and ministers.

However, Mabandla went too far, especially when the Corruption Commission sought to subpoena Tibiyo records and began to look at Prince Mfanasibili

Dlamini and Tibiyo managing director Sishayi Nxumalo, then the two most powerful men in Swaziland after the King.[57] The Commission was curtailed in August 1980, although Mabandla retained considerable power. Then in June 1982, shortly before his death, the King named Prince Richard V. Dlamini, one of Mabandla's staunchest royalist opponents, as Foreign Minister.

In the period after King Sobhuza's death, the royalists were soon involved in bitter internecine squabbles. Prince Mabandla was dismissed on 18 March 1983; soon after, he fled to South Africa and was given refuge in Bophuthatswana.[58] In June 1984 Nxumalo and Foreign Minister R.V. Dlamini tried to dismiss Prince Mfanasibili. Nxumalo also announced that high officials, apparently including Mfanasibili, were involved in a R13m customs union fraud.[59] But Nxumalo and R.V. Dlamini were outmanoeuvred; they and the police and army chiefs were sacked. In ill health for some years, R.V. Dlamini died within a few weeks. In October 1984 the other three were detained and later charged with high treason. However, the conflict continued. A year later in October 1985 Prince Mfanasibili was himself dismissed and on 31 December Dr Nxumalo and the former police and army chiefs were pardoned and released.[60] In February 1986 Prince Mfanasibili and Dr Msibi were themselves detained, and the former police commissioner charged with defeating the ends of justice by the earlier detentions.

These internal manoeuverings had their counterpoint in relations with South Africa. The 1984 crackdowns on the ANC and announcement of the security pact followed not only Pretoria's new carrots, but also the fall of Prince Mabandla. In May 1984 a Swazi delegation went to Pretoria to agree the establishment of the trade mission in Mbabane. Early in 1984 the 'cholera' ban on South African fruit and vegetables was relaxed.

On the other hand, the later sacking of R.V. Dlamini and Nxumalo did not please Pretoria, nor was it happy with the Customs Union fraud. R.V. and Nxumalo were particularly close to South Africa, and both had been involved in both the land deal and non-aggression pact negotiations. The Johannesburg *Star* said R.V. was Foreign Minister Pik 'Botha's favourite among his African peers, and probably the most pliant'.[61] After Nxumalo's sacking, Pik Botha sent a telex to the Swazi government saying he hoped the fraud investigation would continue. On 19 June 1984, just a fortnight after the dismissals, the South African government announced that it was abandoning the land deal, and that Swaziland would have to negotiate directly with the bantustans concerned.[62]

Swaziland still tries to show some independence from South Africa. Despite South African objections, Swaziland did host the 1985 SADCC Annual Conference, and government officials have stressed their unwillingness to negotiate with the bantustans over the land deal.[63] But, as the new South African 'trade commissioner' in Mbabane commented 'We can live with that. Clearly, Swaziland has to publicly offset its special relationship with South Africa. We want to deal with a country that is not seen as a puppet of South Africa.'[64]

Delinking from South Africa seems off the agenda, though the new king has yet to make his mark. Swaziland has signed a security agreement, allowed South Africa to open a *de facto* embassy, and publicly opposed sanctions against South Africa — important South African demands.[65] When Foreign Minister Pik Botha visited Swaziland for the opening of the Trade Mission, he was informed by his Swazi counterpart, Mhambi Mnisi, that he no longer needed a passport to visit the Kingdom.[66] This was more than a gesture and reflected strong links between the two ruling classes. The conservative royalist faction must remain close to Pretoria out of economic necessity. Also, because of its feudal structure, this elite would be directly threatened by the social changes in an ANC-ruled South Africa. Thus, more than in any other independent state in the region, the ruling class in Swaziland is dependent on its South African links to maintain its position.

The final irony of the tale is that in 1981 when Swaziland was moving away from South Africa, the apartheid state dangled a whole range of enticements in front of the Swazi elite. But once the Swazis were trapped, most of these disappeared. The extra customs union money was a one-off payment and there was no long-term renegotiation. Virtually all the new industries which were exporting to South Africa, and which made Swaziland at least a partial industrial success story, have closed. And the land deal itself has been shelved. Only the railways project continued — and that is mainly of benefit to South Africa. For all its concessions, Swaziland has earned little more than a South African mission.

11. Lesotho
Bellowing from the Mountain-Top

Lesotho is a tiny country totally surrounded by South Africa. It is the highest country in the world.[1] It has few natural resources, and only 13% of the land is arable. This unique and hostile geography has ensured Lesotho political independence, but at a price of total economic dependence on South Africa.

A century and a half ago Moshoeshoe I led his people into the mountains where they could hold out against the advancing Boers. He was forced to concede to them the richest farmland — now the eastern part of South Africa's Orange Free State — and eventually he had to ask Britain to assume responsibility for his country. But Moshoeshoe I ensured that his people never fell under South African control, and in 1966 Lesotho finally became a sovereign and independent state.

Britain did nothing to develop its colony, instead turning Lesotho into a labour reserve for South Africa. The result is a litany of dependence — more than half of the able-bodied men work in the South African mines and their earnings are nearly half of GNP. Most food and virtually all manufactured goods come from South Africa, and two-thirds of government income is from the Southern African Customs Union. (see Chapter 9)

Lesotho has developed a unique, contradictory, and increasingly tense relationship with South Africa. Uncowed by economic and geographic domination by South Africa, Lesotho has become outspokenly critical of apartheid and the Pretoria government. In part it has been protected by the fact that South Africa could crush Lesotho so easily; international opinion does come to the aid of the underdog, limiting what Pretoria can do. Nevertheless, South Africa has openly and continuously meddled in Lesotho politics, sent guerrillas against the government and directly invaded, closed the borders, and issued innumerable threats of heavier action. In January 1986 it imposed a border blockade that triggered a coup. The picture is made more confusing by Lesotho's growing economic links with South Africa.

POLITICS AND SECURITY

Lesotho is now a thorn in Pretoria's side, but it was not that way at independence, when South Africa saw Lesotho as firmly within its orbit. It seemed in practice that Lesotho would have little choice. When it became independent in 1966, there were only three majority-ruled states within 2000 kilometres; Zambia had come to independence two years before, Malawi only a few months and Botswana only four days earlier than Lesotho. The liberation struggles in Zimbabwe and the

Portuguese colonies were just getting off the ground. So Lesotho had few alternative models. There was no chance of international support, either: two decades ago southern Africa was far from the international spotlight; only the 'pariah states' of Israel, the Shah's Iran, and Taiwan paid any attention to Lesotho — because they wanted its support in the UN. Thus it is hardly surprising that at independence many Basotho accepted the British colonial view that close relations with South Africa were unavoidable.[2]

Despite the apparent inevitability of co-operation, Pretoria was worried by the rhetoric of the established Basutoland Congress Party (BCP) and felt the need to ensure a sympathetic government in Lesotho. It established direct links with Chief Leabua Jonathan's Basotho National Party (BNP), whose manifesto for the 1965 pre-independence elections said that it was 'in the interests of the people' for Lesotho to co-operate with South Africa. South Africa provided the BNP with campaign funds and use of a helicopter; Jonathan was the only party leader permitted to electioneer among Basotho miners in South Africa; South Africa sent 100,000 bags of grain as famine relief — not to the Lesotho government, but to Chief Jonathan personally to distribute.[3]

The BNP won a narrow victory,[4] and, as promised, turned to Pretoria for development assistance. By 1968 there were 83 South Africans working in Lesotho, including four magistrates, the chief electoral officer, and a senior information officer. By the following year, the Chief Justice, the Judges of Appeal, the Attorney General, and the Commissioner for Trade and Industry were all South Africans. There was co-operation between security forces, and South Africa gave money and equipment to the Lesotho police. South African business, particularly Anglo American and Rembrandt, also provided help.

The South African government, however, provided no financial assistance, although it was giving at least limited help to Malawi at the same time.[5] This probably reflects the view in Pretoria that a country which was totally surrounded and completely dependent needed no bribes to keep it in line, while a country that was far away and had few natural links required financial incentives to build a relationship with the apartheid state.

The 1970 election, however, showed that Pretoria had not done enough. The BNP went into the 1970 elections on a platform stating that the experience of the first five years 'confirmed us in our belief' in the importance of co-operation with South Africa. The BNP was overwhelmingly defeated by the opposition BCP.

Even South African political analysts had to admit that a key factor in the defeat had been Leabua's close ties with South Africa,[6] and that Lesotho had gained so little from them. In Lesotho, grassroots nationalism is mixed with a hefty dose of anti-Boer feeling. As well as remembering the history of a century ago, the Basotho still feel their economic subservience to South Africa and resent being politically subservient as well — they are not prepared to allow Lesotho to become just another bantustan. Furthermore, nearly all Basotho men have worked in the mines and experienced apartheid firsthand; indeed, Basotho played a leading role in strikes and in the National Union of Mineworkers set up more recently. The opposition BCP and its leader Ntsu Mokhehle became much more popular than the BNP and Jonathan, in part because the BCP was overtly anti-Pretoria.

Direct intervention

The 1970 election forced Pretoria into its first major move from the path of constitutionalism in the region. As his election defeat became clear, South Africa offered immediate and substantial support to Chief Jonathan, who abrogated the constitution and remained in power.[7]

But the intervention proved to be as unsuccessful as it was drastic. In the year following his coup, Jonathan recognised that he had lost touch with grass-roots sentiment in Lesotho, and switched policies — in some cases trying to take on the election-winning attitudes of the BCP. The change was dramatic. In 1966 and 1967 Jonathan had met with South African Prime Ministers Verwoerd and Vorster, and had lectured foreign statesmen and even the OAU on the importance of talking to South Africa. Suddenly he spoke out against apartheid, warning Pretoria of the dangers of violent change. In the UN, Lesotho switched from a mixed position (similar to Malawi) in 1971 to open hostility to South Africa (similar to Botswana and Zambia) in 1972.[8] In 1972 Jonathan also appealed to the Ivory Coast and other states considering closer links with Pretoria not to take any action — a total reversal of his own stand just a year before.

In that year, too, Jonathan began to appeal for international aid to help reduce dependence on South Africa. It was becoming apparent that aid from Scandinavian countries and the United Nations was more available if it was linked to an anti-apartheid stand, while being pro-Pretoria had generated no money at all.

Pretoria did not take the defection of its proxy lightly. In the four years following the Jonathan coup, there were two bungled coup attempts against him — both probably linked to South Africa. The first, in 1972, was co-ordinated, according to Information Minister Desmond Sixishe, by Fred Roach, a Briton in the pay of the South African security service seconded to Lesotho as Commander of the paramilitary Police Mobile Unit (PMU).[9] The plot was discovered, and Jonathan expelled the South Africans. Ironically, it had been Roach who organised the military side of the 1970 coup, ensuring that all opposition was crushed. The second came in 1974 when a faction of the opposition BCP tried a coup, but it was poorly organised and was quickly crushed by the PMU. Later, in one of the periodic reversals that typify Lesotho, a faction of the anti-Pretoria BCP turned to its erstwhile enemy for help. South Africa helped the perpetrators to escape, and allowed the coup leader, Ntsu Mokhehle, to return to South Africa.

In the following years the divisions between Pretoria and Maseru widened. There were a number of incidents which increased tensions. South Africa blocked the development of several industries in Lesotho under the customs union agreement. A South African refugee was kidnapped by South African security from Lesotho (although returned later); a Mosotho was killed at a South African border post and another died in detention in South Africa; several Basotho mine workers were shot and killed during a strike.

In the mid-1970s, however, Pretoria had one particular prize it sought from Lesotho: recognition of its bantustans. The aim was no less than to secure permanent international acceptance of apartheid by granting blacks full political rights — on just 13% of South Africa's land area. In 1976, the first of these bantustans, Transkei, was declared 'independent'. It is difficult to accept now how many influential voices in Europe and America were then calling for recognition. Lesotho, as a full member of the United Nations, could set the precedent. It borders on the Transkei, and, because of the lack of internal roads, parts of eastern Lesotho were almost cut off from the populated west without road access through Transkei. When Lesotho refused to recognise Transkei, South Africa in effect closed three border posts, thus hampering Lesotho's internal and international trade. Lesotho accused South Africa of trying to blackmail it by forcing it to deal with Transkei officials on the border posts, and appealed to the United Nations for international assistance. South Africa responded by suddenly withdrawing a long-standing subsidy on Lesotho's grain products. But Lesotho held out, and with the failure of the recognition campaign internationally, and the problems caused in Transkei by lack of access to Lesotho, the pressures were relaxed.

Meanwhile, Lesotho moved into mainstream African politics. It became more active in the OAU. In 1975 Lesotho was represented at the Mozambique independence celebrations; the following year it named an ambassador. In 1978 Jonathan made a five-day state visit to Mozambique and at a state banquet noted that Lesotho is 'surrounded on all sides by the enemy oppressor'. In 1978 Lesotho hosted a UN anti-apartheid symposium. Lesotho became the first of South Africa's neighbours explicitly to reject P.W. Botha's proposals for a Constellation of States (Consas). Instead Lesotho became a founder member of SADCC in April 1980, and in January 1982 it hosted the annual SADCC conference. With SADCC it has secured funds for an international airport, a ground satellite station, and internal east-west road links.

Picking up the Stick: the LLA

Lesotho's rejection of Consas, its growing links with the Front Line states, and its support for the ANC caused a change of tactics in Pretoria. P.W. Botha issued a public warning that Lesotho 'should not go too far'.

For the first time, South Africa turned to military pressure, using a surrogate force similar to those in Mozambique and Angola. The campaign began in May 1979 when bombs caused extensive damage to the Maseru post office, the electricity corporation headquarters, bridges, electricity pylons, and telephone posts. Incidents continued into 1980. Several BNP supporters were assassinated, and Lesotho's paramilitary forces killed a number of guerrillas in several clashes.

Ntsu Mokhehle and his external wing of the BCP took credit. He said they had established the Lesotho Liberation Army (LLA) to overthrow Jonathan.[10] It seems hard to imagine that LLA guerrillas could cross South Africa with arms and explosives without at least tacit approval from Pretoria, which quickly showed that it was, indeed, in charge. Jonathan met with P.W. Botha on 20 August 1980 in a caravan on Peka Bridge, over the Caledon River which forms one of the borders between the states. After the meeting, LLA activity suddenly stopped. It was never revealed what was said, and what concessions — if any — Jonathan made, but several ANC people were asked to leave Lesotho.[11]

South Africa was clearly not satisfied for long, however, particularly over the ANC, and in early 1981 the LLA attacks began again. Over the next three years there were about 100 incidents, including attacks on electricity and water installations, shops, fuel depots, and Maseru hotels and airport buildings. A few roads were mined and there were several mortar attacks on police stations. Works Minister Jobo Rampeta was assassinated, and there were nearly successful attempts on the lives of Jonathan and Agriculture Minister Peete Peete, probably the second most important man in government after Jonathan. Also assassinated was Koeyama Chakela, the most prominent BCP politician to return during an amnesty in 1980.

Several raids were aimed at Western donors. In September 1981 bombs in Maseru damaged the United States Cultural Centre and destroyed the car of the West German ambassador. In January 1982 the annual SADCC conference was in Maseru. The morning it opened, small bombs went off in Maseru — damaging the Danish-funded abattoir. The point was clear, because the Danish Foriegn Minister was an opening speaker at the conference.

The role of South Africa was obvious even to the South African press. The Johannesburg *Star* in November 1982 analysed the previous year's incidents and found that all but two were within four kilometres of the Caledon River border with South Africa.[12] Some were literally a few metres over the border, and most were close enough to allow LLA men to run over the border, plant a bomb or fire a few shots, and then run back to South Africa; several were only shelling from the South African side. Farmers on the border said there were tracks to show where vehicles had driven through their farm and across the shallow river.

Why the LLA failed

This hit-and-run nature of LLA attacks is one indicator of its failure to establish roots inside Lesotho. From Pretoria's viewpoint, the LLA has proved strikingly unsuccessful, in contrast to UNITA and the MNR. Indeed, from January 1984 LLA attacks were temporarily abandoned as a tactic, and South Africa moved to political and economic pressure, in the new context of Nkomati. Cross-border raids were renewed later in the year and in September 1985 a Maseru suburb was shelled from the South African side of the border. But the LLA has failed to establish a momentum.

At first sight, the LLA's failure is a surprise. With many of the same characteristics as create openings for the MNR in Mozambique, UNITA in Angola, and dissidents in Zimbabwe, Lesotho must have seemed to the South Africans ideal for a puppet insurgent group. Jonathan was much less popular than the BCP; indeed, more than a decade after he fled, Mokhehle remains personally popular inside Lesotho. Ironically, this was South Africa's only long-term gain from its backing of the 1970 coup, since the perception of the injustice done to the BCP in 1970 has provided a bedrock of opposition to Jonathan ever since.

Furthermore, South Africa could count on the same military over-reaction that it generated in Angola, Mozambique, and Zimbabwe. The first actions of the LLA were followed by a wave of repression which further alienated the general public. In late 1979 the Lesotho Paramilitary Force (LPF, the renamed Police Mobile Unit) reacted ruthlessly to the first LLA incidents in the northwest (a BCP stronghold), killing innocent civilians and sending several hundred Basotho fleeing to South Africa. There was less generalised repression in response to the renewed LLA activity in 1981, but several critics of government were killed.[13]

Yet, despite the unpopularity of the then government and its paramilitary force, the LLA was never able to establish bases and support networks inside Lesotho. This was largely due to the Lesotho government's political response. In 1980 Jonathan announced an amnesty. Some BCP members returned home, splitting the party, and Jonathan included some BCP factions in the government.[14] More importantly, the government waged a highly effective publicity campaign, mainly through local meetings, in which it stressed that LLA raids all came from South Africa. Although it seldom turned people against Mokhehle personally, the campaign did lead to public acceptance that the LLA was acting as an agent of South Africa. Since the apartheid state was even more unpopular than the government, this denied the LLA public support. That in turn, made it possible for the paramilitary to locate and defeat even large groups of LLA that came over the border.

The LLA's clear dependence on South Africa also served to re-establish support for Chief Jonathan internationally. In 1980 both Zambia and Botswana, which had provided a haven for BCP refugees, declared Mokhehle a prohibited immigrant, forcing him back to South Africa. Likewise the extensive Swedish aid programme, for example, is closely related to Sweden's perception of Lesotho as a victim of apartheid — a perception clearly strengthened by the LLA attacks from South Africa.

ATTACKING THE ANC

In Pretoria, however, Lesotho is perceived as a key base for the ANC. Crude propagandists portray the entire unrest inside South Africa as the work of communist agitators infiltrated from the neighbouring states; more sophisticated South African analysts acknowledge that the structures of apartheid create black discontent, but fear the influence of the ANC will forestall limited reform to contain the unrest. Either view requires an assault on the ANC. The propagandist view — which has considerable value to Pretoria in convincing right-wingers in Europe and the United States, as well as at home — demands particular attention to supposed ANC bases in neighbouring states, especially when disorder is greatest in South Africa.

During the 1970s, Pretoria became increasingly vocal about Lesotho's role as host to South African refugees. There is a steady stream of about 100 a month, which becomes a flood each time there is trouble in the townships. Some move on, sometimes to join liberation movements. But many stay and settle; officially, refugees now number more than 11,000. Not all are there for political reasons. Some, for example, are students at the university at Roma, simply because they can get a better education than at black universities in South African bantustans. Others are people who have once lived in South Africa and have moved to Lesotho to avoid the unrest in the townships. For the South African government, however, the presence of refugees means recruiting and supply bases for the military wing of the ANC. Its worries increased as Lesotho's relations with the ANC improved in the late 1970s, when an official ANC representative was permitted.[15]

In 1979, Pretoria began to hit directly and publicly at ANC members in Lesotho. ANC activity had increased inside South Africa in the late 1970s, and Lesotho had given increasingly vocal support to the liberation movements. In July 1979 ANC supporter Father John Osmers had an arm blown off by a parcel bomb. In December 1979 when a flight from Swaziland to Lesotho was forced to land in South Africa due to bad weather, the South Africans detained an ANC man on the plane; he was only returned to Lesotho the following May, after extended negotiations. In June 1980, the ANC's chief representative, Thembi Hani, escaped when a bomb in his car went off prematurely. In February 1981, the house of a prominent ANC-linked lawyer, Khalaki Sello, was damaged in a grenade attack.

South Africa directly tied support for the LLA to Lesotho support for the ANC. A South African journalist, apparently citing Pretoria government or security sources, noted complaints that in December 1980 and April 1981 Lesotho refused to hand over fleeing ANC guerrillas and instead tried them inside Lesotho on illegal firearms charges. Each time, he wrote, 'there was an increase in LLA activity in Lesotho. The deduction is that Pretoria expresses its disapproval by keeping a less than strict eye on the activities of LLA cadres in South Africa.'[16]

The then Foreign Minister Mooki Molapo said that at a meeting in Cape Town on 19 August 1981 South Africa's Foreign Minister Pik Botha told him 'there would be no LLA if you removed all refugees from Lesotho. If you want us to do something about the LLA camps, you mlust do something about the ANC.' Botha then went on to offer to exchange BCP leader Mokhehle for ANC representative Hani. Lesotho refused. As Jonathan noted later, the whole exchange confirmed South African control of the LLA.[17]

9 December 1982

By late 1982, South Africa was using both economic pressure and the LLA to try to push Lesotho away from the Front Line states and from support for the ANC. Nevertheless, Lesotho was entirely unprepared for the events of 9 December. Soon after midnight, more than 100 South African commandos simultaneously attacked a dozen flats and houses — some in the centre of Maseru. In all, 42 people were killed — 30 South Africans and 12 Basotho. Seven of the dead were women; three were children. Some were ANC, including the Lesotho representative, Zola Nguini, but there was no evidence to support the claim that these were terrorist bases. Among the dead was 'Matumo Ralebitso, the daughter of a former government minister who was an assistant librarian at the National University of Lesotho.

By dawn, the killing was over, and the South Africans telephoned the shocked Lesotho government. It was not to gloat or apologise, but to say that 64 South Africans had lost their way and failed to rendezvous with their helicopters as prearranged. Lesotho was told not to obstruct the return of the wayward commandos. It didn't.

This was — to date — the biggest South African invasion of any country except Angola and Namibia. The escalation to use of South African troops against a non-Marxist, Commonweath country was a response to the growing strength of the ANC inside South Africa. In part, the ANC had gained freer access to Lesotho and was using it as a route to enter South Africa; so the raid was a vain attempt to stop this. Equally important, however, was the need to reassure whites inside South Africa that the threat came from external agitation, and a strike at Maseru offered high drama. In addition, the raid marked an increase of the general pressure on Lesotho and on SADCC, which was to hold its annual conference in Maseru the following month. Finally, South Africa calculated that the West would not react. In this, they were right: there were protests, but no action was taken.

To rub salt in the wounds, there were three dramatic raids in Maseru in the following weeks. One was the attack on the water tanks near the abattoir during the SADCC meeting. A week later, five bombs exploded at the Maseru reservoir. Then on 13 February, in the most successful raid, one of Maseru's three main fuel depots was blown up. A helicopter like the one involved in the 9 December raid flew overhead (and, some observers claimed, actually dropped the bombs) while just a few hundred metres away on the South African side of the Caledon River several vehicles were parked to watch the excitement.

In the following months, there were more LLA raids, with an increasingly obvious South African presence; attempts on Prime Minister Jonathan's life were made in June and August 1983. The second was on 4 August 1983 in Maseru, when a car bomb exploded only seconds after Prime Minister Jonathan's car had passed. The device was much too sophisticated to have been set up by the LLA.

Tightening the screws

Pretoria also tightened the economic screws. In October 1982, South Africa had refused to trans-ship British aircraft tyres and small arms, leaving them stranded in Durban and Johannesburg. Later an Italian helicopter was also blocked. Lesotho was given a donation of crude oil, which it had refined at Maputo, but South Africa refused to transport it.[18] By early 1983 Lesotho was complaining about delays in customs union payments.

Pressure was stepped up with a series of border disruptions which began in May 1983 and continued sporadically throughout the year. Some were outright closures, which caused shortages of meat, milk, and other foodstuffs in Maseru; others were just slow processing of passports and unusually careful searches of cars, or the withdrawal of border staff, causing long queues to build up. Sometimes Basotho were prohibited entry but others were allowed to pass. In some cases, the South Africans announced that they were to intensify border controls, and sometimes they simply did it.[19]

There were a series of meetings between Lesotho and South Africa in mid-1983. Three issues dominated discussions — security, the new communist embassies (see below), and renegotiating the customs union to include recognition of the bantustans. Lesotho only conceded on the first. Initially, South Africa wanted Lesotho to expel 3,000 South African refugees. Lesotho raised the matter at the UN in August. Then South Africa cut the number to 600, and finally to a named list of 68. Of those, 26 had never been in Lesotho, while 20 had come and gone; the others left Lesotho in September. Nevertheless, border disruptions continued into October.

Pressure to sign an Nkomati

With the signing of the Nkomati non-aggression pact with Mozambique on 16 March 1984 and the revelation two weeks later that a pact had been signed with Swaziland in 1982, Pretoria made clear it wanted similar accords with its remaining neighbours and further stepped up the pressure.

South Africa demanded three things from Lesotho which were not in Nkomati. First, Lesotho would have to give the name of every refugee who arrived, and South Africa would decide who could stay in Lesotho. Second, South Africa wanted formalised consultations at the level of officials, without prior reference to cabinet, to allow security people to act on their own if they thought there was sufficient danger. It was open encouragement for Lesotho security to be unfaithful to the politicians, according to Evaristus Sekhonyana, who was Foreign Minister at the time.[20] Third was the definition of a 'hostile act'. Sekhonyana said: 'We asked them, "Supposed the university students just hold a meeting and criticise apartheid. Is that a hostile act?" And they said yes..They expected us to crack down internally.'

Perhaps to stress its new role as peacemaker, South Africa turned off the LLA in January 1984. But it increased political and economic pressure. In early May, South Africa threatened to impose border controls so strict that they would strangle Lesotho, and it threatened to repatriate Basotho miners. It halted negotiations on the Highland Water Scheme (of which more later) and it delayed customs union payments of M50m. Sekhonyana was negotiating with South African Foreign Minister Pik Botha. Pik was particularly anxious to have Lesotho sign before he left with P.W. Botha on 28 May for his European tour, because it would give him more international credibility. 'Pik just wanted a passport from Lesotho to go to Europe,' Sekhonyana said.

Sekhonyana admitted that he expected to sign some kind of agreement. Suddenly, instead of signing, Jonathan recalled Sekhonyana and sacked him as Foreign Minister. (Sekhonyana remained Planning Minister, a portfolio he had held continuously for more than 15 years — sometimes in addition to others.) Jonathan then made an international appeal for help. 'When I was a young boy and was faced with a bully, my only chance of survival was to scream as loud as I could, and this was what we did. South Africa was hoping to strangle us into signing quietly,' explained Information Minister Sixishe.

'There is no need for a non-aggression pact between an elephant and an ant,' Sixishe commented later. In any case, 'Nkomati has been a good lesson for us of the unreliability of the other partner.'

In August, Pik Botha went on television to threaten further sanctions against Lesotho unless it signed, and broke off all water talks. Sporadic LLA activity resumed for the first time in several months. Jonathan threatened to take the whole matter to the United Nations, going personally to present Lesotho's case.

Finally, the new Foreign Minister, Vincent Makhele, met Pik Botha in Cape Town on 28 September. In exchange for Jonathan dropping his plans to go to the UN and for some additional ANC 'voluntarily' leaving Lesotho, South Africa agreed to stop its economic pressure. It returned to the water talks, and released the British arms and the Italian helicopter. But east bloc arms in Maputo were still not permitted transit and Pretoria continued to press for a non-aggression pact.

Pretoria tries to widen internal political splits

South Africa's relative failure with the LLA became clear by late 1983, just as cracks began to appear in the Lesotho leadership. South Africa seized the opportunity to try to re-establish its political position, lost in 1971.

The split emerged over the decision to permit embassies from the eastern bloc. In the late 1970s, Lesotho had established diplomatic relations — on a non-residential basis — with Cuba, the Soviet Union, and other eastern bloc states. Jonathan visited East Germany in September 1982. After the South African raid on Maseru on 9 December 1982, Lesotho turned more to the East. Jonathan went to China and eastern Europe in May 1983, and returned to announce that both China and the USSR would shortly open embassies. The South African government saw red.[21] It angrily reminded Jonathan of his anti-communist past, and of his pledge in 1965 that 'as long as I am Prime Minister, I will not allow into Maseru a single embassy of any communist country.' Insiders say Jonathan was surprised by the hostility of the reaction; he pointed out that even Washington has Soviet and other communist embassies. As one South African analyst noted, 'close ties with the Soviet Bloc are perceived by Chief Leabua above all as a shield to protect Lesotho against South Africa. Similarly, his great-grandfather Moshoeshoe I had sought the protection of the British Empire against the Boers.'[22]

Internal reaction was led by key leaders in the Roman Catholic Church, which had been among the early backers of the BNP before independence. They now took a very straightforward line that communism was a worse evil than apartheid; thus an alliance with South Africa is acceptable to oppose communism. The Roman Catholic Church is still heavily influenced by conservative French Canadian missionaries, and has drawn increasing attack from BNP leaders — many of whom were educated by them.

Pretoria exploited this new mood, by shifting away from military attacks, and instead intervening directly in politics for the first time in a decade. On 5 January 1984 there was an unprecedented luncheon at a government guesthouse in Pretoria. On the Lesotho side were various dissident politicians including former foreign minister C.D. Molapo and Phoka Chaolane of the legal, internal branch of the BCP. On the South African side were Pik Botha, his deputy Louis Nel, and the chief of the security police, General Francois Steenkamp. At Botha's urging, they formed the Basotho Democratic Alliance (BDA), and Botha promised funds. There was no attempt to hide the meeting, and the participants talked openly to the press.[23] When Lesotho complained, Pik Botha simply reminded his neighbours that South Africa had given Jonathan the financial support to win his 'first and only' election, and privately briefed journalists about its role in the 1970 coup.[24] Later South Africa put pressure on Basotho miners to join the BDA.[25]

The BDA was presented as an 'anti-communist' front. Undoubtedly the most dramatic conversion was that of C.D. Molapo. As foreign minister, he had bitterly attacked Pretoria, particularly in the United Nations after the 9 December 1982 raid. He talked of the ANC's 'very noble struggle', and accused South Africa of trying 'to manipulate and control neighbouring states'.[26] But he resigned in June 1983, ostensibly in protest against the opening of east bloc embassies.

High Lesotho officials claim that despite his rhetoric in the UN, Molapo (and others) had changed sides before the 9 December raid and the opening of the communist embassies. In a statement to parliament after the raid, Jonathan declared 'that South Africa had infiltratred even our government ministries.'[27] He implied that some people had advance knowledge of the raid.

South Africa also had links in the police. South Africa claimed it warned Lesotho security in advance of the 9 December 1982 raid, and it is clear the LPF did not intervene.[28] Just four months later, on 27 March, seven South Africans were caught in a raid on a border post — and then quickly released without government authorisation. This South African link with Lesotho security is one reason why Minister Sekhonyana and others were so opposed to the provision of the proposed non-aggression pact allowing security officials to meet without ministerial approval.

Economic divisions create political splits

Economic factors underline many of the divisions in Lesotho politics as well as attitudes toward South Africa. At independence, the two main parties were linked to different groups of businessmen. One group was the Basotho Traders Association (BTA), which represented small traders, and which strongly supported the BCP. The other was the Chamber of Commerce, which represented those, particularly foreigners, who had received exclusive trading licences under the colonial government and thus had close links to South African business.

After the BNP won the election, it did business with South Africa and Chamber of Commerce members. The BCP opposed this, and called for businesses to be given to Basotho. In 1969 the BTA ran a campaign to boycott South African traders, especially Frasers. It was called Theko-'Moho, or 'buying together'; it soon had its own wholesaler and branches in most districts. But many BTA traders were linked to the BCP and at the time of the 1970 coup were arrested and went bankrupt. In part their place was taken by BNP politicians, who set up bars and supermarkets, often with loans from the newly formed Lesotho Bank.

The essential factor in business success is regular contact with South Africa, because that is the source of supplies and services. This inevitably colours political judgement. Information Minister Sixishe told me: 'By being involved in business, a politician is more susceptible to temptation. Furthermore, any business here is highly linked to South Africa, and this gives South Africa a grip on people. Because of my anti-apartheid stands, South Africa does not allow me to enter — if I was in business, that would mean I had to close up shop.' He suggested, for example, that Minister Sekhonyana was sacked as Foreign Minister because his close business links led him to favour a non-aggression pact with South Africa.

Factions, elections and a coup

By late 1984 the BNP had split into two factions. One wing was headed by Vincent Makhele, who had replaced Sekhonyana as Foreign Minister, and Desmond Sixishe, the Information Minister. This group was closer to Chief Jonathan, and was strongly and vociferously anti-South Africa and pro-ANC. It also had republican overtones, wanting further to curb the role of the king and the chiefs. The other wing was loosely grouped around Sekhonyana; it wanted to 'normalise' relations with Pretoria, and wanted to increase the role of the king (to increase their own legitimacy).

The third political group was the five tiny right-wing opposition parties (including the BDA and internal BCP), which tended to issue joint statements and which were strongly pro-South Africa, anti-ANC, and anti-communist.[29] They had little real following. Although South Africa was one issue which divided these three groups, the factional struggle was more related to personal ambitions, and to jockeying for position in an attempt to replace the ageing Chief Jonathan.

The army and the king both played important roles. The 1500-man LPF, Lesotho's tiny army, was divided. The bigger element, under LPF commander Major General Justin Lekhanya, supported the Sekhonyana group. A smaller LPF faction was close to Makhele, whose group also controlled the BNP Youth League and the radio. The Makhele group armed the youth league as an alternative military force, and training was provided by North Korea.

Both BNP groups began to look to the king for respectability (despite the republican intentions of one faction). Jonathan had banned the king from all political activity, but began to use him on international missions, and increasingly allowed him to speak for himself — particularly on South Africa and sanctions. In 1985 King Moshoeshoe II attended the Commonwealth conference in the Bahamas, the UN General Assembly, and the SADCC summit in Arusha.

At the SADCC meeting, he said: 'Sanctions against South Africa are but a reflection of international opprobrium against the policy of racial discrimination. ... The effects of sanctions are very clear to us, and they will call for great sacrifices among our peoples. We cannot stand against the sanctions campaign.'

Under growing pressure both internally and internationally, Chief Jonathan announced that elections would be held on 17 and 18 September 1985. This was a last attempt to legitimise the unpopular Jonathan government, and the candidate selection process was seen as a way of allowing BNP factions to fight for dominance. It succeeded in neither goal. The government made it virtually impossible for opposition parties to nominate candidates, and none did.[30] Prime Minister Jonathan simply declared BNP candidates elected; but no one, including the LPF, accepted the outcome.

In the following months, both factions prepared for a coup. The BNP Youth League engaged in increasing thuggery while the Lekhanya army group quietly moved arms to their stronghold.[31]

Meanwhile, South Africa stepped up its pressure on Lesotho. Foreign Minister Pik Botha visited Maseru on 13 August 1985 and met with Information Minister Sixishe in October to demand the expulsion of the ANC.[32] LLA activity increased. In November, the ANC received its own warnings and tried to fly out 150 members — only to have South Africa turn back the plane.[33] Then on 20 December the South African military raided Maseru for a second time, killing six ANC and three Basotho. It was more discreet than the raid three years before; the attack involved only eight men, some white, using hand guns with silencers. This time, South Africa even denied responsiblity.[34]

The funeral on 29 December 1985 was a major public occasion, with the ANC Treasurer General coming from Lusaka, and with speeches by the king and Prime Minister. King Moshoeshoe II read at length from the Freedom Charter and from the Kairos Document and said that blacks fighting apartheid were like the British fighting the Nazis.[35] Chief Jonathan read out a telex from the South African State President requesting talks, and said there was no point — P.W. Botha should talk with Nelson Mandela and the ANC instead. The following day, the UN Security Council unanimously condemned South Africa for the 20 December raid, and demanded it pay compensation.

In reply Pretoria imposed a border blockade on Lesotho on New Year's Day. Technically it was not a blockade, but intensive security checks that allowed only one car per hour to pass. Lorries of fuel and food were stopped; those with fresh vegetables only passed when the produce had rotted.[36] Rail services across the border were also cut. Serious shortages of petrol, paraffin, fresh meat and vegetables, and medical supplies developed. The post was also disrupted, which is particularly important as many migrant workers send money home by post.

Nevertheless, South Africa did not impose a total blockade. All Lesotho's electricity comes from South Africa and this was not cut. And migrant miners, on whom Lesotho depends for its main income, were able to cross the otherwise closed borders to South Africa. So it was clear that the pressure could have been intensified.

South Africa asserted from the first that the primary target of the blockade was the ANC. Neil van Heerden, Deputy Director General of Foreign Affairs, said that South Africa was demanding that Lesotho 'eliminate' the ANC — 'that is the bottom line'. It remains unclear if it was an original goal of the blockade, but the elimination of Jonathan soon became a second goal. Both publicly and privately

South Africa expressed its distaste for the Prime Minister. At one point, Pik Botha denounced him as the greatest destabilising factor in Lesotho.[37]

As intended, the blockade triggered activity by all three political groups. Four right-wing opposition politicians went to Pretoria for talks with Pik Botha on 13 January. The republican faction of the BNP planned its own coup, allegedly scheduled for 21 January, when the Youth League and allied army units were to attack the rest of the LPF as the soldiers collected their pay from the Lesotho Bank on Kingsway, Maseru's main street. It is also alleged that the republicans intended to depose the King, Chief Jonathan, and Maj-Gen Lekhanya.

When the rest of the army learned of this planned coup, they moved. On 15 January they surrounded the Prime Minister's office and successfully disarmed the Youth League, but then seemingly drew back from a coup. On 17 and 18 January there was fighting between the two army factions and those allied to the republicans were defeated, with between seven and 17 soldiers killed — the only deaths.

Also on 17 January, a Lesotho delegation including LPF commander Lekhanya went to Pretoria for talks with a delegation headed by van Heerden. Nothing was said in Lesotho, but in South Africa press reports apparently emanating from the Foreign Ministry said South Africa had indicated to Lekhanya that it would encourage a move against Jonathan.[38]

So on Monday morning, 20 January, the army took over the government and installed Lekhanya as head of the military council. South Africa signalled its partial approval by allowing through two trains, one with eight petrol tankers; within hours of the coup, Neil van Heerden was in Maseru. But the blockade was not lifted. The same day, a team nominated by Lekhanya and headed by Evaristus Sekhonyana met Pik Botha in Cape Town. Botha stressed that the ANC had to go, and provided a list of 90 top priority expulsions.[39] The ANC was immediately ordered to round up its people, and many were at the airport by Thursday, but delays caused by problems chartering a plane meant that the first group did not leave until Saturday morning 25 January. The blockade continued until then, but as soon as the plane was in the air, South Africa raised its border gates and normal traffic began to flow. More ANC left the following week, although an ANC representative and a few others were allowed to remain — an arrangement not dissimilar from that reached with Mozambique as part of the Nkomati Accord. One other concession was also made quickly to South Africa — Radio Lesotho stopped broadcasting material critical of South Africa.

The coup itself was widely popular, and there were celebrations in the streets of Maseru. People seemed jubilant in equal measure over three things — the end of the border closure, the end of the Youth League, and the downfall of Jonathan himself.

Initially, at least, Maj-Gen Lekhanya seems to have been a reluctant plotter.[40] And in his first speech, he announced that 'the military council of Lesotho decided to vest all executive and legislative powers in HM the King, with ... the military council to act as an advisory body.' The King took his new role seriously, and did not do what South Africa must have expected. In his first speech to the nation, on 27 January, he declared his intention 'to pursue an independent foreign policy'. This means, he continued, that Lesotho will:

● defend 'her existence as a sovereign, independent, and non-aligned state';
● 'remain the traditional and historical hospitable hosts of refugees';

● strive to develop good relations with all neighbours based 'on the principle of non-interference in each other's internal and external affairs, without across the border raids and economic blockades'; and
● 'remain committed to SADCC'.

In a press conference the following day, Maj-Gen Lekhanya stressed that Lesotho would maintain all its diplomatic links, including those with the socialist bloc,[41] that Lesotho would never hand over refugees to South Africa, and that Lesotho would not sign an Nkomati-type agreement — 'a piece of paper you call an agreement wouldn't solve anything.' Another official stressed that the King's previous statement on sanctions still remained government policy.[42]

Even more dramatic was the new cabinet, announced on 27 January. Immediately after Maj-Gen Lekhanya as Minister of Defence and Interior, two outspoken critics of South Africa headed the list. Khalaki Sello was named Minister of Law, Public Service and Constitutional and Parliamentary Affairs. In 1962 he had been jailed for two years for membership of the ANC and he remains a strong ANC supporter; indeed, his house in Maseru was bombed in 1981. Next was Dr Michael Sefali, named Minister of Planning and Economic Affairs. He is Soviet-trained and the Director of the Institute of Southern African Studies at the National University of Lesotho, and has written about destabilisation.

The only member of the previous government is Sekhonyana, included on the insistence of Lekhanya. As Foreign Minister he had nearly concluded an Nkomati-type accord and South Africa would have preferred him to return as Foreign Minister. Instead, he was given the politically less sensitive post of Finance Minister, precisely because he was felt to be too close to Pretoria. The only member of the four man opposition delegation that went to Pretoria to be included in the government is Bennett Khaketla, whose conservative and nationalist views ensure he would defer to the king rather than P.W. Botha. Notably absent is C.D. Molapo, whom South Africa would be particularly anxious to have in government, but who has no local following.

On the day after the new government was appointed, Dr Sefali flew to Harare to head a strong delegation to the annual SADCC conference, which was then already under way. He was given permission to give a special statement in which he accused South Africa of aggression and destabilisation against Lesotho, and stressed that 'the new government of Lesotho has a resolve to resist any attempts (covert or overt) aimed at reducing her to a status of subservience.'

Many details of the coup remain to be disclosed — especially South Africa's role. It seems likely that a coup of some sort would have taken place in early 1986 in any case (and South Africa must have known about the plotting going on). Thus its blockade simply speeded up the action. Although it seems obvious that South Africa wanted Jonathan overthrown, it remains unclear if it just started the blockade and waited to see what would happen, or if Pretoria intervened directly.

What seems apparent, however, is that South Africa must have expected a more sympathetic government, and miscalculated.[43] This may have been due to Pretoria's misjudgements of both the King and Lekhanya, and to its exaggerated view of the role of the opposition parties. The four opposition politicians who had gone to Pretoria on 13 January were C.D. Molapo (who had met Pik Botha to form the BDA), C.D. Mofeli (leader of the United Democratic Party), G.P. Ramoreboli (leader of the internal BCP), and Bennett Khaketla (leader of the royalist Marematlou Freedom Party). In a joint interview with Mofeli and

Ramoreboli,[44] the former noted that 'Pik Botha, and we ourselves, assumed that the opposition parties would have a role in a new government.' Ramoreboli added that 'of course Pik Botha expects something from us if we are in government — he has seen our literature and knows we want better relations with South Africa.' The two stressed that all five opposition parties agree that Lesotho should:

- sign an Nkomati-type accord;
- publicly oppose international sanctions against South Africa;
- ban all ANC, and not even allow a representative;
- permit South Africa to open an embassy;[45]
- give some kind of formal recognition to the bantustans; and
- expel all communists.[46]

This is, of course, exactly what Pretoria wants, so it must have been music to the Bothas' ears.

The opposition leaders also told Pik Botha that he should arrange a meeting between heads of state, P.W. Botha and King Moshoeshoe II, bypassing Jonathan. And they probably suggested that it was Jonathan, not the king, who had been writing the King's outspoken speeches (which is unlikely as their sections on participation and democracy sounded to Basotho ears like attacks on Jonathan). In any case, South Africa has generally had good success dealing with feudal leaders, particularly in the bantustans, but also at various times in Swaziland. So it was probably happy to assume that whatever he might be saying now, King Moshoeshoe II would come around to its way of thinking — as some of the more outspoken bantustan leaders eventually did.

Similarly, South Africa had had dealings with Lekhanya in various security meetings, and probably saw the LPF commander as a conservative army man not much interested in politics, and willing to accept South African demands. Thus a Lekhanya led coup with prominent roles for King Moshoeshoe II and opposition politicians must have looked very promising to Pretoria. The outcome must have come as a shock, and further South African pressure seems inevitable.

ECONOMIC DEPENDENCE
The rising political tension between Lesotho and South Africa has not been matched on the economic side. Indeed, economic dependence on South Africa has increased even further. This is due to the sharp increase in mine wages and customs union revenue, which brought relative prosperity, as well as to the newly rich who profited from the new wealth and built trading links with South Africa.

The ties that bind

The mountains seem beautiful to the tourist but they contain few of the natural resources which have made surrounding South Africa so wealthy. This is no accident, for the bulk of the good farming land occupied by Sotho-speakers in the last century was seized by the Orange Free State. The first development of mines in Kimberley and the Rand brought prosperity for some, as Basotho farmers supplied grain to the miners. Since the last century, however, ties with South Africa have dragged Lesotho back into poverty, in a classic case of active under-development.[47] In a combination of South African government action and British colonial acquiescence, Basotho farmers were denied access to South African markets and forced back on to inhospitable land. As the land became overpopulated, Lesotho became a labour reserve for South Africa. Now, most Basotho men have worked in the South African mines. Agriculture is for those who stay behind — largely women. Lesotho produces a decreasing proportion of its own food, and virtually all consumer goods are imported from South Africa.

The mine strikes of the early 1970s, combined with the rise in the gold price, forced the first ever increase in real mine wages. Between 1971 and 1976, real wages tripled.[48] This shifted the whole balance of the Lesotho economy. At independence, imports represented only two-thirds of GDP (meaning, more or less, that Lesotho produced more than it imported and that a significant portion of mine wages was spent inside the country). In 1975 imports exceeded GDP for the first time, and by 1983 imports were 138% of GDP. Real income and real GNP per capita rose, but the extra money was spent on imports — which jumped ten-fold in ten years.

But the higher mine wages had a number of side effects which further integrated Lesotho into the South African economy. One was to make agriculture seem less attractive, and the area farmed decreased steadily. This, in turn, meant more food imported from South Africa. A second effect was a sharp increase in customs union revenue, which is roughly 18% of imports. At independence, two-thirds of government income came from Britain; now two-thirds comes from South Africa. This gave more reason for bureaucrats and politicians not to offend Pretoria. The third effect was to provide new opportunities for traders, and thus increase their dependence on South African sources of supply.

The growing dependence on mine wages gives South Africa immense power, and it increasingly wheels out the threat of repatriating miners. For example, when South Africa suggested that Mozambique get an additional quota of miners in exchange for signing the Nkomati Accord, this number would have been taken away from Lesotho.

In fact, the number of miners is already falling, and Lesotho can no longer afford to depend on mine labour. In 1971 less than one-quarter of miners came from South Africa, whereas now it is nearly two-thirds. The number of Basotho miners has decreased steadily since 1977. This has not had a direct impact on the government, so far, because remittances are still rising. This is because South African mines have virtually stopped recruiting young men, while keeping the older, more skilled men. Indeed, it seems clear that the mines are sufficiently dependent on skilled Basotho for the mine operators to resist any attempt to reduce their numbers much faster. But as these men retire, both numbers and remittances will fall sharply in the early 1990s. That, in turn, will reduce Lesotho's ability to import, and thus cut government revenue from the customs union. Thus Lesotho must find jobs now and sources of revenue in the coming decade.

Creating other jobs

Considerable attention has been given to agriculture, and to labour-intensive public works like road building and maintenance. Given the poor land and competing incomes in South Africa, however, much government emphasis is on industrialisation, largely through the Lesotho National Development Corporation (LNDC) set up soon after independence. By 1978 LNDC firms represented 60% of the manufacturing sector and accounted for over 80% of manufacturing exports.[49]

Initially government priority was to attract firms producing for export. Its promotion was much the same as that of Botswana and Swaziland. It offered various subsidies and incentives, and stressed that firms had access to South Africa for sales and supplies, while also having access to the EEC and United States (because Lesotho was a least developed country) and to Africa and the Middle East (not being politically tainted by being in South Africa).

The new firms did create jobs, but with very few local linkages. A few use local wool and mohair for craft products, but most import the raw materials and export the finished product. One of Lesotho's largest exports is now umbrellas; all the components are imported from Germany and South Africa, the umbrellas are assembled in Lesotho, and they are shipped back to Germany. One firm imports wood from South Africa and exports knocked-down furniture to Europe. Clothing and shoe factories import raw materials and export the finished products to South Africa. A new firm is importing milk from South Africa and exporting ice cream back.

Because these industries had little impact on the Lesotho consumer, the mid-70s boom in mine remittances had little indirect effect. One study showed that 80% of rands remitted to Lesotho simply went back to South Africa. Ficksburg, just over the border, was described as a 'boom town' in the late 1970s. A survey in 1982 showed that 58% of Ficksburg shop turnover was accounted for by Lesotho-based customers.[50] This meant that Lesotho was losing not simply jobs for shop assistants, but most of the economic impact that might have been created by the multiplier effect of the increased mine wages.

Consequently, LNDC changed its priorities to emphasise import substitution and supplying the local market.[51] A brewery, flour mill, and bakery have all been built. The main stress, however, has been to pull the retail outlets into Lesotho by building large shopping centres.

South African discouragement

Yet LNDC's 8,000 jobs created in its first 15 years of operation remain many fewer than hoped — less than the fall in the number of migrant miners for example, let alone the number of young people coming onto the job market. As in the colonial past, this is in large part due to South Africa. Some is automatic, the inevitable tendency of investors to prefer to locate in already-developed areas, where supply, marketing and service facilities are already available. But some South African actions have been more direct. In the early 1970s South Africa prevented the opening of a Japanese car assembly plant, and made it impossible for a TV assembly plant to survive (see Chapter 9).

Undoubtedly transport is South Africa's greatest weapon. South Africa forces Lesotho firms to use the railways, either directly to SAR's 2km spur into Maseru, or to border towns like Ficksburg, even when road transport would be quicker and cheaper. A World Bank study noted that 'there are long delays and pilferage'.[52] An UNCTAD study said that South Africa frequently holds up goods, allegedly due to documentation problems, and then forces the Lesotho recipient to pay storage charges. Lesotho and the EEC tried to set up a pilot scheme for shipping goods directly to Lesotho in sealed containers, but this was successfully blocked by Manica, the South African shipping agency.[53] One company, Lesotho Bag, said it would only open in Lesotho if South Africa guaranteed it a road transport permit to bring raw materials from Durban — which was agreed only after long delay. Lesotho sources also argue that the border disruption has discouraged firms from moving.

Various South African disincentives have deterred new industry from locating in Lesotho. One problem is that users pay a higher charge for electricity than those in South Africa — an important factor for a small firm like Tranalquip which makes mining equipment in Lesotho and spends 30% of its costs on power. South African bantustan incentives have probably discouraged some new firms. So far, however, Lesotho has only lost two small handicraft factories to the bantustans.

These South African policies, unlike the economic squeezes described earlier, have not been orchestrated to punish or reward particular moves by the Lesotho government. Rather they are part of wider long-term policies to protect South Africa's own industries and support its own bantustans. They are perhaps the clearest sign to the region of the *economic* disadvantages hidden in Pretoria's scheme for a constellation of states. Not surprisingly, the founding declaration of SADCC stressed the economic arguments for reduced dependence on South Africa.

From South African supply to South African ownership

There is a further problem for Lesotho. In one sense, the projects promoted by LNDC have changed the nature of dependence on South Africa, rather than eliminated it, since almost all industries in Lesotho are controlled by South African firms.[54] LNDC's managing director Lengolo Monyake argues that this is because the intitial stress on the advantages of locating in Lesotho to gain access to US, EEC, and South African markets was mainly of interest to South African firms.[55] But even with companies producing for the local market, ownership is predominantly South African. The brewery is run by South African Breweries.[56] A government-owned flour mill grinds South African wheat for the local market, while the bakery that makes it into bread was recently sold by LNDC to a South African firm. Most dramatically, all the new shopping and distribution centres are being built with and for South African firms — OK (owned by SA Breweries), Metro (Sanlam), and Frasers.

There is no doubt that such developments bring advantages for Lesotho. For example, in the case of the shopping centres, the Lesotho government gets the 8% sales tax that it would not get if the shopper bought across the border. Both OK and Frasers are buying locally made products, not just for their Lesotho shops, but also for sale in South Africa. And, as Minister Sekhonyana told me: 'It is no small point that we have minimised the indignities, and Basotho no longer have to run the gauntlet at the border.'

Yet ownership by South African firms remains dependence, and one must ask why. Are there no local entrepreneurs? The money is there: the central bank talks of 'high liquidity' and 'slack demand' for loans. Even for big projects, is it not possible to go to Europe rather than South Africa, for example for a brewery?

One part of the answer may be the internal difficulties of government policy. As James Cobbe noted, 'in very few instances can the government be claimed to have made a clear policy decision that actually promotes economic independence when [the decision] involved change away from the status quo that would impose significant costs on an influential section of the population.'[57] Perhaps also those businessmen whose base and orientation is within Lesotho have historic links to the BCP and BTA, whilst the businessmen linked to the BNP are orientated toward South Africa.

Yet here again, the main problem is the historic role of South Africa. 'It is hard to destroy what took decades to build,' noted Sam Montsi, LNDC managing director from 1977 to 1982, and now a consultant in Maseru. 'Britain developed southern Africa with dependence on South Africa — even Portugal could not break that.'[58] To compete with giant South African supermarket chains, within a customs union, would undoubtedly be difficult.

Chief Jonathan's original orientation toward South Africa encouraged this. Dr Anton Rupert of Rembrandt became Lesotho's industrial advisor in 1966. He seconded a senior Rembrandt official, Wynand van Graan, to set up LNDC. Van Graan served as managing director until South Africans were expelled in 1973. 'The people who assisted us to get started were South African. Anton Rupert gave us our first MD. So naturally we looked to South Africa,' admitted LNDC's managing director.

Sometimes it is more than that. When LNDC began discussions about the brewery, they did talk to non-South African firms. 'If you look at the brewery development in this region, it is clear that South African Breweries will stifle any opposition. So we just talked to them in the end,' Montsi said.

The diamond mine: Anglo and Lesotho

From the moment of independence, the Lesotho government hoped that a diamond mine would free it from its thralldom to the Customs Union as a source of revenue. Diamonds were known in the country; indeed, there are hand diggings in several places in the mountains, and Anglo briefly worked two small sites in the mid-1960s. Repeated surveys were called for from international donors; foreign mining companies were wooed. But Lesotho's geology seems cruel, and in 1973 both RTZ and Lonrho rejected the two chief prospects, at Letseng-la-Terai and Mothae.

In 1975, however, De Beers agreed to mine diamonds at Letseng-la-Terai. It was the highest diamond mine in the world and relatively small and low grade, but it did produce a high proportion of large stones. It opened in 1977 and had a dramatic effect on the internal economy. With 700 Basotho, it was the country's largest private employer; it accounted for half of all exports and added M3m per year to government revenue. But all this disappeared again when De Beers closed the mine in 1982.

Letseng-la-Terai is a key example of Anglo's involvement in southern Africa. Commercially, the mine was marginal, as the earlier rejections by RTZ and Lonrho showed; profits were possible only if sufficient numbers of large stones were found. Indeed, in 1981, the executive director of Anglo, D.A. Etheredge, said that Letseng-la-Terai 'exists today only because the decision to open it was in the hands of Mr Harry Oppenheimer who saw it as a helpful venture in one of the poorest countries in the world.'[59] In other words, its opening was explicitly political — Oppenheimer saw that Lesotho had gained little from its links with South Africa and that relations were deteriorating. Anglo wanted to encourage co-existence between South Africa and its neighbours. Lesotho, as the source of a high proportion of Anglo's mine labour, was an obvious candidate. The closure of the mine reflected Anglo's reassessment of the position in 1982. Economically, the hoped-for run of large stones had not materialised and the market for them had collapsed. Politically, the Lesotho government refused a renegotiation of the tax provisions on the mine, and relations with Pretoria had deteriorated. If

Lesotho insisted on biting the hand that fed it, there was no point in keeping open a marginal mine.

The Highland Water Scheme

Water seems the only export that could replace diamonds. For Pretoria, this has been a carrot to dangle in front of Lesotho, and so it remains; but Lesotho's resources are also becoming more needed for South African industry, so the bargaining is not completely one-sided.

The Orange (Senqu) River rises in Lesotho and then flows into South Africa, where it eventually forms the boundary between South Africa and Namibia and flows into the Atlantic Ocean 200km away. For 30 years there have been various proposals to tap water from the Orange and send it north to the Transvaal and the Johannesburg industrial zones. Recently, with forecasts that the area will run short of water before the end of the century, this has become a more pressing issue. One choice is to simply pump the water out of the river where it flows into South Africa. But this is estimated to cost two-and-a-half times as much as a massive dam and tunnel system inside Lesotho. This would allow Lesotho to sell water, which would become what Jonathan called Lesotho's 'white gold'.

The EEC has been funding Lesotho's studies (South Africa is doing a parallel set), which propose a $4bn project involving five dams which would flood high valleys, plus more than 100km of tunnels. It could provide 70 cubic metres per second of water to South Africa by the year 2025. Tentative agreement has been reached on a $1bn first stage to provide 19 cubic metres per second by 1995. This should earn Lesotho M100m to M250m per year. The project would also generate electricity for Lesotho, which currently buys all its power from South Africa. Lesotho would be expected to pay most of the cost. The World Bank has been approached to be the lead agency in arranging a funding package, probably to include donor agencies like the EEC as well as commercial banks. But South Africa would have to guarantee the loans to Lesotho.[60]

The project has always been immensely political. Inevitably there is dispute about the merits of an internationally funded project that will sharply increase Lesotho's links with South Africa. To be sure, there is a mutual dependence, but Lesotho's water is aiding South Africa's further industrialisation. Some argue that Lesotho might as well sell to South Africa something it already gives for nothing. Minister Sekhonyana says that both the ANC and PAC have given their OK, as they expect to control South Africa before it is finished. SWAPO has taken the position that a legitimate Namibian government must be a party to the talks, as its downstream rights are involved.

There are political tensions between Lesotho and South Africa over the project, with both sides cutting off negotiations at various times to put political pressure on the other party. This has led to concern about just who will control the project when it is built. South Africa's fear that Lesotho might turn off the water has been resolved by a technical solution — the power station will be placed in such a way that if Lesotho cuts off the water, it also turns off its own electricity. But there is still some hard negotiating left to agree the balance between Lesotho and South Africa over the management of the project, and a price for water has yet to be set. Lesotho hopes that South Africa has little time left for delaying negotiations if it wants the first phase finished in time to head off the projected

Transvaal water shortages.

The sheer size of the Highland Water Scheme, combined with the dreams of vast projects and the regional political implications, overshadows what should be a major consideration. That is the question of alternatives. This project will create few jobs (2,000 for construction and 200 once it is running), so it is really just a way to earn money. If that massive capital investment were available for a series of smaller development projects in Lesotho, would it create more jobs as well as reducing dependence on South Africa?

Even Sekhonyana, who had been planning minister for 15 years, admits that too little has been done on irrigated agriculture for local consumption. He is no longer a fan of the Highland Water Scheme — 'it will remain a debt for our grandchildren and in ten years will only give us M100m a year. We could achieve more if we irrigated agriculture and cut food imports.' He points to the $75m Oxbow scheme now under consideration, which could produce half of Lesotho's electricity (saving $2m per year) and irrigate a large area of good farmland in the Hoholo valley. This and similar projects would give a much better rate of return than the Highland Water Scheme, Sekhonyana claims.

No-one has ever asked how many of these alternative projects might be created. But it is worth noting that at the relatively high cost per job of Lesotho National Development Corporation projects (about M19,000 per job) the M2.5bn for the initial stages of the Highland Water Scheme would create 132,000 jobs. This is more than all the Basotho miners in South Africa. Unfortunately, this is a meaningless calculation. This huge amount of money is available precisely because South Africa will guarantee the loans.

Do outside agencies encourage dependence on South Africa?

The Highland Water Scheme, a massive project with contracts for foreign companies, is the kind of scheme aid donors prefer. Lesotho is the second highest per-capita aid recipient in the region,[61] and that level of aid is often justified as a way of reducing dependence on South Africa. Too often, however, aid agency actions go in the opposite direction. Donors are reluctant to use labour intensive, job creating construction techniques;[62] they avoid the smaller, local contractors; and they are chary of projects that will reduce dependence. Donors claim this is because they are smaller, harder to administer, and may involve higher initial costs for locally produced goods; larger, more experienced South African firms are cheaper and more efficient, whereas Basotho managers will need more training. Privately they stress that local projects are often opposed by politicians and others who will gain more from projects linked to South Africa.

For the large Western countries, the Highland Water Scheme is also attractive precisely because it ties Lesotho and South Africa more closely in what seems a mutually beneficial economic arrangement. The British retain their pre-independence perspective that there is no alternative. The United States has made no secret of its view that SADCC will only succeed if it includes South Africa. It is the view of foreign investors too. As the LNDC's former managing director noted, 'When we started promoting export based companies in 1978 we went to firms in the United States, Britain, and Germany. They said, "We have branches in South Africa — talk to them. You can't expect us to go to your little country." So we promoted in South Africa, and most firms come from there.'[63]

The same perception of the necessity of integration led the United States and Britain to support South Africa in its demand for a non-aggression pact after Nkomati. Minister Sekhonyana commented that Britain and the United States thus 'accept the idea of a Monroe doctrine in southern Africa, with South Africa playing a dominant role. Nkomati-type agreements are seen as giving South Africa some kind of legal umbrella to intervene in neighbouring states — as happened with Grenada.'[64]

Can Lesotho resist the bear hug?

Because of the way it was established Lesotho's new government is acutely sensitive to South African economic power. 'The economic blockade that this country has been subjected to in the past four weeks has exposed the inadequacy of our post-independence economic strategy,' declared King Moshoeshoe II in his 27 January 1986 speech. 'We need to strive for a more accelerated economic development of the country, with a view to achieving self-sufficiency in basic supplies.' Unfortunately, this has been said before, and as we have seen, there are strong forces inside and outside Lesotho resisting changes to economic policy. Similarly, Maj-Gen Lekhanya pointed out that the blockade showed the need for Lesotho to have an air corridor to link it to other SADCC states.[65] But that, too, has been suggested before.

It is too early to say what political course the new government will take (as this chapter is written only one month after the coup). Some suggest Lesotho will try to follow a course like Botswana: constant dialogue with Pretoria but no security agreement; criticism of apartheid but no gratuitous verbal attacks on South Africa; restrictions on refugees but no overall expulsion; and a strong role in SADCC. But will South Africa allow this? It is likely to resist another Botswana, and demand further concessions from the new Lesotho government. First, it wants a security pact. Second, it probably wants Sello and Sefali out of government and C.D. Molapo in. Third, it will oppose economic delinking (as that would limit the power of future blockades). Fourth, it will probably push, as in Swaziland, for some sort of diplomatic recognition or a 'trade mission'. Fifth, it wants public opposition to sanctions. And sixth, very specifically to Lesotho, South Africa will try to force out the socialist embassies.

Nor is the ANC problem solved. Trying to keep the ANC out of Lesotho is like trying to bail a leaking boat — refugees will come in as fast as they are flown out and this will provide a channel for the ANC. Thus South Africa could well demand some vetting of refugees and some South African police presence in Lesotho.

Lesotho's freedom of action is severely circumscribed; in December and January South Africa showed just a small part of its military might, with a raid much smaller than that in 1982, and just a small part of its economic might, with a partial blockade. It would take a strong government to resist a really tight blockade, especially if combined with military action. However, the present government is still weak. Relations between King Moshoeshoe II, Maj-Gen Lekhanya, lower officers, and various politicians have still to be clarified. Thus South Africa could intervene and might thus provoke further coups if the government does not bend sufficiently. Continued support for the LLA and for opposition politicians is another card Pretoria can continue to play.

The January 1986 blockade only provoked a coup because of divisions within

Lesotho. Jonothan's progressive foreign policy could not be maintained when it was not matched by progressive internal policies which ensured that the people supported the government. Inside Lesotho, anti-Pretoria stands counted for less than the bullyboy tactics of the BNP youth league. As Botswana shows, a unified government and people are better able to resist South African government pressure.

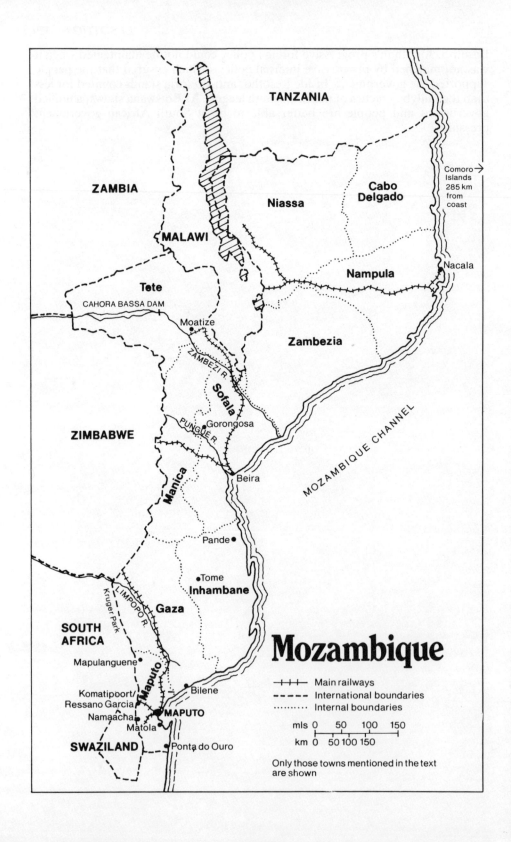

TANZANIA

ZAMBIA

MALAWI

Niassa

Cabo
Delgado

Comoro →
Islands
285 km
from
coast

Nacala

Tete

Nampula

CAHORA BASSA DAM

Moatize

Zambezia

ZAMBEZI R.

Sofala

PUNGUE R.

Gorongosa

ZIMBABWE

Beira

MOZAMBIQUE CHANNEL

Manica

Pande

•Tome

Inhambane

SOUTH
AFRICA

Mapulanguene

Gaza

L. IMPOPO R.

Kruger Park

Bilene

Komatipoort/
Ressano Garcia

Maputo

Namaacha

MAPUTO

Matola

SWAZILAND

Ponta do Ouro

Mozambique

┼┼┼ Main railways

- - - International boundaries

······ Internal boundaries

mls 0   50   100   150

km 0   50 100 150

Only those towns mentioned in the text
are shown

12. Mozambique
Ports and Railways

Mozambique and Angola came to independence in 1975, and were the first states in the region to fight long and bitter liberation struggles successfully. These wars radicalised the Frelimo and MPLA leadership, leading them to follow a Marxist line; South Africa's support of Portugal also accelerated their move away from Pretoria. The apartheid state responded by hitting Mozambique and Angola harder than other states in the region.

Both geographically and politically Mozambique was a threat to apartheid. Situated on the coast and with trade patterns oriented toward Europe, Mozambique was not heavily dependent on South Africa and could afford to reduce the ties. Later, its position as the natural port for much of the hinterland made the country central to SADCC, and thus a direct economic threat to South Africa. Politically, the prospect of a successful non-racial, socialist state independent of South Africa but still on its borders, would question the very core of the apartheid ideology. Indeed, Frelimo's victory in 1974 did prove an inspiration to the quiescent movement inside South Africa.

SERVICE ECONOMY — TRANSPORT AND OTHER LINKS

Colonial Mozambique had little importance in its own right; it was seen by both Portugal and Britain as serving other colonies by providing services — transport and migrant labour, and later electricity and tourist facilities. But it did lead to the unusual position where Mozambique is the only country in the region to have had a net balance of payments *surplus* with South Africa.

The shortest route to the sea

The railway from Lourenço Marques (now Maputo) to South Africa opened in 1895; under a special agreement in force for most of the century, it carried half the Transvaal's imports and exports. The line from Beira to Rhodesia opened in 1897, and a line from Beira to Malawi in 1922. Later expansions only took place after World War II: Rhodesia-Lourenço Marques in 1955, Swaziland-Lourenço Marques in 1964, and Malawi-Nacala in 1970.[2]

In 1973 Mozambique handled a large proportion of regional imports and exports: one-fifth of South African, two-thirds of Rhodesian, half of Swazi, and all of Malawian. Some copper from Botswana, Zambia, and Zaire also passed through Mozambican harbours. Maputo was the largest port in southern Africa, handling more cargo than any port in South Africa. Maputo was also the main port for Rhodesian sanctions-busting, particularly for oil deliveries.

When it became clear to the South African government that Frelimo would win, however, cargo was moved away. South African traffic fell from 6.2m tonnes in 1973 to 4.4m in 1975. The ports at Richards Bay and Durban were developed and modernised, in part to take traffic that would once have gone through Mozambique. In March 1976 Mozambique imposed sanctions on Rhodesia, ending that traffic.[3] Thus by 1979 most of the region's traffic was passing through South Africa (see Table 1).

Table 1. *Port traffic (m tonnes)*

	1973	1975	1979	1981	1982
Total	18.3	14.9	10.9	9.1	9.0
Transit for					
South Africa	6.2	4.4	4.0	3.0	2.2
Swaziland	3.0	2.8	0.7	0.7	0.7
Zimbabwe	3.3	2.2	—	0.9	1.1
Malawi	0.7	0.6	1.0	0.9	0.7

Nevertheless, Maputo remained an important port for South Africa. It was still the closest and thus cheapest for the eastern Transvaal. In 1979 the then general manager of South African Railways (SAR) said simply, 'It is an economic necessity that the railway line to, and harbour of, Maputo should remain accessible to South Africa.'

Indeed, South Africa has always used Maputo as a kind of 'internal' port. Fuel oil came up the coast from Cape Town and Durban in small tankers and was transferred to railway wagons to be sent to Swaziland and the eastern Transvaal. Coal was railed from the Transvaal to Maputo and sent in boats down the coast to power stations. For these bulk cargoes, it was cheaper than sending them long distances through South Africa by rail.

The independence of Zimbabwe and the founding of SADCC raised the possibility of shifting the majority of regional imports and exports back to Mozambican ports. But they had been starved of investment for over 15 years. Portugal had always built on the cheap; for example the Nacala-Malawi railway was built of undersized second-hand rails laid on sand, and it was hardly surprising that despite running at very low speeds the trains often fell off the track. During the last decade of colonialism Portugal put in no new investment and did little maintenance; in the first years after independence Frelimo had trouble enough keeping the trains running. At the same time South Africa had made substantial new investments in bulk cargo and container handling in the ports and in railway electrification.

In 1980 the Mozambican ports and railways were still able to move regional cargo, and by 1982 half of Zimbabwean cargo was passing through Mozambique. But massive investments were needed to handle that cargo efficiently. At its first annual conference in Maputo, SADCC asked donors for US$880m to rehabilitate and upgrade regional ports and railways; $645m of that was for Mozambique.

Migrant labour but no investment

Mozambique became one of the main suppliers of mine labour to South Africa as part of the agreement to send Transvaal cargo through Lourenço Marques. From

1908 until 1976 there were always more than 80,000 Mozambicans in the South African mines, and the number exceeded 110,000 in 1966, 1970 and 1975. During this time Mozambicans were normally more than half of all foreign workers, and during 1970-74 there were actually more Mozambicans working in the mines than South Africans.[4]

Numbers were cut back substantially after independence, so that in 1977 there were only one-third as many Mozambicans in the mines as there had been in 1975.[5] But mine wages had risen substantially, in part due to the wave of strikes in South Africa in 1973 and 1974, so the drop in income was not severe; indeed, migrant labour is now a more important source of foreign exchange than any single export. But the drop in the number of miners has not been matched by new jobs inside Mozambique, creating a significant unemployment problem.

As well as migrant labour and ports and railways, Mozambique provided one other service to South Africa and Rhodesia. A substantial tourist trade built up, with families coming for the beaches, fishing, and beer and prawns, while thousands of men went to 'LM' and Beira for nightlife and interracial sex banned in South Africa. At independence, there were more than 30,000 prostitutes in Lourenço Marques. The border was later closed to tourists, and is only now being slowly reopened.

South Africa made little direct investment in Mozambique. Most foreign capital was British or Portuguese. Inevitably, South African firms dominated freight and forwarding, and still do.[6] Anglo and Barlow Rand had small holdings which they retained after independence. Metal Box transferred its ownership of the Mozambican subsidiary from South Africa to the UK parent.

Two important firms pulled out, however. South African Breweries owned the best hotel, the Polana, as well as a brewery, but abandoned them. Iscor, the South African parastatal iron and steel corporation, had a share in the Moatize coal mine, but the foreign owners virtually abandoned the mine and Mozambique eventually nationalised it after two serious accidents.

The most important project in terms of South Africa was the Cahora Bassa dam, one of the largest in the world. When it finally began full operation in 1979, it supplied 10% of South Africa's entire electricity demand. The project was not designed to earn money, but rather to link Portugal and South Africa and further bring South Africa into the war against Frelimo. In 1969 the Portuguese government signed a contract with the South African Electricity Supply Commission (Escom) to supply power at no profit and at less than the cost of coal to generate a similar amount of electricity.[7] This meant that the negotiations to end the liberation war had the bizarre aspect of Portugal trying to force Frelimo to take the dam, and the latter refusing to accept what it called 'the great white elephant'. In the end, Mozambique received 18.3% of the equity and was to receive more as debts were paid off, but Portugal took full responsibility for paying off those debts. In practice, independent Mozambique earned not a penny from the dam, but at least suffered no losses.

South Africa as magnet

Toward the end of the colonial era, Johannesburg became the metropole and the cultural focus in place of Lisbon. Whites increasingly went to South Africa for shopping, health care, holidays, and further education. Indeed, white South Africa was seen as an extension of Europe rather than part of Africa.

Furthermore, the 'third white tribe' in South Africa is the Portuguese; there were more than 500,000 there even before 1975 so whites in Mozambique could happily go to South Africa without speaking either English or Afrikaans.

For many blacks, Soweto became the cultural Mecca, as well as the model of the consumer society. The Mozambican black middle class image of South Africa was only of Soweto, high mine wages, and overflowing supermarkets; they knew virtually nothing of the bantustans.

South Africa overtook Portugal to become colonial Mozambique's main supplier. Even basic foodstuffs like onions came from over the border. South Africa was particularly important as a source of spare parts and servicing for machinery because it was so convenient; a telephone call to Johannesburg meant that a part or an engineer could be on a train or plane in a day or two, whereas goods take three or four months to arrive from Europe.

Despite the tensions that arose after independence, South Africa remained a major source of supply. The Planning Commission was even moved to point out that South African goods tend to be more expensive than those available in Europe. It noted that too many ministries were buying from South Africa simply because they did not plan ahead far enough to order in Europe, and so needed items in a hurry. But there was never a policy decision against buying in South Africa.[8] And it proved hard to overcome habit, lack of planning, and racism.

A linked factor is that the people who do the buying in many ministries and parastatals in Mozambique are white, because blacks were barred from business and education in the colonial era; thus whites who were privileged before independence remain the only people who can do these jobs, and Frelimo is strongly 'nonracial', promoting people only on merit and qualifications. But most buy through Portuguese-speaking agents in South Africa or Swaziland, many of whom are people who left Mozambique after independence. Working through agents is more expensive, but buyers find it easier to place an order by telephoning someone who speaks Portuguese, and who is probably the 'friend of a friend' anyway, than to telex or write a letter in English or French.

The final reason, in Mozambique as elsewhere in the region, is that the middle class — black and white — likes to go to South Africa for shopping and entertainment. It is much easier to justify a trip to South Africa, which is only 70km from Maputo and can be done by car or train, than one to Europe; South African business agents will happily lay on the necessary tranport, accommodation, and spending money.

ECONOMIC SABOTAGE

After a somewhat confused period (see below), Pretoria did not initially move against Frelimo. For example, cargo through Maputo port, having been cut by one-third at independence, was not further affected for some years. South African Railways (SAR) retained various rules requiring certain shippers to use Maputo, and traffic remained steady at 4m tonnes per year up to 1979. The main exception was with respect to migrant miners. The number was cut sharply in 1976, and in April 1978 South Africa ended the highly profitable system under which Mozambique was paid part of miners' wages in gold at the official price rather than the free market price.[9]

Sanctions

Then in 1980, with the independence of Zimbabwe and the founding of SADCC, the position changed. The SADCC transport commission was set up in Maputo,[10] and the first annual SADCC conference was held there in November 1980. South Africa responded with a commando raid on Maputo on 30 January 1981 (see below), a railway embargo on cargo to Maputo for two weeks in mid-March, and another military incursion on 17 March. In January, February and April 1981 it also imposed *de facto* rail embargoes on SADCC members Botswana and Zimbabwe (see Chapters 14 and 15).

South Africa imposed *de facto* sanctions on Mozambique. Substantial amounts of cargo were rerouted away from Maputo, so traffic fell steadily from 4m tonnes in 1979 to 1.5m tonnes in 1983. Furthermore, it was the cargo with high tariffs that was moved; for example steel exports and CKD car kit imports were both ended in 1981. Whereas before 1980 SAR had prevented shippers from shifting away from Maputo, now it forced them to, for example, by only providing wagons to go to Durban. Ferrochrome was shifted from Maputo to Richards Bay.[11] And in 1983 South Africa ended fuel shipments through Maputo. Only coal traffic increased, and coal is a particularly low value, low tariff cargo; by 1983 export and internal power station coal constituted more than half the South African cargo passing through Maputo.

The sanctions may have been informal, but they were effective. Nor were they confined to state action. For example, in 1981 Anglo American suddenly and without explanation abandoned its two cashew factories in Mozambique, Antenes and Mocita. This was politically important, because cashew nuts are Mozambique's biggest export and Anglo had stayed on after independence; the gesture seemed political because by 1981 other private companies were no longer pulling out.

South Africa also moved against migrant workers, expelling 12,000 farm labourers working in the eastern Transvaal in 1982. (There is no sure way of counting, but there are perhaps 50,000 more Mozambicans working on farms there, most illegally.)

Finally, there were a host of smaller incidents, some of which could simply have been incompetence. For example, deliveries of chlorine from South Africa for the Maputo water supply suddenly stopped just when a cholera outbreak was reported. A vital water pump from the Maputo water supply was sent to South Africa for an overhaul, and was not bolted down properly on the return trip so it arrived back in Maputo damaged. An aeroplane engine sent to South Africa for servicing came back with a nut not screwed on, nearly causing a crash.[12]

But the really serious economic damage was done by the Mozambique National Resistance (MNR or Renamo), described in more detail below. It concentrated on road and railway links and development projects, causing economic chaos and disrupting the links that were vital for the development of SADCC.

MILITARY INTERVENTION

South Africa's initial response to Mozambican independence was confused. In late August 1974 the Rhodesian and South African secret service chiefs, Ken Flowers and General H.J. Van den Berg, were called to Lisbon by the Portuguese Foreign Minister Mario Soares. He told them that they could no longer count on

Portugal as an ally in southern Africa, and that within days Portugal would sign an agreement with Frelimo. (That occurred in Lusaka on 7 September.)

In response, the then defence minister and now State President, P.W. Botha, decided to invade Mozambique to support a settler uprising, and armoured cars arrived at the border town of Komatipoort. In an extraordinary series of events, however, the convoy is reported to have been disabled by BOSS, the South African security service, which prevented the invasion on the instructions of Prime Minister Vorster.[13] It was a period when Vorster was pushing his *détente* exercise with black Africa; he went on to visit the presidents of the Ivory Coast and Liberia in September 1974 and February 1975, and in August 1975 met with Kaunda at Victoria Falls. Thus he may have felt that an invasion of Mozambique would scuttle *détente*. Also, Van den Berg erroneously believed that Portuguese troops would defend Frelimo against South Africa. A year later, however, Botha won out over Van den Berg and invaded Angola.

For five years after the aborted invasion, South Africa took little direct military action against Mozambique.[14] Attacking Frelimo was left to Ian Smith, although with ample backing from Pretoria. But in 1980, Rhodesia was defeated while P.W. Botha had become Prime Minister in Pretoria. Ronald Reagan, the new President of the United States, promised warmer relations with P.W. Botha and seemed most unlikely to object if South Africa was more aggressive against its socialist neighbours. So South Africa effectively declared war on Mozambique.

Direct attack

The South African Defence Force made at least a dozen attacks inside Mozambique in the next three years (in its own right, as distinct from supporting the MNR). The first and undoubtedly most successful was in the early morning of 30 January 1981, when commandos came over the border and drove 70km to Matola, a suburb of Maputo. With perfect accuracy they destroyed three houses on tree-lined streets in otherwise quiet neighbourhoods, killing 13 ANC members and a Portuguese passer-by. At one house, the ANC fought back, killing two commandos and injuring others. One of the dead was wearing a helmet painted with swastikas and the slogan 'Sieg Heil'; he turned out to be a British mercenary, Robert Lewis Hutchinson. He had moved from the British Army to Rhodesian SAS and then down to South Africa after Zimbabwean independence.

Investigating the raid, the authorities discovered that the truckloads of commandos had been helped to enter Mozambique. They found that the CIA and South African security were cooperating and had penetrated the Mozambican government much more deeply than Frelimo expected. A high official in the army general staff (who blocked the initial report of the incursion) and a member of Frelimo's Central Committee were agents.

On 17 March 1981 a South African patrol walked up the beach and over the border into the Mozambican resort of Ponta do Ouro in what may have been a test to see if Mozambique had improved its border defences. It had, and one South African soldier was killed in the ensuing battle.

There were three raids in the six weeks before the second SADCC annual conference on 19-20 November 1981 in Blantyre, Malawi. All were near Beira, a port which serves Malawi, and all were on the port and railway in what must have been intended as a clear South African gesture of defiance towards SADCC.

The first, on 14 October, was a South African failure. A Mozambican patrol

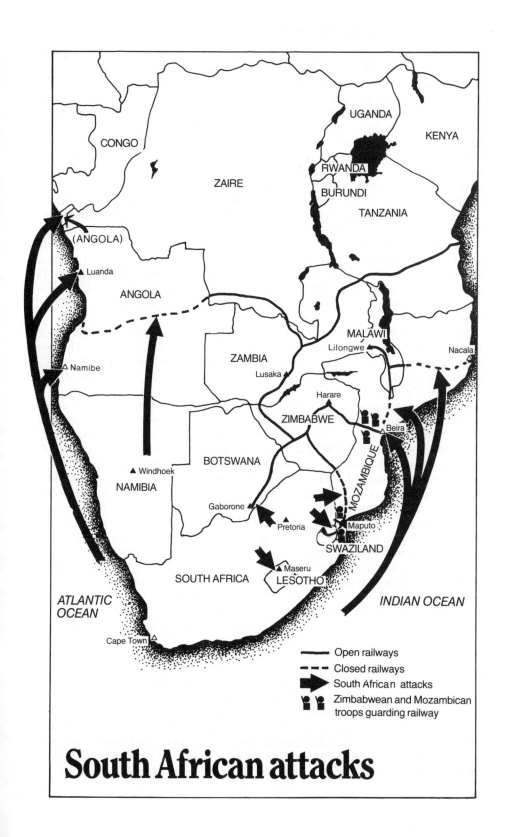

South African attacks

Legend:
- Open railways
- Closed railways
- South African attacks
- Zimbabwean and Mozambican troops guarding railway

came across a group laying a mine on the Beira-Zimbabwe railway, and shot the mine, which exploded blowing up the group. Found among the remains was a white ear. In their camp, a man's pack was found, and in it notebooks for a novel the man was writing. More than a year later, the London Sunday newspaper, the *Observer*, concluded from the handwriting and other evidence that the man was Alan Gingles. Sandhurst trained, Gingles left the British Army and joined the Selous Scouts in Rhodesia, then moved to the SADF (South African Defence Force). At the time, the South African army had indeed announced that Gingles had been killed 'in action against terrorists' in the 'operational area', but ridiculed Mozambican suggestions that the SADF was involved in the mining.[15]

Two weeks later the South Africans were more successful, and hit two bridges over the Pungue River just 50 km from Beira. The bridge carrying the road and oil pipeline was destroyed and one carrying the railway damaged, cutting all traffic between Beira and Zimbabwe.[16] The raid was almost surely the work of the South African Reconnaissance Commandos, and was very similar to one on road and rail bridges over the Giraul River in Angola in November 1982. (See Chapters 13 and 15). Then South Africa added insult to injury by destroying the marker buoys in Beira harbour on 13 November, less than a week before the SADCC conference.

Eight months later South Africa hit again. On 17 August 1982 Ruth First was killed by a parcel bomb in her office at Eduardo Mondlane University. She was research director of the Centre of African Studies and active in promoting ANC-Frelimo cooperation. She was the wife of Joe Slovo, an ANC and South African Communist Party leader.

Less than a week later on 23 August South African commandos came over the border to the town of Namaacha (which is close to the point where Swaziland, South Africa, and Mozambique meet). It was a somewhat strange raid, apparently aimed at the ANC but based on intelligence which was long out of date. Two Mozambicans and a Portuguese aid worker were killed and three Mozambicans kidnapped. One of those kidnapped, Maputo teacher Jeronimo Simbini, made it back to Mozambique more than two years later. He said he had been taken to Phalaborwa in the eastern Transvaal and interrogated for several days about the ANC in Namaacha. After that, he was given a new name, a South African pass book, and military training which included parachute jumping and endurance training. Then he was placed in the 5th Reconnaissance Commando, which is based in Phalaborwa and is partly responsible for the MNR. Eventually in November 1984 he was given leave, and he returned to Mozambique (where he was detained by the security service, Snasp, until April).[17]

The Reconnaissance Commando hit Beira on 9 December 1982, blowing up the depot which held fuel for the Zimbabwe pipeline and for Malawi. Commandos came ashore from a boat and carefully attached two limpet mines to each tank (the commandos caught in Angola two-and-a-half years later intended a carbon copy of the Beira raid). Damage was estimated at US$20m in lost oil and damaged facilities. And the raid caused a fuel crisis in Zimbabwe (see Chapter 15). It was discovered that a crucial role had been played by personnel working for Manica Freight Services, the Anglo- and Safmarine-owned shipping agency better known for its earlier role in sanctions-busting.[18] The Beira director of Manica, a Briton named Dion Hamilton, was later sentenced to 20 years in jail by a military tribunal for possession of arms and 'acts equivalent to terrorism'; his deputy, a Portuguese man named Benjamin Fox, was sentenced to eight years. Hamilton and Fox had known about the raid in advance. It seemed that Hamilton — a private pilot, yachtsman, and parachutist — had provided the information that the Reconnaissance Commando needed for the raid, and probably for the raid on the bridges a year before. Fox served as a liaison man for the MNR, and the Manica office in Beira was effectively an MNR office.

On 23 May 1983 a dozen South African jets hit Matola and another Maputo suburb, Liberdade (Liberty). The South Africans called it Operation Skerwe, Afrikaans for 'shrapnel', and the planes strafed the two suburbs with special fragmentation rockets. After the raid, bits of shrapnel were embedded in trees and dug into the ground. The South African Defence Force said it had destroyed ANC bases and killed what it called 41 'ANC terrorist'. In fact, it killed three workers at the Somopal jam factory as they arrived for work, a soldier guarding a bridge, a child playing, and an ANC man washing a car. At least 40 other people, mostly women and children, were hurt by shrapnel. The raid was an explicit response to an ANC bomb in Pretoria. A week later, anti-aircraft fire in Maputo brought down an Israeli-built remote controlled spy plane which had been sending close-up TV pictures back to South Africa — probably a test to see if Mozambican defences had improved.

The next raid came on 17 October, when commandos bombed the ANC office in Maputo. Five people were injured. The office was not secret; it was in a block of flats and was often visited by foreign journalists passing through Maputo. One and a half years later when South African commando Wynand Petrus du Toit was caught trying to blow up fuel tanks in Angola, he admitted participating in the Maputo raid on the ANC office as well. Finally on 7 December two ANC men were hurt when a tiny house in the high density suburb of Xipamanine was bombed.

The Mozambique National Resistance

Although spectactular, South Africa's direct attacks on Mozambique were really a sideshow in its undeclared war on Frelimo. The main action was the Mozambique National Resistance (*Resistência Nacional Moçambicana*, variously called MNR, RNM, or Renamo). The MNR was initially set up by the Rhodesians to be a fifth column inside Mozambique. Its first members were men from various Portuguese special forces units who fled to Rhodesia in 1974. These included the commandos, *flechas* (the secret police private army), special paratroops, and other particularly brutal anti-Frelimo units. Many of their members either felt abandoned by the Portuguese or afraid of retribution from the people who had suffered at their hands. These initial groups increased their numbers by raiding Frelimo re-education camps (open prisons in rural areas) and recruiting people with no vested interest in Frelimo. A particularly important group was cashiered Frelimo petty officers, many of whom had been detained because they believed that after a decade in the bush, they had an automatic right to take cars, houses, and women. Both of the MNR's leaders had been corrupt Frelimo officers, Andre Matzangaissa, who was killed by Frelimo in 1979, and his successor Alfonso Dhlakama.

This makes the MNR very different from UNITA or the LLA in that it was entirely created by a security service with no initial base in an opposition movement or alternative liberation movement. In time it did garner small amounts of support, but its lack of roots is shown most clearly by the total failure of the MNR's backers to develop a programme or find a credible leader for it.

There are claims in South Africa that the MNR was created by BOSS, the South African secret police.[19] But this is denied by reliable sources both in Mozambique and Rhodesia. What is clear is that there was ample cooperation between South Africa and Rhodesia, as shown by the case of Amaro Silva, a Maputo school teacher who crossed the border into South Africa in 1978 and turned himself over to the police. The South Africans passed him on to the Rhodesians, who sent him for training at an MNR camp in Bindura, Rhodesia. He was then sent back to Maputo in an unsuccessful attempt to assassinate Robert Mugabe; instead he bombed a cafe in Maputo's *baixa* (city centre) area, injuring 50 people. He was caught by police but escaped in 1981 and went back to South Africa. This time he was used with other MNR men to kidnap ANC member Joe Pillay in Swaziland (see Chapter 10). Then he served in Namibia, and finally returned to Mozambique with the MNR, where he was caught again and this time executed.

Rebuilding the MNR

With independence in Zimbabwe, South African military intelligence took over the MNR. Its radio station began broadcasting from Pietersburg in the Transvaal instead of Rhodesia; bases were set up in Phalaborwa and elsewhere in the eastern Transvaal, particularly near the Kruger National Park, which runs for 350km along the Mozambican border.

The MNR leaders moved to South Africa in February or March 1980; Commander Andre had been killed in October 1979 and the main MNR bases were captured in October 1979 (Gorongosa) and June 1980 (Sitatonga). The MNR was truly in tatters and needed rebuilding almost from scratch. But by June 1980 both Mozambique and Zimbabwe reported that South Africa was now backing the MNR and South African helicopters were seen over Mozambique's Manica province.

As well as rebuilding it, South Africa also changed the nature of the MNR. Rhodesia had used it as a fifth column and for intelligence about ZANU movements inside Mozambique, which required that it develop some rapport and credibility with local people. South Africa seemed interested only in using it for terrorism, disruption, and destruction.

For Mozambique, 1980 was a year of peace, promise, and excitement. The war with Ian Smith was finally over, and resources could finally be turned to building the economy. But it was not to be.

By late 1980 the MNR had opened bases in central Mozambique which were being supplied by air from South Africa. By mid-1981 the MNR had re-established a central base on the Gorongosa mountain, and were attacking the Beira-Zimbabwe railway (with the help of South African soldiers like Gingles); the only road linking Beira and Maputo was closed and the electricity line to Beira was cut repeatedly. In a slightly odd move, the MNR also cut the line linking the Cahora Bassa dam with South Africa.[20] In 1982 they began attacking the Beira-Malawi railway,[21] and moved south nearly to the Limpopo River, 150km north of Maputo.

The level of South African support was sizeable. Mozambique complained of more than 40 overflights in an 18-month period during 1980-81. There were repeated reports of air drops, usually of large crates containing several tonnes of weapons, ammunition, and other supplies; often they were dropped at night into a cleared space surrounded by marker fires. Supplies were also sent up the coast and dropped on the beach; for example, on 20 August 1982 the private South African 'fishing boat' Plumstead was caught coming down the coast returning to Durban, but it had no fish, no fishing tackle, and no refrigerator.

One South African goal was to attack SADCC, and in particular to disrupt and block traffic from Zimbabwe and Malawi. Thus railways were a specific target of MNR attacks. In three years, 93 locomotives and 250 wagons were destroyed or damaged; 150 railway workers were killed.[22] South Africa also wanted to paralyse the Mozambican economy by disrupting transport. Roads as well as railways were mined, and traffic attacked. In dozens of horrific massacres, MNR guerrillas derailed trains and wrecked buses, then shot at the passengers as they climbed from the wreckage and burned the vehicles with the wounded still inside. Hundreds of private cars, vans and lorries were also attacked. The goal seemed to be to make people afraid to travel. Another target was Mozambique's new development projects, particularly internationally-funded mines, farms and factories.

Finally, the MNR set out to destroy the rural economy. The MNR burned peasant grain stores and mined roads. It destroyed 900 rural shops in 1982 and 1983. In 1982 alone the MNR burned 140 villages, destroyed 102 medical centres and rural health posts, and destroyed or forced the closure of 489 primary schools.[23] Teachers were often a special target; many were killed or had their ears hacked off.

The effect was devasting. Combined with the worst drought in decades, the MNR precipitated virtual economic collapse. Key exports, particularly of tea, cashew nuts, cotton, and sugar were badly hit; internally there was starvation due to the lack of marketing.

MNR recruitment

For an organisation with no historic roots, the MNR was very effective, and it is necessary to look at how it recruited guerrillas. The most important factor was force — armed bands would simply kidnap hundreds of young men (and women); many escaped, but those caught escaping were killed. Those who stayed were given rudimentary training, and often forced at gunpoint to kill someone, and thus made part of the band. Illegal immigrants in Swaziland and South Africa were also recruited, often by the South African police; sometimes they were given no choice and sometimes given the choice of jail or the MNR.

Some people were taken by the MNR but stayed willingly, for example people taken from re-education camps (an important method of recruiting). Also, some kidnapped peasants stayed just for the adventure of being an armed bandit. Life in MNR camps, with women, marijuana, stolen food and radios, and luxuries like captured motorcycles, was much better than the grinding poverty of being a hoe farmer.

Finally, there was a political factor. Like so many newly independent countries, Frelimo's economic policies initially stressed big development projects at the expense of the peasant farmer. By 1982 there was little in rural shops and money was becoming valueless, so peasants were already producing less for the market. In many areas, the peasants saw no particular reason to defend the government, and so would not report MNR bands who passed through. Sometimes an MNR group would come into an area, rob the local shop and distribute the goods to the peasants, and often hold a party (with cattle stolen from another zone); so people at first thought the MNR guerrillas were 'Robin Hoods' who actually provided them with things, and only later realised the MNR was there to stay and had to be fed. The war itself creates discontent, as MNR disruption means even less in the shops, but all too often it is the government which carries the can and not the MNR. However, the MNR never seems to present a political programme; at meetings it simply says Frelimo and communism are the causes of Mozambique's problems and the MNR will do better.

As elsewhere in the region, South Africa could count on over-reaction to recruit for it. In several provinces, the army forced people to move into villages to keep them away from the MNR.[24] Not surprisingly, people who might have been neutral or pro-Frelimo before became embittered, and welcomed the MNR into their zone. In other areas, young men were simply press-ganged into the rapidly expanding army, and some felt that if they had to fight for one side or the other, they would choose the MNR. And there were a number of cases of abuse of power by the army and local officials, which also helped MNR recruitment. In other instances, villagers supported the MNR to get back at a village secretary who unfairly flogged people, or a local military commander who raped village women. In several cases mistreated or unfairly dismissed workers have helped the MNR burn factories.

The result is a curious mix of people who hate the MNR bitterly because of atrocities, many who are neutral and just trying to keep their heads down, and some who actively support the MNR. When one group of MNR men who had all been captured in the same area were interviewed, several talked of local support and of collaborators who collected food from neighbours and brought it to MNR camps, while another had been nearly killed by villagers who discovered he was part of the MNR.

Frelimo's own reaction to the revitalised MNR was very slow. It really did not believe what was happening until well into 1982, and then was ill-equipped to respond. One problem was that it was most worried about a conventional ground invasion, in part because this is what had happened in 1975 in Angola (and had been attempted against Mozambique in 1974), and in part because the border is only 70km from Maputo and the terrain is ideal for tanks and armoured cars. Thus it disbanded the guerrilla army that had successfully defeated the Portuguese and built a modern conventional one. This army did turn back Rhodesian invasions, and could at least delay a South African ground invasion and probably impose unacceptable casualties.

But that meant Frelimo had to build a new counter-guerrilla force starting in 1982. Many ex-combatants were drawn back into the army to create a home defence force built up of provincial units fighting the MNR in their home areas. Emphasis was also put on arming the local population in militias, particularly to guard key economic installations. Both the army and local party militants put great stress on changing economic policy to give more support to peasants, which was done at Frelimo's Fourth Congress in April 1983 — too late to have much effect.

NKOMATI

Under this enormous and growing pressure, Mozambique became the first country to sign a public peace treaty with South Africa (although it soon emerged that Swaziland had signed one secretly). It turned out to be a futile action — ample evidence to the rest of SADCC of the pointlessness of trying to negotiate with the apartheid state. But is important also to understand why Frelimo was forced to such a pass, and how South Africa internationalised support for the MNR.

By 1983 Frelimo was being pummelled from all sides. The worst drought in memory was moving into its third year, while South African attacks and support for the MNR were increasing. Together these were cutting exports just when the world economic crisis was pushing down commodity prices and raising interest rates. And Frelimo had recognised its own economic policy errors too late, and, under pressure from drought, world recession and South Africa, was not able to implement sensible reforms.

Mozambique had two unsuccessful ministerial level meetings with South Africa, in the border town of Komatipoort, on 17 December 1982 and 5 May 1983. The 23 May 1983 air raid was South Africa's answer.

Frelimo made a conscious policy decision to court the West, in the (eventually successful) hope that Britain and the US would put pressure on South Africa and provide food aid. Mozambique signed an agreement with West Germany which required it to recognise West Germany's control over West Berlin (which Mozambique's main trading partner and strongest political ally, East Germany, does not accept). In less than a year, five Mozambican government ministers visited the US to stress that, despite its socialist policies, it saw South Africa as the main enemy, not the United States. President Machel visited western Europe in October 1983, stopping in Portugal, France, Britain, Holland, and Belgium (where he also talked with the EEC).

Great stress was placed on the role of Western private investment. In London Machel had a secret meeting with Anglo's Harry Oppenheimer to try to persuade him to put pressure on his government to back off. And on 29 February 1984, Machel had a highly publicised meeting with Lonrho's Tiny Rowland, at which it was agreed that Lonrho would give US$4m in food aid and invest in various new projects. Inevitably, Lonrho became involved in politics. Its managing director for Mozambique was a cardiologist, Marquand de Villiers, who ran the business from his Pretoria medical suite. De Villiers was a friend and golf partner of John Vorster, and claims to have been part of the *détente* exercise and to have been involved in the Victoria Falls meeting between Vorster and Kaunda (see Chapter 19). De Villiers tried unsuccessfully to mediate between Frelimo and the MNR. And it was De Villiers who stressed Lonrho's political role in the region by commenting that 'President Samora Machel is a moderate, and he is undeniably the leader of the people of Mozambique. We will support him actively, as we have supported UNITA's Jonas Savimbi in Angola the last 14 years.'[25]

Crisis

A famine in 1983 showed just what pressure Machel was under. In January 1983, when it was clear that rains had failed completely yet again, Mozambique warned that 'hundreds would die' without extra food aid. Donations *decreased*.

The worst province was Inhambane. The MNR was burning grain stores, mining roads, attacking food relief lorries, and killing anyone caught escaping from MNR-controlled areas to try to get to refugee camps in government-controlled zones. At the height of the famine, in August 1983, South Africa dropped ten tonnes of supplies to the main MNR base at Tome, Inhambane — not food for the starving, but more mines, arms, and ammunition to attack the relief lorries. Thus the problem for the international community was that this famine was not an act of God, but an act of war — a direct tactic of South African destabilisation. So providing food relief in Inhambane meant taking sides in the undeclared war South Africa was waging on Mozambique.

Finally, in October 1983, Mozambique's Western overtures paid off. The US decided that Machel really was 'turning to the West' and called for substantial food aid for Inhambane. Once the US said it was OK, bureaucratic difficulties suddenly fell away. Western governments fell over each other to fly in aid that Mozambique had asked for in January. But it was too late — over 100,000 people died.[26]

Almost inevitably, South Africa benefited. Aid had to be sent in great haste because it had not been organised when Mozambique had asked nine months before. So the EEC and other donors turned to South Africa for supplies and airfreighting.[27]

Another response to Mozambique's appeals to the West was pressure from the US, Britain, and Portugal on South Africa to be seen to be talking to Frelimo. Suddenly, meetings on 20 December 1983 and 16 January, 20 February, and 3 March 1984 produced tentative agreement. Meanwhile, at the end of January Mozambique asked for its debts to be rescheduled. After a decade of debate, the Council of Ministers agreed that Mozambique should join the IMF and World Bank.[28]

Frelimo put on a brave face, and with maximum pomp and ceremony Samora Machel and P.W. Botha signed the Nkomati non-aggression pact on 16 March — in the same white railway carriage that had been used for the Victoria Falls talks nine years before (see Chapters 5 and 19).

Mozambique had become an important access route for ANC guerrillas, although apparently training was carefully done elsewhere. After Nkomati Mozambique expelled nearly all ANC and guerrilla access ended.[29] South Africa was supposed to stop supporting the MNR. It did shut down the MNR radio, but little else, as we shall see later.

Mozambique's colleagues in the Front Line states were, in general, not pleased with Nkomati. They thought it was foolish and put them under pressure to sign similar accords. But Frelimo was on its knees and probably had little choice; in any event it had negotiated a successful settlement with the Portuguese and had pushed ZANU into a not unacceptable negotiated deal at Lancaster House, so its record was reasonable. Had the Accord succeeded and brought peace it would have been hailed by all as a victory. In the event, it only confirmed the conventional wisdom of the region — the Afrikaners were not to be trusted. It was, Julius Nyerere said later, a 'humiliation'.

Economic gains?

At the 20 December 1983 talks, South Africa wanted to talk about economic issues and tourism. Mozambique said this was putting the cart before the horse and wanted to concentrate first on the MNR and security issue. But South Africa pushed, particularly demanding that its tourists be able to return to Maputo. Mozambique conceded, and from the 16 January meeting there were four separate commissions: security, tourism, Cahora Bassa, and general economic links.

At the time of the signing, much was made of the potential economic impact of Nkomati. South African businessmen would revitalise the shattered Mozambican economy, proving the advantages of white capitalism over integrated socialism and killing SADCC once and for all. Later, Pretoria officials made clear that South Africa had little money to put in, but stressed that it expected to be a conduit for foreign capital because it was the 'natural' economic centre of the region and had long experience in dealing with the black states.[30] Margaret Thatcher had already made clear to Machel, during his October 1983 visit to London, her view that South Africa would remain the centre of the region and thus that any new British capital would naturally be routed through South Africa. The US and West Germany made similar points.

This was a direct challenge to SADCC, and it reacted angrily. 'We hear whispers that Western economic private investment will come to SADCC countries through South Africa and not directly,' said President Nyerere at a SADCC summit in July 1984. 'We should denounce such blackmail in support of apartheid.' Later that month the then chairman of the SADCC standing committee of officials, Lebang Mpotokwane, said that enterprises, agencies, or countries 'cannot be seen by us to be cooperating' if they treat SADCC states merely 'as appendages of South Africa'.[31]

In fact, SADCC need not have worried. No such investment materialised; the only finance so far has come from Lonrho, and from various companies looking for oil (including Shell, Exxon, Amoco, and BP). There were several smaller contracts; for example, Mozambique granted fishing licences to several South African firms. And the South African Industrial Development Corporation gave Mozambique a R8m (then about $3m) credit line for South African firms to rehabilitate Mozambican sugar mills.[32]

A new deal was agreed on Cahora Bassa, which might in the long term earn Mozambique some money.[33] Finally, there was a small increase in low tariff South African port traffic, mainly coal exports and sulphur imports. Rennie (Old Mutual) organised R4m for port rehabilitiation — half for the coal terminal and half for new cranes. As is common, the money was put up by the shippers who are paid back out of rebates on their port charges.

Escalation

Far from bringing peace, Nkomati brought an escalation in the war. The capital city had been relatively exempt from the war, but after Nkomati there was an attempt to invade or at least surround and cut off Maputo. MNR men captured later said that in January and February 1984, just prior to the Accord and at a time when it was clear an agreement would be signed, there was a massive resupply effort in order to keep the MNR going as long as possible. Paratroops were dropped into southern Mozambique and MNR men in Gaza province, 150km to the north, were given instructions to filter south to the capital.

On 5 April, less than three weeks after the Accord, the MNR for the first time cut the power line from South Africa to Maputo. In June there were attacks on the roads from Maputo to South Africa and Swaziland; in one instance workers from the South African construction company Murray & Roberts were kidnapped on the way to work in Maputo port (they were later released). In the next few months the MNR came over the border from the Kruger Park and attacked the main road and railway north from Maputo, including frequent grisly attacks on passenger cars, buses, and commuter trains. Attacks on the rail and power links with South Africa (and Swaziland) continued through 1985 and into 1986: in December 1985, the Mozambique government directly accused Pretoria, as well as the MNR, of the sabotage of a railway bridge. Rail traffic was increasingly diverted away from Maputo, which handled only about one million tonnes of South African goods in 1985, 33% down on 1983, and only a sixth of the level at independence.

Tens of thousands of Mozambicans fled to South Africa from MNR in the border zone. The Southern African Catholic Bishops' Conference based in Pretoria declared that 'the atrocities committed by the MNR have also risen to a horrific level' and the refugees show 'extreme fear of the MNR'. The bishops reported that in the Mapulanguene area, as well as the normal rape, torture, and kidnapping, the MNR had killed old people and cut off their heads to use as seats and had boiled children alive in front of the parents. And they noted that the MNR men carried the same rifles as the South African Defence Force.[34]

There were few incidents inside the capital itself, but travel outside became risky, pushing up the price of food and firewood inside Maputo. Combined with regular power cuts, it increased the demoralisation in the capital.

Mozambique was increasingly stretched by the war, finding itself unable to feed, clothe, and arm its rapidly increasing number of soldiers adequately, and lacking the helicopters and four-wheel-drive vehicles needed for effective anti-guerrilla campaigns. Zimbabwe assigned more than 3000 of its soldiers to guard the road, railway, and oil pipeline from Beira (and later the road across Tete province that links Malawi and Zimbabwe). On 12 June 1985 Mugabe, Nyerere, and Machel met in Harare and Mugabe agreed to more than triple the number of troops and take a more active role. Under the new arrangement, the Zimbabweans were to do more of the fighting, while Mozambique agreed to provide political and economic backup in an attempt to restore life in the areas cleared of MNR by Zimbabwean troops.[35] The Zimbabwean troops came to Mozambique in much larger numbers as soon as their security role in the Zimbabwe election finished in early July. Their first big success came at the end of August, when Zimbabwean helicopter gunships and paratroops helped to capture the main MNR base, Casa Banana,[36] in the foothills of the Gorongosa mountain, which the Mozambicans had been trying unsuccessfully to take for nearly two years.

Internationalisation

As well as increasing the intensity of the war, Nkomati brought one other important change — internationalisation of support for the MNR. Malawi had already become an important rear base for the MNR. In August 1982 an invasion of northern Zambezia and Tete provinces was launched from Malawi. MNR men were flown from South Africa to Malawi, and then transported over the border. On 27 October 1982 the Mozambican Foreign Minister Joaquim Chissano went to Malawi for talks with Life President H. Kamuzu Banda and apparently persuaded him to withdraw support. The invasion collapsed as suddenly as it had begun. But in early 1983 it resumed again. There were obviously sharp divisions both in South Africa and Malawi over this, especially after Nkomati; for example, soon after the signing of the Nkomati accord, Malawi expelled the MNR representative there, allegedly at the insistence of Pik Botha.[37] Yet the use of Malawi as a rear base increased — leading, ironically, to the cutting by the MNR of Malawi's second rail link to the sea, the line to Nacala (see Chapter 18). Samora Machel went to Malawi in October 1984, but failed to persuade Banda to stop support. Throughout 1985, the MNR was able to use Malawi to launch invasions, and South Africa used it as a base for supply flights.

South Africa also set up MNR bases in Swaziland and began to attack the road and railway linking Swaziland and Maputo (see Chapter 10). The MNR meanwhile established a representation in Kenya. Finally, the Comoro Islands became a source of supply for the MNR, allegedly with supplies coming from Europe via Saudi Arabia. The Comoros are just 300km off the coast of northern Mozambique and have had close links with South Africa since mercenaries overthrew the government and installed President Abderramane Ahmed Abdallah in 1978. South African Airways began a weekly service from Johannesburg in 1983 and South African firms began expanding the tourist infrastructure. Abdallah visited South Africa in 1983.[38]

After Nkomati, supplies continued to flow. Boats from South Africa and the Comoros landed on the coast, while planes made drops all over the country. December 1984 was probably a typical month, with at least a dozen confirmed air drops of supplies: two in Gaza province from South Africa, two in Cabo Delgado province from the Comoros, six to Tete province from Malawi, and two to Sofala province — probably planes from South Africa to Casa Banana.

Right-wing groups in Europe began to support the MNR. When Foreign Minister Joaquim Chissano visited Britain in July 1985, he gave Foreign Minister Geoffrey Howe names of Britons aiding the MNR and asked that action be taken against them. Mozambique alleges that Israel is providing military support to the MNR in Malawi, and hints that the CIA may be giving at least approval and perhaps support through Germany, Saudi Arabia, and Malawi.

The most important connection, however, remains the Portuguese. The ultra-conservative Portuguese millionaire Manuel Bulhosa, who owned the refinery in Maputo before independence, has provided some of the funding and given salaries and facilities to MNR spokesmen in Lisbon. The Portuguese government is also involved: at least one serving Portuguese officer, Lt-Col Silva Ramos of Portuguese Military Intelligence, went to the main MNR base at Tome, Inhambane, in May 1983. Portuguese in South Africa also help, and South African military intelligence sold a supply plane for the MNR to a private group so that supplies could be dropped without using government planes.

Varying goals

The internationalisation of support and the subsequent wheeling and dealing led to a confusing picture which remains opaque. But a number of essential points can be made.

In the run-up to Nkomati, there seemed to be agreement within the State Security Council that, at least for a period, South Africa would need to be seen to be abiding by Nkomati. Thus in the two months before the signing, South Africa gave the MNR six months worth of supplies, new plans, and newly trained men. Furthermore, it set up as many alternative supply routes as possible, involving Europe, Malawi, Swaziland, the Comoros, and Portuguese inside South Africa. As we note below, South Africa still pulls the strings, but the puppet now has more independence and more puppet masters. Perhaps the South African military was worried that it might eventually be forced to abandon support for the MNR.

The presence of Zimbabwean troops along the Beira-Mutare corridor effectively cut the MNR in half. The northern group was supplied via Malawi and the Comoros and could be semi-autonomous. This raised the possibility that South Africa might finally reach a settlement with Mozambique in the south, where its economic interests are concentrated, while the MNR continues destabilisation in the north — perhaps trying to promote a breakaway state.

Mozambican officials made a big play of splits within South Africa, saying that the Foreign Ministry wanted to abide by Nkomati and businessmen wanted to invest, but that they could not control middle levels of the army and the 'Portuguese connection'. There is no doubt that divisions exist, with probably three lines of thought: overthrow the government because Marxists can never be trusted, continue keeping Frelimo in chaos, or co-opt the Machel government. The first group did lose out when Nkomati was signed.[39] But it seems likely that even P.W. Botha and the State Security Council have not yet chosen between the latter two options.

In the initial glow of Nkomati, Prime Minister P.W. Botha was able to make a triumphal visit to Europe; dozens of businessmen flooded into Maputo. Since then, South Africa's world image has deteriorated to the point where Nkomati makes little difference, while the businessmen were shocked to find the level of Mozambican underdevelopment and to realise that there were few quick sales to be made. Thus much of the pressure from diplomats and businessmen that led to the signing of Nkomati has now evaporated. Meanwhile, the MNR's disruption is keeping the Maputo-Zimbabwe railway closed and diverting traffic to South Africa. So the South African leadership is probably happy for the MNR to continue as it is.

South Africa used Nkomati to evict the ANC from Mozambique without having to give up anything significant itself. This led to the assumption that it was possible to extract further concessions from Frelimo. And it is clear from an examination of the documents captured from Casa Banana that some policy change was made in July 1984. It appears that increased support was to be permitted (see Chapter 6). But there was no agreement as to just how far to go, or even as to what concessions were desired.

South Africa is pressing for more formal diplomatic recognition. It also wants its troops to be allowed into Mozambique, because this would give credence to its claims to be regional policeman. This has been suggested for a variety of purposes: to guard returning MNR men, to guard South African workers repairing railways or power lines, and even to assist in simple agricultural development tasks. Mozambique has always refused.[40]

Outside South Africa there are also different demands and different aims for the MNR. Bulhosa wants his refinery back, so the MNR made explicitly neo-colonial demands for Portuguese who fled at independence to be able to return to their previous privileged positions, and to reoccupy the houses, farms, and businesses they had abandoned when they departed in unnecessary panic. The Portuguese government seems not willing to go that far, but it does apparently want to push Frelimo to become more pro-Western and more open to foreign capital. It felt it had US support for this, and that as a reward it would be made an intermediary. Portugal has no capital to invest, but because of language and its colonial experience, it was openly saying that US capital should go to Mozambique through Portugal.[41] In this, Portugal was directly competing with South Africa to serve as a sub-imperialist power.

In practice, there were sharp divisions amongst international business as to whether more concessions were required. US, British, and large South African and Portuguese firms wanted more concessions. After a seven-hour meeting with President Samora Machel, the American financier David Rockefeller stressed that 'Mozambique has a long way to go before foreign investors are going to find it an attractive place to put their money.' He suggested that Mozambique should join the Rand Zone and South Africa's Consas-linked development bank.[42] Smaller South African and Portuguese companies, as well as Italy, argued that the point had been won — saying that as with Mugabe in Zimbabwe, talk of socialism was now largely rhetoric (or was linked to health and education services which were essential in any case) and that Mozambique was genuinely open to foreign capital. Italy has become Mozambique's biggest foreign partner, with more than US$300m in dam and electricity projects. The MNR's backers supported the former line, and stepped up attacks on foreign workers, including South Africans, Italians, and Portuguese.

South African support continues

South Africa always denies at the time that it is supporting the MNR (Renamo). But Pretoria has finally admitted supporting it in the past. 'Naturally there was a time when we helped train and support Renamo,' Foreign Minister Pik Botha said in the South African parliament on 25 April 1985. 'We helped Renamo. I want to affirm today that under similar circumstances, we would do it again.'[43]

After Nkomati, South Africa tried to argue that it had clean hands. It claimed the MNR was an independent organisation outside South African control, supported by Malawi, the Comoros, and in South Africa only by private former Portuguese citizens. To back this up, it was South Africa itself that leaked to journalists much of the information about the Comoros and the 'Portuguese connection'. For a time even the Mozambique government seemed convinced. Eventually the evidence of continued South African support for the MNR became overwhelming. Security Minister Sergio Vieira said later that it was clear South Africa was planning to violate the accord even before signing it.[44]

The South African press reported that in April 1985, a year after the Nkomati signing, South African police in areas near the border town of Komatipoort were still detaining alleged illegal immigrants from Mozambique, who would then be visited by white men asking if they wanted to join the MNR. One man who has relatives in Mozambique but is South African and has a reference book ('pass') was arrested twice and told that he could avoid repeated further arrests only by joining the MNR.[45]

Links with the main base at Gorongosa were stepped up after Nkomati. When the base fell in August 1985, the Mozambicans found a log book recording the comings and goings at the base. An angry President Samora Machel summoned Foreign Minister Pik Botha to Maputo on 16 September and accused Pretoria of violating Nkomati. The Mozambicans did not detail their evidence; instead Machel mentioned some of what was recorded, and as proof tore just two pages out of the log book and gave them to Pik Botha.

Three days later Pik Botha held a press conference to admit a host of violations.[46] After Nkomati South Africa had extended the landing strip at the Gorongosa base. South African planes flew arms and other supplies there, and ferried MNR and SADF officials between South Africa and Gorongosa; in at least one case the SADF sent a submarine up the coast to pick up an MNR leader. Botha also admitted that South Africa maintained radio contact, in violation of a section of the Nkomati Accord explicitly banning this. Most damning of all, Pik Botha admitted that his then deputy, Louis Nel, had flown into Gorongosa for meetings with Dhlakama three times during June, July, and August 1985.[47]

South African arrogance remained undiminished, however. A deputy foreign minister going into a foreign country without permission to talk to anti-government guerrillas, and the sending of submarines into a foreign country's territorial waters, were dismissed by Pik Botha as mere 'technical violations' of Nkomati.

One final story shows South Africa's continuing role. After Nkomati the MNR increasingly cut the road and power line between South Africa and Maputo. The electricity line was hit eight times in the period from October 1984 to February 1985. Then on 21 January 1985, just a week before the SADCC meeting in Swaziland, the MNR damaged a key railway bridge on the Maputo-South Africa line, just 14km from the South African border. It was repaired with South African help. Another bridge was hit on 6 February, and again repaired with South African help. Incidents along the road, railway, and power line were all close to the South African border, and it was clear that South Africa was involved. In one case the MNR were seen running back over the border, and in another Mozambique said a white South African officer had been captured. Not unrelated was the fact that until late 1984 South Africa needed Maputo for coal exports, and had been under pressure by coal mine operators in the eastern Transvaal to allow the export of more coal by the cheaper Maputo route. But the recession in South Africa was beginning to bite, and South African Railways (SAR) was about to lay off workers at the port of East London when coal was suddenly diverted from Maputo because of the line closures.

Then on 26 March Maputo was hit by a disaster not of South African making. A cyclone blew down 31 pylons on the electricity line — more than the MNR had hit in its whole campaign. The US government gave Mozambique $250,000 for an emergency purchase of coal in South Africa for Maputo's coal fired power station, and this was due to start arriving at the beginning of April at the rate of 1000 tonnes per day. For three weeks, SAR refused to provide wagons. Mozambique made a public protest, calling it 'an open boycott of support action given priority by the international community'. Finally on 27 April SAR told Mozambique it would give priority to the coal shipments. The only problem was that the night before a railway bridge 8km from the border had been sabotaged.[48]

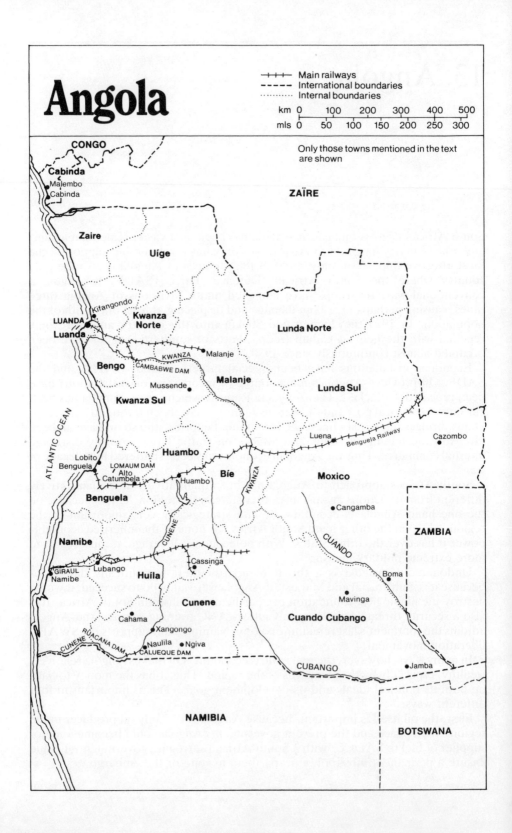

Angola

- ┼┼┼ Main railways
- ‑ ‑ ‑ International boundaries
- ⋯⋯ Internal boundaries

km	0		100	200	300	400	500
mls	0	50	100	150	200	250	300

Only those towns mentioned in the text are shown

CONGO

Cabinda
Malembo
Cabinda

ZAÏRE

Zaire

Uíge

Kifangondo

LUANDA
Luanda

Kwanza
Norte

Lunda Norte

KWANZA
CAMBABWE DAM
Malanje

Bengo

Malanje

Lunda Sul

Mussende

Kwanza Sul

ATLANTIC OCEAN

Luena
Benguela Railway
Cazombo

Huambo

Lobito
Benguela
LOMAUM DAM
Alto
Catumbela
Huambo

Bié

KWANZA

Moxico

Cangamba

ZAMBIA

Benguela

Namibe

CUNENE

Cassinga

Huíla

CUANDO

Boma

Lubango

Cunene

Mavinga

Cahama

Cuando Cubango

GIRAUL
Namibe

Xangongo

RUACANA DAM
CUNENE
Naulila • Ngiva
CALUEQUE DAM

CUBANGO

Jamba

NAMIBIA

BOTSWANA

13. Angola

South African aggression against Angola has been on a vaster scale than against any other country in southern Africa. Not only has it rebuilt and supported the most effective opposition movement in the region, but Angola is also the only country where the South African 'Defence' Force (SADF) is waging a conventional war. Its troops have launched major invasions of Angola three times, causing perhaps $12,000m damage and displacing at least one-tenth of the population. In 1975 they penetrated 800km into the country and were only repelled with the help of Cuban troops. Parts of southern Angola have been occupied almost continuously since 1980.[1]

Economic installations have been special targets of both UNITA and the SADF. Oil provides Angola's main source of income, so oil installations have been repeatedly attacked. The Benguela Railway which serves Zambia has been cut since 1980; local port and railway installations have been frequently attacked. Dams, bridges, electricity lines, the iron mine, factories, and so on have all been hit. And the mining of roads and attacks on traffic have seriously disrupted internal commerce. Thus the Angolan economy has been shattered by a decade of war.

South Africa's approach to Angola has been qualitatively and quantitatively different from its actions against any other state in the region. This is because on the one hand Angola is economically and strategically very important in the region, while on the other hand South Africa has none of the inherited economic power it has over the other states. With no economic leverage, it must resort to more extreme military measures.

Undoubtedly, Angola is a threat to apartheid. It is politically dangerous because it is multi-racial and Marxist; if Angola were allowed to succeed, it would destroy the ideological foundation of apartheid capitalism in South Africa. It is also a security threat. Angola openly allows ANC training camps. And Angola adjoins the continent's last remaining colony, Namibia, and supports the SWAPO liberation movement.

In many ways, however, the real issue is economic. Oil makes Angola relatively wealthy, especially by the standards of the region. Thus it has the money to back up both its political ideals and its development goals. This is important in four different ways.

First, the oil itself is important, because Angola is the only oil producer in the region. With peace and the present government, Angola could become a major supplier of fuel to SADCC; with a South African surrogate government, it could ensure a permanent oil supply for apartheid in spite of the embargo.

Second, the oil income means that Angola cannot be economically squeezed in the same way as Mozambique, and thus cannot be forced into an Nkomati-style non-aggression pact. With no diplomatic or economic leverage, armed force is South Africa's only weapon.

Third, just as gold paid for the industrialisation of South Africa, so oil can pay for Angolan development — on a Marxist rather than a capitalist model. But such development requires peace, so a primary South African goal must be simple destabilisation — preventing the peace needed for development.

Finally, Angola is potentially important to SADCC, not just because of oil and the Benguela Railway, but also because it could be an economic force for the whole region. Thus South African aggression sharply reduces the role of a key SADCC member.

South African action is determined by opportunity as well as need, and in some cases the opportunity has been generated by previous action. The most valuable opportunity for South Africa was provided by the fragmentation of the original liberation movements, which never coalesced into one group as in Mozambique. This invited intervention, and South Africa supported UNITA even before independence, helping to create the conditions that prevented a coalition government at independence. Once South African intervention had prevented the movements from coming together, UNITA became the obvious surrogate army to keep pressure on the Angolan government. It was more useful and more powerful than the other three surrogate armies South Africa later created or adopted, because UNITA had a genuine history and an historic base. It was thus an excellent agent of destabilisation, and could potentially be propelled into government.

The second opportunity was created by the United States, which in 1974 and 1975 encouraged South Africa to come in on the side of UNITA (indeed, South Africa believed it had a promise of US military and economic help).

The third opportunity was created by the first two. South African and US pressure forced Angola into a much closer relationship with the eastern bloc than had been intended; Angola called in Cuban troops only because of the South African invasion. But for cold warriors this provides further justification for South African aggression, and permits South Africa to delay Namibian independence and link it with a Cuban withdrawal. This allows South Africa to create a circle: continued aggression requires the continued presence of Cuban troops, which South Africa says prevents the independence of Namibia and justifies US involvement. Thus South African attacks serve a useful political function by keeping the tension high.

The fourth opportunity is not connected to the other three, but rather to South Africa's lack of historic involvement. Disruptive actions against several of the other states in the region have been curbed by diplomatic or economic considerations, particularly a desire not to disrupt existing trade links. With no such links in Angola to disrupt, the military has a freer hand. Thus South Africa wages an entirely military campaign against Angola both because it can and because it has no other weapons.

In this context, it is possible to suggest a series of immediate and longer term goals. In the short term, South Africa wants to:

● cause as much general chaos and disruption as possible, to prevent development and create discontent;

● hit particular key economic targets, especially oil facilities and the Benguela railway;
● attack SWAPO and the ANC; and
● promote and support UNITA, both as an agent of destabilisation, and as a possible political force.

It seems likely that in the short term, at least, South Africa wants to keep the Cubans in Angola. This is seen both as a way of drawing the US into backing South Africa, and as an excuse not to settle in Namibia. If Angola were to withdraw the Cubans, however, on its past record South Africa would be likely to invade and try again to install UNITA. South Africa has been unwilling to remove that threat, making clear, for example, that it is not prepared to end its support for UNITA, even in exchange for the departure of the Cubans.

In the longer term, South Africa wants to change the government of Angola. In part, this is because Angola is the one state in the region where it feels it has a chance to install a surrogate government — namely UNITA. But also South Africa knows that a peaceful Angola under the present government represents a major threat and that there can be no Nkomati-style accommodation with Angola.

Divided struggle — to 1974

Because of the importance of UNITA, and because major South African intervention began earlier here than elsewhere, it is necessary to look more closely at the pre-independence period of Angola. Three groups waged armed struggle against the Portuguese in the 1960s and early 1970s. They were divided on both class and ethnic grounds.[2]

The FNLA was based in Bakongo refugees in neighbouring Zaire (previously Belgian Congo). Its leadership was formed from traditional chiefs, businessmen, and small traders which, combined with a Baptist education, gave it a conservative orientation. It built a small army in exile which largely waited for the Portuguese to withdraw; although active in the two northern provinces it seemed to gain little popular support.

UNITA's leaders, including its head Jonas Savimbi, were largely Congregationalist-educated Ovimbundu. It had support among peasants, particularly the Ovimbundu, who form the largest single ethnic group and live mainly in the rich central highlands. Savimbi had been a member of the FNLA until he broke with it in 1964, accusing it of tribalism and serving American imperialism. He then formed UNITA among Angolan refugees in Zambia. The MPLA leadership tended to be Mbundu and Methodist-educated; its base was in the urban proletariat and public sector workers, particularly in Luanda. While class and ethnic origin played a role, it is important not to look at support for the various groups either in strictly class or strictly ethnic terms. For example, UNITA and MPLA both drew support from Ovimbundu workers, while some non-Ovimbundu peasants supported UNITA.

By 1967, all three groups were fighting inside Angola, but the MPLA was better organised and more active. UNITA was in the central highlands, west and south of Luso (now Luena), while the MPLA was active further east. Documents released after the coup in Portugal, as well as interviews in Angola after independence, show that UNITA had contacts with the Portuguese secret police, PIDE, from 1969. In 1971 UNITA and the Portuguese military came to a written agreement. The military wanted to stop the MPLA's westward movement and they worked on the probably correct assumption that UNITA hated the MPLA more than the Portuguese. The agreement authorised UNITA control of an area near Luso, in exchange for UNITA opposing any MPLA advance into that area.[3]

In general, the CIA and the South Africans backed the Portuguese, but the 25 April 1974 coup in Portugal changed the entire picture.[4] In its other colonies, Portugal eventually accepted the inevitability of independence led by the liberation movement. But in Angola, with the largest number of whites (350,000) and with the liberation movements divided, Portugal saw an opportunity for a neo-colonial solution. UNITA quickly, and FNLA later, signed cease-fires with Portugal and entered secret negotiations. Both accepted General Antonio de Spinola's view that Angola was not ready for independence, and that there could be only gradual decolonisation.

But the MPLA rejected neo-colonialism and held out. By mid-1974 it controlled 11 of 16 provincial capitals (FNLA controlled two in the north, UNITA three in the centre). With Spinola's overthrow in September 1974 and the advent of successively more radical governments in Portugal, the MPLA signed a cease-fire in November. In January 1975 there was an all-party conference in Alvor, Portugal, which agreed on a transitional government of MPLA, UNITA, FNLA, and Portuguese representatives, with independence on 11 November 1975.

CIA and South Africa move in — 1975-76

Portugal may have opted out, but the CIA and South Africa did not accept the Alvor agreement. According to John Stockwell, the former chief of the CIA Angola Task Force, within days of the Alvor agreement the US government decided to step up CIA involvement, and by July it had authorised $14m for FNLA and UNITA.[5] The goal was 'to prevent an easy victory by Soviet-backed forces in Angola'. In other words, the CIA could not prevent an MPLA dominated government, but it could create as much chaos as possible so that it would not be 'easy' for the MPLA.[6]

The first action was in the north. In February 1975, with US and Zairian encouragement, the FNLA began attacking the MPLA in northern Angola and then in Luanda, in direct violation of the Alvor Accord. The fighting in Luanda intensified in July, but Luanda was the MPLA's home ground and it evicted the FNLA (and UNITA).

With South African help and encouragement, Mobutu committed two elite Zaire battalions in an attempt to take Luanda before independence day, 11 November. By the end of October, the joint FNLA-Zaire column had reached Kifangondo, 20km from the capital. Two South African planes landed with long range artillery and South African artillerymen, who began shelling Luanda on 9 November. The following day the joint FNLA, Zairian, and South African armoured column moved across the valley toward the capital. John Stockwell tells how CIA and South African observers sat on a ridge to watch the capture of Luanda. Instead, it was a rout, because the Cubans had arrived two days before with heavy weapons.[7] The FNLA and Zairian troops fled in panic; South Africa sent a frigate up the coast to rescue its artillerymen.[8] At midnight of 10/11 November, the MPLA declared independence.

Meanwhile, with CIA encouragement, South Africa had moved in support of

UNITA in the south. On 9 August 1975 more than 1,000 troops with armoured cars and helicopters were sent to 'guard' South African workers on the Ruacana and Calueque dams, part of a major hydroelectricity project near the Namibian border.[9] During August and September South African troops crossed the border in several places. Throughout central and southern Angola, the South Africans began sending in supplies for UNITA (and the FNLA, then also present in those areas), and setting up training camps for UNITA.

Finally, on 16 October 1975 the South African army invaded. The MPLA was no match and retreated before the advancing armoured column as it moved up the coast. By 15 November it had moved 700km north and was only 200km from the capital. The arrival of the first Cuban troops halted any further advance of that column. But in November and December two other South African armoured columns entered Angola further east, and they continued. One took Luena on the Benguela railway on 11 December.

Whenever South African forces captured a town, UNITA and the FNLA moved in to set up local administrations. On 23 November they announced the formation of a joint government of the Democratic Republic of Angola. But within a month they had fallen out, and there was fighting between UNITA and FNLA troops in several cities.

In these circumstances, the MPLA appealed for help from the eastern bloc. Cuba and the Soviet Union were not prepared to allow the US and South Africa to defeat the MPLA, and they poured in support during December and January. Meanwhile the CIA role became public and the US Congress took umbrage. A ban on the expenditure of US military funds in Angola, except to gather intelligence, was passed by the Senate in December and the House of Representatives in January. It was signed into law by President Ford on 9 February. It became known as the Clark Amendment, after Dick Clark, chairman of the Senate subcommittee on African Affairs, and one of those who first proposed it.[10]

By then it was clear that Pretoria would not get the support it expected from Washington, and in mid-January South African troops began to withdraw, leaving UNITA in the lurch. On 27 March, the withdrawal was completed. As they retreated in front of Cuban and Angolan forces, the South Africans destroyed much of the remaining infrastructure. Hundreds of road bridges were destroyed, including 50 major ones. Angola estimated the total damage at $6.7bn.[11]

South Africa withdraws and UNITA collapses — 1977-79

With the South African retreat, UNITA was expelled from the main towns. There seem to have been atrocities on both sides, with retreating UNITA forces killing several hundred MPLA supporters and advancing MPLA forces killing UNITA supporters in retaliation. UNITA clearly retained strong support. MPLA officials later estimated that at least 350,000, and possibly more than one million, peasants in Bie and Huambo provinces fled into the wooded highlands to follow retreating UNITA guerrillas.[12] Most of the Angolan leaders of the Congregational Church joined UNITA in the bush. During the following three years, UNITA guerrillas totally disrupted commerce and food production in the central highlands, formerly the granary of Angola.

The Benguela Railway was the main outlet to the sea for minerals from Zambia and Zaire's Shaba province, and thus is of more strategic importance in Angola than anything but oil. During the liberation war, Zambia and Zaire had supported UNITA, in part out of fear of the Benguela falling under 'communist' control, while the MPLA had carefully not attacked the line so as not to offend those two states. During the 1976-78 period, UNITA made the Benguela a particular target, destroying 20 of 25 diesel locomotives, and virtually closing the railway.

Low-level South African activity continued, particularly at first. Between 3 April and 30 July 1976 there were 17 South African raids in Angola. During the following three years, there were several more raids, and nearly 200 minelaying operations. And there was continued support for UNITA; for example in 1977 a joint UNITA/South African column moved nearly 200km north into Cuando-Cubango province in the southeast.[13] Nevertheless, South African action was at a much lower level than before or later.[14]

As South African support for UNITA decreased and the MPLA mounted a series of successful offensives, the MPLA gained the upper hand over UNITA by mid-1979. In the central highlands, tens of thousands of ragged, disenchanted UNITA supporters flooded out of the bush to return to their old villages. Sporadic UNITA raids continued, but for the first time in many years people travelled freely on the main roads through the central highlands. The foreign press could fairly talk about 'the recent rout of UNITA'.[15] The Benguela Railway was reopened to international traffic for the first time since 1975. The first Zairian manganese reached the sea in August 1979, and in July 1980 Zambian copper was exported through the Atlantic Ocean port of Lobito. An EEC-organised donors conference raised $18m, and rehabilitation of the railways was started.[16]

1980 was to be Angola's best year ever. War was at its lowest level and the economy hit its peak. Much of the damage caused by the 1975 invasions had been repaired. Angola held its first parliamentary elections. The MPLA held a special congress to look optimistically towards socialist development.

South Africa moves back

The South African defeat in Angola in 1976 was an important factor in the final collapse of the Vorster government in South Africa (along with the Soweto uprising, the information scandal, and various other causes). Until the government crisis inside South Africa could be resolved, it was impossible to mount any further large-scale operations against Angola. But P.W. Botha had been Minister of Defence at the time of the 1975 invasion; when he became Prime Minister, one of his first actions was to step up pressure again on Angola.

On 26 September 1979 the South African Air Force (SAAF) bombed Lubango and Xangongo. Lubango is the provincial capital of Huila province and is more than 200km north of the border. The mid-morning raid destroyed, among other buildings, one of the largest furniture factories in Angola killing 26 workers. A month later helicopter borne troops returned to the area of Lubango to sabotage a railway line by blowing up bridges and a tunnel. In November South African ground troops captured the village of Naulila, 30km north of the Namibian border in Cunene province.

For several months there was relative calm. Then in April and May 1980 there was a series of South African air and ground force raids on villages in Cunene and Cuando-Cubango, some more than 50km inside the border. Cuando-Cubango is one of Angola's largest provinces, but it is semi-desert and has only 2% of the country's people.

Up to this time, South Africa had played down its incursions. But in June the

South African Defence Force (SADF) announced 'Operation Smokeshell', a full scale invasion of parts of Cunene and Cuando-Cubango, which involved a larger military force than the 1975 invasion.

In an unusual raid in September 1980, the SADF moved into a zone far from previous actions, and captured and destroyed Mavinga, a town in central Cuando-Cubango 250km from Namibia, for reasons that will become clearer in the discussion of UNITA below.[17]

The Carter administration in the United States seems to have served as a restraining hand on the South African military. With the election of Ronald Reagan, that was removed, and the SADF quickly lashed out in both Mozambique and Angola. From the beginning of 1981, there was permanent war in southern Angola. President José Eduardo dos Santos said that in the first 11 months of 1981 there had been 53 South African troop operations, more than 100 bombing raids, and 1,600 reconnaissance flights.[18]

The biggest was 'Operation Protea' in which more than 5,000 South African troops occupied all the main towns in Cunene for several weeks. Angolan troops by then were much better trained and equipped than they had been when they faced the South African invasion in 1975, so they were able to stop the South African advance at Cahama, 110km north of the border. But the air force penetrated further, severely damaging Cahama. On 5 September it strafed a party of 36 journalists, superficially injuring BBC correspondent Mike Wooldridge and calling down unfavourable comment on South Africa in, among other papers, the *Daily Telegraph*.[19]

During Operation Protea, towns were flattened and an estimated 130,000 refugees were sent fleeing north. Others were kidnapped and taken to Namibia; cattle were driven to Namibia as well. The idea seemed to be to create a cleared buffer zone; after Operation Protea, several thousand South African troops remained in occupation of a 70km-deep strip of southern Cunene, including the provincial capital of Ngiva.[20] South African newspapers reported that in 1982 the SADF started operating the Ruacana/Calueque hydro-electricity scheme, sending power to Namibia.[21]

During the following two years there were major South African attacks almost weekly, but several are worth special note:

● In December 1981 SAAF planes made their first bombing raids into the huge and sparsely populated Moxico province, more than 350km from Namibia.
● On 16 May 1982 the SAAF attacked Angola's only iron mine, at Kassinga, 250km from Namibia. Mining equipment was destroyed and a power station and the railway line were damaged.
● In August 1983 South African ground troops captured Cangamba, in Moxico province 450km from Namibia.
● Operation Askari in December 1983 and January 1984, in which the SADF pushed 300km north, capturing Kassinga and bombing Lubango and other towns. The SADF pulled back only after suffering heavier losses than expected, and being privately warned by the Soviet Union not to escalate the conflict.[22]

In addition there were a series of sea-borne commando raids:

● Lobito oil terminal, 12 August 1980.
● Luanda oil refinery, 30 November 1981, causing $12.5m in damage and preventing the export of $24m in oil while the refinery was closed for four months. A white body was found after the raid.

● Road and rail bridges over the Giraul River near the port of Namibe were seriously damaged on 7 November 1982.
● Cabinda oil pipeline, 12 July 1984.
● Limpet mines used to sink two cargo ships in Luanda harbour, 29 July 1984.

South Africa claimed that all its raids into Angola were only against SWAPO bases, and it is clear that some attacks were aimed at SWAPO. But most were either to cause economic damage or to assist UNITA. There is ample evidence that the SADF was picking out Angolan military and economic targets. Angolan military camps were hit, and traffic on roads frequently attacked from the air.

Perhaps the most clearly economic target was the Kassinga iron mine, which had been damaged in the 1975 invasion and had not operated since. South Africa makes much of Angola's economic links with the eastern bloc, but in this case Angola signed an agreement with Voest-Alpine, an Austrian parastatal which also has contracts with the Zimbabwean and South African iron and steel parastatals. Voest-Alpine had contracted to take 1.1m tonnes of iron per year, and to rehabilitate the Kassinga mine. In late 1981 140,000 tonnes of stockpiled ore was shipped to Austria; the rehabilitation was well under way when the SAAF bombed the mine and ancillary facilities on 16 May 1982. The Giraul River bridge, which was hit by South African commandos on 7 November that year, was important primarily as the export route for Kassinga iron ore. In Operation Askari the town of Kassinga was occupied. The iron mine is probably the most important economic installation in southern Angola, and it seems obvious that South Africa did not want a Western-backed project in the buffer zone that it hoped to create.

The Lusaka accord

By early 1984, South African and UNITA military action had displaced more than 600,000 people — nearly one-tenth of the population.[23] Tens of millions of dollars of damage had been done, and the internal economy was almost totally disrupted. As part of its new peacemaking image, in early 1984 South Africa made a limited agreement with Angola on troop withdrawal. It was largely organised by US diplomats trying to find something to show for constructive engagement. After several days of negotiations in Lusaka between South African and Angolan military and US diplomats, the accord was agreed on 16 February 1984 by Pik Botha, Angolan Interior Minister Alexandre Rodrigues, and Chester Crocker.

It called for the withdrawal of South African troops from a triangle with the Namibia border as its base, the Cunene and Cubango rivers as its sides, and Kassinga as its apex. The zone corresponds approximately to Cunene Province. It was called the 'area in question', and thus referred to in conversation as the 'AIQ'. It was divided into five strips, demarcated simply by drawing horizontal lines on a map. South African troops were to move south out of them at roughly one strip per week, finally leaving Angola by the end of March. A Joint Monitoring Commission composed of Angolan and South African military personnel would oversee the withdrawal. It was agreed that no 'outside forces' — that is UNITA or SWAPO — would move into the zone.

The accord was extremely limited, covering only the western half of the Namibia-Angola border. This was because South Africa refused to even discuss its support for UNITA, so the AIQ excluded Cuando-Cubango province where the main South African activity was support of UNITA. Instead, the AIQ was defined only to include those areas occupied by South African troops during Operation Askari.

Diplomatic sources gave the following explanation for the limited nature of the accord. Both sides were anxious for a military disengagement. Operation Askari had been unexpectedly heavy going for the South African forces. SWAPO had retreated, as usual, and the SADF faced FAPLA, the Angolan army. FAPLA proved well equipped, trained, and disciplined, and fought more skilfully and harder than the SADF expected. Improved anti-aircraft batteries prevented the SADF from using its air power, leading to larger than expected SADF losses. For its part, FAPLA had resisted the invasion only by throwing its best troops against the SADF. UNITA was expanding rapidly in the north, and FAPLA wanted to move troops there. Thus both sides were anxious for a troop withdrawal, and accepted the limited nature of the accord. On the US side, the accord was seen as a preliminary 'confidence building exercise'. It was, one diplomat explained, intended to 'try to get a conveyor belt going'; once Angola and South Africa were on the belt, the US hoped they would be carried into agreements on Cuban troop withdrawal and a Namibia settlement.

The text of the accord has never been published, and left a number of issues vague. The most important were, first, the position of UNITA and SWAPO groups already in the AIQ, and second, what happened when the withdrawal was completed.

In some respects, the accord was adhered to, at least initially. The Angolan and South African military got on well within the Joint Monitoring Commission (JMC). SWAPO promised Angola that it would reduce its activity in the zone, and did so. And the withdrawal continued, albeit very much more slowly than had been agreed at Lusaka.

Both UNITA and SWAPO groups were found by the commission in the AIQ. In each case, it was claimed that they were not new (and thus not in violation of the accord). South Africa admitted that it had installed UNITA units in the area during its occupation, and that some were trying to stay behind after the withdrawal. It was never clear, however, if, as the Angolans claimed, South Africa was delaying the withdrawal to allow more time for UNITA to move in or, as the South Africans said privately, that they had hoped UNITA would move in but that in fact so many UNITA troops were tied up further north that Jonas Savimbi refused to commit people to a zone in which he had little interest. As to SWAPO, South Africa publicly accused Angola of violating the accord by allowing SWAPO into the zone. Privately, it accepted that in the three years it had controlled the zone, the SADF had been unable to stop SWAPO infiltration, and so could hardly expect Angola to do so.

The withdrawal did begin, albeit slowly. In May the South Africans finally pulled out of Ngiva, the capital of Cunene province, which they had occupied since August 1981. But just south of Ngiva, the SADF stopped its withdrawal; it had left four of the five strips but remained in occupation of a 40km wide strip between Ngiva and the border. Finally, on 2 July 1984 the South African foreign ministry announced that it was halting the withdrawal, 'pending a response from Luanda on key issues'. (See Chapter 6 for a more detailed discussion of these demands.)

The announcement that it would not carry out the Lusaka accord came less than a month after the triumphal visit of Pik and P.W. Botha to Europe, at a time when they felt most self-confident and arrogant. There was also an internal backlash in

South African government circles at any proposals for ending support for UNITA and the MNR.

Then, suddenly and without warning, in April 1985 South Africa announced that it would withdraw its troops. With much fanfare, it did so. But it left behind a company of 60 men controlling the Ruacana/Calueque hydro-electricity scheme, which the SADF was running to supply power to Namibia. Angola protested. Pik Botha called on Angola to negotiate 'at ministerial level' about the continued supply of power.[24] Angola refused, and several weeks later the South Africans withdrew from there as well.

Resurrecting UNITA

By 1979, UNITA was effectively defeated, and no longer a major threat to the Angolan government. Thus the immediate goal of the new P.W. Botha government in South Africa was to rebuild UNITA, to prevent peace from breaking out in Angola. The formation of SADCC in April 1980, and the key role to be played by Angola, made this task all the more urgent.

Thus the central purpose of the South African invasions was to resurrect UNITA. At the height of the 1981 Operation Protea, one ' Johannesburg newspaper headline said baldly: 'SA raids will strengthen UNITA'. It explained that military sources expected UNITA to 'cash in on the situation'.[25] And UNITA did move in behind the SADF. As one refugee from Operation Protea commented: 'It is obvious that UNITA and the South African forces work together. UNITA fighters wear the same boots and carry the same rifles as the South African soldiers.'[26] And captured UNITA guerrillas talked of being trained by South Africa in Namibia, and of being brought to UNITA areas by South African helicopters.

Sometimes South Africa uses its special '32 Battalion', also known as the 'Buffalo Battalion', to support UNITA and for liaison between SADF and UNITA. It is also used for torture and terror tactics inside Angola. This special battalion is under military intelligence, and is composed largely of Angolans, with some former Rhodesians and a sprinkling of western mercenaries. Details of it were revealed by two men who defected, a British mercenary and an Angolan who had been part of FNLA and was recruited by South Africa with other FNLA members into 32 Battalion in December 1975.[27]

In some instances, the SADF assists UNITA with direct military actions. In September 1980 the SADF had moved far off its normal path to capture Mavinga, a remote town in Cuando-Cubango. UNITA clearly followed, because in early 1981 the United Nations High Commission for Refugees reported 10,000 refugees fleeing into Zambia from UNITA. Then Savimbi set up his forward headquarters in Mavinga,[28] and UNITA expanded its activity into sparsely populated areas of Cuando-Cubango and Moxico in southeast Angloa.

Undoubtedly the most dramatic example was the capture of Cangamba in August 1982. As *The Times* (London) explained simply: 'For the first time, a large UNITA force tried to take a government position. It seems they failed, and the South Africans intervened.'[29] Lt-Col Ngongo, Angola's deputy army chief of staff, explained what happened.[30] In March, during the dry season, artillery, Panhard armoured cars, and lorryloads of food and ammunition were driven from the Caprivi strip and up the isolated (and then dry) banks of the Cuando River to near Cangamba. On 2 August a massive attack was launched against Cangamba, with heavy artillery and several thousand UNITA men. But the Angolans defended the town, and on 9 August UNITA was forced to withdraw, leaving behind hundreds of dead guerrillas. Then on 14 August the SAAF bombed the town, effectively destroying it. Only then did the Angolans withdraw, leaving the shattered town to UNITA forces brought in by helicopter.

With this kind of support, UNITA spread rapidly through much of southern and central Angola. In the south UNITA moved into areas just north of the South African forces, for example attacking the Namibe-Lubango-Kassinga railway. By 1983 UNITA dominated much of the semi-desert provinces of Cuando-Cubango and Moxico, and foreign journalists were being taken to the forward base at Mavinga.[31]

In the centre, the Benguela Railway was the priority target, and it was closed in late 1980, only a year after it had begun international operation again. By 1982 UNITA was active in all four central provinces, and travel had become difficult again in the central highlands. In May 1985, for example, the peasants near Huambo produced a bumper harvest — but much of it rotted as a result of lack of transport and the absence of consumer goods, which left the peasants with little incentive to sell their crops. Both were direct results of UNITA disruptions of commerce.

By late 1982 UNITA was active north of the railway, particularly in Malanje province. This was particularly worrying for the authorities, because Malanje was a strong MPLA area and it was a priority for agricultural development projects. By 1984 UNITA had moved into the northern province of Uije where it began to attack coffee plantations within 100km of the Zaire border. It was also active in Kwanza Norte, on the road between Malanje and Luanda.

UNITA forces were able to launch increasingly bold attacks. On 19 January 1983 they sabotaged Angola's second biggest dam, at Lomaun, causing flooding and cutting power to two important cities, Lobito and Benguela. On 12 March 1983 UNITA raided Alto Catumbela, capturing 66 Czechs and destroying a paper factory and power station. In April 1984 a car bomb in Huambo killed at least 24 people. On 27 September 1984 guerrillas destroyed a dozen locomotives in the railway yard in the port of Benguela. UNITA hit the diamond mines in the northeast of the country in February and December 1984, in April 1985 and in March 1986. The 150km-long electricity line to Luanda was cut several times.

UNITA problems — and further intervention

All was not going well with UNITA, however. There were clear fears about the impact of the Lusaka and Nkomati Accords. Would South Africa abandon UNITA as it had promised to abandon the MNR in Mozambique? In May 1984, three months after the Lusaka Accord, Jonas Savimbi met separately with Chester Crocker and Pik Botha.[32] In July, just as agreement was being reached to resupply the MNR, Defence Minister Magnus Malan flew to Angola to reassure the UNITA leader. In September, Dr Savimbi was an official guest at P.W. Botha's inauguration as State President.

South Africa pushed UNITA north and west, in an attempt to put pressure on the capital, Luanda. But the move north was not entirely successful; UNITA became overstretched and suffered major defeats. Hundreds of guerrillas were killed or captured. The Angolans found 40 tonnes of assorted weapons and explosives that had been parachuted into Malanje by South African planes between 19 and 27 April 1985, but which UNITA had not been able to pick up. According to the government, it included more than 500,000 rounds of ammunition, 1,000 mortar shells, 1,800 hand grenades, more than 1,000 mines, and nearly 7 tonnes of explosives. There were also large quantities of UNITA propaganda.[33]

With UNITA overstretched, the South Africans pulling back, and the Angolan army and especially the air force significantly improved and re-armed, Angola launched a highly successful offensive against UNITA in August 1985. Pushing south from the Benguela railway, the government recaptured Cazombo (150km south of the railway and 100km from Zambia). Then it moved south and hit Mavinga. This was more than the South Africans could accept, and they launched a new raid into Angola in September. It was ostensibly to attack SWAPO, but diplomats and the Western press all said it was to defend UNITA.[34] The Buffalo Battalion was sent in. For six days (28 September to 3 October) South African planes bombed Angolan positions near Mavinga.[35] South African armoured cars moved in to defend the town, which served as UNITA forward headquarters.

Finally, Defence Minister Magnus Malan was forced to admit that South Africa was backing UNITA, and declared that South Africa would not allow UNITA to be defeated. Malan said that South African support for UNITA served the 'interests of the free world'. He called UNITA an 'anti-Marxist people's movement' and claimed that Savimbi 'stands for the same norms and values in which we believe'.[36] South Africa sent a high-level delegation to the US to argue that, with the withdrawal of the Clark Amendment, the US had to step in and support UNITA again.

The strongest confirmation of the South African role in Angola was the failure of the 21 May 1985 raid on Gulf Oil installations in Cabinda. Two South African commandos were killed. One, Captain Wynand Petrus du Toit, was captured, and gave a press conference in Luanda on 28 May.[37] He said he had been a member of a special forces unit, the Fourth Reconnaissance Commando since 1982.[38] His previous operations had included the destruction of the Giraul Bridge near Namibe in 1982, an operation inside Angola linked to Operation Askari, and the raid on the ANC office in Maputo, Mozambique, on 17 October 1983 (See Chapter 12).[39]

For the Cabinda raid, he underwent four months of preparation. He was leader of a nine-man team which was taken up the coast on an Israeli-built ship. The team landed in inflatable boats and made their way up to the town of Malembo, where they were supposed to blow up six oil storage tanks.[40] Instead, they were caught by Angolan soldiers guarding the installation. The team carried UNITA propaganda material and a small tin of paint so that they could paint 'Viva UNITA' on the road. As du Toit explained, on 'most of the operations that we usually do, ... UNITA claims the responsiblity. If this attack was done successfully and UNITA got the responsibility for the attack, then it shows UNITA is also active in the northern part, in the province of Cabinda.' (Savimbi had publicly set the Cabinda oil installations as one of UNITA's targets, but in fact its guerrillas seem never to have penetrated Cabinda.)

Although UNITA remains primarily a South African surrogate, the Pretoria government has always tried to find other support for it (as it has done more recently with the MNR). In March 1981, soon after his inauguration, President Ronald Reagan called for the repeal of the Clark Amendment, which banned US aid to UNITA. At the time, Congress refused, but it was repealed, somewhat unexpectedly, in July 1985. Six months later, President Reagan welcomed Savimbi to the White House (see below). Although there has never been any proof, there have been repeated suggestions that the CIA was aiding UNITA despite the Clark Amendment.[41]

UNITA also has support in other right-wing US circles. A group called Citizens for America organised a meeting at UNITA's headquarters in Cuando-Cubango in June 1985 which included right-wing anti-government forces from Laos, Afghanistan, and Nicaragua.[42] Savimbi's January 1986 visit to the United States, organised by the public relations firm Black, Manafort, Stone, Kelly Inc., was much welcomed by the Conservative Caucus, a group of 29 conservative organisations in Washington.

UNITA also had traditional support from Zambia and its President, Kenneth Kaunda, who was unhappy with the Marxist MPLA. It was not until November 1976, a year after Angolan independence, that Zambia finally closed down the UNITA office in Lusaka. In July 1983 Kaunda came out firmly and declared 'we do not support UNITA'.[43]

The British multinational Lonrho is also known to have supported UNITA. For example, the *Daily Telegraph* reported that in 1974 Lonrho's head, Tiny Rowland, provided Savimbi with a plane (a Hawker Siddeley 125) and two British pilots, and that Lonrho had paid for UNITA representatives including Savimbi to visit London.[44] When President Samora Machel challenged Rowland on this when they first met, the Lonrho head replied that he had backed Savimbi only because Kaunda asked him to; Machel reportedly accepted this explanation.

Elsewhere, it has been alleged that Morocco is a firm backer of UNITA, and even that government ministers in West Germany and particularly Portugal have close links with the movement.[45]

Much the most confusing link is provided by Israel and Zaire. Israel assists Mobutu with the training and equipping of the Zaire army; the Israeli Defence Minister, Ariel Sharon, visited Zaire in late 1981 and in January 1983.[46] There are repeated reports of substantial quantities of Israeli arms, as well as other support, going to Zaire for Angolan dissidents.[47] The CIA and South Africa also work through Israel and Zaire in their support of the Zairian-based dissidents. Some of this goes to UNITA, which is said to have bases in Zaire. But in 1981 there was a joint US-South African effort to resurrect the FNLA, either directly or as a new organisation named Comira (without FNLA head Holden Roberto but with foreign mercenary assistance).[48] By 1983 the revived FNLA had moved back into northern Angola. But it was a shortlived offensive. The Angolan army made a big push, while the government announced a special amnesty for FNLA soldiers. In 1984 and 1985 at least 2,000 FNLA guerrillas and thousands of civilian supporters gave themselves up to the government, and the offensive collapsed.[49] The government victory was less notable than it might have been, however, because it appears that UNITA rather than the government took over from the FNLA in some areas.

And yet, UNITA is a presence

There is no question that UNITA has spread partly, in the words of the London *Guardian*, 'by sowing terror and destruction, and systematically creating starvation'.[50] In other words, by battering local people into accepting and feeding

UNITA. Such actions have been extensively documented, and cannot be over-emphasised. And it is obvious that the chaos in Angola, and UNITA's position today, is due largely to South African and other foreign involvement. But that is not the entire story.

The contradiction is spelled out by the case of Elias Njivaluco, who was captured in March 1985. He had been with UNITA since 1976 and was part of the UNITA group which sabotaged the Lomaun hydroelectricity dam in 1983. He said his battalion had been in Mussende, 350km southeast of Luanda, in June 1984, when four plane-loads of South African material was dropped, and the battalion was given orders to move north toward Malanje. 'We were assured that we would find massive support from the people, which didn't happen.' With constant harassment by the army and with no local support, most members of the battalion were eventually captured or killed.[51]

But Njivaluco had been with UNITA, inside Angola, for nine years. And it is clear that the lack of support in Malanje came as a surprise precisely because UNITA had received popular support elsewhere. Even the government admits that, in the words of President José Eduardo dos Santos, 'There are those who are misled into staying in the bush, either because they believe in certain family or tribal ties they have with some UNITA elements, or because they do not yet understand the presence in our country of the Cuban internationalists.'[52]

It is also apparent, in sharp contrast to the MNR in Mozambique, that UNITA is using its foreign help to establish alternative governmental structures. For example, the French organisation Médicins Sans Frontières and the South African army have assisted UNITA in setting up a working rural health service.[53] There are some agricultural developments as well. And with substantial South African support, there is regular trade across the border into Namibia.

Meanwhile, in the late 1970s when the MPLA was in control of most of the country, it made a number of mistakes which made it easier for UNITA to return. Paul Fauvet, a journalist sympathetic to the MPLA, wrote in 1980 about the tens of thousands of former UNITA supporters streaming out of the mountains, and warned then that 'the *regressados* may be disillusioned with UNITA, but that does not yet mean they are all committed supporters of the MPLA.'[54]

Despite such warnings the MPLA failed to rebuild its base among the peasants. It had always been based in the urban male working class and civil service and the Central Committee report to the 1980 Congress stressed that 'the working peasantry, owing to its living and working conditions and the concepts derived from them, is not in a position to assume the leading role in the struggle'. This is so because the peasant has 'the seeds of capitalism, since he owns a small plot of land and means of production and hopes to expand them more and more'. Thus the party must be composed of workers rather than peasants. Of the 31,098 members of the party at the time of the 1980 Congress, only 4% were peasants, compared to 37% workers and 45% 'office holders'. Only 9% were women. (By contrast, peasants were 54% of the members of Frelimo in Mozambique in 1983; 26% were women.) Thus the MPLA was poorly represented in rural areas; peasants had few links, either through mass organisations or through the party, to Luanda. Inevitably, this fuelled an existing distrust of the more privileged bureaucrats of Luanda — a distrust which has increased with the emerging stories of corruption in high places.

UNITA can also build on tribalism, because so few in the Luanda leadership are Ovimbundu. A visitor to the central highlands in 1980, at the peak of MPLA control, noted that nearly all the provincial officials and local military commanders were non-Ovimbundu. They did not speak the local language or know the local people; there were obvious tensions between the local people and officials sent from Luanda.

A central issue, however, is that peasants have gained so little from the revolution. In part this can be traced to a Luanda-based, highly centralised planning process that stressed the 'modern' sector. It was a combined technical and political choice — it appeared that only modern factories and state farms could make the big productive gains needed, only they could form the material basis for socialism, and the workers in those enterprises were to be the leading force in political change. The role of the 'traditional' sector, particularly of peasants, was downplayed — politically they did not have a place, while their potential economic contribution was vastly underestimated. Inevitably, resources — of both money and scarce skilled people — went to the modern sector. The continuing war made matters much worse, constantly drawing skilled cadres to defence and away from productive sectors. As a result, the rural areas received very little in terms of agricultural inputs or consumer goods.

'Living conditions of peasants differ little from those that existed in colonial times,' while 'the differences between the town and countryside are not only not disappearing but are tending to increase,' admitted the Central Committee report to the 1980 MPLA Congress. It went on talk of 'the lack of minimally adequate supplies to the countryside' leading to worker absenteeism, and a lack of incentive for peasants to produce for the market. That Congress called for an urgent review of the support for peasants, but four years later a Politburo member could still admit 'We have made tremendous errors in agriculture. ... We haven't supported the peasants enough in recent years.'[55]

The war has, of course, made it extremely difficult for the MPLA to carry out rural development projects. And it is not always easy to find suitable projects on which to spend oil revenues when there is such a shortage of skilled people. But whatever the causes, the lack of MPLA cells or mass organisations in rural areas to build support for the government, the absence of material gains for the peasants, and the perceived differences with Luanda must rank with terror and South African backing as reasons for the rapid spread of UNITA. As always, South Africa can build on the weaknesses of its victims.

THE ECONOMY

Angola is potentially the richest of the Front Line states, with a population of 8 million people, much fertile land with relatively reliable rainfall, and considerable mineral potential. In colonial times, the economy was structured as part of the wider Portuguese empire. There were 350,000 white settlers, many of them farmers, producing coffee and other exports. The industrial sector was extremely small.

In this economy subservient to Portugal, South Africa played a very small role. Partly this was because of colonial policy, emphasising links with Portugal itself. Partly it was a simple matter of distance, for Angola is separated from South Africa by 1000 km of Namibia. Unlike Mozambique, Angola supplied no migrant labour, and its ports were too far to be of use for South African transit traffic. A few Boer settlers did make the long trek in the 19th century, establishing themselves in southern Angola as traders and cattle farmers, but most families returned to South Africa in the 1920s.

The only major South African involvement which remains is in diamonds, which in 1983 provided 5% of Angola's exports but in the 1970s considerably more. Angola is a relatively small diamond producer, compared with Botswana, Namibia or South Africa. But output is sufficient to be of interest to De Beers, the diamond arm of Anglo, in its constant efforts to maintain control of the world diamond market (see Chapter 17). Today the diamond mines are owned 77% by the government, 17.4% by Société Générale de Belgique, and only 1.7% by De Beers. But the mines were until 1985 managed by Mining and Technical Services (MATS) and the diamonds are sold through the Central Selling Organisation, both firms owned by De Beers.

Angola has lost vast amounts of money through diamond smuggling, especially since 1981. At a huge trial in 1984, the government estimated that smuggling had cost it $140m in just two years. Contacts in Portugal and even in the former US embassy in Luanda were involved; in Portugal a company was set up purely to process smuggled diamonds. UNITA seems to have played a major role. For example, one group of journalists who went behind the lines with UNITA in 1983 were accompanied by an English diamond dealer who had come to buy the smuggled diamonds.[56]

De Beers plays a complex role in Angola's diamonds.[57] At De Beers' suggestion, Angola hired a British security firm and was able to tighten security and thus decrease smuggling. Indeed, it is suggested that one reason UNITA began attacking the mines directly was to steal stones that had previously been sold to it. Nevertheless, Angola may have felt De Beers did not do enough to curb the illegal trade. Perhaps Angola was worried that De Beers had links with UNITA and with South African security services which were too close for comfort. In any case, in June 1985 it was reported that Angola was not happy with MATS and was looking for another operator.

Immediately to the south of Angola lies the most populated part of Namibia, the 'homelands' of Ovamboland and Kavango to which South Africa confined the bulk of the black population of Namibia. In colonial times there was considerable local trade across the border, which in practice is an arbitrary colonial line dividing pre-existing African societies.[58] War in both northern Namibia and southern Angola has devastated this trade. Now the bulk of cargoes are more sinister. UNITA smuggles out rare hardwood and ivory, using a South African firm Frama Inter-Trading.[59] Press reports suggest timber sales of several million dollars a year; a South African newspaper reported that in 1982 and 1983 UNITA sold more than 100 tonnes of ivory — the tusks of 10,000 elephants — worth more than $5m.[60]

What colonial links Angola did have were rather north and east, to Zaire and Zambia. Until 1975 the Benguela railway was the main route for their mineral exports. It is today a major SADCC transport project, but its disruption by UNITA has forced Zaire and Zambia to export through South Africa. In 1981 the giant Belgian firm Société Générale bought control of Tanganyika Concessions which owns 90% of the Benguela Railway.[61] This too reflects Angola's central African links, for Société Générale has a very prominent role in Zaire, especially in mining. Its interests in Angola extend to energy (see below) and also to control of the main shipping agency, AMI. Société Générale is not entirely independent of South Africa, however: it has long and close links with Anglo American in mining throughout the region,[62] and a major interest in the De Beers industrial diamond business.

South Africa's economic role in Angola since independence has been very simple: the economy has been devastated by war. Defence spending absorbs perhaps three-quarters of the national budget and half of export revenues. Internal trade has been prevented, production disrupted and planning rendered near impossible. Production and exports of crops, manufactures and most minerals are all well below pre-independence levels. Diamond exports, for example, fell from 2.1 million carats in 1974 to 1.0 in 1983 (plus smuggled diamonds). Coffee production in 1984/5 was estimated at only 15% of its pre-independence level.

Oil

The great exception to this severe economic crisis has been oil. Despite sabotage attempts and the general state of the economy, its development has proceeded remarkably smoothly.[63] Production has risen from 135,000 barrels per day before independence to 278,000 in December 1985 and is expected to reach 500,000 in 1991. Oil sales in 1985 earned $2,500m.

Exploitation is by joint venture between the state oil company Sonangol and some of the largest Western oil companies: Chevron (through its subsidiary Gulf) and Texaco (USA), and Petrofina (Belgium). Other firms actively prospecting include Mobil (USA), Agip (Italy), Total and Elf-Aquitaine (France), Hispanoil (Spain), BP (Britain), Diminex (Federal Republic of Germany) and Petrobras (Brazil).

The Luanda refinery is managed (and 40% owned) by Petrofina, which is owned by Société Générale and the other major Belgian group, Bruxelles Lambert.[64] Petrofina is on particularly good terms with the MPLA because it rehabilitated the Luanda refinery in half the expected time after the South African sabotage. This was an important political gesture, as was Italy's agreement to rebuild the Lobito oil tanks which had been destroyed in 1980.

Similarly the transnational corporations regularly express their appreciation of the businesslike attitude of the Angolan petroleum administration. The president of Gulf Oil, for example, told the US Congress that the Angolan government has a 'responsive and supportive' attitude towards foreign business.

Angola also leads the SADCC energy sector, which has been promoting regional co-operation in electricity supply and a variety of other areas. Almost all the energy projects are fully funded, with support especially from Canada, Norway and, increasingly, the World Bank.

On the basis of oil revenue, Angola has become an extremely important trading partner for the West, in addition to its attractions for oil investment. In 1982 62% of its imports were from Western Europe and 20% from the Americas. Indeed, Angola seems to be looking consistently West. In 1985 it finally joined the EEC's Lomé Convention. The major iron ore development is with an Austrian state company. The largest project to involve the eastern bloc has Brazil as the major partner; it is the $900m Kwanza River dam, which will have turbines from the Soviet Union, but the $600m engineering contract is with Brazilian firms in exchange for oil. Although Angola nationalised Portuguese companies soon after independence, taking control of more than 85% of all firms, it did not touch non-Portuguese firms. Now there is even a return to private banks; in June 1985 the French Paribas became the first foreign bank to open in Angola.

Angola and the United States

The United States is therefore in an extraordinarily contradictory position. Angola is its fourth largest trading partner in Africa, and is keen to expand: a first trade mission visited the United States in October 1985. Angola has more economic involvement with the United States than with any other country. Chevron (Gulf) is Angola's biggest oil company with investments of around $600m; it was a Gulf installation that the South Africans tried unsuccessfully to attack in May 1985. Other major US oil companies are also involved. The US government's Export-Import Bank has underwritten more than $100m in exports to Angola; US banks are also lending extensively. Angola has an impeccable record for repaying its debts.

Nonetheless the United States still refuses diplomatic recognition to the Angolan government, and in 1986 swung firmly towards UNITA. In January President Reagan received Jonas Savimbi at the White House, saying 'We want to be very helpful to Dr Savimbi and what he is trying to do.' Savimbi met the Defence Secretary and the chairman of the Joint Chiefs of Staff. At the State Department, he was greeted by the chief of protocol, an honour normally reserved for members of government. A package of $10 to $15 million in covert CIA aid was simultaneously being discussed by the administration with Congressional committees, and a group of senior Congressmen were pressing for overt assistance to UNITA. [65]

The State Department has now recognised — though not resolved — the contradiction between support for UNITA on the one hand, and growing and profitable economic links with Angola on the other. The right-wing Conservative Caucus simply calls for Chevron to withdraw. The State Department, which in 1984 had said, 'We feel strongly that US business participation in Angola is in the long-term interest of both our nations', was in January 1986

> telling American companies active in Angola that they should take note that they are in the middle of a war zone, that they're also in the middle of a rather hot political debate in this country, and they should be thinking about US national interests as well as their own corporate interests as they make their decisions ... Much of the hard currency earned by the Angolan government with the help of these firms goes towards imports of military equipment and payments for Cuban troops. This supports war rather than the search for peace.[66]

The contrast with the US Government's attitude towards US investment in South Africa was plain to all.

The political contradictions in US policy are even greater than the economic ones. First, the US government argued that support for UNITA would induce the Angolan government to agree to a negotiated regional solution in southern Africa. As Congressman Jack Kemp, one of the sponsors of the pro-UNITA Bill, put it 'Aiding UNITA does not prevent a political settlement...if negotiations succeed, it will be because UNITA has put pressure on the Marxists to remove foreign forces and move towards free elections.'[67] Events almost immediately indicated that aid to UNITA would rather lead to an escalation of war; as Savimbi met with President Reagan and the US Defence Department, the Soviet Foreign Minister and the two most senior Soviet generals met with Angolan government officials, and warned that the USSR might consider increasing military aid to Angola if Mr Savimbi received an aid commitment in Washington.[68]

Equally serious are the assumptions underlying the Kemp position. As the *Washington Post* put it:[69]

> It is necessary to be clear, however, about just who was responsible for the impasse in that negotiating effort. It was considerably more South Africa than Angola. And that is what is so troubling about the idea of new aid for Jonas Savimbi. The country that tended to cooperate with Washington is being 'rewarded' with the threat of American support to an internal challenger. The country that defied Washington — stonewalled in the talks on Angola/Namibia, set out to sabotage a big American oil installation in Angola — is being 'penalised' by the offer of/ an implicit American alliance of tremendous strategic and political value. This is diplomacy?

It appears that the United States has fallen into a trap dug by South Africa. The US government repeatedly makes clear its opposition to apartheid. Yet, as this chapter has demonstrated, the devastation of Angola is largely a result of South African intervention, both directly and in support of UNITA. The war in Angola is not an internal freedom struggle. It is part of Pretoria's wider defence of apartheid, and seems designed particularly to embroil the United States. US aid to UNITA has clearly enlisted the United States government in Pretoria's 'total strategy'.

THE FUTURE

The position in Angola remains circular. Oil profits generated with the aid of a US multinational go to pay for Cuban troops and eastern bloc military equipment to fight against South African destabilisation — and in particular to defend the workers and equipment of the US firms against that destabilisation.

Extrication from the quagmire is dependent on events outside. The level of South African military involvement is so massive as to dominate all other issues, and the repeal of the Clark Amendment can only further encourage US and South African involvement. US public opinion is important but fickle; it forced the Clark amendment in the first place, but then allowed its repeal at the same time as it was supporting sanctions against South Africa. The struggle inside South Africa itself is vital to Angola; in the short term it could at least force South Africa to pull back troops to police the townships and perhaps force a settlement in Namibia.

In some form, the Angolan government can hold out almost indefinitely, but it is the Angolan people who are paying the price of two decades of foreign interference.

14. Zimbabwe

I. South African Military Intervention
WITH TERESA SMART

At the centre of the region both politically and geographically, Zimbabwe was the biggest threat to South African hegemony. Robert Mugabe's joint policies of socialism and reconciliation raised the threat of a prosperous multiracial state which would really give the lie to apartheid. And Zimbabwe is crucial to SADCC: it is literally the hub of regional transport and would thus be central in redirecting traffic away from South Africa, while as the most developed state it raised the prospect of industrial development independent of South Africa. However, 15 years of sanctions had substantially reinforced Rhodesia's dependence on South Africa,[1] so that by 1980 hardly any aspect of the modern economy was not substantially influenced by South African interests — mining, manufacturing, retailing, transport, finance, agriculture, and energy.

In the years after independence in 1980, Zimbabwe tried to delink and reduce its dependence on South Africa — but cautiously, in an attempt to avoid the massive military intervention that took place in Mozambique and Angola. South Africa responded in an often sophisticated and complex way. Military and security actions (detailed in this chapter) included attempts to kill Mugabe, widen the splits between ZANU and ZAPU, and promote a dissident movement. In addition the South African state was responsible for massive disruptions of fuel supplies and transport links (discussed in the next chapter). But in Zimbabwe the South African private sector has an influential role which is different from its role in other states in the region. It too has acted against the interests of Zimbabwe in an attempt to maintain its power and Zimbabwe's dependence (detailed in the following chapter).

Despite the relative sophistication of specific South African actions, however, its policy toward Zimbabwe has been confused and contradictory. Often it seemed to lack a clear goal. The victory of ZANU and Robert Mugabe in the March 1980 election and the founding of SADCC came as rude shocks to the South Africans, who were convinced that Bishop Muzorewa would win and take Zimbabwe into Consas. In the months that followed, there was no policy toward Zimbabwe. By early 1981, South Africa's State Security Council had clearly decided to hit Zimbabwe hard. There was substantial sabotage and Zimbabwe was subjected to *de facto* sanctions. The main goal seemed simply to show Prime Minister Mugabe who was boss in the region, and to cause as much disruption as possible without overt military intervention. In many cases, it was simply a policy of opportunism, making use of a fifth column of whites in Zimbabwe who were intending to leave but were willing to stay on for a while and work for South Africa.

By late 1981 there was growing opposition to this strategy within South Africa. Anglo American, the head of South African Railways, and others argued that the aggressive policy was harming South Africa's economic interests, and pushing Zimbabwe to delink from South Africa. In any case it made more sense to them to deal with the Mugabe government and try to co-opt it. It may also have been argued that the Zimbabwe government had survived the pressure, and was, if anything, being strengthened by it. The December 1981 attempt to kill the Prime Minister was probably a last ditch attempt by the military 'forward' strategists before a decision was taken to reduce the pressure. In late 1981 and early 1982, the economic sanctions were lifted.

Since then South Africa seems to have followed a two-pronged policy. First, it has used military and economic means to try to increase Zimbabwe's dependence on South Africa and disrupt SADCC; the main aspect of this has been to block railway traffic to Mozambican ports. Indeed, an important target of destabilisation in Mozambique has really been Zimbabwean rail traffic. Second, there has been a steady but limited attempt to create disruption, particularly by supporting dissidents and infiltrating agents and guerrillas. This was eased off in 1984 when South Africa was pretending to be a regional peacemaker and was trying to force neighbouring states, including Zimbabwe, to sign non-aggression pacts. But it was turned on again in late 1984.

Pretoria has not (yet) launched an overt military attack by SADF troops. When a number of ANC landmines exploded on South African farms near the Zimbabwe border in late 1985, General Malan responded: 'It is clear that the ANC is going out of its way with this sort of action to force conflict between South Africa and its neighbours. South Africa will not tolerate such actions, and I must warn that this could lead to a situation similar to that of SWAPO in Angola' — in other words, South African attacks. In the event, South African and Zimbabwean military commanders met to discuss the situation and, in addition, Pretoria was later reported to be planning a high-voltage electrified fence along the border.

In practice, it seems that South Africa may be more constrained in dealing with Zimbabwe than with some other states in the region. It has much less power over Zimbabwe than over, say, Lesotho. The United States seems to have put pressure on Pretoria on some occasions in support of Zimbabwe. And South Africa's strong economic interests in Zimbabwe probably block the kind of overt destabilisation applied to Mozambique and Angola. But, as Chapter 16 shows, this does provide another source of power.

SABOTAGE AND ASSASSINATION

There had been very close links between South African and Rhodesian security services during the independence war and during the 1980 election. At independence, and especially after the ZANU victory, at least 5000 people — white and black — with military or security links crossed the border to South Africa. They included members of the police, Special Branch, Selous Scouts, Abel Muzorewa's 'auxiliaries', and even the Mozambique National Resistance (MNR). Some joined the security apparatus there, and in subsequent years appeared in Mozambique and Angola as well as Zimbabwe, or helped to organise actions against those states.

Most whites left the security services and went to South Africa. Some stayed to work for the new government — a few still do. But a core had already been recruited by the South Africans; using ZANU's policy of reconciliation as a cover, they recruited more agents and attacked Mugabe. Zimbabwe's July 1980 decision that the South African diplomatic mission in Harare would be downgraded to a trade mission was, according to Mugabe, because diplomats there had been recruiting spies and mercenaries.

Explosions

South Africa's role was shown by three dramatic blasts. On 16 August 1981 explosions rocked the Inkomo Barracks for more than four hours and could be easily heard in Harare, 30 km away. Inkomo was one of the new army's main arsenals, and Z$50m of arms and ammunition — much of it brought back to Zimbabwe by ZIPRA and ZANLA guerrilla forces — was destroyed.

Later the government said that there had been a series of three main explosions at hourly intervals, suggesting that an agent had placed explosives with timing devices among ammunition or gas canisters. An engineer and bomb expert who had had free access to Inkomo Barracks, Captain Patrick Gericke, was detained. He was sprung by the South Africans in a cloak and dagger operation on 15 November. The South Africans kidnapped the wife and two children of Fred Varkevisser, the investigating officer on the case and the only man with authority to take Gericke from the cells in Harare. They forced Varkevisser to release Gericke on the pretext of further investigations; all were then flown to South Africa.

Five months later, on 18 December 1981, a bomb shattered the ZANU headquarters at 88 Manica Road in downtown Harare, killing seven people and injuring 124. The bomb went off on the roof over the third floor conference room where the ZANU central committee was due to meet. Robert Mugabe and many of the cabinet would have been present, and were clearly the target; all would have been killed had the meeting not been delayed. In the event, the dead were workers and customers in a neighbouring bakery, which was also destroyed, while the injured were Christmas shoppers on the packed street outside.

The finger for this raid points at Geoffrey Price, one of the most conspicuous examples of the cost of the post-independence reconciliation policy. During UDI, Price had been active in the government's anti-ZANU disinformation campaign. In the 1980 elections he had been assigned to promote Bishop Muzorewa's campaign. Using South African funds he hired helicopters and organised rallies. After ZANU won, Price stayed on and was made director of close security in the Central Intelligence Organisation (CIO), becoming responsible for Mugabe's personal protection.

Price had built up a good reputation and seemed to be one of those with a 'professional' view of security — to support whatever government is in power —[2] and was therefore not initially suspected. In January, however, as investigations proceeded, two other white security officers were detained; they admitted to being part of a spy ring organised by Price.[3] In the few days between the detention of the two officers and their confession, Price took leave for a 'brief' trip to visit relatives in England; from there he went to South Africa.

The third spectacular raid was on the Thornhill air base near Gweru in mid-Zimbabwe on 25 July 1982. Saboteurs put explosives in 13 fighter and trainer aircraft, and caused Z$30-50m damage. Even now there is no certainty about who carried out the Thornhill raid (see below), but widely accepted reports from South Africa say that it was former Rhodesian SAS men acting on behalf of Pretoria.[4] It seems likely that South Africa was particularly worried that — with white help — Zimbabwe was building up an effective air force.

Continued sniping

In addition to the the three big attacks, there was a steady series of small incidents. In the period around Christmas 1980 a group of white raiders wearing combat fatigues and using bogus requisition papers stole Z$250,000 worth of arms from Cranbourne Barracks, Harare. At the same time the army discovered incendiary devices with time delay fuses in the fuel tanks of more than 30 vehicles at the King George VI Barracks.

A bomb was discovered in the car of ANC representative Joe Gqabi in Harare on 24 February 1981. Discovery did not deter the South Africans: on 30 July he was shot and killed as he came out of his house. In 1982 there were a series of raids across the Limpopo River into southern Zimbabwe, especially near Beit Bridge. In early May explosions damaged the railway and electricity and water installations in Beit Bridge. Later in the month South African soldiers fired across the river and killed a woman, then came across and abducted 15 others.

On 18 August there was a gunfight in a remote area in the south-east near the borders of Mozambique and South Africa. Three white men were killed, part of a group of 17 whites and blacks which had recently infiltrated from South Africa. From maps they were carrying, it is believed they intended to sabotage the railway line that runs to Maputo. South Africa admitted that all 17 were members of the South African armed forces who had previously been part of the Rhodesian forces; of the three dead, two had been in the Rhodesian Light Infantry and in the SAS.

In December 1982 one of the few remaining white Bulawayo policemen, CID Supt Eric Roberts, was shot and killed in his drive. Roberts had conducted several investigations of whites acting against the Zimbabwe government, and it is known that one of his former police colleagues had come to see him before the murder. The killing has never been fully explained, but is believed he was assassinated by former colleagues who were upset at his working for the new government, perhaps after they failed to recruit him. There were also at least two attacks, in April 1982 and January 1983, near Harare on the power line that feeds Mutare.

In March 1983 South Africa opened Radio Truth. This is a clandestine anti-government station, broadcasting from the Transvaal every morning in English and every evening in Ndebele. Its message is hardly subtle; it defends South Africa and claims that the former colonial government had been a 'pro-Western Christian democracy', while it points out that 'quietly but inexorably the tentacles of Marxism are embracing all spheres of life in our country.'[5] Radio Truth was probably connected with anti-Mozambique and anti-Angola stations that broadcast from the same area.

Agents

South Africa is believed to have several camps in the northern Transvaal to train Zimbabweans and others, and to be still sending agents into Zimbabwe. This is supported by evidence presented before Zimbabwean courts. In one case, two black former members of the Rhodesian security forces were sentenced to life imprisonment for their actions. They admitted that in March 1980, just after the ZANU election victory, their superior, Dep. Insp. Graham Banfield, offered them jobs in South Africa. The type of work was not specified, they said, but with Banfield they crossed the Limpopo into South Africa, where they were met by white South Africans and former members of the Selous Scouts. The two men admitted that at various camps they underwent training which included guerrilla tactics, compass reading, unarmed combat, demolition, and even parachuting. In January 1982 they returned to Zimbabwe with other South African agents, and were eventually captured.

By then Banfield was in South Africa training Zimbabwean agents and was involved in one of the odder cases to become public. In November 1981 he persuaded a Bulawayo businessman to fly a black former Rhodesian policeman from a remote airfield in the northern Transvaal into Zimbabwe. It was easy enough in a very big country where there are still quite a few private planes. But they were caught.

Another former member of the Rhodesian security forces was Benson Dube. He said he went to South Africa looking for work and was picked up and sent to a camp where there were about 50 other Zimbabweans.[6] After training, he was part of a heavily armed group of 15 sent back into the Beit Bridge area in October 1982. On 1 December they were involved in a clash with security forces in which a Zimbabwean policeman was killed. Soon after, he was captured, and later sentenced to hang.

There have been a number of similar cases. Alfred Malaphela went to South Africa looking for work in October 1981. In Messina he met a friend serving in the SADF (South African Defence Force) who offered him a job. Malaphela underwent 18 months' training and returned to Zimbabwe where he was involved in several clashes with security fores. He was sentenced to 15 years. Another case involved 19 year-old Bigboy Ngulube, who went to South Africa in February 1984. He too met someone from the SADF who offered him work. But he was only given two weeks' training; he asked to go back home to Zimbabwe and was told he could if he observed Zimbabwe military movements.[7] It is clear that South Africa has been training agents and sending them to Zimbabwe, and that it continues to do so.[8]

Disinformation

In 1983 there were two disinformation campaigns. One involved the distribution of a series of leaflets. They were mainly just sets of anti-government newspaper clippings, for example from the British *Daily Telegraph* and *Daily Mail*, sometimes with a few typed additions, like an anti-communist quotation from Pope Pius XI. They were posted from a variety of places — West Germany, Switzerland, different parts of London, and within Zimbabwe. They were sent to hundreds of people in Zimbabwe, mainly businessmen, ranging from small shopkeepers to officials of the Confederation of Zimbabwe Industry.

Meanwhile, a series of threatening letters was sent to a variety of addresses. All were signed by 'Joe Moyo for ZiPRA High Command' (with the particular orthography 'ZiPRA'). All were typed. Generally they accused the recipients of supporting the government, and warned that action would be taken against them which 'may be attributed to ZiPRA'. One letter went to Qantas after it was announced that the Australian airline was to fly to Zimbabwe instead of South Africa and there was to be an Australian cricket tour. It was a 'friendly warning to Qantas' and to 'the cricket side who intends touring Zimbabwe', and claimed, 'We do not want anything to happen to Australians. We do not want them caught in the crossfire.' Another letter was sent to district councils to warn school headmasters not to use army trucks to transport students. A warning was sent to the newly elected white Senator Max Rosenfels, and three months later he was ambushed on his farm. Others threatened white farmers. Embassies were told to warn tourists from their countries to stay away.

By comparing the typing, the security services discovered that the two campaigns were linked. The same typewriter was used for the letter to Qantas and the quotation from Pius XI on one pamphlet. Others of the Joe Moyo letters were typed with the same typewriter as was used to address some of the envelopes for the pamphlets. The next step was to look for the typewriters. Comparison of the material with letters sent officially by the South African trade mission in Harare showed that they had run the disinformation campaign. One man from the trade mission was quietly expelled, but nothing was ever said publicly about the disinformation campaign.

DISSIDENTS

South Africa has organised anti-government forces in Zimbabwe, just as it did in Angola, Mozambique, Lesotho, and Zambia. In each of the five countries, Pretoria was able to make use of local discontent with the government. But the nature of the opposition movement in each case is very different, with South Africa sometimes drawing on an existing group (such as UNITA in Angola) and sometimes creating a new one (such as the LLA in Lesotho). In Zimbabwe, it focused its attention on a dissident movement in the southern part of the country, particularly Matabeleland. In fact, it failed to co-opt that movement, but it did use the dissidents in three ways. First, it used them as a cover for its own anti-government forces infiltrated into Zimbabwe. Second, it provided supplies to the dissidents to keep them active against the government. Finally, it helped to generate the discontent which fuelled dissident activity.

Because they were the focus of South African interest, it is useful to look briefly at the dissidents themselves. There seem to be three different categories. The first is composed of former ZIPRA (ZAPU) guerrillas who returned to the bush in opposition to the government. The second is groups of armed bandits without political motivation who claim to be dissidents only as a cloak. And the third is the groups of infiltrated South Africans.

Dissident activity proper only began in 1982, but it had its roots in the integration of the three pre-independence forces — ZANLA, ZIPRA, and the former Rhodesian army — into a new national army. On the whole, the integration was a remarkable success, especially considering the animosities felt by the various forces. But the process did take two years, and between November 1980 and March 1981 there were clashes between ZANLA and ZIPRA in which several hundred men were killed. During this period, both ZANLA and ZIPRA guerrillas stockpiled arms. Some former ZIPRA guerrillas blamed ZANLA for the clashes and also believed that ZIPRA guerrillas and commanders were being marginalised in the army integration exercise. Some former ZIPRA men deserted from the new national army. At a national level, there were also increasing tensions between Robert Mugabe's majority ZANU and Joshua Nkomo's ZAPU.

Probably the single most important event was the discovery in early 1982 of arms caches on farms owned by the ZAPU company Nitram. This convinced ZANU of ZAPU's duplicity. Within six weeks Robert Mugabe dismissed Joshua Nkomo and three other ZAPU ministers from the government. Nitram and other ZAPU firms were taken over by the government. And Dumiso Dabengwa, the former ZIPRA intelligence chief, and Lookout Masuku, the former ZIPRA commander, were arrested and accused of involvement in the arms caching. (At their trial a year later, both Dabengwa and Masuku were acquitted, but they were immediately redetained.)[9] The expulsion of Nkomo and the continued detention of Dabengwa and Masuku fuelled discontent. But in many ways the worst blow was the confiscation of Nitram and other properties, since several hundred men were thrown out of work and some evicted from homes on the farms; many others had invested some of their demobilisation money in Nitram, and lost what they saw as their only hope. Hundreds of former ZIPRA men returned to the bush in Matabeleland in early 1982. Most took weapons with them, and there were incidents of armouries being robbed.[10]

Some dissidents were able to establish bases in remote country near Lupane, which ZIPRA had controlled during the liberation war. Some turned to banditry elsewhere. From March 1982 dissident activity grew rapidly in Matabeleland. It has continued ever since and in late 1985 dissidents were still holding out in the remote forests and hills of Matabeleland. Dissidents in the bush attacked shops, farms, villages, schools, and road traffic. More than 500 people have been killed by dissidents, including at least 50 ZANU officials and a number of policemen. A particular target are white farmers (and members of their families). At least 30 have been killed, including Senator Paul Savage in 1983, and more recently six between November 1985 and January 1986. Some local people accused of being 'sell-outs' have been killed or mutilated. Several dozen buses have been burned; trains have been attacked and railway lines sabotaged. The kidnapping (and apparent murder) of six foreign tourists on 23 July 1982 drew the most international publicity.[11]

In response the government sent in the army and imposed a series of curfews. The rules in curfew areas varied, but generally people were not allowed more than 50 yards from their own homes — usually at night, but sometimes 24 hours a day. Shops were closed and bus and car travel banned or severely limited. Since this was at a time of the worst drought of the century, when peasants had no crops and were dependent on shops and aid distribution for food, the curfews caused hunger.

In 1983 and again in 1984 the Fifth Brigade was sent in. It was ill-trained and undisciplined, as well as entirely ex-ZANLA. Almost immediately there were reports of brutalities and killings of civilians. Undoubtedly there were exaggerations and false reports both locally and in the foreign press; it was very difficult to confirm stories within the curfew areas. But as the Zimbabwean magazine *Moto* commented, allegations against the army came 'from sources too varied and reliable to be discounted'.[12] Hundreds of people were killed.

South Africa steps in

The curfews and army activity alienated many local people. Thousands of refugees fled to Botswana, and the dissidents continued to enjoy some local support and gain recruits. South Africa took advantage of this discontent. A Zimbabwe government briefing paper admitted that 'the recent efforts of the Fifth Brigade in Matabeleland have offered the South Africans another highly motivated dissident movement on a plate.' As with the MNR, LLA, and UNITA, South Africa has tried its best to make use of the Zimbabwe dissidents.

South Africa has tried to create what the Zimbabweans have dubbed 'super-ZAPU' — a small group of highly trained fighters, ideally ZIPRA ex-combatants, which it can superimpose on the existing dissident movement. Although most Zimbabweans trained in South Africa seem not have served with ZIPRA, there are a few ex-ZIPRA guerrillas who have been trained in South Africa and sent back into Zimbabwe, and a handful have been caught. Arms and ammunition have also been supplied.

Some attempts have been made to recruit former ZIPRA who fled from Matabeleland to the Dukwe refugee camp in Botswana. The liaison man has been Malcolm 'Matt' Calloway, a member of the Rhodesian Special Branch who stayed on after independence and joined the newly created Central Intelligence Organisation (CIO). He served first as CIO head at Hwange, where he made contacts with ZIPRA guerrillas at Gwaai River Mine waiting to be integrated into the national army. Next he moved to Beit Bridge, on the border. Then he crossed the Limpopo and joined South African intelligence. He was definitely working as a South African agent while he was at Beit Bridge, and probably at Hwange as well. His recruiting seems to have been based on people he knew at Gwaai who showed up at Dukwe. Several 'super-ZAPU' have said they met Calloway, mostly in Botswana.[13]

The case of Hillary Vincent is particularly interesting. He was a former ZIPRA guerrilla who had been at Gwaai before being demobbed. In March 1982 he met Hillary Tafara and went back to the bush with him. Tafara already had South African links, and the two Hillaries met Calloway in Francistown in January 1983 to talk about training and arms. Three loads of arms were brought across the border from South Africa to Botswana in April, July, and November 1983 in Land Cruisers and VW Combis. Hillary Vincent was caught by the Botswana authorities in December 1983 and turned over to Zimbabwe. After interrogation, he agreed to identify two of the caches of South African arms in Botswana, which proved to contain 70 AK47 and RPK light machine guns, ammunition, mines, rocket launchers, and 285kg of plastic explosive.

RPK and AK47 machine guns similar to those supplied by South Africa to Hillary Vincent have been used by dissidents in Zimbabwe.[14] Other evidence of outside (surely South African) supply is that while ZIPRA received no weapons from its Eastern bloc suppliers after September 1979, some weaponry found on dead or captured dissidents was made afterwards. For example a new RPG7 rocket launcher was recovered in March 1983 near Plumtree with a manufacture date of 1981 still stamped on it.

Perhaps the clearest example was 7.62mm ammunition for AK47s with the head stamp '22-80' on the base of the cartridge case. The '22' identifies them as being made in Romania, while the '80' denotes the year of manufacture. Such shells were made after independence and thus never supplied to or used by ZIPRA in the liberation war. Some men captured just after coming over the border from South Africa had boxes of 22-80 shells. By mid-1983 they were the most common cartridge cases found after dissident raids, and had been used in the attacks on Senators Savage and Rosenfels.

Three groups

Southern African involvement with Zimbabwean dissidents is much less than with opposition groups in other countries. Security sources estimate that the number of trained 'super-ZAPU' infiltrated into Zimbabwe can be counted in 'tens' and the number of weapons supplied in 'hundreds'. There are no air drops and no radio communication as in Mozambique — groups go in and out of Zimbabwe on foot for breaks and to collect ammunition and instructions.

One reason is strong antagonism by organised ex-ZIPRA dissidents to South Africa. It seems that most ex-ZIPRA dissidents will have nothing to do with 'super-ZAPU' groups, and there have been fights between the two. This comes in part from the Zimbabweans' experience in the South African mines and long and close links in the past between ZIPRA and the ANC.[15] One instance occurred when Hillary Vincent and Hillary Tafara went into Zimbabwe in September 1983 and met with a group of dissidents in Nsize forest in Lupane. Tafara was harassed about his South African links. At one point he was accused of being super-ZAPU and disarmed and beaten. Eventually the Hillaries had to withdraw to Botswana. After his capture, Vincent vociferously defended Tafara, saying he only pretended to be super-ZAPU in order to get arms and ammunition from South Africa. Ammunition was an exception. The dissidents were running short of supplies and were prepared to use South African-supplied 22-80 shells.

Thus in the confusing scene in Matabeleland there seem to be three forces who will have little to do with each other. The first is organised former ZIPRA guerrillas and their later recruits who have returned to areas they controlled in the liberation war. They do not have the tightly organised leadership structure they had during that war, but they do have some support from the population and they have political goals, such as the release of Dabengwa and Masuku and the return of ZAPU properties. The second group are simply bands of men who have kept their weapons and turned to armed banditry.

The third are men infiltrated from South Africa. Although they have been rejected by the 'true' dissidents, they have been able to take some advantage of discontent. An example is Zwelindabe Nzima, sentenced to death for the killing of the policeman near Beit Bridge with the South African-trained Benson Dube. A former ZIPRA guerrilla, Nzima had not received any further training. He explained that a group of men (who later turned out to be from South Africa) passed through his village and asked him to join them. He said he recognised that they were carrying the same kind of weapons he had had during training in Angola. 'I was willing to go back to the bush and fight, so I joined them,' 21 year-old Nzima explained. 'I just like staying in the bush, and I was going to fight for Nkomo because I would like him back in parliament.'[16]

South Africa infiltrated few 'super-ZAPU' in 1984. In May 1984, two months after Nkomati, the South African security chief, P.W. van der Westhuizen, went to Harare for talks with Zimbabwe National Army Chief of Staff Sheba Gava. The *de facto* truce was broken in August 1984 when a group entered Zimbabwe and there was a clash with security forces on the Botswana border about 70km from

South Africa. Security sources said some of those killed had South African supplied uniforms and weapons.[17]

Clearly the main role of 'super-ZAPU' is simply to agitate and cause disruption. But there are strong suggestions that it has an anti-ANC role. South African-infiltrated groups have been most active in Matabeleland South and near Beit Bridge. This leads to the suggestion that South Africa is trying to create a buffer zone against ANC infiltration. This would work in two ways — first, the 'super-ZAPU' could attack any ANC units and, second, the presence of huge numbers of Zimbabwean regular soldiers would make it very difficult for ANC cadres to move through Matabeleland as they would be picked out as strangers and thus presumed dissidents. UNITA performs a similar role for South Africa against SWAPO in southern Angola.

OVER-REACTION

Some South African interventions have been dependent for their success on the Zimbabwean reaction or over-reaction to them. One example may well have been the aftermath of the raid on the Thornhill air base in 1982. The police arrested six white Zimbabwe air force officers who had previously been members of the Rhodesian air force, including Air Vice Marshall Hugh Slatter. In the end they were acquitted but expelled from Zimbabwe. With them went nearly all the white pilots and ground staff inherited from Rhodesia. The result was that Zimbabwe's air force was grounded, because there had been no time after independence to produce fully-trained black airmen. Thus, the Zimbabwe reaction compounded the damage done to the air force by the original South African attack. Was this the real goal of the South African attack, rather than just luck? It cannot be ruled out.

South Africa is sophisticated enough to play both sides — on the one hand to use white agents for sabotage, while on the other hand trapping whites sympathetic to the Zimbabwe government by setting them up (as at Thornhill) or accusing them of carrying out just the sort of action that is in fact being done by others (as with Lancashire Steel — see Chapter 16). Another motive is bitterness on the part of white Rhodesians who fled that some of their white former compatriots are now helping what they still see as the enemy.

Similarly, the troubles in Matabeleland are heaven-sent for the South Africans, since they create new dissidents. It is felt in Lesotho and Mozambique that South African intervention is intended to create just such a reaction, in the knowledge that provocative actions normally bring a massive over-reaction by the military with mistreatment of local people, thus accelerating a downward spiral of dissent and reaction.

In public statements, the Zimbabwe government has frequently lumped together all 'dissident' actions and blamed them on the ZAPU leadership, whether they are the work of dissident ZIPRA, 'super-ZAPU' or bandits. There are hints that South Africa recognises this, and uses 'super-ZAPU' for spectacular and nasty raids just when calm has been restored in order to stir the pot again. There is no hard evidence, but some raids in the Beit Bridge area, where South African intervention is more frequent, fit this pattern.

Plotting division

South Africa's biggest piece of luck in Zimbabwe must be the ZANU-ZAPU split. Had the rift been healed after independence, there would probably be no dissident movement in which South Africa could intervene. In fact, however, this may not have been entirely a matter of luck at all. Nothing can be proved, but there is a strong possibility of South African manipulation of the arms caching affair which was to become the basis of the Dabengwa-Masuku trial, and which in turn played a key role in exacerbating the ZANU-ZAPU split.

The arms stockpiling in late 1980 was organised by a senior ZIPRA officer. Curiously, he spent only 36 hours in custody, despite admitting his central role in the caching; he was also virtually the only witness at the Dabengwa-Masuku trial not considered an 'accomplice'.[18] In contrast, other witnesses were treated as 'accomplices' and were still in detention at the time of the trial. This suggests strongly that at the time of the arrests this key figure was already serving as a Zimbabwe police or security agent. He admitted at the trial that as part of his job at the time of the arms caching he had regular contact with Matt Calloway, the then CIO (security) head in the next town. Calloway later defected to South Africa and became the contact and recruiting man for 'super-ZAPU'. Probably Calloway was already working for the South Africans in 1980. At the least, he would have learned the details of the arms caching, and South Africa must have learned them from Calloway. And there is the possibility that Calloway actually encouraged the hiding of the arms on his own initiative or at the suggestion of Pretoria.

It seems likely that South Africa also had a role in the 'discovery' of the arms and the decision to prosecute Dabengwa and Masuku. In late 1981, security was still white-dominated; Price remained head of Mugabe's personal security until January 1982. The officer who led the investigation in 1982 later defected to South Africa. At the trial it was clear that strong pressure had been put on witnesses to blame the top ZAPU leadership — which of course precipitated the final ZANU-ZAPU split. South African agents were thus curiously close to the hiding of the arms, the investigation of the caches, and the eagerness to implicate ZIPRA leaders.

The South African agents in the CIO may also have been in a position to manipulate the timing of the discovery, and even the supply of information to Prime Minister Mugabe. Even the British press reported in 1981 that arms had been stockpiled, and surely the CIO knew the details. But it was not revealed to the government till early 1982, which was certainly a convenient time for the South Africans. 1981 had been a good year for Zimbabwe — as noted in the next chapter, serious South African economic pressures had been resisted, while the integration of the army was going well and white confidence in the government was increasing. More drastic measures like the assassination of the Prime Minister and the creation of internal divisions may have seemed the only answer. Or, having failed to kill Mugabe in December 1981, did South Africa turn to the reserve plan: splitting ZANU and ZAPU?

15. Zimbabwe

II. South African Government Economic Actions

As well as its overtly military action, South Africa also moved against Zimbabwe's economy, concentrating particularly on manipulating the special links it had built up with Rhodesia during the UDI period. This necessarily involved the private sector, and especially the monopoly groups, which are discussed in more detail in the following chapter. But the South African state also took steps to disrupt transport and cut back on trade and migrant labour concessions.

As well as causing general disruption, Pretoria tried to keep Zimbabwe dependent on South Africa, particularly for fuel. And it tried to extract a key political concession: at least tacit diplomatic recognition. After independence, Zimbabwe refused to have formal diplomatic or ministerial contacts with South Africa. It was no longer allowed to maintain a full diplomatic mission, although a trade mission was allowed to remain. Contacts between officials in the railways and security and trade ministries continued normally. All contact between ministers was banned, however, as it was felt such contact would imply recognition of the apartheid government; this became symbolic on both sides, and it was this, more than any other single point, that Pretoria tried (and failed) to reverse.

TRADE & LABOUR

Non-renewal of trade agreements

During the UDI and sanctions period, South Africa became Rhodesia's main trading partner. Under a special bilateral trade agreement, Rhodesia was allowed access at reduced duties to South Africa's protected market, and by independence it took three-quarters of Zimbabwe's manufactured exports (excluding steel and processed minerals). South Africa also became a key supplier of inputs and consumer goods.

The first step toward lessening the special relationship built up prior to independence came in July 1980, only three months after independence, when the South African Credit Guarantee Insurance Corporation (CGIC) limited cover on new exports to Zimbabwe to 25%. CGIC said that it was a political decision, and it was noted that senior government officials were on the committee that took the decision. The main purpose was to force the Zimbabwe government to make a high level request for the full CGIC cover to be instituted, but Zimbabwe never did.[1]

Then on 24 March 1981 South Africa gave one year's notice that it would abrogate the bilateral trade agreement.[2] In all, Z$54m of goods went to South Africa under the agreements in 1980, particularly clothing, radios, and steel rod and wire, as well as small quantities of cigarettes, furniture, travel goods, exhaust systems, and pharmaceuticals. Nearly 7000 jobs were involved in producing these exports.[3] Not all of these exports and jobs would have been lost if the agreement had ended, but some goods such as clothing would have been non-competitive at full duty. Thus the cancellation of the agreement would have a serious impact on the economy. This was underlined by South Africa making the announcement while the Zimbabwe government was hosting Zimcord (Zimbabwe Conference for Reconstruction & Development) during which it hoped to raise substantial amounts of assistance from international donors.

The demand, as before, was minister-to-minister talks, which Zimbabwe refused. Finally talks did take place at the level of officials. South Africa came under strong pressure from the USA, which argued that it was in South Africa's own best interests to maintain the economic power it had with the trade agreement. (At the same time, the United States was also arguing that Pretoria should stop its transport disruptions — see below.) Then in mid-March 1982, less than a fortnight before the agreement was due to expire, and largely as a result of US pressure, South Africa relented and extended it. But much of the damage had already been done; South African buyers had found other sources for many of the goods, and the uncertainty remains because Pretoria can always give notice again.

Migrants sent back

Like the other colonies in the region, Rhodesia had sent migrant labourers to South Africa. Fewer than 40,000 men were involved, and it was less important for Rhodesia than the other states. (In fact, Rhodesia recruited migrants from Mozambique and elsewhere to work in *its* mines.) Nevertheless, migrant remittances were worth about Z$25m per year to Zimbabwe at independence.

In February 1981 Zimbabwe stopped formal recruiting of new miners in Zimbabwe by Wenela, the main South African recruiting agency; this was because Zimbabwe did not want to continue a government-to-government recruiting agreement. Nevertheless, Zimbabwe stressed that its citizens were free to continue working in South Africa if they wished. But South Africa responded by expelling many who lacked formal contracts, and refusing to renew work permits for others when their contracts came up for renewal; by late 1982 there were only a few hundred Zimbabweans left in the mines although several thousand continued to work in other sectors in South Africa, particularly domestic service.

TRANSPORT

Rhodesia developed as an exporter of minerals and agricultural products, and given its landlocked position, railways played a particularly important role. For the first half of the century, there were only two routes to the sea, to Beira in Mozambique and to South Africa via Botswana. In the 1950s another was opened along the Limpopo valley to Maputo. Only with Mozambique independence looming and the possibility of sanctions, was a direct link to South Africa built at Beit Bridge. The 145 km long line was constructed in only 93 days, and opened in October 1974.[4] The distances tell much of the tale:

	Length	Opened
Harare-Beira	602 km	1898
Harare-Maputo via Chicualacuala	1269 km	1955
Harare-Durban via Beit Bridge	2066 km	1974
Harare-East London via Botswana	2370 km	1897

Thus shipping goods through Mozambique costs half as much as shipping via South Africa.[5] This was reflected in the choice of routes during colonial times for imports and exports, with 65% going via Mozambique in 1970:[6]

	1953	1967	1970	1975	1980	1981
Via Mozambique						
Beira	55%	31%	13%	29%	1%	3%
Maputo	—	47%	53%	34%	—	25%
Via South Africa						
via Botswana	45%	22%	33%	27%	51%	20%
via Beit Bridge	—	—	—	9%	49%	52%

Portugal had refused to impose sanctions against Rhodesia, but independent Mozambique did so in March 1976 (after Rhodesia made its first raids into Mozambique). This diverted all of Zimbabwe's imports and exports via South Africa. After independence, Zimbabwe intended to return to the cheaper Mozambican routes. It took some months to rehabilitate the lines, as parts of them had been out of use for four years. (Indeed, during the war Rhodesia had pulled up 100 km of track on the Maputo line on its side of the border in order to use it to repair damage to other parts of the railway caused by ZANU and ZAPU guerrillas.) But both lines were open by November 1980.

A central focus of SADCC is to rehabilitate these lines, and Maputo and Beira ports. In 1981 perhaps one-third of Zimbabwe traffic went through Mozambique, and in 1982 it was over half. Zambian and Zairian traffic also passes through Zimbabwe on its way to the sea, and it was hoped to transfer this to Mozambique instead of South Africa as well.

Oil is a particularly essential import. In 1965, just before UDI, Lonrho opened an oil pipeline from Beira to just over the border at Mutare. It was closed when the British blockaded Beira harbour. But the British did not blockade Maputo so oil went to Rhodesia via South Africa, in a sanctions-busting operation now well documented.

Embargoes

At independence in 1980, South Africa used its control of transport and oil in parallel with actions over trade and military interventions. As we noted in the previous chapter, the goals of this delicate and explicit action seemed complex. In part it was 'using its economic muscle to show Zimbabwe who is boss', as one Johannesburg newspaper put it, and trying to bludgeon Zimbabwe into political and diplomatic concessions.[7] But it was also an effort to create chaos in the newly independent state, to prevent the multiracial state from being successful. A successful majority-ruled Zimbabwe would undermine the basic tenets of apartheid.

The squeeze was gradual at first, with South Africa simply holding up cargo. By November 1980 there were complaints of delays of up to three weeks, and more than 50,000 tonnes of goods stuck in South Africa. Then in January 1981 South Africa imposed an effective but unannounced embargo on goods for Zimbabwe, Botswana, and Zambia — just when a flood had cut the newly opened line to Maputo. By March there were an estimated 300,000 tonnes of Zimbabwean goods stranded in South African ports. There was a fertiliser shortage in Zimbabwe, and three fertiliser ships were diverted to Maputo.[8]

The responsibility did not rest entirely with South Africa. There were three other factors. First, Zimbabwe's post-independence drive to retool and reinvest, combined with the post-sanctions demand for previously unavailable consumer goods, pushed up imports 47% in 1980 and another 26% in 1981. This was being paid for partly by the inflow of aid after independence, but more by a massive increase in exports, including a record maize harvest of over 2m tonnes in 1981.[9] Thus with the end of sanctions, the railways had to handle much more cargo. Second, South Africa also had a brief boom in 1980, so it had more cargo of its own on the railways. Third, many of the white artisans who had kept Rhodesia Railways (RR) running on string and sealing wax left, so National Railways of Zimbabwe (NRZ) had trouble keeping its ancient and diverse fleet in service. Locomotive availability dropped sharply. This meant that turnaround time in Zimbabwe fell and NRZ had trouble moving the higher volumes of cargo. This was exacerbated by similar problems of lack of skilled people in the Mozambican ports and railways.

But South Africa was crucial, and the main point was its reversal in attitude to its northern neighbour. South African Railways (SAR) had gone out of its way to keep RR running prior to independence despite sanctions, and RR had become dependent on this.[10] Now SAR went out of its way to disrupt. For example, RR had never been self-sufficient; SAR had leased RR 3000 wagons and nearly 50 locomotives, as well as seconding technicians to keep them going. In July 1980 SAR began pulling back its technicians, which compounded the problem of white Rhodesians leaving.

On 11 March 1981 the *Financial Times* (London) predicted that 'Zimbabwe's increasingly hostile stance towards Pretoria — mirrored in Salisbury's vote in the UN General Assembly last week in favour of sanctions against South Africa — could elicit an economic response.... It is highly likely that South Africa will withdraw some of its rolling stock and diesel locomotives.'

A fortnight later, Pretoria announced the end of the bilateral trade agreement. Two weeks after that, on 4 April, SAR said it wanted back the 24 diesel locos leased to NRZ. (Mozambique later loaned nine locomotives and Zambia four, but that did not make up the entire shortfall.) After that, the harassment increased. Import cargo was delayed in South Africa, sometimes for several weeks, because the South Africans claimed documents were not in order, or because of alleged congestion within South Africa. Exports were delayed so that they missed the boat.

South Africa forced much Zimbabwean traffic through Port Elizabeth instead of Durban. This caused two problems. First it was a longer rail trip and thus took longer and tied up wagons. Second, as there are no grain storage facilities wheat imports had to be loaded directly into railway wagons — thus tying up wagons and causing extra demurrage charges on ships delayed in port.

The then mining minister, Maurice Nyagumbo, alleged that some whites within NRZ were exacerbating the crisis with deliberate sabotage. This was confirmed by Rex Chiwara, one of the first blacks in NRZ management after independence and later assistant general manager.[11] He cited as an example whites sending empty wagons to Wankie Colliery, on the wrong side of country, instead of to where they were needed. They also tried to block the transfer of traffic to Mozambican ports.

Fuel imports, especially of diesel, were increasingly subject to delay; sometimes wagons arriving from South Africa were empty. Fuel was brought by road from Zambia and by rail from Mozambique; nevertheless, reserves fell to as low as two days supply. Petrol station opening hours were restricted; an informal fuel rationing system was imposed on large users. Lack of diesel disrupted the collection of the bumper maize harvest, and delayed ploughing for the coming season.

By September there was a public outcry. Eddie Cross, then general manager of the Zimbabwe Dairy Marketing Board, gave a speech in Johannesburg accusing the South African government of sabotaging and disrupting the Zimbabwean economy.[12] Energy Minister Simba Makoni accused Pretoria of deliberately delaying diesel deliveries.

The reply came in Parliament, where the South African Transport Minister Hendrick Schoeman implicitly admitted that South Africa was deliberately delaying Zimbabwean cargo. He said that the problem could only be solved if an approach was made by Zimbabwe at ministerial level, and that the government in Harare must give high level assurances that the African National Congress would not be allowed to operate in Zimbabwe.

Finally in November South Africa backed down. Without ministerial level talks, South Africa agreed to lease 26 locomotives.[13] More important, however, the disruptions in South Africa came to an end.

Within Zimbabwe, things improved rapidly for reasons largely unrelated to South Africa. Before the end of the year, the first of 500 Indian and Pakistani artisans began to arrive, and the first of 70 old Garratt steam locomotives being rehabilitated wi in Zimbabwe returned to service. In January 1982 the first 25 of 60 diesel locomotives ordered from the US and Canada arrived. At the same time, the drought had begun; the 1982 harvest was smaller and the economy moved into recession. By May 1982 NRZ said it had surplus capacity for the first time since independence.

At its peak in August and September 1981, the transport crisis was costing Zimbabwe Z$5m per week in lost exports, according to the then Transport Minister Josiah Chinamano.[14] It could have been much worse, but a special Railway Priorities Committee acted with great skill. It assigned the available capacity to exports with the highest value per tonne, such as cotton and tobacco, so as to minimise balance of payment problems. Low value coal and coke exports fell to less than one-third their normal volume.

By the end of the year, more than 60,000 tonnes of sugar, significant amounts of asbestos, and huge amounts of maize — more than Z$100m in goods — were still stored inside the country, awaiting export.[15] Maize is a low value crop, and more than 1m tonnes were simply left in massive canvas covered piles throughout the country; clearing this backlog meant that more maize was exported during the drought year of 1982 than the good year of 1981. The disruption in maize exports in 1981 was particularly unfortunate, however, because the UN World Food Programme was exporting Zimbabwe maize to Kenya, Tanzania, Mali, Senegal, and several other countries; a daily maize train ran from Mutare to Beira, where the grain was put on ships. It was a case of black Africa feeding itself, and a public relations triumph for newly independent Zimbabwe. But it would have been even more dramatic and effective if Zimbabwe had been able to allocate more transport to the maize exports.

A narrow window

The South African press attributed the backdown on the transport squeeze, as well as the withdrawal of the trade agreement cancellation, which happened soon after, to pressure from Western embassies, particularly that of the US.[16] But another consideration must be that South Africa had a very short period of time in which pressure could be effective. The level of confusion within Zimbabwe would never be as high again, and black and white Zimbabweans committed to the new country were beginning to take control of transport undertakings like NRZ. The new government moved as quickly as it could to buy new locomotives and contract foreign technicians, and these were due to arrive in 1982. Arrangements were being made to shift cargo to Mozambique. The Lonrho oil pipeline was being repaired and as soon as it reopened South Africa would have less control over Zimbabwe's fuel.

South Africa had tried explicitly and deliberately to destabilise the economy of the newly independent state, in sharp contrast to Prime Minister Mugabe's repeated assertions that he wanted to maintain normal relations with South Africa. In addition to transport pressure, there was the ending of the trade agreement and the expulsion of migrant workers, as well as raids such as the one on Inkomo barracks. But by the end of 1981, Zimbabwe was getting its act together, and South Africa had little choice but to ease off the pressure if it expected to retain any influence at all north of the Limpopo. It is believed that this was the line the US took in trying to persuade South Africa to back off.

In that short period, however, the impact was severe. The delay in renegotiating the trade agreement cost tens of millions of dollars in temporarily lost exports. The expulsions of migrant miners probably cost Zimbabwe an extra Z$50m in foreign exchange earnings in the 1981-83 period. Like the transport disruptions, this was an action which had to be taken quickly to be effective, as Zimbabwe itself had stopped recruiting. On top of this came the cost of lost exports and disruptions caused by fuel shortages. Finally, there was the really serious cash-flow problem caused by delayed exports, which exacerbated the growing balance of payments deficit. This was particularly important because it forced Zimbabwe to turn to the IMF, which imposed a series of limitations on the new government. In September 1981, at the height of the transport crisis, Finance Minister Enos Nkala was at the World Bank/IMF meeting in the US seeking, in his words, balance of payments support 'as soon as possible'.[17]

South Africa clearly hoped to extract concessions, or alternatively disrupt Zimbabwe's very promising start. But there were also two more specific goals, which Pretoria continued to pursue in other ways in following months. The first was to attack SADCC. Transport is the keystone of SADCC, and Zimbabwe is at the heart — not only is it the main exporter in the region, but it controls the traffic of Zambia and Botswana. If NRZ could be crippled, it might also cripple the dream of SADCC and resurrect the constellation of states. This was widely discussed in the South African press at the time.[18]

The other issue was Zimbabwe's massive maize exports. One of South Africa's oft-cited arguments for white rule is that black Africa cannot feed itself. Now, the newly independent Zimbabwe was exporting maize — including to countries like Zambia and Mozambique that had previously bought from South Africa. What was worse, the good rains meant South Africa, too, had a surplus that it wanted to sell. The South African generated rail crisis curtailed low value maize exports. Again the South African press was open about the implications,[19] noting that South Africa might be called on to fill the demand that Zimbabwe could not meet.

Sabotage in Mozambique

When it became clear that Zimbabwe had survived the 1981 squeeze, it also became increasingly clear that Zimbabwe wanted to route its trade through Mozambique. SADCC would succeed, and South Africa would lose its leverage (as well as considerable revenue from Zimbabwe transit traffic). South Africa decided on a very deliberate policy of sabotage. One of its tools was the Mozambique National Resistance (MNR), a surrogate group first created by Rhodesia, but which was taken over by Pretoria in 1980.[20]

Perhaps because of the maize train, the Beira-Mutare railway became the first target. By mid-1981 the MNR was attacking this line, but not with consistent enough success to create problems. In October, South Africa stepped up the pressure, for two reasons. First, it had decided to ease off on the southern route. And second, the SADCC annual conference was to be held in Blantyre, Malawi, on 19-20 November. On 14 October a white British man, later discovered to be an officer in the South African army, was blown up trying to mine the railway. Two weeks later on 29 October, the railway and road bridges over the Pungue River, 50 km from Beira, were sabotaged. The raid was almost surely carried out by the South African Reconnaissance Commandos.[21] The road bridge was destroyed, and with it a section of the oil pipeline which hung from the bridge, delaying the reopening of the pipe. The attack on the railway bridge was less successful — a pillar was blown up leaving the bridge hanging in mid-air but still intact. The pillar was rebuilt and the bridge reopened on 17 December. The maize train resumed operation, but rail traffic was still somewhat disrupted as road vehicles had to be ferried over the railway bridge for several months.

Oil

The oil pipeline finally opened on 19 June 1982, carrying all of Zimbabwe's diesel and petrol (although not aviation fuel and lubricants, which continued to be railed — some via South Africa).[22] Not only did this substantially release Zimbabwe from Pretoria's grasp, but the pipeline would save Zimbabwe Z$36m per year in transport costs.[23] In the following weeks the MNR stepped up its raids on the Beira railway and pipeline (and began raids on the Maputo railway). Zimbabwe responded in November by sending its own troops into Mozambique to guard the pipeline, which largely ended MNR raids on it. South Africa answered on the morning of 9 December 1982 with a raid on the oil storage depot in Beira harbour.

Almost surely done by Reconnaissance Commandos coming in from the sea, the raid did US$20m in damage.

Mozambique moved quickly to send fuel by rail from the Maputo refinery. But that line runs through semi-desert near the South African border, and was an easy target for MNR men coming across from South Africa's Kruger Park. The MNR stepped up its raids; some fuel got through, but Mozambique lost some tank wagons.

This left the old UDI sanctions-busting route from Maputo, but via Komatipoort in South Africa and then Beit Bridge.[24] In fact, this line was still in use because of an inherited problem — aviation fuel and specialist oil products could not be sent up the pipeline, while Zimbabwe's jumbo tank wagons were too big for the still somewhat fragile direct Limpopo valley line. This route had remained in use for three trains with 78 tank wagons per week, even during the 1981 crisis (albeit with difficulties).

As an emergency measure, diesel and petrol were put in the jumbo tankers. But South Africa cut off this line as well; the tank wagons simply never arrived at Beit Bridge. South Africa tightened the screw by even preventing motorists from taking cans of petrol or oil across the border.[25] There was a major petrol crisis in Zimbabwe during the Christmas holiday period, leaving tourists stranded and normal economic activity severely disrupted. South Africa offered to sell petrol to Zimbabwe, but only if it signed a long-term contract of at least three years.

After three weeks, NRZ officials went to Johannesburg to negotiate, but were told the problem could only be solved, as usual, on a minister-to-minister basis. Zimbabwe refused. NRZ stressed that whatever else was going on in the region, there was a binding SAR-NRZ contract which included those three fuel trains each week — if SAR was tearing up this part of the contract, then it was tearing up the entire contract, and Zimbabwe no longer had any responsibility to carry transit traffic for Zambia and Zaire. Ending transit traffic would mean substantial cost to SAR, and seriously escalate the dispute. SAR officials consulted their ministers, then backed down and released the nine trains. Three had been stabled at Messina, just over the border from Beit Bridge, and crossed into Zimbabwe within hours.[26] By 13 January, enough temporary patching had been done in Beira to allow fuel to be pumped directly from tankers into the pipeline (rather than into storage tanks as before), quickly ending the fuel shortage.

In the following years, Zimbabwean troops were able to protect the Beira line. But MNR raids increased on the Maputo line, effectively closing it by mid 1984.[27] According to Zimbabwean sources, disruptions were:

	No. of disruptions	Days closed
Maputo line		
1982	25	75
1983	38	144
1984	30	221
1985	closed	
Beira line		
1982	7	24
1983	negligible	
1984	13	32
1985	6	24

Only in 1982 did more than half of Zimbabwe's imports and exports move via Mozambique. By 1983 the raids on the Maputo line were so severe that cargo was again being shifted to South African ports; by mid-1984 the line was permanently closed. There were some public complaints that shipping costs through South Africa are Z$10-50 per tonne higher than through Mozambican ports.[28] Eddie Cross, head of the Cold Storage Commission, estimates that Zimbabwe is now losing Z$100m per year in invisibles and higher transport costs as a result of the disruptions.[29]

Disruptions continued in South Africa as well, particularly on the line through South Africa that links Beit Bridge and Maputo. As MNR raids increasingly closed the direct line, Zimbabwe tried to ship through South Africa to Maputo certain cargoes such as sugar and steel for which there are special handling facilities in Maputo. South Africa does not like this, as it feels those cargoes should go through South African ports. So for three months in 1983 and again for two months in 1984 cargoes on this line were significantly delayed.[30] Then the MNR began to attack the part of the line between Komatipoort and Maputo; seven MNR raids, including some on important bridges, closed this line for 100 days during 1985.

Forwarding agencies and containers

One curious aspect of the whole 1981-82 period was that Mozambique was prepared to handle more cargo than Zimbabwean shippers would send. At the height of the crisis, in August and September 1981, there were public statements by Zimbabwean and Mozambican officials calling for more cargo to be sent via Maputo and Beira instead of South Africa. Even the local representative of Safmarine, the South African national shipping line, commented that despite the problems in South Africa, importers were not making full use of Mozambican ports.[31] This was also true in 1983-85 when the Maputo line was closed by the MNR: cargo was transferred to South Africa instead of Beira — despite the fact that Zimbabwean troops were protecting the line.

This occurred for a complex mix of political and technical reasons. The technical one was that in the late colonial period, Portugal invested virtually nothing in the Mozambican ports, while South Africa invested extensively, especially in Durban. During the 1976-79 period of Mozambican sanctions against Rhodesia, South Africa continued its investment, developing the bulk port at Richards Bay and in 1977-78 rapidly containerising. Whereas Maputo had been much more efficient than Durban in the early 1960s, providing a faster turnaround time with similar technology, now Durban was an entire technical generation ahead, providing faster turnarounds and much better computer and communications facilities. SADCC projects will reduce this difference only in coming years. Thus Mozambican ports are cheaper and politically preferable, but more troublesome for the shippers.

Thus an important reason why relatively little cargo goes via Mozambique is that it was the private and parastatal sector, not government, which controls the choice of port. It prefers South Africa on the grounds of efficiency, but also for historic and social reasons.

Import and export flows are largely in the hands of freight forwarding agencies, and in Rhodesia there were two main agencies. One was Manica Freight Services, owned by Anglo (40%) and the then South African state-owned Safmarine

(60%), and the best known for sanctions-busting. The other was Rennies, also a South African company.[32] (In 1985, the two were merged.)

Ocean shipping is dominated by cartels known as 'conferences' which set schedules and rates, with each member of the conference running some of the ships. As the national shipping line, Safmarine is the major partner in the conferences that serve South Africa, and Safmarine acts as their local agent. Government regulations give conferences to which Safmarine belongs the right to carry 87.5% of South African imports on those routes. In the colonial era, Rhodesia and Mozambique were served by the South African conferences, which still dominate traffic to Maputo and Beira.[33]

Manica, which is owned by Safmarine, acts as Zimbabwe agent for it.[34] In interviews, Manica makes no bones about the fact that it acts for its 'principal' Safmarine, and preferentially directs cargo to it.[35] Thus it is hardly surprising that when import or export routing is left to the agents (which is quite common), Manica usually chooses a South African port and a conference ship.

This process was accelerated by containerisation, which was pushed very hard by the South African government (through Safmarine) in 1977. In 1980, the first year of independence, Zimbabwe shippers were given substantial inducements to containerise. Arguably containers are more efficient, but it was certainly a way of tying Zimbabwe to Durban to provide business for the expensive new container facilities.[36] The following year, containers were often exempted from the various South African delays and embargoes, again as an inducement to containerise.[37] Tobacco, coffee, tea, and nickel exports were all containerised by 1982.

There are special container conferences. Safmarine is the major partner in SAECS (South Africa — Europe Container Services), which provides most container ships calling at Beira and Maputo as well as South African ports.[38] Manica manages the container pool, handling about three-quarters of SAECS containers in South Africa. It is also Zimbabwe agent for SAECS, organising containers there through the Safmarine computer in South Africa.

Using conference ships and South African ports costs Zimbabwe a lot of money. As well as the extra cost of shipping to South African ports, conference ships are significantly more expensive than the non-conference 'outsider' lines. These are no longer the tramp steamers of adventure novels, but modern general cargo and container ships that are not part of the cartels and tend to run a slightly more irregular schedule. One way to find the cheapest route is to put a contract out to public tender. When the shipping of EEC milk powder to Zimbabwe was put out to tender, the cheapest price was obtained using the USSR's non-conference Besta Lines, and shipping the milk in containers via Beira. Clearly neither Manica nor Rennies were the shipping agents. Yet, despite evidence that the Beira route is cheaper, relatively efficient, and reliable now that it is guarded by Zimbabwean troops, it is still used at less than half its capacity.

The shipping agencies say that it is the client who decides how a cargo is sent. But it is the agent who 'advises' the client. In any case, the two South African shipping agencies bias the case in favour of South Africa in a variety of ways, so that it *is* simpler and often more efficient to send cargo via South Africa. One role of the agents is to keep a watchful eye on the progress of a cargo and sort out any difficulties. This is easier with South Africa because of better communications and computer links.

In some cases, agents will put together packages — for example giving a fixed price to export all cotton. That sort of package always involves conference lines and South African ports. It is much easier for a civil servant or marketing board official to allow the agents to deal with the whole package, than to have the hassle of putting together a cheaper package using a mix of outsider and conference lines and several ports. Similarly, some of the same people are dealing with shipping now who dealt with it during sanctions busting. They are happy to deal with their old friends at Manica and Rennies. This is reinforced by propaganda about the inefficiencies of Mozambican ports and the likelihood of MNR attack. Despite delays and holdups in South Africa, the shipping agents argued that it was still better to ship that way.[39]

Manica also makes it difficult to use Maputo and Beira, even if shippers want to. It acts differently with respect to the two countries, actively managing the progress of freight through South Africa, while washing its hands of freight to Mozambique and pleading lack of information. Manica is also reluctant to provide containers for exports through Mozambican ports; since it controls 90% of containers, there are few available elsewhere.

Also, it refuses to provide 'through bills of lading' and insurance for cargo passing through Mozambican ports, while providing these for goods through South Africa. A through bill means that the freight remains in a container door to door, to or from the 'port of Harare'. The shipping agency handles all clearance at the intermediate port; without it there are delays, and the Zimbabwean who is shipping or receiving the goods may have to go to Maputo or Beira to ensure the passage. Thus through bills are far more efficient for companies in a land locked country like Zimbabwe. The smaller non-South African forwarding agents in Harare are all happy to provide through bills and insurance for cargoes through Mozambique.

Overt military intervention plays a key role. It is, after all, MNR and South African raids that create the instability that allow Manica and Rennies to warn their clients against Mozambican ports. It is significant that in late 1981 and again in late 1982, when shippers were becoming convinced of the merits of Beira, there were the raids on the Pungue River bridge and the oil depot which damaged that confidence.

Manica personnel played a role in these interventions. Dion Hamilton, the Beira head of Manica, provided the information that allowed the South African Reconnaissance Commandos to raid the oil depot and the bridge. His deputy at Manica, Benjamin Fox, was identified as the man who had been taking arms and instructions to MNR bases near Beira.[40] All of this ties up to a final chicken-and-egg problem. Not enough ships call at Beira now because so little cargo goes through the port. Thus agents can argue that it makes no sense to send cargo to Beira because there will not be a ship.

At the same time it has to be admitted that inaction by the Zimbabwe and Mozambique authorities is also partly responsible for the failure of more shippers to use Mozambican ports. For example, at independence a UK-based SAECS member, Overseas Container Lines (OCL), expected to be pressed to stop shipping to Zimbabwe via South Africa. It was afraid that if this occurred, it would lose cargo to outsider lines, so contingency plans were made for a special conference without Safmarine to serve Mozambique. To OCL's surprise, they were not pressed to stop using South Africa, so the new conference never materialised.

The Zimbabwe government could use the influence it has over private shippers and marketing boards. For example, on grounds of foreign exchange limitations, it could require shippers to demonstrate that they were using the cheapest route — probably by demanding that marketing boards tender for transport. The government could also press the marketing boards to stop using Manica and Rennies. And it could make better use of its control over NRZ. Some tobacco was eventually sent out via Beira (with no difficulties and much publicity) because the government forced NRZ to tell shippers that some wagons would be available only to Beira and not South Africa. Finally, the government could provide guarantees to shipping lines that enough cargo would pass through Beira to make it worth their calling there; even if it were necessary to pay a penalty at first, with enough political backing it should generate enough cargo quite quickly. One shipping agent said flatly: 'Beira needs at least a nudge from the government but this has never happened. Shippers have never been pushed to use Mozambique.'

Mozambique sometimes does not help. For example, there is a war going on, but it has often painted glowing pictures that were obviously false. Zimbabweans had more knowledge of difficulties than the Mozambicans realised, and were not fooled. The inability to get accurate information with which to plan meant that even government officials who would normally be sympathetic to Mozambique accepted the excessively gloomy pictures painted by Manica. A possibly important move to reduce dependence on South Africa took place in late 1984, when Mozambique formed a joint venture freight forwarding agency with AMI, part of Société Générale de Belgique. It will have offices in Beira and Nacala, and could be the vehicle to reroute cargo away from South Africa.

Outside agencies also have an influence on choice of port. For example, the Indian shipping line refuses to call at South African ports, so goods for the Indian subcontinent (like wattle) are sent out through Beira. The World Food Programme made a political choice to use Beira to export maize, and was in 1982 the biggest user of the port. But when the United States sent food aid in 1983 due to the drought, it was sent to Port Elizabeth. This meant SAR had a large number of empty wagons returning, so it offered a special contract price on asbestos that was cheaper than Maputo — winning away traffic.

Rate-cutting

The transport saga took another twist in 1984, when the recession both in South Africa and in world shipping in general forced ferocious rate cutting. Outsider lines were taking increasing amounts of cargo from the conferences, while the railway to Beira was guarded by Zimbabwean troops and thus increasingly attractive. Thus both SAECS and SAR were forced into more drastic measures to retain Zimbabwean traffic.

The main argument (other than regional cooperation) in favour of Mozambican ports had been that they were cheaper. So in mid-1984 SAECS and SATS began to undercut even on price — but with two twists. The first was that SAECS put a surcharge of up to 20% on containers it carried through Beira, so ensuring that Durban was cheaper. Second, SAR began giving sizeable contract discounts. In late 1984 shippers gave these as typical rates for a container from Harare to Britain (in Z$):

	Rail	Ship	Total
Via Beira	850	1650	2500
Via Durban — normal	1150	1350	2500
Via Durban — contract	975	1350	2350

As is clear, the key factor is the SAECS surcharge on Beira, so that under normal circumstances outsider lines would still be cheaper. Thus SAR contract rates are important in cutting prices further. Contract discounts are typically for more than 1000 containers per year *in both directions.* The large number needed for the lower rate ensures that most exports continued to go through South Africa, while the requirement that containers be full in both directions ensured that imports came through South Africa as well. In 1984 when SAR began offering bigger discounts on large contracts, it also raised non-contract prices substantially, in an effort to force customers into contracts. Additionally, for some Zimbabwe exports like sugar, the discounts were only offered if exporters guaranteed to use South African routes for extended periods. The collapse of the South African rand in 1985 further reduced the real cost of SAR tariffs.

THE FUTURE

The most striking characteristic of South Africa's actions has been its ability to shift with the times and respond to new situations, often in subtle ways. The most overt destabilisation, like attempts on Mugabe's life and direct embargoes on traffic through South Africa, have been phased out. They have been replaced by quieter intervention in Matabeleland, attacks on railways in Mozambique, and rate-cutting. All of this fits more neatly with its continued influence in the private sector. But no one forgets that Pretoria has demonstrated its willingness to use a much bigger stick.

16. Zimbabwe

III. The Private Sector and South Africa

WITH COLIN STONEMAN

Zimbabwe has been influenced economically by South Africa since before colonial times. Cecil Rhodes' 'Pioneer Column', which came up from South Africa, included both English-and Afrikaans-speaking South Africans, and from that time there have been close family and cultural ties with the ruling white elite in South Africa. For the first three decades of its existence, Southern Rhodesia was controlled by Rhodes' British South Africa Company.

Consequently, there has always been a tension among the whites (often in the same person) reflecting a natural empathy with South Africa, on the one hand, against a desire to fight its influence, on the other. This was well summed up in a close vote in 1922 when the settlers opposed joining the Union of South Africa, and instead chose 'responsible self-government'(with reserved powers to the British crown in foreign affairs and 'native interests').

British capital initially dominated foreign investment in Zimbabwe, but often indirectly through South African subsidiaries; few companies had subsidiaries only in Rhodesia.[1] In several key cases, control of 'British' firms passed to South Africa: South African Breweries transferred its headquarters from London to South Africa, while in 1966 Anglo American grouped all its interests into Anglo American Rhodesia, taking nominal control from some London-based firms in the group. UDI and sanctions accelerated this trend.[2] Thus South African capital has grown both through direct investment and indirectly through the common link with Britain, and now controls about one-quarter of productive investment in Zimbabwe (see Statistical Annex).

During colonial times, international trade was largely with Europe and was directed predominantly through the Mozambican port of Beira. During the UDI/sanctions period (1965-79), trade increased with and through South Africa. Sanctions were also the main cause of shifting trade patterns. In 1965 Britain was still Zimbabwe's main trading partner, while by independence trade with South Africa was three times as large as with any other single country. The South African economy has been highly protected through both import controls and high tariffs, but special exemptions were made for various Rhodesian products.[3] This arose partly through commercial reciprocity, but it was encouraged by South Africa's geopolitical strategy during the UDI period. The most recent trade agreement was signed in 1964, and permitted a variety of goods to enter South Africa under reduced tariffs, subject to quotas. This proved to be of great importance to infant industry in Rhodesia, and until recently about three-quarters of all exports of manufactured goods were to South Africa.[4] Nevertheless, only three sectors really benefited: clothing, radios, and rod and wire from Lancashire

Steel (see below). Given the disparity in the sizes of the economies and Zimbabwe's difficulties in other markets, the South African market naturally has become much more important for Zimbabwe than has *its* market for South Africa.

This history puts the Zimbabwean economy in a much more complex relationship to South Africa than that of any of the other countries in this study. In part, South Africa fills the role of metropolitan power in both economic and social terms, It is also the nearest more industrialised country, and is linked by telex, telephones, good roads and railways, and regular flights. Many whites (and some blacks) have been educated in South Africa; many have worked there and have relatives there. This means that many Zimbabweans (and not only whites) naturally think in terms of people and institutions in South Africa.

If that were the extent of the links, the story would be much simpler. However the long independence struggle and the relationship which developed between the white minority regimes in South Africa and Rhodesia left a legacy of another kind of links. Roughly half of the whites left Zimbabwe at or soon after independence, and many of those who stayed do not support the new government (for example, a majority voted for Ian Smith's Republican Front in the 1985 elections). They often feel that white South Africans share and therefore understand what they see as a unique set of problems ignored by the rest of the world — the problems of maintaining a racial hegemony.

There is a spectrum of white opinion, ranging from an active South African fifth column inside Zimbabwe, through the unenthusiastic, to outspoken Zimbabwean nationalists. Some actions of the fifth column were noted in Chapter 14 and it is probably safe to assume that most (but not all) of the active agents of South Africa have now left Zimbabwe. The nationalists are playing a particularly important role in business and strongly oppose the antics of the Republican Front and the sabotage carried out by South African agents.

For the middle group, South African links provide an alternative and an opportunity. For example, transfer pricing is used all over the world as a way of moving money out of developing countries. But in Zimbabwe, it is often businessmen moving money to South Africa where they have long-established contacts and where they may hope eventually to move themselves. Similarly, they will be resistant to attempts to delink from South Africa. Finally, they will share the racism of some South African businessmen.

Thus the Zimbabwean economy is linked to South Africa not simply as a developing economy to a more industrialised one, but also through a complex web of geographic, social, and political interactions. Furthermore, these occur in a framework of South African destabilisation and pressure for regional hegemony sketched in the initial chapters of this book. For example, in 1981 the largely white business community was acting in a climate created by active South African sabotage and extensive economic pressure, when many of their close friends had left for South Africa or were planning to do so. Business decisions, even if made on apparently economic grounds, were inevitably coloured by perceptions of the future of Zimbabwe, SADCC, and links with South Africa. More recently, decisions about business links with Mozambique or shipping goods through Mozambican ports have been made in a climate created by South African destabilisation in Mozambique, and with anti-Mozambique propaganda by Renfreight and other South African agencies in Zimbabwe. At the same time, nationalistic business people (both white and black) were taking an increasingly important part in the economy, and the government was playing a major role.

Because Zimbabwe's relationship to South Africa is so complex, this chapter sets out not simply to document active South African sabotage. It also looks at the continuing South African role in the economy. And it looks at Zimbabwean efforts to reduce the powerful role of South Africa, which have been more sophisticated than those of any other state in the region.

The study of South Africa's role in the economy is intrinsically important, because it is a SADCC (and a Zimbabwe government) goal to reduce dependence on South Africa. But it is also important because that dependence provides the basis for South African manipulation and sabotage. Few of the examples are clearcut. If a businessman smuggles money to South Africa, would he have been just as likely to do so to Switzerland? It is impossible to say, but what is true is that the particular relationship with South Africa makes it easier and more likely.

KEY COMPANIES

Almost all companies in Zimbabwe have extensive South African links, but not all are South African. The most important are the South African companies Anglo American, Barlow Rand, and Old Mutual, and the British firms Lonrho, RTZ, and Turner and Newall.

The eight biggest companies listed on the Zimbabwe Stock Exchange are: Delta, Hippo Valley, Zimbabwe Alloys, and National Foods (all controlled or dominated by Anglo), David Whitehead (Lonrho), Hunyani (Barlow), Plate Glass (Barlow), and TA Holdings (Zimbabwean).[5]

Both Delta and Hunyani have put proposals to the government to permit at least 50% Zimbabwean ownership, but it remains unclear if control would still rest with the South African parent.

Anglo American Corporation of South Africa

In terms of either turnover or total capital invested, 'Anglo' is the largest single economic entity in Zimbabwe apart from the state. Since 1966 it has controlled the assets in Zimbabwe of the former British South Africa Company, which effectively owned Southern Rhodesia (including mines, farms, and railways) until 1923. Anglo controls the production of products as diverse as sugar, beer, and coal. It is not quoted directly on the Zimbabwe Stock Exchange, preferring to be the main (or controlling) shareholder in seven or eight listed companies (see Table overleaf).[6]

In addition to the six major firms in the Anglo group, Anglo has dozens of wholly owned subsidiaries in finance, transport, property, agriculture (Mazoe Citrus Estates) and industry (especially linked to mining: Clay Products, Boart, Hogarths). Through interests in South African parent companies, it dominates the fertiliser industry, which is crucial in an agricultural country.[7] In the milling sector it has 49% of Blue Ribbon Foods and at least 24% of National Foods, the country's largest miller with seven of the 13 maize mills.[8] It has a small holding in Zisco (the Zimbabwe Iron and Steel Corporation).[9] Anglo is also important in fuel: all Zimbabwe motor fuel now contains 15% ethonol made from sugarcane at Anglo's Triangle sugar mill and 1% benzol produced at the coking plant of the Anglo-run Wankie Colliery.

Listed companies controlled or dominated by Anglo (Z$m)

Company	Capital employed	Turnover	Operating profits	Anglo's share
Anglo Group				
Bindura Nickel	163.6	77.0	12.7	69%
Border Timbers	27.8	15.2*	0.3*	65%
Hippo Valley	105.6	60.9	5.6	41%
RAL Holdings	12.0+	...	3.0	53%
Wankie Colliery	148.0	78.5	14.7	23%
Zimbabwe Alloys	87.4	76.0	14.3*	65%
Other				
Delta Corporation	160.7	254.1	23.9	control via SAB
National Foods	73.9	205.0	18.5	24%

for comparison, the largest predominantly Zimbabwean firm is

TA Holdings	84.0	180.0	9.6	—

All data for the 1984/5 financial year, except * half-year results at annualised rate.
(+ = authorised capital)

Finally, Anglo's 1983 takeover of South African Breweries gave it control of Delta, the largest single company in Zimbabwe in terms of turnover or market capitalisation, and Edgars retail chain. Delta has a monopoly on brewing through subsidiaries National Breweries (lager beer, gross turnover Z$88.5m) and Chibuku Breweries (traditional sorghum beer, Z$76.3m). It dominates the retail trade (OK Bazaars and Springmaster, Z$85m). And it is important in a number of other areas including tourism (Zimbabwe Sun Hotels, Z$19.7m), soft drinks (Unibev, including Coca Cola, Z$30.1m), and wine and liquor (through a large shareholding in African Distillers). In addition, Delta has investments of Z$49.2m in other companies, which earned Z$8.3m out of a total profit of Z$11.1m in 1983/84.

Barlow Rand

Barlow Rand is another major South African presence in Zimbabwe, although much less visible than Anglo. Thomas Barlow & Sons (Rhodesia) changed its name to Astra Corporation after independence, and claimed to be owned by Bommenede Houdstermaatschappij (Ned) B.V. of the Netherlands. But this is purely a holding company established in April 1981 by Barlow Rand; the link is admitted privately, but never officially.

Barlow's main holding in Zimbabwe is Hunyani, Zimbabwe's largest pulp and paper company, employing Z$42m capital and with a turnover of Z$47.5m in 1983/84.[10] The Astra Group includes three vehicle distributors — Zemco (earthmoving), Puzey & Payne (car, truck, and bus), and Farmec (tractor) — as well as Astra Engineering (contract engineering), Astra Paints, Zimbabwe Handling Equipment Company, and the Component Rebuild Centre (a new automotive engine overhaul firm). Before its sales of Imco to Tinto Industries in 1984, Astra claimed assets of US$57m.

Old Mutual

Old Mutual is the largest life insurance operator in Zimbabwe, with more assets than all other life insurance companies combined.[11] It is a sister company to Old Mutual in South Africa, which is the largest assurance company there. In 1981 Old Mutual (South Africa)) had assets of R5140m and Old Mutual (Zimbabwe) of Z$392m, which had risen to Z$608m in 1983. Both are 'mutual societies', which means that they are officially owned by their policy holders.

Technically the two Old Mutuals are independent companies, and the official line is to stress the distinction. In fact there are very close links. Indeed, Old Mutual (South Africa) had assets of R5140m and Old Mutual (Zimbabwe) of Societies as the 'South African Mutual Life Assurance Society' with headquarters in South Africa and board membership determined in South Africa. Staff move freely between the two companies; until 1984, all senior staff of Old Mutual (Zimbabwe) were seconded from South Africa.[12] There was overlapping management of investments, and the Zimbabwe company was dependent on use of the Old Mutual computer in Cape Town (for which a fee was paid).

Although each Old Mutual invests mainly in its own country, both have invested in the other country. A special loophole in the exchange control regulations (now closed) was designed to allow Old Mutual (Zimbabwe) to invest in South Africa. By late 1985 new Zimbabwe legislation was enforcing a formal divorce; in future Old Mutual (Zimbabwe) will choose its own board.[13]

Old Mutual (Zimbabwe) is probably the largest single institutional investor in companies listed on the Zimbabwe Stock Exchange, with assets valued at Z$272m in 1983.[14] It is also active in property, and has launched or completed eight new developments worth Z$90m since independence, as well as buying out the Zimbabwe interests of the British property company MEPC for Z$16m.

Old Mutual (South Africa) is now the dominant force in shipping in Zimbabwe. It owns the South African national shipping line Safmarine (see Chapter 15) and its Zimbabwe subsidiary Zimarine, as well as the main freight and forwarding agency Renfreight. Old Mutual (South Africa) also owns a majority of Rennie-Grinaker (Anglovaal of South Africa owns the other 40%), which owns Kariba Batteries, Grinaker Construction, Jagger Wholesalers, 25% of Thomas Cook travel agents, and several major hotels.[15]

Lonrho

The *Lon*don and *Rho*desia Mining and Land Company, founded in 1909, was one of a number of firms given concessions by the British South African Company. None were spectacularly successful until Lonrho's take-off under Tiny Rowland in the 1960s. In Zimbabwe the company expanded first into the motor trade (in which Rowland's first successes had been achieved), then strengthened its holdings in both mining and ranching by judicious takeovers. Then Rowland masterminded the construction of the Beira to Mutare oil pipeline. Closed in late 1965, soon after UDI, the pipeline had only operated for ten months (until reopened on 19 June 1982) and cannot be said to be a hugely successful investment; indeed, Lonrho tried to sue British oil companies for breaking sanctions during UDI as the pipeline company had the contract for oil supply and any action which prolonged the life of the Smith regime delayed the income-earning prospects of the pipeline. Despite this, there were reports of Lonrho's own sanctions-busting activity.[16]

The Lonrho empire in Zimbabwe is dominated by Coronation Syndicate (Corsyn) and David Whitehead. The former controls three gold mines which produce 30% of Zimbabwe's gold, making it the largest gold producer in the country. It is owned by one of Lonrho's South African subsidiaries, Tweefontein United Collieries, whose major asset it is. Corsyn's Zimbabwe stock exchange listing was suspended as the proportion of minority shareholders increased in South Africa and fell in Zimbabwe. It is not clear that Zimbabwe benefits in any way from having these key assets owned through South Africa.

David Whitehead is a textile company which dominates the Zimbabwean market and is the main Lonrho-controlled listed company. In addition there are about fifty Lonrho subsidiaries in Zimbabwe, in most sectors, making the group more diversified than Anglo or other large companies. They include ranches with 85,000 cattle, the main producer of wattle, the main coffee grower, a freight and forwarding agent (Kuehne & Nagel), and firms making window frames, furniture, and records. It is also a major force in vehicle assembly and repair.

Banks

Banking is dominated by two British banks, Standard and Barclays. Both have strong South African links; roughly one-quarter of Standard's overall profits come from South Africa. Anglo has shareholdings in the South African subsidiaries of both banks, and during the UDI period had board members on both banks in Zimbabwe. The other three commercial banks are Zimbank (48.7% government, bought from Nedbank of South Africa which retains 12.2%), BCCZ (53% Bank of Credit and Commerce International, 47% government), and Grindleys (UK). The most important merchant bank is the Anglo-owned RAL Merchant Bank. The largest finance house is UDC, which was taken over in 1984 by a South African-linked firm, Edesa, and changed its name to Edesa Holdings.[17]

ATTITUDES

South Africa is so dominant in the economy that the attitudes of South African companies and managers are extremely important. Some are openly hostile to black-ruled states, and these attitudes are influential on both blacks and whites in the Zimbabwean subsidiaries.

Racism in the boardroom

With independence and the end of sanctions, a specialised Zimbabwean company set out to expand into the SADCC market. Its exports to Mozambique, Botswana, Zambia, and Malawi jumped 25-fold between 1980 and 1983, and it was fairly billed as 'A remarkable success story' by *Industrial Review*, the journal of the Confederation of Zimbabwe Industries (CZI). The firm embarked on a major expansion, using loans and reinvested profits, and buying new machinery through the US Commodity Import Programme (CIP), which allows firms to buy US machinery in local currency.

The company seemed in all respects a Zimbabwean firm, with an aggressive, nationalistic Zimbabwean managing director. In fact it is owned by one of the South African monopoly groups. When the managing director proposed to the South African parent a further expansion, he was firmly squashed by the parent board. Again using the CIP he planned to expand without any cost to the parent; but he needed Zimbabwe dollars, and proposed to raise them by enlarging the capital base and selling shares locally (for Zimbabwe dollars). It was this which was unacceptable. One director in South Africa summed up the opposition when he declared simply: I'm not getting into bed with kaffirs.'

Not all South African companies operating in Zimbabwe have this attitude. Some have given their local managers considerable freedom, and even encouraged reinvestment. The point is that in at least some cases, business is *not* always colour blind, searching out profits wherever they can be made; racism directly affects some boardroom decisions in South Africa. It is not that South African businessmen reject profits from black countries; in these instances there is a much more subtle process at work. 'Even if they criticise racial policies inside South Africa, businessmen there are convinced that blacks can't make a go of it — so in their mind it's foolish to invest or expand,' explained the spurned managing director. 'In any case, South Africans are very parochial. And they have been brainwashed by the media and by the claims of the thousands of ex-Rhodesians who are praying for Zimbabwe to fail.'

Of course, profit considerations do play a role. When it exported to Zambia and Malawi, this company began competing with a South African subsidiary of its parent company. Although the competition was not large, it must have had some influence on the board's decision as well. Forced to decide between small profits for a white-run home company and potentially larger profits in a black state, the board chose the former, and expressed its decision in explicitly racist terms.

The Anglo alternative and SAB

Anglo American takes precisely the opposite line, and has shown in both Zambia and Zimbabwe that it is happy to be even a minority partner — so long as it retains control. Anglo may or may not like black governments, but it does make profit-oriented decisions, and is willing to deal with majority-ruled states.[18] For example, in sharp contrast to the attitude of the firm cited above, Anglo has sold additional shares to the public in its Zimbabwe Alloys.

Wankie Colliery is the best example of how Anglo works. In 1982, Anglo negotiated the sale of 40%, and thus nominal control, to the government. The government paid more than double the current price of Wankie shares on the Zimbabwe stock exchange while Anglo kept effective control. Anglo retained 23% of shares and the right to appoint three of the ten directors, including the managing director, and it continued to run the mine.[19] As the new chairman, Douglas Kadenhe, reported in his annual statement in April 1983: 'Mine and managerial arrangements together with administration and technical services have remained unchanged.'

It is a perfect arrangement for Anglo. It gains protection through state participation, while retaining control. It has guaranteed profits, through a coal price agreement which ensures profits based on capital employed; indeed, the sale was linked to a massive expansion of Wankie (see below) at no direct cost to Anglo, but which would increase the capital base and thus potentially raise Anglo profits above what they were before Anglo sold a 'controlling interest' to the state.

Even so, Anglo's attitude toward Zimbabwe is sometimes less sympathetic than that of other transnationals. For example, in early 1981 Anglo announced that it had abandoned plans to expand Zimbabwe Alloys' chrome production. At precisely the same time the US company Union Carbide announced plans to spend Z$20m to expand chrome mining. Japanese mining experts, who happened to be visiting Zimbabwe at the time, attributed Anglo's decision to a purely political desire not to invest in Zimbabwe.[20] Alternatively it may have been made on economic grounds. But nearly 90% of the world's chrome comes from Zimbabwe and South Africa, and Anglo may simply have preferred to support chrome production at home. Or it may have been a long term ploy to extract concessions — two years later the government lent Anglo Z$6m to keep Zimalloys and Bindura Nickel open.

Anglo's overall approach contrasts most sharply with that of South African Breweries, before it came under Anglo control in 1983. SAB pulled out of Angola, Mozambique, and Zambia after independence in those countries. In Angola and Mozambique, SAB had made significant new investments in the early 1970s on the assumption that the MPLA and Frelimo would never come to power, but then abandoned those investments in panic in 1975 without even asking if it would be allowed to continue operating. The extent to which racism overshadowed SAB's profit considerations is shown by the fact that other South African companies still operate profitably in all three countries, and some of SAB's investments have been taken over by other private firms. Only in the BLS states, where it can guarantee a virtual turn-key operation, and where it is essential to keep competitors out of the customs union market, has SAB expanded.

This would be more important for South Africa than Zimbabwe, except that SAB owns Delta, the beer, retail, and hotel firm which is the biggest company in Zimbabwe (see above). As in other countries, SAB began running down its operation after independence. It narrowed its operations to fields of traditional expertise at a time when many other companies were diversifying: Springmaster, the largest furniture manufacturer was sold in 1984, while Delta retained the Springmaster retail outlets and expanded elsewhere in the retail sector.[21] It also moved key directors and experienced managers to South Africa, especially for expansions in the bantustans, while at the same time resisting localisation. The press accused Delta of appointing token, powerless black managers.[22] Some resigned in frustration on finding chains of command revised so that when they replaced a white manager, staff (especially whites) who had previously reported to that manager were assigned to report to another white rather than to them.

Then there seemed to be a change in attitude. Blacks were appointed to important posts; for example, Tom Mswaka, formerly Permanent Secretary in the Ministry of Economic Planning and Development, became managing director of the National Breweries subsidiary. The change was signalled most strongly in an unusual advertisement in a Zimbabwe supplement to the (London) *Guardian* on 23 August 1985 headed 'partners in a growing, progressive nation'; it declared that 'Delta Corporation has confidence in the future of Zimbabwe' and noted that

Delta is seeking 'opportunities for investment' that 'complement national goals'.[23]

It is too early to tell if the shift is real, but four factors suggest it could be. First is the Anglo takeover, which led to the departure of many old SAB managers in South Africa, and probably means Anglo attitudes overriding the feelings of the old SAB men. This would be linked to the second factor, nationalistic Zimbabweans still inside Delta who may not be as anxious as some of their old managers and former colleagues to 'take the gap' and move to South Africa. Third, Delta, in spite of itself, made massive profits in 1984/85.[24] And fourth, the sheer size of Delta makes it much harder for SAB to simply abandon its interests as it did a decade earlier in neighbouring states. What now seems most likely is a rearrangement similar to that of Wankie Colliery, in which Anglo sold a majority share to the government but retained management (and thus effective control).[25]

Does it matter?

Within Zimbabwe, managers and government officials argue that there *is* a real difference between South African-based corporations and other transnationals. 'South Africans have limited experience and a colonial mentality; they don't even like to visit black states. Non-South African executives have wider horizons — they can see the profit potential here. It makes a real difference to report to an American or European, and not to report through South Africa,' one manager told us.

Clearly, there are exceptions. Some firms, particularly Anglo, seem anxious to stay and are reinvesting; despite their tensions with the government, they see potential for future profits. And Zimbabwean managers of even the most racist firms often have a free hand to push ahead independent of central policy. Nevertheless, there are special problems with South African companies. And it is often racist South African businesses which influence the Zimbabwean economy.

Reflecting this view, several firms, including the German chemical company BASF, BAT (formerly British American Tobacco) and GEC changed the position of their Zimbabwean subsidiaries. Until independence they had been subordinate to the South African subsidiaries, but they were all restructured so as to report directly to the parent company.[26]

ACTIONS

Excessive dependence on South Africa is dangerous precisely because it permits actions to be taken which are not in Zimbabwe's interests. These are rarely 'political', in the sense that most private South African businesses are not actively trying to destabilise Zimbabwe. They do not often take actions to support their government's policy if it will mean a loss of profits. Nevertheless, as we have seen in the previous section, the social and geopolitical position of South African business executives sometimes leads them to take different (and less profitable) decisions than would be taken by local firms or even by other transnationals.

In this section, we look at several specific actions taken by South African firms which have been harmful to Zimbabwe. On the one hand, their damage has been so strong that in some quarters they would be considered 'economic sabotage'.

Yet in another sense they were simply decisions to maximise profit. In the two main examples, South African firms acted simply to increase their earnings from steel and coal. They were perfectly 'rational' capitalist actions, and were probably legal. Yet both cost the Zimbabwe economy dearly. The reason for their inclusion here is that they were possible largely because of the special relationship between South Africa and Zimbabwe inherited from the UDI/sanctions period; non-South African firms would not have been in a position to act in that way, nor would they have wanted to. What these examples show, then, is not that South African firms set out to sabotage the Zimbabwean economy, but rather that the special dependence on South Africa leads to rational, profit-maximising decisions which seriously harm Zimbabwe.

Lancashire Steel

One of the most dramatic manoeuvres, in which South African interests destroyed the competition of an independent Zimbabwean rival, was the attack on Lancashire Steel. Interestingly, conflicting pressures prevented them gaining South African government support until the final coup de grace.

Lancashire Steel was until June 1984 a subsidiary of the British Steel Corporation, although it was run by its local managers and largely ignored by its parent. It produces steel rod and wire from billets supplied by Zisco. Under the bilateral trade agreement, it exported 1000 tonnes a month to South Africa. This satisfied barely 2% of the latter's market, but it was worth Z$5m per year and was important for Zimbabwe as a toehold in manufactured exports.

The problem for Lancashire began with the partial denationalisation of the South African steel industry in the late 1970s. Haggie Rand (part of Anglo) has a near monopoly on rod and wire.[27] Users are tied in to a system involving high basic monopoly prices, with significant discounts for captive rod and wire user companies. The industry is highly protected, so that export prices must be half or less of domestic prices. And it is immensely profitable — despite the severe depression of the early 1980s which meant it operated at scarcely 30% of capacity, Haggie Rand made profits of 20% of turnover.

There was a rapid rise of a group of 'independent' wire users, dependent on the cheaper (and, they claim, better quality) rod and wire from Lancashire. The independents were putting severe pressure on Haggie Rand's customers, stimulating demands for greater discounts. Over a six year period, Haggie (with Iscor, the South African parastatal Iron and Steel Corporation) tried to have a 25% duty imposed on Lancashire imports (in 1978 and 1984); to buy it out (1981 and 1983); to ensure that rod and wire were excluded from the renegotiation of the bilateral trade agreement (1982); to press Zisco to deny it supplies (1982); and to have the quota cut (1984). All of these failed, in part because the South African government did not back Haggie's attempts to change the trade agreement.

Haggie's final ploy was to offer to buy the entire 1000 tonnes a month, if Lancashire agreed not to sell to the independent wire users. The Lancashire management refused, pointing out that this would put the independents out of business. As soon as that happened, Haggie could cancel the contract — and Lancashire would have no export market at all because its previous customers would have gone out of business. The matter was raised in the Zimbabwean and South African press, and even in the South African parliament. The Johannesburg *Star* warned that such a move would force Lancashire out of business, and lead to a South African monopoly over wire in the entire SADCC region.[28] But Haggie won in the end, and thereby hangs the tale.

Iron and steel is an incestuous industry in southern Africa, in part because of the sanctions period. Two aspects are particularly important. One is that Haggie Rand also produces rod and wire in Zimbabwe, using Zisco billets. The other is the role of the Austrian iron and steel parastatal, Voest-Alpine, which is involved with Iscor, Zisco, and in Angola. Voest-Alpine's controversial Kurt Kuhn was managing director of (the then) Risco in the 1970s;[29] he played a prominent sanctions-busting role in its expansion and only resigned in 1979, just before Zimbabwe's independence. He returned as managing director in 1982, with a Voest-Alpine team funded through an Austrian government technical assistance loan, and planned a Z$200m rehabilitation. It was not put out to tender, and is to be done by Voest-Alpine. West German firms point out that they supply Voest-Alpine, which adds a significant markup; it was also reported by a university study that there could have been Z$50m more in local content. Despite the size of this contract, however, Kuhn's critics argue that he and Voest-Alpine had a relatively greater and longer term interest in remaining in favour with the much larger South African steel industry, where more large contracts could be gained.[30]

Whatever the reasons, it became clear that Haggie Rand (Zimbabwe) was supporting the efforts of Haggie Rand (South Africa) to break Lancashire, and that Zisco was backing Haggie Rand (Zimbabwe) against Lancashire. The government, of course, looked to Zisco for advice, so it too was turned against Lancashire. This showed up in various ways. For example, all steel exports are subsidised, but Lancashire found that it was getting a subsidy of only Z$80 per tonne when Haggie was getting Z$140 per tonne for the same products to the same countries (for example, to Malawi). And when Zisco raised its prices by 25% in late 1982, permission for Lancashire to pass on the price rise was delayed for several months, causing a two-month shutdown and critically affecting its competitive position in the long run.[31] Tension grew between Zisco and Lancashire Steel as Kuhn and Zisco pressed the Lancashire board of directors to accept the Haggie offer.[32] On one visit to Lancashire, Kuhn said Zimbabwe only had room for one rod mill, and implied it wasn't Lancashire.

About this time, Haggie, Zisco, and some government sources began to allege that Lancashire Steel was badly and corruptly run. They said that Lancashire was undercharging, implying that part of the difference was going into bank accounts in South Africa. This was certainly not true, but such transfer pricing is so common in other sectors that the allegation was readily believed. Apparently briefed by Zisco, Industry Minister Kumbirai Kangai said publicly that Lancashire had been grossly mismanaged and stripped of its assets by the managing director, and had been selling steel wire to South Africa at R120 per tonne too little.[33] No evidence for these allegations ever emerged, and the Minister had almost certainly been misled; for example, Lancashire was selling wire at R120 per tonne below Haggie's 'official' price, but Haggie never sold at that price either because of its discount system.

Eventually, burdened by debts, in June 1984 Lancashire Steel was taken over by the government and Zisco, who appointed a new board. Its first act was to sign the exclusive contract with Haggie. Nominally it was, indeed, for R120 per tonne more. But it was different from the old contract in two key ways: prices were quoted in rand rather than Zimbabwe dollars, and prices were quoted for wire and rod delivered in Johannesburg rather than loaded on railway wagons in

Zimbabwe. The latter point meant that Lancashire had to pay all shipping costs and customs duties (which Haggie and Iscor were trying to raise). When all that was taken into account, combined with the fall in the rand with respect to the Zimbabwe dollar, plus SATS' increased rail charges, it turned out that Lancashire earned less money than before!

Kuhn's contract expired and he left Zisco at the end of 1984, taking many staff (some Voest-Alpine and all those recruited through his own Geneva-based agency); but the damage had been done. An independent and nationalistic Lancashire board had been purged, and Haggie had gained effective control of Lancashire's exports. The irony was that the key had been for South Africans to accuse an honest management of defrauding Zimbabwe in a way that is so easy and so commonly done with the collusion of South African business that everyone believed it.

The end, sadly, was all too predictable. In August 1985 the South African government imposed a new 50% tariff on steel imports, which was expected to kill Lancashire's 'exports stone dead'.[34] But worse may be to follow, for Haggie in South Africa may now feel that Haggie Rand Zimbabwe has fulfilled its role in destroying competition, and may simply close it down. In that event, rod and wire production in southern Africa will contract to an exclusively South African base.

The Hwange power station

Zimbabwe's largest single development project, the Z$1bn Hwange coal-fired power station,[35] is another example of how government policy and SADCC regional goals were subverted. The story is complex, because it can be argued that the main participant, Anglo, was acting entirely from a profit motive — the coal-fired power station provided a market for coal from the Anglo-controlled Wankie Colliery.[36] But the story is important here because the development of the power station aided South African goals set out earlier in this book. In particular, the justification of the power station was that Zimbabwe should not cooperate with its neighbours, and should not buy electricity from Mozambique or Zambia. Thus the very act of making this case discouraged SADCC cooperation, and supported an important South African goal.

It sometimes is argued that other transnationals in the same position would have made the same choice, and no doubt some might have. What is important is that, for historical reasons already set out, Anglo was in that powerful a position. Furthermore, other TNCs and national industries more in tune with Zimbabwean goals probably would not have pursued this policy. Thus the South African ownership is important because it made the whole action possible, because it was predicated on the sort of anti-SADCC argument that came naturally to a South African firm, and because it ultimately supported South African goals.

Most of Zimbabwe's electricity is generated by the Kariba dam between Zambia and Zimbabwe, with some electricity imported from the power station on the Zambian side. A massive coal-fired power station was proposed (in the first instance, during UDI) to make Zimbabwe nearly self-sufficient in electricity. It consists of three parts: the expansion of Wankie Colliery, Stage I of the Power station, and another power station called Stage II which itself has two phases.[37]

There is some economic justification for Stage I. It will burn low-grade coal which is currently discarded, but which must be dug out because it is on top of the higher quality coking coal. Thus the fuel will be unusually cheap, while Wankie will get some earnings for coal it previously wasted.

The second stage was very different, and much more controversial. The power would be more expensive than from Hwange I, in part because Hwange II would not simply consume waste coal, but would require the digging of additional higher grade coking coal for power station use. It would be cheaper to buy hydroelectricity from Zambia or Mozambique than thermally generated power from Hwange II. Furthermore, Zambia and Mozambique wanted to sell electricity to Zimbabwe, while under the plan Zambian power exports to Zimbabwe would fall to lower levels than during the 1970s when the two countries were supposedly at war.

As well as going against theoretical pledges to increase regional cooperation, the project also seems likely to harm Zimbabwean trade in a practical way. Zimbabwe expects to export manufactured goods to its neighbours, and one of the few things they could provide in exchange is electricity. Finally, a vast amount of capital was being assigned to an unnecessary project; that money could be used elsewhere, while Zimbabwe was being saddled with large repayments on an unnecessary foreign debt.

The main justification for the second stage of the power station was self-sufficiency, and this was backed up both by political arguments and by a technical argument which seemed to show that there was no choice but to build Hwange II. The main study behind the proposal included a very high forecast for electricity demand, and it warned that if new supplies were not provided quickly, Zimbabwe would run out of electricity.[38] The obvious supply alternatives in Zambia and Mozambique were eliminated in different ways. Zambia was forecast to have economic growth as rapid as Zimbabwe's, so that it would quickly use up all its surplus power and have none to sell to Zimbabwe. Zambia publicly protested that this would not be the case, but it was ignored.[39] A second power station in Mozambique's Cahora Bassa dam would have provided the same amount of electricity at less than half the capital cost, as Mozambique was proposing at just that time; this was avoided simply by not mentioning it in the report, apparently on the grounds that Mozambique was not in the World Bank so could not be considered for a World Bank funded project.

Technical claims were backed up by a political campaign against Mozambique and Zambia. Zimbabwe's still largely white technical elite argued that a relatively industrialised and advanced Zimbabwe was superior to its neighbours, and should not be dependent on them. It was able to present a basically white-supremacist case as a more subtle Zimbabwe-national case that was more acceptable to the new black civil servants and ministers. It also said that Zambia was difficult to negotiate with, and sometimes threatened to cut off Zimbabwe's power. This is probably true, but objectively Zambia was no harder to negotiate with than Anglo.[40]

The argument against Cahora Bassa was that South African backed MNR rebels would cut the power line, so that any supply from Mozambique would be insecure. In effect, they said that South African destabilisation should be allowed to prevent regional cooperation, and supported continued dependence on a South African company instead. In the event, the argument was turned on its head when anti-government forces in Zimbabwe sabotaged electricity lines serving Mutare in 1982. Under government pressure, a reluctant Electricity Supply Commission decided to upgrade the link with Mozambique as a way of securing power in eastern Zimbabwe should there be any further such sabotage actions.[41]

Stage II, Phase 1 was approved in 1982, despite objections. However, approval of Stage II, Phase 2 was not as easy to obtain; despite pressure from Wankie and ESC, it had not been agreed by late 1985 and may have been shelved indefinitely.

Financial chicanery

Hundreds of millions of dollars have been smuggled from Zimbabwe to South Africa since independence, according to former Home Minister Simbi Mubako.[42] Some has literally been smuggled out in the form of currency, gold, jewellery, and drugs. But probably more has been moved through various forms of transfer pricing and false invoicing. This sort of deal is particularly easy because of the secret networks which were set up via South Africa as part of sanctions busting during the UDI period. The South African agents always took a cut, and it was simple to ask them to stash away money for the Zimbabwean partner.

Cone Textiles, one of the largest textile companies in Zimbabwe, paid a R1 per kilogram surcharge on dyestuffs imported from Yorkshire Chemicals (UK) via Comitex (South Africa), which cost Zimbabwe at least Z$2m before it was discovered. In another case, the general manager of Halsted Brothers in Mutare was allocated foreign exchange to buy fire bricks from his brother in South Africa; instead his brother sent packing cases full of wood chips.[43] In both of these cases, people were charged but absconded to South Africa.

In other instances there are no formal charges and no publicity. For example, four Zimbabwean pharmaceutical dealers had their foreign exchange allocations cut off after they were detected transferring money to South Africa through overcharges by parent companies there. In one of the cases, the manager of the Zimbabwean firm set up a South African company for the sole purpose of 'selling' drugs to the Zimbabwe firm at triple the previous price. All these cases involve imports, but there are also instances of underinvoicing exports.

Propaganda

Malicious propaganda is also an important component of South African destabilisation. False information planted by the South African government and exaggerated reports from Johannesburg-based newspaper correspondents are widely considered to be an important factor in discouraging new Western private investment in Zimbabwe. Sometimes, this is backed up by very pessimistic forecasts of Zimbabwe's economic prospects.

For example, the conservative Johannesburg *Financial Mail* was moved to contrast 'the persistent gloom painted by the published reports of the Harare economic gurus of Zimbank and RAL Merchant Bank' with the 'more cheery assessment from the Reserve Bank of Zimbabwe'.[44] RAL is Anglo's bank, and has been subject to some criticism on this issue. There was a public row when a RAL economist painted a particularly discouraging picture to a Saudi Arabian prince who wanted to invest in Zimbabwe.[45] Zimbank is now 48.7% owned by the government, with a minority 12.2% holding by the South African Nedbank.[46] But faced with many demands for scarce skilled staff, the government has not yet been able to change the old management and outlook. A high civil servant admitted: 'We may have the most shares, but we don't yet have *control* over Zimbank.'[47]

HOW ZIMBABWE RESPONDS

The Zimbabwe government recognises the dangers of continued dependence on South Africa, and it has followed as sophisticated a path to delinking as any country in the region. It has a cautious but reasonably consistent policy of extending local control wherever possible, but not taking actions which would provoke a South African reaction. Some would argue that it has been too cautious, and the government has clearly been out-flanked on issues like Lancashire Steel. Nevertheless, in a quiet way, it has significantly reduced dependence on South Africa, and is continuing to do so.

Reconciliation was the watchword at independence, as Robert Mugabe tried not to lose the skills of the white population, as had happened in Mozambique five years before. It worked to the extent that about half of Rhodesian whites still live in independent Zimbabwe. Africanisation has spread fairly fast in the civil service, but has yet to make a signficant impact on managerial levels in most of industry. Some of these managers, and the owners of some of the remaining small industries, are pro-Zimbabwe and nationalistic, so there is the nucleus of a 'national capital' in Zimbabwe unlike other SADCC states.

Others retain close links with South Africa and reconciliation necessarily means a degree of reconciliation with South African business. Indeed, despite the socialist and anti-apartheid stance, there has been little effort to reduce trade with South Africa and only a few South African companies have been nationalised.[48] Some influential figures in the government argue that the continued presence of South African companies and personnel provides some guarantee against the sort of destabilisation suffered by Mozambique and Angola, and it may have helped to end the 1981 pressure on Zimbabwe.

Localisation

There have been a number of strategic nationalisations (albeit agreed with the previous owners). Some, like the CAPS pharmaceutical firm and Lancashire Steel, were not South African. But the key ones were South African, and that particular foreign ownership probably pushed the government into early nationalisation. As well as Wankie, the government bought the daily newspapers and then the main newsagents (Kingstons) from Anglo-controlled companies. And a controlling interest in Rhobank (now Zimbank) was bought from Nedbank. There have also been repeated hints that at least some in the government want it to have a bigger role in the South African-dominated milling industry, and in Delta.[49]

There have been several private takeovers of South African owned firms. Soon after independence, the Thomas Meikle Trust acquired a majority holding in the South African-owned Zimbabwe Engineering Company (formerly Rescco). In 1984 the Cairns food group bought 60% of National Chemical Products from Sentrachem of South Africa, which meant that production of potable alcohol had passed into local hands. In 1985 the local Apex group bought out the South African-owned Abercal.[50]

The Preferential Trade Area (PTA) for Eastern and Southern Africa could encourage more local takeovers, and is providing a quiet area of struggle between the government and South African business. The PTA includes most SADCC states, plus east African countries such as Kenya and Ethiopia. It is a free trade area which depends on tariff reductions on an agreed list of items to increase trade.[51] Since its introduction in 1984, the PTA has generated significant amounts of new Zimbabwean exports. Hunyani Pulp and Paper, owned by Barlow Rand of South Africa, has been one of the beneficiaries, and its general manager, Chris Molam, is one of the PTA's strongest proponents. Molam is also vice-chairman of the Confederation of Zimbabwe Industries (CZI) trade promotion committee.

The problem for Hunyani is that under PTA rules, companies qualify only if a majority of managers are nationals and at least 51% of the equity is held by nationals. Furthermore, the rules are very clearly drawn — it does not matter where the company is registered, but rather who are the genuine beneficial owners. Zimbabwe has an exemption from this only until September 1986; after that, companies like Hunyani will no longer qualify. A campaign has been launched to extend the exemption and modify the rules, either by allowing companies like Hunyani that are locally registered and listed on the local stock exchange, even though they are foreign owned, or by allowing foreign owned companies that are at least locally managed.

The Zimbabwe government is being placed under pressure by some South African-owned businesses to push for changes within the PTA. So far, it has resisted. Officials argue that they knew full well what they were doing when they signed the agreement. Indeed, the rules are *intended* to support local business and prevent transnationals from using the PTA as a route into the region. And they hope it will force South African companies to increase local shareholdings to over 50%. There are indications that in 1986 Hunyani will do just that. It is also clear that the government has tried to block increased South African holdings. There have been no public statements, and when South Africa has protested, Zimbabwe has denied that there is such a policy. But in practice the Foreign Investment Committee rejects virtually any proposed South African investments. (The Haggie Rand attempt to acquire Lancashire Steel was one such rejection.)

However, Zimbabwe is unable to prevent foreign-owned companies from changing hands. One ironic aspect of disinvestment from South Africa is that Zimbabwean babies get thrown out with the South African bathwater. The biggest example of this was the Hong Kong firm Jardine Mathieson's sale of Rennie to Old Mutual. Most Rennie operations are in South Africa, and this was quite explicitly a disinvestment from South Africa. But Rennie (through Rennie-Grinaker Zimbabwe) controlled Kariba Batteries, Holiday Inns, and Rennies shipping in Zimbabwe, which thus passed from Hong Kong to South African control. In a similar case, the Dickinson Robinson group (UK) sold its South African and Zimbabwean holdings to Gencor (Sanlam — South Africa).

Control

More important than actual ownership, the government has asserted control over several key sectors. Probably the most important was the establishment of a Minerals Marketing Corporation, which will eventually take over the sale and export of most minerals, while leaving their production to the transnationals (many of whom, in the case of Zimbabwe, are South African or South Africa-based). This is based on the widely held assumption that transnationals gain their biggest mining profits through transfer pricing, and thus it is most useful to intervene in the marketing. In announcing the MMC, mining minister Maurice Nyagumbo said simply: 'The rip-off is ended'.

The government is also trying to Zimbabweanise Old Mutual, as noted above. It began by monitoring the insurance giant, and discovered at least two clear cases in which money was invested in South Africa when, even in Old Mutual's own terms, equally good investments were available in Zimbabwe. So in 1984 it put some of its own people into the company, and began forcing Old Mutual to separate from the 'sister' Old Mutual (South Africa). Computers will be delinked, and the practice of overlapping managements and investments will be ended — hopefully by 1986, according to government sources.

Another important step was to take control of reinsurance. At least Z$45m per year left the country in reinsurance premiums, mainly to South Africa. All eight local reinsurers were registered in South Africa; even two of the big names in reinsurance, Munich Reinsurance and Swiss Reinsurance, worked through South African subsidiaries. To control this, a government run Zimbabwe Reinsurance Company was set up in 1984 and is initially taking a compulsory 20% of all reinsurance business.

OUTSIDE AGENCIES

Zimbabwe and South Africa, of course, are not acting in isolation from the world context. A number of foreign agencies also influence their relationship, and can provide important support to SADCC and Zimbabwe's attempts to delink from South Africa. Unfortunately, many aid decisions are not made in a regional context; too often agencies look at Zimbabwe in isolation, or look at their Zimbabwean projects entirely differently from their SADCC projects. Often individual funding decisions are made without considering the South African implications.

Industrialisation is the key issue. With a relatively large and diversified engineering sector and the only integrated steel mill in black Africa, Zimbabwe must be the cornerstone to developing a SADCC manufacturing capacity independent of South Africa. However, Zimbabwe's industry developed behind the wall of sanctions; this means much of it is inefficient and its machinery is obsolete. In turn, this means that protection will be required for some years until firms modernise, and a significant amount of new machinery is required.

The World Bank

The World Bank plays a particularly important role in Zimbabwe and in the region as a whole. It has become an important financer of SADCC transport projects, and is supporting regional integration. And it has also provided vital funding for industrial rehabilitation. Yet several important World Bank decisions relating to Zimbabwe have gone against regional goals.

For example, a condition of a 1981 industrial rehabilitation loan was that a study of the 'international competitiveness' of Zimbabwean industry be commissioned first.[52] The methodology of the study was a completely unsophisticated application of the principle of 'comparative advantage', ignoring all the caveats the economic textbooks stress when discussing this principle. Its conclusion was that there were compelling economic grounds for closing down large sectors of more advanced industry immediately (including steel-making and some engineering) and for phasing out others. Zimbabwe should then concentrate on food processing and other relatively simple industry in which it currently had a 'comparative advantage'. No weight was given to arguments for protection of infant industry, to the need to build up a capital goods sector (as argued by the OAU and UN institutions), or to the importance of integrating the domestic economy. The only criterion was: Could Zimbabwe make an immediate financial gain from purchasing a commodity (frequently from South Africa) instead of producing it?

The World Bank thus seems to see Zimbabwe as a supplier and processor of primary products, less industrialised than at present, and more closely integrated with the South African economy. The fact that the lower cost South African industries concerned were built up under high protection, and that many are low cost only because of export subsidies which could be withdrawn, is not considered relevant.

The World Bank also strongly backed the Hwange thermal power station project, which went against regional cooperation goals, saddled Zimbabwe with unnecessary foreign debt, and unnecessarily raised electricity costs.

The problem, then, is a conflict of goals. On one side, the World Bank is actively supporting SADCC. But on the ground in Zimbabwe, it is also taking decisions which work against SADCC.

The International Monetary Fund

The IMF's standard package includes restrictions on government spending, cutting subsidies, devaluation, liberalising foreign exchange control, using the cheapest supplier even if it is politically unacceptable, and in general moving to a more open economy. In Zimbabwe, this has the direct effect of preventing the restructuring of the economy while limiting the amount of protection that the government can give to its industry. The IMF is not intentionally pushing Zimbabwe into the arms of South Africa; rather, its standard prescription plays directly into South Africa's hands by increasing dependence on the neighbour to the south, and no exception has been made for the special political conditions of the region.

Zimbabwe joined the IMF within five months of independence, largely because IMF membership is necessary to draw World Bank loans. It drew its first small IMF allocation in April 1981; as is normal with the first loan, no conditions were attached. Negotiations then began in earnest for a much larger loan, and the IMF took a larger role in the new country's financial planning. Just at this time, South Africa began to apply pressure to Zimbabwe, creating the transport crisis which cost Zimbabwe more than Z$5 million per week in lost exports (see Chapter 15). This created a crisis which forced the Zimbabwe government to take the IMF medicine.[53] It may be entirely coincidental that South African destabilisation forced Zimbabwe to accept what many believe to be thoroughly inappropriate IMF policy prescriptions, which in turn just happened to steer Zimbabwe in a direction which pleased South Africa. What is clear is that the IMF's lever on Zimbabwean economic policy was much strengthened by South African destabilisation.

Even if IMF 'stabilisation' policies were universally accepted as appropriate for countries whose internal policies have generated unsustainable external imbalances (and there is considerable reservation on this issue, even on market capitalist premises), it would *not* follow that they would be appropriate where imbalances were externally (and possibly temporarily) caused. Action against the destabilising force would seem more appropriate. But the IMF apparently took the opportunity to force a range of policy directions that were contrary to Zimbabwe's professed aims of redistribution, socialism, and increased self-reliance. With the recent example of the fall of the Manley government in Jamaica after a period when there was both sustained opposition to its policies from the IMF and also externally directed violence and destabilisation, it is understandable that the Zimbabwe government should have played safe and acceded to IMF demands.

Foreign aid in support of trade and industry

A central part of SADCC and PTA programmes to reduce dependence on South Africa, and thus reduce South African power in the region, is to increase trade between the majority ruled states and to support and expand the region's industry. Aid agencies have made a contribution to this. One simple example is the assembly in Zimbabwe of Land Rovers and lorries used by aid agencies in Mozambique and other countries, rather than their direct import from Europe. Larger projects are involved too. Morewear Industries won a 6.5m ecu EEC-funded contract to rehabilitate Zambia Railways wagons, and has recently won a much larger contract for the Tazara.

Even when sympathetic aid agencies and parastatals are involved, however, this does not always happen. Substantial EEC aid is going to the state owned copper mines in Zambia, while Zimbabwe has a significant mining equipment manufacturing sector. But of 55m ecu in recent soft loans under Sysmin, only 1m ecu went to Zimbabwe. And here the South African hand appears again. Despite nominal state ownership and management, South Africans still dominate the Zambian mines. One Z$1.5m order collapsed recently when a white simply said he was unwilling to buy from 'kaffirs'. EEC arguments that the Zimbabwean firm was the low bidder and thus had to be given the order were of no avail.[54]

Paper — two ways of looking at South African participation

A SADCC-supported project to expand a South African-owned paper company raised eyebrows in aid circles, but it also brought to the fore disputes about just how to reduce South African involvement. The paper industry in Zimbabwe is dominated by South Africa — Barlow Rand owns the biggest paper maker, Hunyani, while Anglo-American owns the main pulpwood producer, Border Timbers. The only other paper producers are the British owned Mutare Board and Paper and the locally-owned Nedlaw. Initially SADCC proposed a $100m integrated pulp and paper mill as an expansion of Hunyani. The project was to be 40% owned by Zimbabwe's Industrial Development Corporation (IDC), 30% by a foreign partner supplying the technology (SADCC suggested Sweden), and 30% by Hunyani (and possibly other local partners from the pulpwood and paper industries). Sweden undertook the initial studies, but then dropped out after the apparent Zimbabwean insistence on South African participation. IDC then paid for a Canadian study.

Some Zimbabweans are critical of what they see as Swedish rigidity in ignoring Zimbabwean attempts to co-opt and take control of South African interests.

Barlow Rand would have only a minority shareholding in the new firm, which meant that Zimbabwe was diluting South African control of the paper industry without actually buying out the South African interests. One government official commented: 'We should use the expertise we have here and build on that base. Even if it is South African, we should take it over and make it work for us.' And he stressed that IDC, not Hunyani, was controlling the project studies.

It is a difficult issue. Anglo-American, for example, has a history of moving to minority ownership without losing control. And these arguments are often used by influential people who want to maintain links with South Africa. Nevertheless, there is a genuine belief by some Zimbabweans that this is the way to co-opt South African capital. Only time will tell.

CONCLUSIONS

The significant presence of South African private sector interests in Zimbabwe presents the government there with serious problems. There is no doubt that the racist attitudes of some South African parent companies create a negative view of Zimbabwean economic prospects which has led to adverse decisions with respect to Zimbabwean subsidiaries. This has the effect of reducing the size and diversity of the Zimbabwean economy and thus increasing its vulnerability to South African destabilisation. In other cases, South African firms, acting on narrow profit-based considerations, have harmed the Zimbabwean economy.

In this way, the South African private sector operates, in practice if not in intention, as an arm of the South African state. Business has not actively tried to destabilise Zimbabwe out of political motives, but it cannot escape the charge that its actions make it a partner in crime. Doubtless, too, the personal and cultural links of many whites in Zimbabwe with families and friends in South Africa reinforce and create racist attitudes in Zimbabwe. To the extent that these attitudes add to racial tension and uncertainty, they too harm Zimbabwe and frustrate government attempts to create a unified society. The Zimbabwe government recognises these problems, and continues to reduce links gradually, both to develop its own economic independence, and to increase integration with other African countries. Only in that way can it minimise opportunities for economic sabotage like Lancashire Steel. But in the short term, much will depend on the outside support it receives for reducing dependence on South Africa.

17. Botswana

Cautious but outspoken
WITH PAUL SPRAY

When South African commandos drove into Gaborone and killed 12 people on 14 June 1985, they broke a pattern that had continued for more than a decade. Until the 14 June raid Botswana had remained economically intertwined with South Africa while becoming more outspokenly critical of the apartheid state — without serious retribution.

Geography is a determining factor. Botswana is the size of France but is largely desert and has only one million people. It is surrounded on three sides by South Africa and South African-occupied Namibia. Britain never took Bechuanaland (the colonial name) seriously and treated it simply as a labour reserve for South Africa, even ruling its colony from the nearby South African town of Mafeking. Botswana's other border is with Zimbabwe — which meant that for the first 14 years of independence it was surrounded by minority ruled states. It also shares a hundred-yard border with Zambia — Botswana borders Namibia, Zambia, and Zimbabwe in this stretch in the middle of the Zambezi River. This is the location of the Kazungula ferry, which provided a lifeline for both Zambia and Botswana during sanctions against UDI Rhodesia.

Despite this overwhelming physical presence of white power, Botswana took the step of joining Zambia, Tanzania, Angola, and Mozambique in the Front Line States (FLS) working for Zimbabwean independence. Botswana's then President, Sir Seretse Khama, took a leading role in promoting an economic arm for the FLS, in SADCC. In 1983 SADCC headquarters were located in Gaborone, which is just 5km from South Africa, in a firm declaration of where Botswana's allegiance lies.

Botswana frequently and loudly criticises apartheid and the Pretoria regime. And it has further offended South Africa by its 'open door' policy to refugees, and its willingness to allow acknowledged members of the ANC to remain in Gaborone so long as they do not openly attack the apartheid state from Botswana. Political independence has been bolstered by diamonds. In value terms, Botswana now produces about 30% of the world's diamonds, about the same as the USSR or South Africa. This makes it in some ways like an oil state, with an enclave producing substantial wealth that has had relatively little direct impact on the majority of the population. The government's 50/50 partner in diamond mining, and the day-to-day manager of the mines, is the South African company De Beers. With imports also largely from South Africa, the economy is dominated by South African links. But the diamond wealth gives Botswana a freedom of action that poorer states like Lesotho and Swaziland often do not have.

TRANSPORT AND MILITARY PRESSURE

South Africa has put Botswana under increasing pressure to try to force it to do four things: stop making anti-apartheid statements, recognise the bantustans, expel South African refugees, and sign a non-aggression pact.

Trains, oil and water

Landlocked Botswana is largely dependent on the rail link with South Africa for imports and especially for exports of its beef (all of which is shipped through South Africa). This link is used to put pressure on Botswana. Sometimes, after Botswana makes a particularly outspoken statement in the UN or OAU, South Africa fails to send refrigerator wagons to the abattoir for a few days. [1] Similarly, there have been fuel shortages due to disruptions in oil deliveries from South Africa, particularly in December 1980 and January 1981, which severely disrupted travel during the Christmas period and eventually brought transport to a virtual standstill for several days in mid-January. South African Railways imposed embargoes on wagons going north in February, April and August 1981 which caused serious shortages — at one point, for example, Botswana shops ran out of matches. [2]

Because of this kind of pressure, in 1980 Botswana built tanks to hold three months supply of oil products. But for more than a year, South Africa refused to provide the fuel to fill them. There is nothing in the customs union agreement which requires members to buy fuel from South Africa. Curiously, Botswana never tried to buy the fuel abroad, even though it could have done so, bringing it by rail from Zambia or Mozambique and paying the appropriate customs duties to the Customs Union, SACU. But this was at a time when South Africa was putting both economic and military pressure on Zimbabwe to prevent it from buying fuel elsewhere, and attacked fuel installations in Angola and Lesotho. So the Botswana government may well have assumed that if Botswana bought the fuel elsewhere, South Africa would simply have blown up the tanks.

In a desert country, water is a key issue. Gaborone's water comes at present from the Notwane River and some groundwater, and may in future come from the Limpopo River. Some farmers in the south draw irrigation water from the Molopo River. These rivers rise in South Africa. Without informing Botswana, dams were built in the catchment area of all three rivers inside the bantustan of Bophuthatswana in 1982, in violation both of international law and of a 1957 agreement between Botswana and South Africa. When Botswana protested, Pretoria responded that the negotiations must be with the 'independent state' of Bophuthatswana — a transparent attempt to force Botswana to give at least tacit recognition to a bantustan. This created serious problems. The World Bank refused to fund an irrigation project on the Molopo unless Botswana came to terms with its neighbours, but South Africa refused to discuss the issue and Botswana refused to talk to a bantustan. Partly because the Bophuthatswana dam reduced the catchment area (but also because of drought), the dam at Gaborone had to be raised earlier than planned — at a cost of P56m, according to President Quett Masire. [3]

Another long-running economic fight has been a proposal to produce soda ash (sodium carbonate) from a huge salt lake at Sua Pan, in central Botswana. [4] The main market would be South Africa, which currently imports all its soda ash.

However AECI (an Anglo company) has a long standing proposal to make synthetic soda ash; the cost would be higher, but South Africa would not depend on its neighbour. It could exclude Botswana's soda ash, making the P300m Sua Pan project useless. Every time Botswana raised this in talks with South Africa, the Pretoria government brought up political issues such as inclusion of the bantustans in the customs union. In 1984 they said the project could only go ahead if Botswana signed an Nkomati-type agreement.[5] The project was also linked to the sanctions issue, with Pretoria expressing fears over security of supplies and demanding assurances that if international sanctions were imposed Botswana would still supply soda ash. But as a sweetener, Pretoria offered to put together a $240 million financing package for the transport and infrastructure costs of Sua Pan — if Botswana did sign a non-aggression pact.[6]

There are other examples of pressure. In 1984 South Africa delayed customs union payments to Botswana. In 1983 and 1984 beef imports from Botswana were cut,[7] primarily because South Africa had a domestic beef surplus in those years but perhaps also from political motives. Foreign Minister Pik Botha stressed that further economic cooperation with Botswana was linked to the signing of a pact.[8]

Incursions

In parallel, South Africa stepped up the military pressure. There were border incidents at least monthly through 1981 and 1982, most involving South African troops in Namibia, especially along the Caprivi strip.[9] South African troops fired on the Botswana Defence Force, fishermen, and game rangers — sometimes from helicopters. Soldiers came across the border in remote areas where they killed, injured, and kidnapped several Batswana civilians.[10] In one incident they hijacked a vehicle belonging to a district council and kidnapped the driver. The mobile clinic had to stop visiting the remote area east of the Okavango River for some time, for fear of attack. There was substantial game poaching. It was also alleged that South African soldiers were coming across the border from Namibia trying to recruit Batswana in remote border areas.

President Masire also objected to repeated illegal overflights by South African planes flying to the Caprivi strip and Angola. Then on 11 December 1982 Botswana shot down a plane. It was a civilian aircraft, but was flown by an employee of the South African Defence Force. It turned out to belong to Frama Inter-trading, a Johannesburg firm which buys teak from UNITA. The logs are floated down the Cuando River into the Caprivi strip; in the military zone there the logs are loaded on to container lorries and driven to South Africa.[11]

Meanwhile, Botswana joined Lesotho, Swaziland and Mozambique in a meeting in Swaziland on 6 April 1981, which denounced South African destabilisation. Mozambique's President Samora Machel visited Gaborone in July. Botswana, which already had a Soviet embassy, began buying arms from the USSR. This provoked outrage from South Africa about Botswana becoming a communist 'base' in southern Africa, followed by a barrage of press attacks. In a series of public statements in late 1981, President Masire accused the United States of backing what he called South Africa's 'intransigent attitude', and warned that South Africa was preparing for an attack on Botswana similar to the one on Mozambique earlier that year. Early the following year, he warned that South Africa was trying to turn Botswana into 'another Lebanon' by exporting the internal war against apartheid out into neighbouring states.[12]

Despite growing pressure from South Africa, Botswana reiterated its 'open door' policy and noted that the flow of refugees was actually increasing. The President personally welcomed home a Motswana who had been an ANC activist and spent 16 years on Robben Island. But Botswana tightened up on the more than 2000 South African refugees there. A few involved in illegal activities were expelled and two ANC men were tried for arms possession. South Africa took its own actions. On 6 February 1982 Peter Lengene, a Soweto student leader who had been in Botswana since 1976, was kidnapped in Gaborone. He was tied, gagged, and bundled into the boot of a car and driven to South Africa.[13] On 31 August 1982 a bomb went off in a SWAPO house in Gaborone. On 22 July 1982 a South African police warrant officer, Jacobus Kok, was caught trying to bribe a Botswana policeman to give information on the ANC and PAC; he was jailed for two years. Botswana came under heavy pressure from Pretoria over Kok, and after less than a year in jail, he was released following what were described as 'representations from the South African government'.[14]

Incidents continued throughout 1983. There were border clashes and more trouble with South African agents. In October a member of the 'Bophuthatswana Defence Force' was arrested and jailed for being in Botswana illegally, and in December the *Botswana Daily News* warned refugees to 'beware' of South African spies posing as refugees.

Another area of South African involvement was in recruiting Zimbabweans from Dukwe refugee camp in northern Botswana and training and arming them to return to Zimbabwe as 'super-Zapu'. This is discussed in more detail in Chapter 14, but one incident involved the Botswana Defence Force directly. On 14 November 1983 a Defence Force patrol came across two vehicles in the bush near Dukwe. When the patrol approached, the occupants opened fire and ran off, abandoning the car and pick-up truck which were found to contain weapons and radios. The *Star* newspaper checked the registration numbers, and discovered that the vehicles had been bought the week before in Pretoria by two English-speaking white men who paid cash but gave false names and addresses.[15] Botswana government sources say they do not know for sure what was going on, but believe the cars were being driven by South African security men and were taking 'super-Zapu' to the border to infiltrate into Zimbabwe.

With the signing of the Nkomati Accord, South Africa stepped up the pressure on Botswana for a similar accord. Masire complained that South Africa 'has bullied Mozambique into this pact' and was applying 'heavy pressure' on Botswana. The US, he added, was supporting South Africa's demand that Botswana sign. He said Botswana would refuse; it had no need for such an accord and South Africa would use it as a pretext to invade Botswana. South African and Botswana officials met three times in early 1984. Masire said that in the meetings South Africa threatened economic pressure, including disruption of border traffic.[16] On 14 September 1984 Dr Gaositwe Chiepe was named foreign minister, perhaps because it was thought that, with her success in driving hard bargains as minerals minister, she would be well able to stand up to Pretoria.

In late 1984 and early 1985 there were repeated allegations by South African officials that ANC guerrillas were coming into South Africa from Botswana. In early February 1985, Foreign Minister Pik Botha said simply that things 'cannot continue as at present', while Bophuthatswana warned that it would pursue 'terrorists' into Botswana. Masire called it a threat of invasion. On 13 February a bomb nearly destroyed the house of Nat Serache, a former *Rand Daily Mail* journalist who fled to Botswana in 1977, where he became BBC correspondent. He was not seriously injured.

Pik Botha and Dr Chiepe met in Pretoria on 22 February. To the surprise of Dr Chiepe, Botha seemed to back off; he announced afterwards that 'the South African government has not insisted on a formal security agreement'. South Africa said later it had asked Botswana to expel certain ANC members. Botswana denied this, but 17 ANC members left Botswana soon afterwards.

As the Botswana High Commissioner in London, Sam Mpuchane, explained, South African pressure for a security pact has always 'been accompanied by accusations that Botswana harboured ANC guerrilla bases and that the ANC used Botswana as a transit route for infiltration into South Africa. No concrete proof was ever produced, despite the longstanding request by the Botswana government for evidence on which it could act. Botswana rather assured South Africa that it stands by its well-known policy of not allowing freedom fighters bases on its soil or allowing them transit to South Africa.' Finally, it seemed as if 'the South African government accepted our assurances'.[17] But on 14 May South Africa hit again when a car bomb killed Vernon Nkadimeng, son of the general secretary of the South African Congress of Trade Unions.

14 June 1985

A month later South African commandos invaded. At 1 a.m. on 14 June they drove over the border and the short distance to Gaborone, where they attacked ten houses with mortars and machine guns and fired at passing cars; 12 people were killed. Also attacked was the office of Solidarity News Service, the second attack on journalists. It was all over in an hour.

Nine of those killed were South African refugees, including three women, a six-year old child, and a 71-year old man who had retired to Botswana. One of the women was a social worker employed by the Botswana government; her husband, a local businessman, was also killed. Other dead included a white draft resister, a graphic artist, and a secondary school teacher. Five had ANC links, but Botswana President Quett Masire 'rejected with contempt' the South African claim that any were 'ANC freedom fighters'. The ANC itself made the same point.[18] But the commandos did not just kill South Africans. Two of the dead were young Batswana girls who had just returned home from a Jehovah's Witnesses prayer meeting. Eugenia Kobole and Kelape Kesupile lived in one room of a tiny servants quarter which was reduced to a pile of cement blocks by a grenade or mortar shell and the girls' bodies mutilated beyond recognition. Apparently they were killed because a nurse who also lived in the tiny servants quarter had a South African refugee boyfriend who sometimes stayed at weekends.[19] Another of the dead was a Somali refugee who worked for a local computer company; his pregnant Dutch wife was seriously injured.

The manager of a local discotheque told how he saw a burning car and ran to pull out the trapped driver when he was stopped by South African soldiers. The shot Motswana driver managed to pull himself from the blazing car and hide in a ditch, and he survived. It turned out he had unknowingly come upon the South African soldiers who attacked the car with grenade and machinegun fire.

Inevitably, there were recriminations after the raid. The tiny Botswana Defence Force did not engage the raiders and apparently made no effort to stop them leaving Botswana. This lack of response led to reports that, as in Lesotho on

9 December 1982, the local security services had been warned in advance not to interfere. The independent *Guardian* newspaper asked: 'how was it possible for the invaders to retreat so smoothly without being scratched — to a point of waving to a crowd near Oasis Motel?' The allegation was angrily denied by the BDF commander, Maj Gen Mompati Merafhe, who also reported that on the day after the raid, South African soldiers kidnapped 32 Batswana and held them for several hours.[20]

Motives

General Constand Viljoen, chief of the South African Defence Force, said his men had attacked 'the nerve centre of the ANC machinery'. Security policeman Major Craig Williamson told a press conference that the houses had been an ANC base. There were suggestions that Gaborone was linked to bomb explosions in Cape Town two days earlier. This is all highly unlikely. Gaborone is 1200km from Cape Town, and there was no evidence in the attacked houses that they were 'bases' or 'nerve centres'. It was a 'terrorist' raid in the strict sense — intended to strike terror into both refugees and Batswana. It seems likely that the raid was an Israeli-style retaliation — a response to a major bomb blast, even if the target of the response is not linked to the initial bomb.

The raid did indeed come after bomb attacks in Cape Town on two 'coloured' MPs, one a deputy minister. The 'coloured' house of parliament was central to the new constitution bringing 'coloureds' and 'Indians' into special roles in the apartheid system. Since so few 'coloureds' had agreed to participate, it was essential to be seen to protect the few collaborators. So the government wanted to respond to the attack. A response was also essential because the Nkomati Accord had clearly failed to curb ANC activity. The ANC was also about to hold, in Zambia, its first major internal conference for 16 years. In these circumstances, Pretoria needed a target. Mozambique could not be attacked because of Nkomati, while Lesotho was under steady pressure already. Meanwhile, Botswana was refusing to sign an Nkomati-type accord, and publicly denouncing South African pressure that it should do so.

Threats and Refugees

In the weeks after the raid, a number of South Africans were asked to leave Botswana. Most were refugees linked to the ANC, but some may have been declared persona non grata by the Botswana government because they had provided information to Pretoria.

South Africa, however, continued its allegations that Botswana harbours ANC bases, with a specific statement from the State Security Council in December 1985. On 4 January 1986 a landmine exploded in South Africa, close to the border, killing two whites. Pik Botha telexed Gaborone: 'While the South African government is always prepared to engage in discussions in order to promote peace and harmony in the region, it at the same time reserves its rights in terms of established international principles to take appropriate measures to protect the lives of its citizens.'[21] Troops concentrated on the border, and Britain was reported to be making urgent representations to Pretoria against military action.

Botswana reiterated its position that it does not allow its territory to be used for attacks against neighbouring states. On 15 January, as if to underline the point, 18 'illegal immigrants' were held by the Botswana Police following raids on houses in three towns, and one of them was charged with possessing six AK47 rifles. South Africa was again invited to point out any supposed ANC bases in the country. Again the government emphasised that if the South African army and police could not themselves completely seal the border, Pretoria should not expect Botswana's smaller forces to be able to do so. On 25 January, Pik Botha returned to the attack: 'That ANC infiltration route will have to be closed — or the Defence Force will take appropriate action.'[22] As President Masire told diplomats in his New Year message, South African threats of aggression haunt Botswana.

Political dirty tricks

The evidence is not firm, but it appears that South Africa has also been meddling in Botswana politics. The first incident was a series of leaflets sent through the post in October 1982. Allegedly from the 'Bamangwato Democrats', they tried to create tribal divisions and argued that President Quett Masire was not the legitimate successor to the late President Seretse Khama (who had been a tribal head as well as a government leader). The leaflets also attacked the government for harbouring South African refugees, and asked whether Soviet arms were 'worth more to one's stomach than oil and maize from a good neighbour.'[23] South Africa was blamed, and it was alleged that this was an attempt to create a split that might be used later to create a group like the LLA or MNR.

The second incident came during the 1984 elections (which the governing Botswana Democratic Party eventually won with a large majority). The main opposition party is the Botswana National Front (BNF), and its secretary general, Mareledi Giddie, said that if elected the BNF would immediately enter into an Nkomati-type accord with South Africa (though the BNF, leader Kenneth Koma, denied that this was party policy).[24] Kenneth Koma was eventually elected to a seat from Gaborone, defeating Vice President Peter Mmusi (who was later given a nominated seat). Mmusi alleged that Koma had met with South African whites, and that the BNF was receiving South African money and cars in exchange for its support of a non-aggression pact. The BNF denied this, but Koma admitted that he and Giddie had met with individual South Africans and had visited Bophuthatswana, which he referred to as a 'neighbouring state'.[25] Since then, however, the BNF has reiterated its strong opposition to apartheid South Africa. In the wake of the June raid, the leaders of all the opposition parties joined President Masire for a special briefing and discussion on the raid, in a public demonstration of national unity.

ECONOMIC DEPENDENCE

In 1973, Botswana's Fourth National Development Plan stated, 'In many respects, the economy remains a satellite of that of South Africa.' At independence in 1966 Botswana was little more than a labour reserve for South Africa, with very little integrating infrastructure and the state dependent on British aid for its tiny recurrent budget, let alone development projects. 20 years later, national income per head is four times greater in real terms, there is a network of roads and rural services, 40% of households have one or more members in wage employment in Botswana, and the state maintains large financial reserves.[26] Botswana has literally struck it rich — the prosperity is based on an entirely new mining sector. Yet the dependence on South Africa remains — today less for jobs than for management, technology and imports. The vulnerability of these links hangs over the future.

Botswana's economy is dominated by mining, which at present involves three products: diamonds, copper-nickel, and coal. All three are now managed by the giant South African Anglo American group. It was not inappropriate that at the funeral of Botswana's first President, Seretse Khama, the heads of state present were immediately followed in their wreath-laying by Harry Oppenheimer. The relationship between Anglo and Botswana is however fairly complex, and not entirely one-sided.

At the centre of the relationship are diamonds. In 1967, just after independence, De Beers (the diamond arm of Anglo) discovered diamonds, an event which was to lead to the transformation of the economy. Production began in 1971, and two further mines were opened later, making Botswana one of the three largest diamond producers in the world (in value terms), as important as South Africa itself. By 1984, diamonds were 76% of Botswana's exports. Botswana had no objection to South African investment, and so, once De Beers had discovered the diamonds, their initial involvement was automatic. But once the size of the deposits became clear, the government's negotiating position was strengthened by the nature of the world diamond market: diamond prices are kept high by a monopoly in marketing (including much of the USSR's sales) organised by De Beers. If De Beers lost control of Botswana's diamonds, they would risk the collapse of world diamond prices. Through a series of renegotiations, Botswana was able to squeeze out of De Beers one of the best mineral exploitation contracts in the world. The mining company Debswana is a 50-50 joint venture, in which neither partner has overall control. The government receives about 75% of the profits. Sorting is done inside Botswana, in a new 11-storey building which dominates tiny Gaborone. But most important, Botswana was able to force a high rate of development and high production levels.

Anglo-American is also now the dominant partner in Botswana's other mining venture, copper-nickel at Selebi-Pikwe. With 4500 workers it is the largest private employer in Botswana, and it has some internal linkages, but is a financial disaster. Despite being developed by some of the world's most experienced mining engineers, when production began in 1973 the smelter did not work. By the time the technical problems had been solved, the price of copper and nickel had collapsed. The project is now technically efficient, but the debt incurred can never be repaid in full, and the very low world metal prices have meant operating losses in some years.

Both the government and Anglo have provided emergency funds to keep the mine running, and under normal circumstances it would probably have closed down. The reason it has remained open provides an interesting case of South African dependence on the neighbouring states. Anglo would almost certainly have refused to help, like the other private investment partner AMAX, were it not for its wish to curry favour with the government in order to safeguard its position in diamonds. Anglo's contribution to the emergency funds is three times that of the government.[27] Anglo has therefore emerged as the dominant private investor at Selebi-Pikwe, whereas it originally was one of two.[28] Anglo's position in coal arose out of the Selebi-Pikwe development, for part of its contribution was to develop the small Morupule coal mine to supply the smelter and power station at Pikwe.

The effect of Anglo links

Anglo's dominance in mining is not welcomed by the government, whose mineral policy objectives include contributing to economic independence by increasing the number of companies involved.[29] The dominance has emerged partly by others' default. The government has encouraged other companies to prospect for diamonds — notably Falconbridge — but they have found none. In any case, when it did find a promising rock formation, Falconbridge came to a technical agreement with De Beers to evaluate it (without consulting the government before making the agreement); such is De Beers' technical pre-eminence in diamonds. Much government time in the early 1980s was taken up in discussions with Shell about a possible export coal mine that would have dwarfed Anglo's Morupule, but the negotiations came to nothing because of expectations of a low world coal price over the next decade. The lack of development of other minerals also reflects poor world prices. If BP's Sua Pan soda ash project goes ahead, Anglo's direct dominance of the mining sector will be diluted — but even then Anglo wuld probably be the major customer.

Anglo dominance has undoubted negative consequences for Botswana. The basic problem is having so much power concentrated in one South African board room. Decisions are bound to be coloured by the course of events in South Africa, and Anglo's wider interests. Meanwhile, South African links are stronger than they would be for another foreign investor. The engineering consultants for the diamond mines are the Anglo American Corporation itself, and there are daily flights of technical personnel to and from Johannesburg. The Botswana authorities put considerable emphasis on monitoring Debswana contracts and purchases of mine supplies, but mine managers from South Africa tend to look there in the first instance and there have been allegations that Anglo-linked companies have sometimes been given priority in contracts. Such strong South African links may impede the development of industry inside the country, and restrict the use of cheaper or more appropriate inputs from elsewhere in the world. More directly, their disruption would be very serious for Botswana. Given Botswana's importance to De Beers, it is unlikely that Anglo would institute such disruption — but the South African government is a different matter.

Anglo dominance also means a fair number of white South Africans in key positions, and inevitably some racism. At an angry meeting in Gaborone in January 1984 the Botswana Diamond Sorters and Valuers Union said that Debswana brought unskilled white expatriates into management positions while more experienced locals were kept in low positions.[30] Although this is not official Anglo policy, and the head of Debswana is a Motswana, the Botswana government has had to insist that particular individuals were removed from their posts.

Beef

With three times as many cattle as people, Botswana has become independent Africa's biggest beef exporter. Beef remains Botswana's second largest export. Cattle are ideal for the arid bush, and there is a long herding tradition.

Cattle are big business. Half of the cattle sold to the abattoir have been raised or fattened on a small number of freehold ranches (occupying about 6% of Botswana's land area). Some of these ranches, including one which supplies 5% of the cattle, are owned by South African citizens.[31] The more important link with South Africa, however, is exports of beef. Botswana's preferred market is the EEC, where prices are well above the world level and to which Botswana has access through the Lomé Convention. But the EEC has strict quotas, and generally accounts for only half Botswana's exports. Furthermore, it is unreliable: an outbreak of foot-and-mouth disease, such as occurred in Botswana in 1977-78 and 1979-81 or even in Britain in 1968, leads to severe restrictions or even complete suspension. In other markets, Botswana faces high transport costs and severe competition — including, ironically, from subsidised EEC exports. So the nearby South African market, which usually accounts for a third of exports, is extremely important.

Yet the South African market too is controlled by a quota, imposed by the South African Meat Board. Since the 1920s, this quota has been raised and lowered in line with the interests of South Africa's own beef farmers. In 1977, for example, carcass sales from Botswana were completely banned. The potential for South Africa to put pressure on Botswana by manipulating this quota is clear: as long ago as 1933, General Smuts suggested to the British Government that imports from Bechuanaland (as Botswana then was) might be prevented if it remained outside the Union of South Africa.[32] Since almost all Botswana's beef exports travel out through Cape Town, disruption could be considerable. Given the nature of cattle raising, the impact would spread into almost every corner of the country.

Manufacturing and commerce

Diamonds, copper-nickel and beef dwarf the rest of the economy, in terms of value of production. Ownership of the tiny manufacturing and commerce sector is largely in South African hands. The most recent figures date back to 1980, but at that time 62% of registered industrial enterprises were foreign owned and 25% in mixed foreign and Botswana ownership. A different survey showed that of foreign-owned industry, 66% of the capital was South African.[33]

The brewery, the second largest manufacturing investment after the abattoir, is controlled by South African Breweries (Anglo). Light industry for the local market, such as chemicals and furniture, is South African. The wholesale and retail trade is largely in the hands of South African firms, so the same names appear in Gaborone as in any city in South Africa — Metro, Edgars, Jet, OK Bazaars, Fraser, and so on. Renfreight is the dominant freight and forwarding agency. The main banks, Barclays and Standard, are controlled from London, but maintain strong links with branches of the same banks in South Africa, Swaziland, and Lesotho; for example, bank staff have been transferred from Lesotho to Botswana. Anglo has close ties with both banks in South Africa. As the London *Financial Times* commented, the Botswana 'economy is deeply integrated into the regional structures that are dominated by, and usually administered by, South Africa. The businessmen [in Botswana] usually operate with an ear to their colleagues in Johannesburg.'[34]

Since the independence of Zimbabwe and the economic rearrangements of the region, Botswana has attracted a number of new firms. It promotes the fact that it has special trade agreements with both Zimbabwe and South Africa. Some of the new companies have simply been fleeing independent Zimbabwe and have tried to export, particularly textiles, back to Zimbabwe. Some South African firms have also opened.

Trade, food and work

The small size of Botswana's economy, colonial neglect and the operations of the Customs Union combined to mean that much of what Botswana consumes is imported rather than locally produced. And, whereas almost 90% of exports go to the outside world, imports are 85% from South Africa. This is perhaps Botswana's greatest vulnerability to short-term destabilisation.

In one critical respect, this dependence has been worsening in recent years: the need to import food. This clearly offers Pretoria a major opportunity for destabilisation in future. There is little rain in Botswana, and even that is variable; nevertheless, at independence the country was self-sufficient in food in normal years and made substantial net exports of grain in good years. Since independence, crop production has plummeted and most food is now imported. For example, grain production fell from 106,000 tonnes in 1973/74 to 51,000 tonnes in 1980/81, although both were good rainfall seasons. At the same time, the population has been increasing, pushing up demand.

Ironically, the problems of agriculture are partly a consequence of economic success elsewhere. The rise in urban incomes, coinciding in the 1980s with five consecutive drought years and the availability of drought relief food, depressed incentives to farm. In a pattern familiar from oil-producing states, the government funded a major expansion of rural services, but found it extremely difficult to spend its mineral revenues on raising rural incomes.[35] Crop prices were kept down by competition from South African crops, much of it subsidised and some (especially vegetables) low quality surpluses 'dumped' on Botswana. The existence of the Customs Union, and the risk of smuggling, deterred the government from major increases in producer prices. The obvious option of irrigation is favoured in the new National Development Plan, but has the disadvantage of not helping the majority of the rural population, in a country which already has one of the most uneven rural distributions of income in the world.

If dependence on South Africa for food has increased, dependence on it for work has fallen in relative terms. In 1943, some 17,000 adult men were at work in South Africa, compared to around 5000 with paid jobs inside Botswana. Forty years later, in 1983, perhaps 39,000 were in South Africa, compared to 100,000 in formal employment in Botswana. The number in South Africa is falling as firms there give preference to citizens: recruitment of Batswana for the mines has fallen from 40,000 in 1976 to 18,000 in 1983. But, as the figures make clear, the greater effect has been the alternatives provided by urbanisation and the expansion of government service in Botswana itself. Nevertheless with the labour force growing by 13,000 a year, and jobs at home by less than 10,000, migrant labour remains important.

Government policy

Given this inherited mass of linkages to South Africa, Botswana government policy has been to reduce dependence in key areas, rather than to attempt generalised delinking. The main goals of economic policy have been the usual ones of a developing country — employment, rural development, income growth, etc — rather than structural delinking from South Africa. Thus, for example, in 1982 a Financial Assistance Policy was established to promote new industries in Botswana, with the aim of increasing employment and local development. To the extent that goods were produced within Botswana, rather than imported, the Policy might also reduce dependence on South Africa. But there was no attempt to exclude South African investors from its benefits — indeed in its first year, nearly half the money went to non-Batswana.

The most serious obstacle to any move to delink is the simple historical legacy of dependence. There are major short term costs to delinking, which are not simply financial. For example, for over a decade Botswana has had a large programme of installing village water supplies, heavily funded by Swedish aid. For several years Swedish suggestions that materials should not be purchased in South Africa were resisted by the Botswana government, not simply because South African supplies were cheaper but because the operators and maintenance technicians were used to South African engines and pumps. Given the dismal African experience of failure of new water supplies for lack of maintenance, this was a serious consideration — and it has parallels across the economy.

The effects of inherited dependence are very broad. As in Lesotho and Swaziland, well-known and tested trade links are to South Africa; this means that, particularly in a crisis, it is the automatic place of first resort. The life style of urban Batswana, including the bureaucracy and other decision makers, is based on South African goods. The collapse of the rand's value has underlined this, as they have become much cheaper.

In some respects, dependence has been aggravated by the economic path Botswana has followed since independence. The capital-intensive nature of the mining sector and infrastructure development has increased the demands for imports and servicing. Imports of consumer goods have been bolstered by the large and probably widening income differentials — another feature diamond-based Botswana shares with oil states. Meanwhile, though employment creation has been a central plank of successive development plans, the government has been very cautious financially, building up large reserves rather than searching out extra productive investment.[36] Financial reserves do allow the state to smooth out cycles caused by fluctuating mineral revenues, and they also provide a buffer against any future South African economic disruption. But they entail considerable costs. A number of productive possibilities remain untried, such as an integrated leather industry where the Botswana Meat Commission has shown great conservatism.[37] The banking system too has at times such as the late 1970s been 'awash with liquidity', but the commercial banks proved unwilling to invest imaginatively.[38]

Trade policy too has been criticised. Brian Egner points out that while 'Botswana is noted for its thoroughly researched, aggressive, and fruitful trading negotiations with the EEC over its beef exports — negotiations that have taken place continuously and simultaneously at political, diplomatic, and technical levels — no such co-ordinated approach has been adopted to secure the maximum benefits for Botswana from its relationship with its main trading partner, South Africa.'[39] Clearly South Africa's demand for political concessions makes renegotiation of the customs union agreement impossible, but Botswana has scarcely tried to make the best of the existing agreement.

Attempts to delink

In its chosen key areas, however, Botswana has made more attempts to delink than either Swaziland or Lesotho. Most important was its withdrawal from the rand zone in 1976 and the establishment of an independent currency. This has allowed some control of inflation, and at other times stimulation of local production, by varying the rate of exchange against the rand. However, the high level of trade with South Africa, the importance of migrant workers' earnings, and the need for domestic producers to compete with South African, restrict the extent to which the pula can be allowed to move out of line with the rand.[40]

Another important decision was Botswana's demand that Selebi-Pikwe use electricity generated from Botswana coal. Donors objected strongly, arguing that it would be cheaper to buy electricity from South Africa, but Botswana held out on grounds of limiting dependence. It won, and proved to be financially more astute as well because during the following two decades South African electricity tariffs rose much more rapidly than the donors assumed, making Botswana's own power cheaper.[41] Botswana again demanded locally generated electricity when the expansion of diamond production (with the opening of a large new mine at Jwaneng in 1982) required more power. The Botswana Power Corporation (BPC) is building a 90 MW power station at the Morupule coal mine linking it to a new eastern grid including Gaborone, Jwaneng, and the already existing Orapa diamond mine. In addition to supplying the new mine, the new station will generate electricity for Orapa previously supplied by an oil-fired power station and thus reduce by about one-sixth the need for oil imported from South Africa.

The Morupule project demonstrates, however, the limits of delinking. The coal will come from Anglo's mine at Morupule. In the short run, Botswana faced a five year power shortage before the new station was ready in 1986; the gap was met by taking a link from South Africa's Electricity Supply Commission (Escom).[42] In addition, as with almost all major construction projects except where aid donors rule otherwise, many of the suppliers and contractors building the Morupule station were South African.[43]

Several other projects have also reduced dependence, including an earth station for satellite telecommunications and a new international airport, which make it possible to fly to and telephone Botswana without passing through Johannesburg. Import licences were introduced for vegetables and poultry to protect local producers. A factory was set up to produce vaccine against foot and mouth disease, because both British and South African vaccine proved ineffective: Botswana is now exporting vaccine to the region. A wheat flour mill was given tariff protection in 1984.

Undoubtedly the most fraught attempt to delink was the brewery.[44] In 1973 Botswana made a policy decision to have a European firm build and operate a new brewery, and Brau Finanz, one of the larger German firms, agreed. In order to protect the firm against South African competition, Botswana agreed to give the infant industry protection under the customs union (for the first time) by charging a 50% duty on imported South African beer. At that time Brau was expanding into several African countries, but it seems to have underestimated the problems and all ended in failure. In 1978, with Botswana government encouragement,

South African Breweries bought out the Brau share, giving it monopoly control over the entire SACU market.

The Botswana government has had hopes of independent surface transport links. The Kazungula ferry link demonstrated both the costs and the limits of a northern highway route to Zambia, and was actually used largely for South African trade northwards. In 1980, Zimbabwean independence, and the expectation of Namibia's, gave rise to hopes of access to both Atlantic and Indian Ocean ports. The collapse of the world coal market, combined with South African intransigence in Namibia, have indefinitely deferred the building of the Trans-Kalahari Railway, while South African sabotage and destabilisation by proxy has closed the routes from Botswana through Zimbabwe to Maputo and made those to Beira appear risky. Thus only minor rerouting of cargo has actually taken place to date.

South African opposition

Botswana's efforts at delinking have however been limited by a number of more predatory actions by both the government and private companies in South Africa. As in Lesotho and Swaziland, it is difficult to convince the dominant South African wholesale and retail chains to stock locally made goods. In at least one case, a Botswana firm found it could export its products to South Africa, but could not get them stocked in Botswana shops. Thus South African dominance of the retail trade inhibits new small industries, including some set up with government help.

Despite the extensive trade between Botswana and South Africa, Botswana hauliers find it difficult to obtain road transport licences in South Africa — so South African firms dominate the trade. One operator obtained a contract to transport machinery to South Africa for servicing; he applied to South Africa for the required licence; soon after, a South African rang the machinery owner 'out of the blue' saying that a transport licence would not be issued to a Botswana haulier, but he would happily do the job. The Botswana operator is convinced the licensing authorities in South Africa informed the firm there.

Attempts to import goods from countries other than South Africa also face problems. Botswana officials complain that South African customs sometimes holds up goods in the ports if similar items are made in South Africa. Pretoria also unilaterally changes import regulations to the detriment of Botswana. For example, Botswana was importing packaged tea from Malawi when South Africa decided to support South Africa's first local tea packer and imposed a duty on packaged tea but not bulk tea. That made South African tea cheaper than Malawian. But in this case, Botswana set up its own tea packer, and switched to importing in bulk.

Perhaps more serious is the common practice by British and other European firms of treating southern Africa as a single market, including South Africa, and to appoint a South African firm as sole agent. In some cases they place such a high mark-up on the goods that it would be cheaper for Botswana to import directly from Europe — but often the manufacturer refuses, saying they have appointed a South African agent. In one instance, Botswana tried to import British electrical equipment from England; the manufacturer refused, but Botswana discovered that it was still cheaper to buy the same goods from the German agent of the British firm and go through all the import problems than to buy the items from the

South African agent. Some Botswana officials estimate that up to one-third of 'imports' from South Africa are in fact re-imports of items from elsewhere.[45]

The South African government has also disrupted some Botswana attempts to industrialise. The most blatant example was the closure of the South African-owned firm in Botswana which recycled jute bags (see Chapter 9). In another case a firm was set up to manufacture electric sockets, but the product was excluded from South Africa on the grounds that it did not meet local standards — because it had an *extra* safety device.

The precarious future

Botswana is regularly hailed in the West as one of the success stories of Africa. It is a multi-party democracy with regular elections. Next door to South Africa, it is a non-racial country where a white Cabinet Minister received the highest popular vote in the 1984 elections. Its real per capita GDP has increased fourfold since independence. Its free enterprise policies, encouraging foreign investment and basing development on the private sector, win it considerable prestige in the West. Even the Johannesburg *Financial Mail* described it as 'the best-managed economy in Africa'.[46]

There are nevertheless serious problems: unemployment is rising faster than new jobs, the rural poor still have very little chance of a secure income because the cattle herd is at its maximum size and very unevenly distributed, and because viable small scale crop production faces very real difficulties. These are major issues, over which there are many arguments and debates within Botswana, with different parties putting forward different solutions.

This debate will be pre-empted, and the achievements destroyed, if South Africa is allowed by the international community to strike with impunity. When Britain was at war with Nazi Germany, Botswana sent ten thousand soldiers.

18. Malawi
Taking from Both Sides

The picture on the front page of Malawi's *Daily Times* for 17 November 1981 showed delegates arriving for the SADCC annual conference. The conference was to discuss efforts to delink from South Africa, especially with respect to transport. On the same front page was a report of the new South African general manager of Malawi Railways returning from meetings in Johannesburg with South African Railways.

Malawi's continued links with South Africa are geographically anomalous, as the two countries share no border and are separated by 700km of Mozambique and Zimbabwe. Yet Malawi has always distanced itself from the other majority-ruled states of the region, and tried to steer a course between them and white-ruled South Africa.

For South Africa, Malawi has never been economically important; there is little South African investment there, although the trade is useful. But as the only country in black Africa to allow a South African embassy, it is important diplomatically, particularly as a sign that Pretoria is still not totally a pariah. More recently, Malawi has proved a useful outpost from which to support the MNR in Mozambique.

For Malawi, the benefits of links with South Africa are less easy to see. There has been some aid, especially at key times when it was not available from other donors. But the real key to ties with South Africa lies in Life President Ngwazi Dr H. Kamuzu Banda, the octogenarian who has almost total power in Malawi. Malawi's relationship with South Africa has passed through three phases which are similar in many ways to the position of Lesotho and Swaziland. In the first phase, from 1964 to the early 1970s, President Banda looked to South Africa for political support, rather like Chief Jonathan in Lesotho, and for economic help as well (which was not provided in the same way to Lesotho). During the second phase, from 1974 to 1978, neither side seems to have put as much stress on the relationship; some links increased while others were reduced. The third phase began in 1979, when Malawi started to take a much more independent line, reducing trade with South Africa and joining SADCC. A similar trend was taking place in Swaziland and, as with Swaziland, South Africa launched a serious campaign to win back its former ally. With Swaziland, the stress was on the carrot; with Malawi, however, there was more of the stick.

Personal Power and Patronage

President Banda has adapted medieval court-style politics to gain control over

Malawi.[1] He carefully promoted and balanced contending interest groups while at the same time gaining increasing power for himself. Members of parliament and ministers were appointed by Banda — who stressed his total power by sporadically dissolving his cabinet arbitrarily, only to reappoint most of the same people. He created the Malawi Congress Party (MCP) and controlled all appointments. Banda created the Young Pioneers, a paramilitary youth group that served as a private army. There were four different security services — the army, police, Special Branch, and Young Pioneers — and Banda named their heads.

Life President Banda also gained economic control through two companies: Press Holdings, which was President Banda's personal company, and Admarc, the parastatal Agricultural Development and Marketing Corporation. Between them, they control the banks, most agricultural estates, and most apparently 'private' companies. Peasants sell their produce to Admarc and spend their money in Press's PTC supermarkets. Together, Press and Admarc control more than half the economy, and until recently both were personally controlled by President Banda. As a result Malawi is often described as a capitalist country without capitalists.

Thus political advancement depended on Dr Banda, and economic gain also came only through the beneficence of the Life President.[2] Furthermore, Banda was careful to ensure that the political and economic areas remained distinct, so that no-one but he had both political and economic power, which would have been essential to wrest control from him. However, Banda has built an honest and efficient civil service. Hiring and promotion are rigidly meritocratic through difficult written examinations, and Banda is ruthless with any civil servant caught abusing his or her position for gain or influence. Thus Banda can dispense with his would-be successors or dismiss his cabinet, but the state machine continues to run smoothly.

Phase 1: Initial South African links

Inevitably, Malawi's initial links with South Africa reflected Banda's own choices. In part, South Africa provided help when no one else would. But probably more important is H. Kamuzu Banda's own conservatism. He does see South Africa as a preferable alternative to the socialism of his neighbours. Despite his own consolidation of power, he seems to hark back to the colonial era and believes that whites are more qualified for many key positions than blacks. Much of this comes together in his new Kamuzu Academy. Banda argues that an educated man must know Latin, Greek, and European history; he modelled his Kamuzu Academy on Eton and said that only whites were good enough to teach there.

The already elderly doctor had been brought back to Malawi by the nationalists who felt they needed a respectable front. But within weeks of independence in July 1964 he consolidated power and purged many of the nationalists in what became known as the 'cabinet crisis'. This was provoked by the nationalists' criticisms of Banda on a variety of grounds, including his slowness in Africanising the civil service, his refusal to accept a £6m Chinese loan for a link to the proposed Tazara Railway, and his closeness to South Africa and Portugal (then ruling Mozambique).[3]

Banda won this key battle, and turned to South Africa for support. In 1967

Malawi established diplomatic relations with South Africa. In 1970 the South African Prime Minister, John Vorster, visited Malawi, and Banda went to Pretoria in 1971. This high-profile diplomatic link with Malawi was clearly important to South Africa, because it demonstrated to the world that at least one majority-ruled state accepted South Africa. Malawi also established diplomatic relations with Israel and Taiwan,[4] and all three helped to train and equip Malawi's various security services. South Africa sent people to fill a variety of key posts, including the first heads of the Malawi Development Corporation, Air Malawi, and Malawi's Ministry of Information.[5]

Initially, Kamuzu Banda had two pet projects — building a new capital in the centre of the country at Lilongwe, and building a new railway to connect with the line in Mozambique going to the port of Nacala (thus ensuring he had two outlets to the sea). The Life President went to Britain and other foreign donors first, but when they rejected both projects he turned to South Africa. Pretoria provided a R11m soft loan for the railway and a R14m soft loan for the new capital. The South African loan financed work on the initial design of the capital city, and many of the senior staff of the Capital City Development Corporation were South African. Precisely because no one else would provide the initial funding, Banda still refers to this South African help, and this relatively small amount of money gave South Africa significant prestige.[6]

For a critical three years, 1969-71, South Africa accounted for about 20% of aid to Malawi — a direct reward for opening diplomatic relations. The other reward was a sharp increase in the number of migrant miners recruited in Malawi; in 1966 there were fewer than 50,000, while by 1971 there were more than 100,000. After that, the aid money stopped. Lilongwe was finished with aid from other donors, and largely with international loans.

Phase 2: A slight cooling

Perhaps because of the end of aid, relations cooled somewhat in the middle 1970s. In 1975 Banda suddenly banned recruitment of miners, ostensibly because of a plane crash, but really because of a shortage of cheap labour for his rapidly expanding tobacco plantations. Recruitment resumed on a much lower level two years later. Dr Banda was also not pleased about the possible role of South Africa in a 1976 coup attempt. South African officers had trained Malawi's Special Branch, which under its head, Focus Gwede, had launched a particularly repressive era with many arbitrary arrests and detentions. Gwede tried to plot a coup in 1976, and was convicted and executed. It remains unclear if South Africa itself had a hand, but certainly South Africa was temporarily eased out of security training.

Despite these problems, economic and informal links with South Africa continued to grow. Imports from South Africa increased steadily. From only 6% of the total at independence, they rose to 23% and equalled imports from the UK in 1974. In 1976 they passed imports from the UK and grew rapidly, reaching a peak of 41% of total imports in 1979. South African consumer goods are particularly important for the luxury market. Malawi produces excellent jam and tinned fruit which is sold throughout the country for under K1 per tin — and is on the shelves of Press shops side-by-side with tins of the same items imported from South Africa and costing K5.

Services also became more important. Regional offices of international accountancy, engineering, management, and other consulting firms are usually in Johannesburg. Contracts are frequently with a London head office, but it is a South African consultant who gets off the plane from Johannesburg. And South African architects designed several prestige projects, including the Kamuzu Academy and the new Reserve Bank (which sits on the top of a hill and dominates Lilongwe — perhaps a physical manifestation of the power of its then head, John Tembo).

Finally, shopping trips to South Africa became important for the new bourgeoisie, such as the new black executives in the banks and Press. They generally dislike white South Africans and derisively call them 'boers', but for them apartheid has a special twist. They like their special status in Johannesburg's 'international' hotels — this makes them 'better' than South African blacks who once looked down on them or their relatives when they worked in the South African mines. And, as for others in the region, the wide range of luxury consumer goods in Johannesburg shops is an undoubted attraction.

During the 1970s the economy expanded. But despite its free-market image, Malawi attracted little foreign investment — South African or otherwise.[7] In part this is because Malawi has no minerals, and Banda has kept the most profitable agricultural area — tobacco production — out of foreign hands and in his own control. But wage levels were also held down rigorously, and, as Jonathan Kydd notes, 'The lack of broad-based growth in incomes limited the scope for expansion in consumer goods production.'[8]

There are only four important South African firms: Optichem imports and compounds specialised fertilisers, Old Mutual is the main insurance company for small life assurance policies, and Renfreight is the main freight and forwarding agency.[9] Roberts Construction has a Malawi subsidiary. In practice, most interest by foreign firms is in direct sales of goods, services, and technology. So there is a significant number of foreign consultants and managers, and this has increased with the larger role of the IMF and World Bank. Press also employed a large number of white farm managers, mostly ex-Rhodesians; the Press management, however, was entirely black, and provided jobs for members of Banda's entourage.

Phase 3: Attempts to delink

The late 1970s brought a variety of changes. The civil servants were gaining power as a result of the growing economic crisis and Banda's weakening hold over day-to-day operations, just as Zimbabwe became independent and the regional picture changed. The technocrats improved working relations with the neighbours and noted that South Africa was not always the cheapest source for imported goods. To South Africa's dismay, Malawi joined SADCC; South Africa's share of Malawi's imports plummeted from 41% in 1979 to 32% in 1981.[10] South Africa responded with money for the first time in nearly a decade. In January 1980 it suddenly provided R12m in new development aid. It also provided R11m in export credits for a massive grain silo in Lilongwe — again a project which had been turned down by other donors.

But if Malawian civil servants were moving away from South Africa, the pressure from the IMF and World Bank was in the other direction. They insisted on expatriate management for the parastatals; this increased South African links because it was easier (and cheaper) to get skilled staff there than in Europe.[11] The new heads of Malawi Railways and Press Holdings were both South Africans. An advertisement for managers in the Johannesburg *Sunday Times* declared that 'South African management expertise and experience are warmly welcomed by Admarc'.[12] The South African government provided a technical team to study the rationalisation of the parastatals.[13]

Targeting SADCC

Malawi's move away from South Africa and towards its neighbours probably reached its furthest extent when Malawi hosted the SADCC annual conference on 19-20 November 1981. In a general attack on SADCC on 29 October South African saboteurs blew up two bridges over the Pungue River in Mozambique which carried the road and railway linking the port of Beira to Zimbabwe. The bridges were to the west of the junction with the line going north to Malawi, however, and did not initially affect it. Then South Africa directed two actions specifically at Malawi. First, it cut off Malawi's oil for a period just before the conference, causing petrol shortages. (South Africa still supplied most of Malawi's fuel). Then on 13 November, just days before the conference, South African commandos destroyed the marker buoys in Beira harbour; with the bridges to Zimbabwe down, Malawi was the main user of the port, and thus it was a particularly pointed gesture.

Just before the meeting the new South African head of Malawi Railways, Norman Husemeyer, went to Johannesburg for talks with South African Railways, which included agreement to lease 83 wagons from SAR. The Malawian hosts invited the South African chargé d'affaires, Sandy Shaw, to the SADCC conference and he made his attendance widely known. Banda kept his distance by leaving Blantyre during the conference. Nevertheless, the mood of the meeting was hostile to South Africa. The *Daily Times* faithfully reported the attacks on South Africa by various speakers. Malawi stressed its support for SADCC and for regional cooperation. In a tacit acknowledgement of concern about Malawi's sincerity, Transport Minister Harry Harawa closed the meeting by saying that the holding of the conference in Blantyre 'is an indication of your confidence and trust in the sincerity of our intentions to make SADCC a reality'. Most strongly, Malawi joined the other SADCC states in a final communique which expressed 'SADCC's concern at South African destabilisation and sabotage actions', notably against the Pungue bridges and Beira harbour marker buoys.[14]

The month after the conference South Africa's Agriculture Minister, P.T.C. Du Plessis, visited Malawi and promised R1.7m for the National Seed Company and for fish breeding research — fisheries having been the SADCC sector that Malawi had been asked to coordinate. He noted that food would be as strategic a weapon in the 1980s as oil was in the 1970s, and offered 15,000 tonnes of wheat at reduced price.

Perhaps Transport Minister Harawa had gone too far in his fulsome praise for SADCC, because he was dismissed on 5 January 1982.

Destabilisation

South Africa stepped up the pressure on Malawi through the Mozambique National Resistance (MNR), its surrogate guerrilla force in Mozambique (see

Chapter 12). In May 1982 the MNR began to attack the line between Beira and Malawi, and by the end of the year it was closed. Increasingly cargo had to be sent more than 3000 km by road to and from Durban instead of 600 km by rail via Beira. It costs two to three times as much to move goods from Durban as from Beira, and in 1982 Malawi had to pay K16m extra in transport costs on imports. For exports, the problem was increasingly that it was unprofitable to send low-value high-bulk cargoes at all; by the end of 1982 more than 50,000 tonnes of sugar was stockpiled, and this had risen to 130,000 tonnes by the end of 1983. Bulk imports came through Beira, so that in late 1982 Malawi faced fuel and fertiliser shortages.

At first, the line to Nacala remained open, mainly handling containerised traffic. But it was subject to a rumour campaign by the largest shipping agency, the South African owned Manica Freight Services (see Chapter 8). According to a study by UNCTAD, in 1983 Manica was lying to clients and saying that the backlog of containers (and thus the delay) was more than double what it really was, and thus advising clients not to use the port.[15] In reality, Nacala handled a record quantity of Malawi cargo in 1983. So in 1984 the MNR began hitting·that line too. Transport ministry officials estimate that the attacks cost Malawi K100m in 1984 in higher freight charges and lower export prices.[16]

South Africa provided some help — linked to closer ties. In early 1983, with Malawi's fertiliser stuck in Beira, South Africa provided a soft loan of K5m to finance the purchase of South African fertiliser to be trucked to Malawi. And in 1985 it granted a K1.1m soft loan for railway and telecommunications upgrading.[17] South African Transport Services offered Malawi a discount on trucking rates — if Malawi guaranteed to send the bulk of its exports by road. South African Foreign Minister Pik Botha visited Malawi in April 1984 to discuss Banda's public appeal for assistance on transport following the disruption of the Nacala line. Shortly afterwards, Malawi and South Africa signed a transport agreement which further reduced the prices Malawi was to pay for tea, tobacco, and fertiliser sent by road.

Deprived of normal outlets to the sea, Malawi found it easier (and cheaper) to buy South African goods. Imports from South Africa began to rise again, from a low in 1981 of 32% back up to 39% in 1983. Malawi made a few protests — in 1983 it very publicly invited a Soviet journalist to visit at roughly the same time as Lesotho was improving its links with the East, and it complained to the South African press that it was buying increasing quantities of South African goods while South Africa was buying little from Malawi. But the protests had no real impact — South Africa had forced Malawi back into the fold.

It is sometimes hard to accept that South Africa could be destabilising Malawi, when Malawi has such close historical links with it. But there was a clear danger in the early 1980s that Malawi, like Lesotho, was moving away from it. And there were clear warnings. There was the fuel stoppage and raid before the SADCC meeting. And there was an obscure article in the Johannesburg *Financial Mail* in 1982 warning Malawi that if its transport links were cut, its economy would collapse.[18]

Undoubtedly the most bizarre aspect is that Malawi is supporting a group which is cutting its own throat, and is thus an agent in its own destabilisation. In 1982, just as the MNR was hitting Malawi's rail link to Beira, Malawi allowed South Africa to set up bases for the MNR inside Malawi. MNR men and equipment were flown from South Africa to Malawi and on to northern Mozambique; in August

1982 the MNR launched a full-scale invasion of Zambezia province from Malawi. On 27 October Mozambique's Foreign Minister, Joaquim Chissano, went to Malawi, where he reminded Banda that the MNR had cut Malawi's fuel supply from Beira. Shortly afterwards, Malawi closed the rear bases for the MNR and the invasion collapsed; Mozambique began to ship Malawi oil via Nacala. But it was a short-lived peace. In early 1983 the bases were reopened, and there was a new invasion of Zambezia.

After the Nkomati Accord of 16 March 1984, more of the support of the MNR was transferred to Malawi. In October 1984, Mozambique's President Samora Machel visited Malawi for talks with Banda. There was a week of pomp and circumstance, but no agreement to stop supporting the MNR. By late 1984 South African-registered planes were making at least two flights per week from Malawi to drop supplies to the MNR in northern Mozambique; MNR bands were moving freely in and out of Malawi without opposition.

There seem to be three related hypotheses to explain why Malawi should back the MNR. One is that South Africa has threatened that if Malawi does not support the MNR, it will cut off Malawi's remaining links with the outside world. This was the second part of the scenario held out by the Johannesburg *Financial Mail*.[19] It could be done quite easily, either through the use of dissidents in Zimbabwe, or just by refusing road transport licences for lorries going to Malawi. The opening of the new British-funded road link to Tanzania is important to counter this particular form of pressure.[20]

The second possibility is that some elements in the political leadership feel that supporting the MNR is a good investment, to overthrow or at least substantially change the Machel government in Mozambique. When the Portuguese were still fighting Frelimo, the Portuguese businessman Jorge Jardim sold Life President Banda the idea of dividing Mozambique in half (like Korea or Germany). The northern part was to be linked to Malawi, giving Dr Banda permanent access to the sea and ensuring a non-socialist neighbour. This concept has re-emerged (see Chapter 12) and support of the MNR may have been sold to him on this basis. Like South Africa, Malawi has a number of Portuguese who left Mozambique before independence and are hostile to Frelimo. South African Military Intelligence has been working through them in Malawi, as it has in South Africa, to form a conduit of support for the MNR.

Finally, it is important to note that the damage to the economy is limited. Malawi's main exports, tea and tobacco, are high-value and low-volume; they are less than 100,000 tonnes per year. That is less than ten lorry-loads per day — a volume which is already being handled through South Africa. The technocrats may realise the harm that the MNR is doing to the economy as a whole, but the living standards of the political leadership are not seriously affected.

The most likely explanation is that Malawi is increasingly divided, especially when Dr Banda takes less day to day control over the running of the country. These divisions are complex and unclear, as factions jockey for position in anticipation of a succession crisis when the Life President dies. Pretoria certainly has an interest in that succession; whether it also has a role in backing particular factions is impossible to say. In any event, those in Malawi who are opposed to destabilisation are probably still too weak to stop South African actions. The army is now playing a central role. South African planes could not land regularly in Malawi to supply the MNR, nor could large MNR bands regularly cross the border, without army acquiescence.

The technocrats and civil servants *are* unhappy. It is they who took Malawi into SADCC and have improved links with neighbouring states, most recently Tanzania. They apparently do not support destabilisation of the neighbours, nor do they look with political sympathy at South Africa. Although they lack the political clout, they have so far ensured that Malawi has said nothing with respect to sanctions — a positive step since any formal statement would necessarily be pro-South Africa and anti-sanctions. And it seems likely that the technocrats will play an increasing role in the future.

Back in the fold?

Has South Africa brought Malawi back into the fold, as it has Swaziland? Undoubtedly it has rebuilt the ties and dependence of the early 1970s, but in a very different way. The links are now more forced than voluntary. South Africa has destabilised Malawi in such a way as to make it an agent of its own destabilisation, as well as that of Mozambique. Thus Malawi's links are even more anomalous now than they were 15 years ago. With its own economic crisis giving little space to provide Malawi with aid, South Africa must depend on increasing amounts of stick to keep Malawi in line.

19. Zambia

Zambia's relationship with South Africa is the most complex and apparently contradictory one in the region. Zambia is one of the Front Line states, Kenneth Kaunda is an outspoken critic of the apartheid regime, and the ANC headquarters, as well as an important and public SWAPO office, are in Lusaka. Yet South Africa has done relatively little to destabilise Zambia, so far, and South Africa has become the largest source of Zambian imports. These contradictions reflect divisions within each country about relationships to the other, as well as Zambia's appalling economic difficulties after a collapse in the copper price, and after the effects of UDI in Rhodesia.

President Kaunda leads a group of nationalist politicians who took power at independence with a commitment to reduce dependence both on Europe and on the white south. Under their leadership, Zambia nationalised the copper mines. It has actively supported the liberation movements, hosting the ANC and SWAPO, and before 1980, ZAPU. Zambia was a founder member of the Front Line states, and with Julius Nyerere's retirement in 1985, Kaunda became its head. All of this has made Zambia a target of the group in the South African military who favour a 'forward policy': they see Kaunda as part of the 'total Marxist onslaught'.

On the other hand, the South African Foreign Ministry is anxious to maintain contacts with Kenneth Kaunda, whom it sees as a 'moderate'. Kaunda has shown himself willing to talk, publicly and privately, with the South Africans, which gives Pretoria some contact with the Front Line states. Kaunda had two public but unsuccessful meetings with South African leaders. On 25 August 1975 he met with Prime Minister John Vorster in a white railway coach on the Victoria Falls Bridge.[1] It is an indication of the conflicts within South Africa that, at the same time, the military was organising a dissident movement for Zambia. Then on 30 April 1982 Kaunda and Prime Minister P.W. Botha met in a caravan on the Botswana-South Africa border.[2] No progress was made on either occasion, but the links were maintained, and Kaunda hosted talks in Lusaka between the South Africans and Angola in February 1984 and the South Africans and SWAPO in May 1984. He also arranged the 1985 talks between the ANC and South African business leaders and opposition politicians.

One other political reason why the South African Foreign Ministry may have wanted to maintain good relations with President Kaunda was Zambia's pre-independence support of Jonas Savimbi and UNITA in Angola. Thus Pretoria may have hoped that Zambia would allow UNITA rear bases and give it political support when South Africa began to rebuild it in 1979. If so, the hope proved ill-founded.

Economically, South Africa has benefited from increased exports and transit traffic for Zambia. South African business sought a political and military climate conducive to continued expansion of economic links. Pretoria's main emphasis has not been on direct destabilisation of Zambia, therefore, so much as on strengthening economic ties. Some of this has been by force — notably the disruption of Zambia's major route to the sea through Angola. But some has been more subtle. Economic links between the two states benefit groups on both sides of the Zambezi. South Africa is an important source of luxury goods for a wealthy Zambian elite, part of which has argued against the nationalist politicians for strengthened links. South Africa gains both profits and leverage from these links, and the business community in South Africa would be strongly opposed to any Mozambican or Angolan-style military destabilisation.

This chapter cannot demonstrate a consistent relationship between South Africa and Zambia, because there is none. Rather it will show how different actors have interacted in different, and sometimes contradictory, ways. But there is a consistent thread running through all the stories, namely that when Zambia is in difficulties, South Africa exploits those troubles.

SECURITY

During the period of Rhodesia's UDI, and especially after the 1973 border closure, Zambia came under increasing South African pressure. In 1975 South Africa trained a dissident group under Adamson Mushala and sent it back into western Zambia the following year. This was an apparent, albeit not very sustained or successful, attempt to capitalise on dissatisfaction in the former Barotseland of western Zambia. Since then, the Mushala Gang has engaged in endemic, low level banditry and disrupted Western Province (which borders Angola and Namibia) and Northwestern Province (which borders Angola and Zaire). Mushala was finally killed by security forces on 26 November 1982. But his gang remained active, and an Italian mineral prospecting team had to withdraw from the zone in 1984 due to attacks. [3]

In October 1979 Zambia was hit by simultaneous Rhodesian and South African invasions. In the southeast, 400 Rhodesian troops invaded, while 600 South African troops came into south west Zambia from the Caprivi strip of Namibia. For the next three years, there were incidents in the 100 km wide strip of Zambia between the Zambezi River and the Angola border. In April 1980 two South African battalions equipped with tanks and armoured cars invaded. Many troops left within a few weeks, but some stayed for the rest of the year. In March 1982 there was an invasion by a company supported by tanks and armoured cars. In these and other incursions, there was widespread mining of roads and burning of villages. Peasants were harassed by South African troops and prevented from cultivating their fields.

South Africa seemed to be trying to clear the strip west of the Zambezi, to make a depopulated area both to prevent access by SWAPO and to open up a route to install UNITA in south-east Angola. At one stage South African troops expelled all Zambian officials, including health workers, from the border town of Imusho; they mined the road from Imusho to Sesheke and in December 1981 impounded the pontoon ferry across the Zambezi to Sesheke. Sesheke is the nearest big

Zambian town outside the zone. Imusho is on one of the access routes to Mavinga, the town South Africa was then establishing as an important forward base for UNITA (see Chapter 13). Thousands of refugees — both Zambians and Angolans who had already fled the joint South African and UNITA push — were forced to leave the area. In April 1981 the Zambian Red Cross reported that thousands of villagers were suffering from famine and disease due to South African raids; hundreds died. Relief agencies dropped food from helicopters and used four wheel drive vehicles through the bush to avoid the mined roads.[4]

After the 1982 meeting between Botha and Kaunda, South African incursions seemed to end. The Sesheke pontoon ferry was returned in September 1982. But problems with UNITA and South African incursions and landmines continued. In the first half of 1985, for example, the Zambian security forces accused South Africa of five border violations, which included the kidnapping of 18 Zambians, and a number of cases of artillery fire into Zambian territory.[5]

The ANC and SWAPO in Lusaka have been targets, though not often. In April 1979, a Rhodesian commando raid on Lusaka included attacks on the Freedom House offices of the ANC and SWAPO, as well as ZAPU and Joshua Nkomo's house. On 2 July 1985, a bomb was thrown over the wall of the ANC headquarters; it occurred a few days after a major ANC conference in Zambia, and was apparently a warning shot, to remind the ANC and/or the government of Zambia of the risks of a raid like that on Gaborone a fortnight earlier. On 13 December 1985, a parcel bomb exploded, injuring two ANC members, and eleven days later two men were killed while attempting to kidnap ANC members from a transit camp in Zambia. In contrast to attacks on ANC offices and officials elsewhere in the region, South Africa may have been afraid to disrupt the delicate balance of its relations with Zambia, and feared that a Gaborone-style raid would alienate the nationalist politicians so much that they would crack down on trading links with South Africa as they did on those with Rhodesia during UDI. The 1985 raids seem to indicate that Pretoria is now adopting a harder line.

TRANSPORT

Cecil Rhodes's 'Cape-to-Cairo' railway crossed the Zambezi River at Victoria Falls in 1905, but it moved no closer to Egypt than northern Zambia. Instead, in 1909 it was linked to the Benguela system in Katanga (now Zaire). For the next 55 years of colonialism, Zambia's outlets through white-ruled Angola and white-ruled South Africa proved adequate for exporting copper and importing consumer goods and machinery. But, just as Rhodes dreamed of a colonial railway, Julius Nyerere and Kenneth Kaunda, who were to head the soon to be independent states of Tanzania and Zambia, talked of a railway that would link Zambia to the newly independent majority-ruled states to the north and reduce links with those still dominated by settlers.[6]

Apartheid was already a political issue, and Nyerere had helped push South Africa out of the Commonwealth in 1961. But the railway problem took on sudden urgency when Zambia's independence on 24 October 1964 was followed only a year later by UDI in Rhodesia.[7] Fuel and other goods had to be brought by road — and even airlift — from Dar es Salaam on what became known as the 'Hell

Run', and substantial copper was exported that way, although the border with Rhodesia was not actually closed. The Italian ENI laid an oil pipeline from Dar in 18 months.

The dream railway was essential. In 1964 the World Bank had refused to fund it, apparently because it had invested £80 million in Rhodesia Railways and did not want to fund a competing line. Britain and other Western countries apparently accepted the World Bank view. So Tanzania and Zambia turned to China. Most Western countries simply refused to believe that the Chinese could do it. And it is an amazing railway, 1870 km long — longer than the distance from London to Moscow — and costing US$450m. The agreement was signed in 1967, work started in 1969, and the first trains ran on the 'Tazara Railway' in 1975.[8]

It was just in time, as the intensifying liberation struggles were disrupting transport links. On 9 January 1973 Ian Smith closed the border with Zambia because it was supporting guerrillas. South Africa objected, because this cut off its K60m per year exports to Zambia, as well as depriving it of revenue from Zambian cargo exported through its ports and railways. On 3 February, Smith backed down — but Kaunda left the border closed. All traffic now moved down the Benguela Railway to Lobito, Angola. But by mid-1975 that line was coming under heavy pressure from South African-backed UNITA forces trying to overthrow the MPLA. By September 1975 Zambia was already using the Tazara, even though it was not actually finished and many of the locomotives had still not been delivered. The official opening was on 24 October, but by then thousands of tonnes of copper had already passed through Dar and several shipments of grain had been brought to Zambia.

The closure of the border was never total. Transit traffic for Zaire continued to pass through Zimbabwe and over the Victoria Falls Bridge. The border was also opened for some emergency shipments in 1975 and 1977. Finally, under heavy pressure from the IMF and business and professional groups within Zambia, Kaunda reopened the border on 26 October 1978, and trade with South Africa resumed. Nyerere and the Mozambican President, Samora Machel, both flew to Lusaka to try to dissuade Kaunda, but received a frosty reception. The transfer was reinforced by Rhodesian attacks on Tazara bridges (in the north of Zambia) and the Kazungula ferry (in the south of Zambia) in 1979.

Except for a brief period in 1980, the Benguela route has remained closed. Since the reopening of the border, roughly two-thirds of copper has been exported via Dar and the remaining one-third via East London. Small amounts of copper have gone via Mozambique at various times. Dar is much the nearest port; the differences in distances are large (see Table 1), and so are the cost differences. In June 1982 the cost per tonne to send copper was only US$73 to Dar, but was US$106 to Maputo and US$111 to East London.[9] Table 2 gives cargo through various ports, and shows the massive and sudden shifts forced by war and sanctions.

The Tazara route has faced some operational problems. The Chinese underestimated the steepness of the mountains and the intensity of the rains, so there have been washouts and the underpowered locomotives burned out. Maintenance has been poor, as well (not the fault of the Chinese). Upgrading Tazara is a priority SADCC project, and at a special donors' conference in April 1985 more than US$60 million was pledged to Tazara projects. More powerful West German locomotives began operation in 1983. The Zambian mines aim to send 80% of copper exports via Tazara and, even when the line is not operating

Table 1. Distance to ports (km)

	Dar	Lobito	Beira	Maputo	Durban	E.Ldn.
Copperbelt	2050	2436	2400	2395	3146	3246
Lusaka	2025	2679	2025	2020	2751	2871

Table 2. International rail traffic

(000 tonnes)	1972	1974	1977	1979	1981	1983
Imports						
via Zimbabwe	709	—	—	439	291	319
via Benguela	122	422	—	—	—	—
via Tazara	—	—	423	191	335	173
Exports						
via Zimbabwe	450	—	—	470	178	231
via Benguela	166	438	—	—	5	6
via Tazara	—	—	570	289	347	648
Transit for Zaire	328	378	490	845	641	585

Excludes coal. 'Via Zimbabwe' includes some trade with Zimbabwe. The rest is traffic through Zimbabwe, nearly all to or from South Africa or South African ports, with only tiny amounts via Mozambique (at various times some copper has been exported and fertiliser imported via Beira). Zaire transit is all via Zimbabwe and thus mostly to or from South Africa and South African ports (after 1980 it includes some Zimbabwean maize for Zaire).

Source: *Monthly Digest of Statistics*, Central Statistical Office, Lusaka.

well, send more than 60% that way. Indeed, some Zimbabwean exporters have begun using Tazara (the long way round, via the Victoria Falls Bridge) for exports to Tanzania and Kenya.[10]

Transport attacks

During the last years of the Rhodesian war, there had been a substantial increase in coordination of Rhodesian and South African attacks, particularly on transport links, as part of a joint effort to force Zambia to use the railway through Rhodesia to South Africa. Vorster noted much later that he had spent a significant part of the 1975 Victoria Falls Bridge meeting trying to convince Kaunda to reopen that line.[11] One alternative had been the Kazungula ferry which links Zambia and Botswana. It was largely a way for traffic between Zambia and South Africa to avoid Rhodesia, and was the main route for South African exports to Zambia when the border was closed. Nevertheless, in April 1979 when the Rhodesians sank the Kazungula ferry, the South Africans refused to allow lorries to go 100 km west through the Caprivi strip to cross the ferry at Sesheke. Bad weather and the increasing war with Rhodesia had meant a bad season, so Zambia was importing maize from South Africa. The cutting of ferry links meant it had to go over the newly reopened railway.[12]

An October 1979 attack on Tazara bridges was also intended to force Zambia to be more dependent on Rhodesian and South African transport links. That raid did K5m damage to road and railway bridges across the Chambeshi river. The railway was later rerouted over the damaged road bridge (and a new road bridge built), but more than 200,000 tonnes of copper had to be sent via East London instead of Dar es Salaam because of disruptions caused by the bridge raid.

Since Zimbabwe's independence there have been several disruptions by South Africa of essential traffic for Zambia. At least three were publicised: South African maize was delayed in 1980, a Canadian wheat donation was held up for eight months in 1981, and fertiliser was delayed in October 1982 when it was needed at the beginning of the agricultural season.[13] The various embargoes on Zimbabwe also affected Zambia. Government officials say there have been other unpublicised examples, in an attempt to create or exacerbate shortages in Zambia. These tend to be linked to anti-apartheid statements by Zambian leaders or allegations of excessive support of SWAPO or the ANC. Some are related to Zambia's attempts to diversify sources of supply, for example of fertiliser.

Over 1984 and 1985 the combination of the falling rand and systematic rate cutting on business which would otherwise travel via Tazara or the Mozambique railway system has become a tactical weapon of economic aggression. This is likely to be a tactic which Zambia will find particularly difficult to resist given its foreign exchange constraints.

ECONOMIC POWER

South Africa retains substantial economic power in Zambia, and as was stressed in earlier chapters, this gives it considerable leverage. This is used first of all simply to retain economic dependence, and to block Zambian efforts to build links with other SADCC states and other suppliers of goods. That, in turn, permits manipulation of transport and supplies for political ends.

Two forces are important in continued South African economic power. The first is Anglo American, which has used sophisticated methods to remain dominant in the copper and engineering industries in spite of nationalisation. The other is the renewed South African trading links.

Copper: Take the money and run — but not too fast

Zambia is a mining-dominated economy. Minerals are 96% of exports and the mining industry requires half of new investment and almost as high a share of imports to continue operation at present levels. The mines proved immensely profitable until the price collapsed in 1975, but since then copper has provided little revenue to the state.

The mines were partly nationalised in 1969 when the state took 51% and left management with the former owners, and further nationalised in 1973 when the government terminated those management contracts. After that, the government appointed the managing directors, but it signed new technical agreements with Anglo and the US firm AMAX, which continued to second foreign technical and management personnel to run the mines. (In 1982 the two mining companies were merged into one, ZCCM — Zambia Consolidated Copper Mines).[14]

Former Anglo American mines dominate ZCCM and Anglo kept a high profile in Zambia despite the nationalisation. Kenneth Kaunda met with the then Anglo chairman Harry Oppenheimer. And the present Anglo chairman Gavin Relly, who a decade ago was head of Anglo in Zambia, was the person who organised the Victoria Falls meeting between Kaunda and Vorster.

More than ten years after the second nationalisation, strikingly little is different. ZCCM's headquarters is in the Anglo building on Cathedral Hill in Lusaka. Some effort has been made to increase the number of black faces in the Lusaka headquarters. But in the copperbelt itself, technical management, as well as sales, accounting, and personnel, remains firmly in white, expatriate hands.[15] As part of their dominance of overall mine management and personnel development, expatriates control the 'Zambianization' of the mines. Thus Zambian 'high-fliers' who have been promoted are precisely those who accept their dependence on expatriate patronage, and who have absorbed a culture in which the 'normal' way of doing things turns out to be the way the international mining companies have always done things.

The top mine engineers remain white, often South African. A detailed study of attitudes on the copper mines in 1984 showed that some of the expatriate managers remain extraordinarily racist, saying that Zambian engineers are lazy and stupid, needing more time to learn than whites. So there is a steady drain of Zambian engineers who complain they cannot get promoted in the mines and move to the private sector.[16]

As well as maintaining control through people, Anglo also kept control of research and engineering. In the colonial era Anglo established the research and development centre for copper and cobalt for the whole Anglo group in Kitwe, Zambia. (The centre for other minerals was in South Africa.) Thus most projects undertaken by Anglo in Zambia were initiated, designed, and implemented locally. More recently (after nationalisation) ZCCM transferred most of this unit, and especially the key engineering design section, to Britain.

Equally important, the nationalisations did not include the vital ancillary engineering industries. Thus Anglo still controls: Scaw (the largest foundry), Deep Drilling (shaft sinkers), Diacarb (drilling equipment), African Wire Ropes (cables), and a variety of other contracting and engineering firms.[17] These services are needed and must be paid for whatever the price of copper, ensuring profits for Anglo. Furthermore, these firms became the main route to repatriate profits, directly as well as indirectly through items imported from Anglo firms in South Africa. Although there has been some Zambianization, the top managers of Anglo firms are still South Africans.

The IMF estimated that 64% of the money Zambia earned from copper sales in 1982 went straight out of the country again — roughly US$550m.[18] An EEC survey found that 'the mines tend to prefer to import final components rather than assist local industry develop their own production'. And expatriate managers openly admit that they prefer to import and do not trust local industry. Furthermore, there are increasing reports of suppliers giving kickbacks to expatriate managers.

Many of the imports for the mines, particularly of equipment, come from South

Table 3: Main imports from South Africa, 1982. (million Kwacha)

Milk for infants	1.2
Poultry and pig feed	1.8
Concentrated essences for beverages	1.5
Synthetic rubber substitutes	1.1
Lubricating oils	4.9
Sunflower seed and other vegetable oil	5.5
Soap, toilet, in tablet form	4.7
Detergents	5.1
Fertiliser	3.4
Fuses, detonators, igniters for mining	2.7
Additives for mineral oils	1.3
Tyres for heavy machinery	2.7
Newsprint	1.1
Other paper	1.8
Iron & steel rods, bars, tubes, angles	9.0
Iron & steel plates & sheets	4.7
Wire rope & cables	2.0
Bolts, nuts, screws	1.0
Interchangeable tools for handtools	2.2
Parts for excavating machinery	1.7
Food processing machinery	1.5
Machinery for stone & ore crushing	2.8
Pumps	9.8
Filtering machinery	1.0
Conveyors, winches, cranes	1.5
Transmission shafts	2.1
Electrical apparatus	2.1
Motor vehicles	1.9

Source: Central Statistical Office, Lusaka.

Africa (see Table 3). In part this is not surprising, as South Africa *is* a world mining centre and some of the Zambian equipment is similar to that installed in South Africa. But there is much more to it than that. Managers still talk about the 'good old days' when they could pick up the telephone to South Africa and have parts on the train a week later, and they admit they still do this; it is asserted to take much longer (and thus require more planning) to order from Europe, despite a special Zambian mining industry purchasing subsidiary in the United Kingdom. Sharing the central office with Anglo makes contact with South Africa even easier.

The role of the engineering companies is also important. Taffere Tesfachaw, who studied these firms, noted that 'the firms I visited which are subsidiaries of foreign firms, particularly Anglo, all import through their parents and not directly'. Because they are supplying the mines, these firms are normally ensured the necessary foreign exchange. All of this happens because so little has changed since nationalisation. Orders are placed by contacting three or four 'normal' suppliers, and very little is done by competitive tender. Indeed, when the World

Bank forced competitive tenders, ZCCM was surprised to receive highly competitive bids from unexpected places like India.

Thus Anglo has been able to retain a substantial influence over the mining and engineering sectors, despite the nationalisations. One effect of this has surely been to maintain dependence on South Africa, as raw materials and supplies are often imported from there instead of from neighbouring states or being locally made. Anglo will tend to source in South Africa for two reasons. First, it will find it profitable to buy from Anglo group members and, second, it will prefer to earn the profits in a convertible currency rather than in Zambian kwacha or, say, Zimbabwean dollars. This increases the costs to Zambia, hampers local industrial development, and provides Pretoria with an economic lever it can use against Zambia.

Squeezed into dependence

Few countries have been so much the victims of the Northern-dominated world economy.[19] Zambia was developed in colonial times as a single commodity country, and after independence that collapsed. Terms of trade fell to the point where Zambia had to exchange nearly three times as much copper for the goods it imported. In addition, Zambia paid a heavy price for the imposition of economic sanctions on Ian Smith's Rhodesia.

This external squeeze has in practice pushed Zambia into closer economic ties with South Africa. During the boom years, development strategy could assume that both imports and state revenue would be readily available. The new industries that were built, for example, required a high level of imported raw materials and parts. Zambia's import dependence increased considerably.

When foreign exchange receipts collapsed, therefore, the economy was plunged into crisis. In particular, the squeeze has led to a form of hand-to-mouth existence which makes planning impossible and increasingly depends on short term credit and paying bills in arrears at the last possible moment before supplies are cut off. The Tazara railway regularly grinds to a halt until Zambia pays its debts; fertiliser was stuck in Beira for weeks because Zambia could not pay the port charges to get it out. Goods are frequently not ordered until supplies run out and the situation becomes desperate. For example, in mid-1985 breakdowns in forward ordering and financing led to the near exhaustion of wheat flour supplies and, more critical, of gunny bags and lorry fuel precisely at the start of harvesting of the first good maize crop in several years. Given Zambia's large commercial arrears and limited export earnings, such breakdowns in the flow even of vital import lines are agonisingly frequent.

South Africa has been the main beneficiary, first because in a crisis it is always the quickest source of supply. For example, the soap company is not able to import essential raw materials, so production stops; with no soap on the market, there is a political scandal, and an urgent order is placed in South Africa. Grain bags are imported from South Africa after the harvest has begun, to keep the maize from rotting on the ground, when a local company has been refused the foreign currency to buy sewing equipment to mend bags.

Secondly, South Africa often appears to be the cheapest source. Zambia now requires government and parastatals to buy from the 'cheapest' source. With planning and finance, that could be Japan, India, or even Europe. But on short notice, it is always cheaper to buy in South Africa than to airfreight from Europe or Asia. And South African businessmen have responded to this by being willing to ship urgent items quickly, based on just a telephone or telex order, and sort out the details later. In a curious and unintentional way the IMF has actually increased Zambian links with South Africa, because it was under IMF insistence that Zambia agreed to buy from the 'cheapest', but it has been unable to impose a suitable planning system.[20]

The main bait offered by South Africa, other than simple geographical proximity, is credit. For example, in May 1985, when Zambia began to run out of fuel because it could not pay for crude oil for its refinery, South Africa magnanimously provided 5600 tonnes of diesel on credit.[21] More generally, South African firms frequently offer 18 months credit whereas neighbouring states typically offer only three to six. That means Lusaka shops can be seen selling South African consumer goods when substantially the same items are available at a lower price from Zimbabwe — but without the extended credit. So even if South Africa is not cheapest overall, it is the 'cheapest' supplier that will allow payment next year.

Why should South African firms be prepared to offer better credit terms than their competitors? Given that the extreme shortage of foreign exchange means that Zambian importers have to wait up to 10 months or more for the foreign exchange to pay their debts, why are South African firms interested at all? Partly because the neighbouring states have been the only viable export market for manufacturers. Partly because the overdraft cost to the exporter of delayed payment is simply added to the price to Zambia. But more importantly, the South African *government* has been prepared to back the deals, with the considerable range of export subsidy detailed in Chapter 8, as well as through direct credit offered by parastatals such as the railways.

Because of speed and credit, South Africa has developed an *image* as the best and cheapest place to buy. Thus in 1983 the chairman of the Mineworkers Union, Timothy Walamba, said that in the face of the 10% wage freeze imposed by the IMF and the continued shortages and high prices of consumer goods, Zambia should buy more from South Africa. 'Much as we have to help our brothers and sisters still under racist regimes, this should not be at the expense of our own people,' he said.[22] Likewise, at the UNIP Third National Convention, the ruling party decided that ZCCM's policy of trying to send 80% of copper through Dar es Salaam was wrong, and that at least 40% should go through East London to avoid having to send empty wagons to collect imports from South Africa.[23]

In response to Zambia's extreme economic crisis, trade with South Africa has indeed risen in the 1980s. This built on an earlier rise after UDI when Zambia's halting of imports from Rhodesia led in part to higher purchases from South Africa. To make this possible, transport links too have had to be strengthened Rail traffic has been supplemented by a special road haulage service, payable in Zambian kwacha, by the parastatal trucking company Contract Haulage. Zambian Airways started a service between Lusaka and Johannesburg in 1980, and offers a discount on airfreight.

It is largely the economic crisis that enabled South Africa to obtain its position. The crisis both discouraged alternative suppliers to Zambia (who feared delay in payment), and led Zambian planners into a pattern of very short-term, hand-to-mouth decisions. The South African government could then exploit the situation by supporting its own traders.

The 'apamawamba'

Yet this is not the whole story. In late 1985, 24 wealthy Zambians were arrested for smuggling substantial quantities of the drug Mandrax to South Africa. The accused include Vernon Mwaanga, one of the country's most prominent businessmen and a former minister. In part, they were allegedly paid cash in foreign bank accounts. But much of the payment was apparently in cars and container loads of luxury goods. President Kaunda set up a special tribunal to hear the cases.

There can be no doubt that a part of the Zambian elite (the so-called 'apamawamba' or 'the ones on top') has in effect challenged the efforts of President Kaunda and the nationalist politicians to oppose apartheid. They have built a public image of South Africa as the 'natural' supplier of goods and services, promoting a line that, whatever the problems of apartheid, 'political' stands will harm Zambian living standards, and that therefore it is in Zambia's interests to deal with South Africa. Of course, the economic crisis has limited the freedom of action even of the nationalist politicians — survival sometimes dictates coming to terms with hostile neighbours or limiting support to liberation movements. But this is an area of some conflict. In the late 1970s Kenneth Kaunda came under heavy pressure from the apamawamba to reduce support for ZAPU and end sanctions against Rhodesia (which he refused to do), and reopen the rail link to South Africa (which he finally did). In 1980 there was even an unsuccessful coup attempt against Kaunda.

The existence of the elite is partly a reflection of the economic path Zambia has followed.[24] The boom years of high copper prices after independence allowed a rapid rise in urban incomes, and so in the consumption of semi-luxury goods. Many of these were imported. Some, like bottled beer and cars, were made locally in new factories, but the factories themselves were highly dependent on imported raw materials. When the copper crash came, a small elite managed to preserve their living standards. The National Planning Commission commented in 1984 that 'as the economy has been declining, the poor became poorer. The size of the rich (group) seems to have become smaller but richer.'[25] This is the base of the 'apamawamba', consisting of private businessmen and others with property, including a group of commercial farmers as well as some high officials in government and parastatals.[26]

This elite in particular requires imports to keep up its living standards, and, as we have seen, South Africa presented itself as the easiest source. This is reinforced for the unscrupulous by the opportunity provided by South African links for illicit incomes, large (as in the drug scandal or emerald smuggling) or small (as in smuggling back luxury goods after business trips there). South African firms facilitate such practices to gain business. An example of the influence of the desire for luxuries was the import of 79 new Mercedes Benz cars from South Africa, supposedly to provide delegates with transport at the February 1984 SADCC conference — when SADCC is aimed at reducing dependence on South Africa. In practice, few of the cars were used for the conference, but they were of course available afterwards.

The point should not be overstated: a commitment to capitalism and to acquiring luxury goods is by no means the same thing as acceptance of apartheid. Nevertheless South Africa gains from the actions of this part of the elite in three ways. First, pressure for South African links undercuts President Kaunda and the nationalist politicians — which means undercutting the image of the head of the Front Line states. Second, and linked, it can be used by South Africa to stress at home the 'practical success' of white rule, and internationally the 'advantages' for neighbouring states of economic 'cooperation' with South Africa. Third, and in many ways most important, the increased links give South Africa further economic leverage. As we have seen, South Africa can and does delay deliveries of goods both to make a political point, and to force Zambia to pay debts (thus making planning even more difficult). The 1978 reopening of the rail link came about from a mix of practical needs and political pressure from the *apamawamba*, and this kind of pressure can always be applied again.

The potential for destabilisation

The consequence of all these factors is a complex and subtle relationship between South Africa and Zambia, with conflicts on both sides. South Africa has succeeded in maintaining and increasing economic dependence, and hence the opportunity for destabilisation, largely because of the economic crisis caused by the plunging copper price. Consequently, there are supporters of the necessity of South African links among the Zambian elite.

Yet through all its immense economic difficulties, Zambia has maintained its position as the site of the ANC headquarters and, in 1985, host of the ANC's most important conference for decades. Furthermore, since the coming to power of P.W. Botha, the South African military has been kept largely at bay. There are perhaps two reasons for this. On the one hand, South Africa's economic leverage is brittle: there is always the danger that, given sufficient provocation, Zambia would cut the ties despite all the short-term costs, as it did with Ian Smith's Rhodesia. South African business, as well as Pretoria's influence, would then suffer. On the other hand, as the level of internal conflict rises in South Africa, Pretoria may again want to turn to President Kaunda's good offices as mediator and negotiator; for that to be possible, it is perhaps important not to antagonise Zambia any further by military action.

But, if military tactics are played down by Pretoria relative to economic and political manoeuvres, this cannot disguise the damage done, by troops in Western Province, by sabotage to the Benguela railway, and by disruptions of essential deliveries of food and fertilizer. More important, it has created the potential for short-term economic destabilisation that Pretoria now holds in its hands.

20. Neighbours' Reactions

Despite all South Africa's pressure, the neighbouring states have not been cowed. No state has recognised the bantustans. Refugees are not returned to South Africa. The strong international representation at SADCC's 1986 conference reaffirmed SADCC's continued importance: some projects have been delayed or deferred by destabilisation, but many have gone ahead. This is the more remarkable given the pressing economic crises faced by many of the states in the region during the early 1980s. But there have also been setbacks.

If we look at the position country by country, Zimbabwe is perhaps the region's most conspicuous success, pursuing a slow but steady programme of economic delinking. Many opportunities have been missed, delayed or sabotaged, but many in the government now have a clearer idea of the role of South Africa in the economy and are working to reduce it. Militarily, Zimbabwe's dissident movement provides fertile ground for South African meddling. But, in a striking example of international cooperation, Zimbabwe has also put thousands of troops into Mozambique, keeping open a line to the sea and in 1985 actually attacking South African-backed rebels there.

Botswana has cautiously delinked, and also served as a key member of the Front Line states and headquarters for SADCC. Other development policies would have led to faster delinking, but the 14 June 1985 raid on the capital, Gaborone, was a reminder of the constraints.

Mozambique is now economically less dependent on South Africa than in 1980, but because of an embargo by South Africa rather than any action of its own. Destabilisation has shattered the Mozambican economy, and it was forced to sign the Nkomati non-aggression pact and expel the ANC. Angola, too, has been crippled by destabilisation. Attacks on railways in both countries have prevented them from becoming the main SADCC ports.

Lesotho became increasingly vociferous, and reaped the penalty in economic, military and political pressure. It has done little to decrease its overwhelming economic dependence on South Africa, however, and one of the main economic development projects — the Highland Water Scheme — would increase links. The 1986 coup brought in a government prepared to negotiate an end to the South African blockade, but maintaining Lesotho's independent stance and potentially more concerned with economic delinking.

Zambia has taken the chair of the Front Line states, so that President Kaunda speaks for the region against apartheid. On the other hand, beset by acute economic problems, Zambia has moved closer to South Africa economically, in part for internal political reasons.

Malawi, which had been drifting away from its previously close ties to South Africa, is being pulled back economically by destabilisation, especially transport disruption. A combination of South African inducements and internal political developments also brought Swaziland more into line with Pretoria. Swaziland signed a non-aggression pact and has even praised President Botha's 'reforms' inside South Africa[1], though the most pro-South African faction in Swaziland has lost power.

The pattern of reaction

The extent of Pretoria's war against its neighbours has been detailed in the preceding chapters, and is summarised in Chapter 1. In many ways, the neighbouring states have reacted by reaffirming their independence, and by closing ranks regionally. Nevertheless, it is worth pointing out two responses which have exacerbated the problem.

The first is over-reaction. One of Pretoria's main weapons has been guerrilla movements, often very vicious, which it either established or rebuilt in four countries. The success of the weapon depended not only on the level of support and training but also on shortcomings and over-reaction in the victim state. In all four cases, military and police brutality and other forms of over-reaction alienated many members of the general public — making it easier for the dissidents to operate and recruit.

In two countries, Mozambique and Angola, Pretoria was able to take over an existing movement, albeit in Mozambique one with very little support. By early 1980, both would soon have been defeated had they not been rejuvenated by South Africa — thus, they are, first and foremost, South African creations. Nevertheless, both countries forgot their own experience of guerrilla warfare, namely that peasant support was essential. Anti-government forces spread faster than expected because of peasant discontent, especially about agricultural policies biased towards big development projects which did not benefit the ordinary family farmer. In both countries, the South African-backed guerrillas created economic chaos, but the government took the blame. Thus peasant alienation — caused by military over-reaction, incorrect agricultural policies, and the destabilisation itself — became South Africa's ally.

In Zimbabwe and Lesotho, Pretoria had to start from scratch to create a movement. In Zimbabwe it first fuelled the discontent, by exacerbating the ZANU-ZAPU split. But once Zimbabwe troops went into Matabeleland, over-reaction ensured recruits and a political dissident movement which it could use as a cover for its own 'super-ZAPU'. In Lesotho, because Leabua Jonathan annulled the 1970 election when his opponents won, there was a ready-made opposition from which South Africa could recruit. But Lesotho did seem the one country that prevented the armed dissidents from gaining a foothold: the government was able to show convincingly that the LLA came from South Africa, and to build on the strong antipathy to South Africa to deny the rebels local support.

The other issue which South Africa has exploited is internal division. Just as different groups in South Africa have different interests in the neighbouring states, so in the region attitudes to South Africa have sometimes been confused by internal division.

In particular, the interests of elites can encourage links with South Africa. As everywhere in the world, government officials, parastatal managers and private business executives expect a privileged life-style, with some luxury goods — though the level they expect varies enormously from country to country. This *need* not involve links with South Africa, but many do see South Africa as a kind of mini-Europe which produces high-quality products. Shopping trips to South Africa became an increasingly important perk. This has been exacerbated by the fall in the value of the rand during 1985, which brought down the prices of South African goods. In Zimbabwe, ZANU's chief political commissar instructed party members to end shopping trips to South Africa, because they flew in the face of the consumer boycotts by South African blacks of white-owned businesses.[2]

A stress on consumption by the elite may also work indirectly to further dependence on South Africa. Delinking requires a clear investment strategy to provide locally the goods and jobs that now come from South Africa. Investment in rural development and production of mass consumption goods seems likely to involve fewer linkages with South Africa than investment in producing goods for the elite — and certainly less than if those goods are imported. Pressure to supply the elite arises with different strengths in different countries, but it is always present and the policy reaction to that pressure is important. Likewise, on some occasions, foreign aid donors have paid little attention to the wider implications of their projects for dependence on South Africa, ignoring the fact that there are groups in all the states whose economic interests lie in closer ties with Pretoria.

Exploiting the contradictions?

Relations with South Africa are inevitably complex, especially for the immediate neighbours. Their military weakness, relative to South Africa, puts a premium on diplomacy. In the same way, their heavy economic dependence, inherited from colonialism, cannot be thrown off at a stroke, and so compromises are required.

An example of the issues involved occurred in Botswana, where a project was undertaken with Norwegian aid to provide road links between villages in the extreme south-west of the country. When an official Norwegian delegation came to inspect the project, they were dismayed to discover that one of the roads suddenly turned into South Africa. The Botswana government argued that there was no realistic alternative to travelling through South Africa in order to reach Gaborone from those villages: the only route entirely within Botswana involves hundreds of kilometres of dirt track across the Kalahari desert. But the Norwegians were concerned about the political implications of financing a link to South Africa, and also questioned the economic consequences of building roads that allowed South African produce to flood into the area and displace locally produced goods.

Most difficult of all is the question of trying to co-opt South Africans and to exploit splits in the façade of apartheid. Swaziland exploits the sports boycott by holding international sporting fixtures and attracting integrated crowds from over the border who come to see things which are banned at home; it bring Swaziland useful revenue, and emphasises the existence of the sports boycott, yet it leaves a strange taste in the mouth as a way of helping white South Africa get around the boycott. Likewise, all three customs union states encourage South African firms to move there and make goods to sell to states that already impose sanctions. If really tight trade sanctions were imposed, should this be seen as a way of splitting South African capital and moving industry to the SADCC states, or alternatively as sanctions busting? This becomes even more problematic as South African companies register front companies in Bermuda or Luxembourg.

Just this sort of issue came up with a SADCC paper project in Zimbabwe, where the Zimbabweans wanted to include in the consortium an existing firm owned by a Dutch-registered South African front company, and Sweden refused to participate. The Zimbabweans were angered, arguing that they knew what they were doing, and that they wanted to dilute the South African interest without losing the existing skilled staff and technology. Was it a case of local interests opposed to delinking, or did the government have a more sophisticated analysis than the donor?

One answer may be to follow the procedure of the Preferential Trade Area of Eastern and Southern Africa, which allows the participation only of companies with both a majority local ownership and a majority local management. This would exclude even re-registered firms, and thus block South African companies from simply moving to the neighbouring states. But it would still allow a more subtle South African control; Wankie Colliery probably qualifies under PTA rules, yet it is openly managed by Anglo, while a number of firms in South Africa are reducing the equity to less than 50% while apparently retaining effective control. Also, the PTA rule would be opposed by the US, Britain, and other countries who would want their companies to move into neighbouring states without a loss of control.

There is no 'right' answer to this question of whether and how neighbouring states can use links with South Africa to their advantage. Obviously it is important to look for alternatives, such as other paper projects without South African participation, or international rather than South African tourism. Most important, however, is to remember the issue, and always ask questions about the roads that suddenly turn toward South Africa.

21. What can be done?

Six years after the independence of Zimbabwe and the founding of SADCC, the war for the control of southern Africa has dramatically intensified. On military, political and economic fronts, Pretoria is asserting its claim to be a regional power. In reply SADCC struggles to reduce its economic dependence on South Africa. So far the war is a costly draw. Pretoria has prevented the neighbours from delinking and has forced them into economic decline, but it has failed to draw them back completely into the fold.

The dreams of 1980, of steady regional progress towards economic growth and independence, have been shattered. Destabilisation now costs the SADCC states more than $4500 million per year.[1] Development efforts are undermined. The political fabric is weakened. Whatever the internal political faults and economic errors of the region's various governments, their effects have been dwarfed by destruction from outside. The neighbouring states clearly underestimated the savagery and cunning of white South Africa. They also failed to predict that the main Western powers would acquiesce in destabilisation and do little to support their attempts to delink.

The international response

In the face of this attack, two responses are required from the international community. First, the neighbouring states need assistance to repair the damage. But to do that alone would just be to treat the symptoms of the disease. The real need is to address the cause. It is clear that South Africa must be stopped. It is also clear, from experience, that diplomatic protest is not enough. The United States protest at South Africa's attempted attack on US oil firms in Angola did not prevent the raid on Gaborone immediately afterwards. The UN Security Council condemnation of the December 1985 commando raid into Lesotho was followed by a South African economic blockade.

If diplomacy fails, the normal recourse of the international community is economic sanctions. Experience in southern Africa does indicate that they can be effective. The present embargo on the supply of arms to South Africa, however much breached, has protected the neighbouring states. It does, for example, limit the kind and quantity of weapons that can be supplied to the MNR and UNITA.[2] It has also prevented South Africa from modernising its air force, a weakness which turned the tide in the invasion of Angola in December 1983.[3] South Africa's own actions in the region have also demonstrated that sanctions can work, especially when combined with other forms of pressure. South African sanctions against Lesotho, combined with military action, did push out the ANC. Sanctions against Mozambique, combined with aggressive destabilisation, forced Mozambique to sign the Nkomati non-aggression pact.

Sanctions against South Africa are of course already on the international agenda. This is not the place to debate the wider issues,[4] but it is important to stress that the Front Line states have a clear position. It was set out by Tanzanian President Julius Nyerere when he opened the SADCC summit in Arusha on 9 August 1985:

> All the major non-white leaders of the anti-apartheid struggle demand that economic sanctions be imposed against the regime. They are not stupid; they know that among other things this means more unemployment for non-white workers. But they believe that sanctions will greatly weaken the South African apartheid system; and it is that which they are fighting with their lives and their freedom. Africa also calls for economic sanctions, and we are not stupid either. We know that South Africa's retaliation may well be directed against neighbouring African states. But we also know that our freedom and our economic development will remain under constant threat until apartheid is defeated.

There have been allegations, particularly by South Africa and the United States, that regional leaders have been speaking out of both sides of their mouths on sanctions. But in mid-1985 they made their positions crystal clear. The Front Line states (Angola, Botswana, Mozambique, Tanzania, Zambia, and Zimbabwe) backed sanctions with a statement at the Front Line summit on 15 September, when they 'hailed' increasing Western pressure on South Africa, 'including economic sanctions against the apartheid regime', and 'called upon these and other countries to broaden and intensify the pressure'. Lesotho has also made clear its support for sanctions. On the other hand, the two remaining states, Malawi and Swaziland, have said little on the subject and seemed not to support sanctions, but nevertheless approved a call by SADCC at its annual conference on 31 January 1986 for co-ordinated pressure on South Africa, including sanctions.

Joaquim Chissano, Mozambique's foreign minister, has frequently made two key points about sanctions. First, they must be organised and applied by South Africa's main trading partners — the US, Japan and Europe. The impact of their sanctions will be greater, yet the relative cost smaller, than sanctions applied by the neighbours. The lesson of sanctions against Rhodesia was harsh; Mozambique lost important port and railway revenue and drew attacks on itself, yet the oil and other goods still reached Rhodesia — through South Africa with British connivance. This time, if Britain leads the way SADCC will follow.

This leads to Chissano's other point, that Britain, the US, and Japan must look at the impact of sanctions on themselves, and not use the excuse of safeguarding the neighbours. They should, in the first instance, look for those sanctions which harm South Africa most and themselves least; only then should they look at the neighbours, and provide compensation as appropriate.

Speaking at the SADCC summit on 9 August 1985, Lesotho's King Moshoeshoe II made his country's position explicit:

> Various sanctions against South Africa are but a reflection of international opprobrium against the policy of racial discrimination. ... The effects of sanctions are very clear to us, and they will call for great sacrifices among our peoples. We cannot stand against the sanctions campaign; thus we call upon the rest of the world that, as it exercises what it feels to be a moral obligation, it should be cognisant that we are not a party to

apartheid. We, therefore, strongly elicit the international community to increase moral support to SADCC states so as to cushion the indirect effects of sanctions to us.

The regional effects of sanctions

The suggestion from the West is that international sanctions on South Africa would have devastating effects on the neighbouring states. The British Foreign Office argues that sanctions are 'counterproductive and damaging to the whole region'.[5]

This is a common resort of those opposed to sanctions; indeed, as we noted in Chapter 7, South Africa has been trying to create dependence precisely so that its allies could make this argument. And there is no question that the continued dependence of the neighbouring states on South Africa means that sanctions would hurt them. Nevertheless, the potential damage has been widely exaggerated. Furthermore, what is likely to hurt is not the sanctions themselves, but South African retaliation.

The position is examined in detail in Appendix 2. South Africa can be expected to increase support for rebel groups, to attempt to stop the flow of oil to the region, perhaps even to send in troops to guarantee its continued access to key facilities such as Cahora Bassa electricity and (were it built) the Highland Water Scheme in Lesotho. Transport would be the main battleground, as it has been since 1980. Under normal circumstances, SADCC ports and railways could handle most of the region's cargo and in many cases at less cost than shipping through South Africa. 20 years ago little cargo passed through South Africa; trade volumes in the region have not grown much since then, while the Tazara railway has increased nominal capacity. The problem is, of course, that South Africa would try to prevent such a transfer of the region's cargo: as now, the railways through Angola and Mozambique would be sabotaged.

Cushioning the effects of destabilisation

The major difficulty for the region caused by international sanctions, therefore, is that Pretoria would step up its destabilisation. It would not be a new problem, but an intensification of the present one. As a result, the kind of assistance needed in the face of sanctions is the same as the help needed in the face of destabilisation. There are two distinct, but linked, kinds of support required: development aid and assistance to resist South African pressure.

First is normal development aid, but targeted in a way that will help the neighbours to ride out destabilisation. A number of existing SADCC projects, particularly rehabilitation of ports and railways, fit into this category, though taking sanctions and retaliation into account might require some modifications. In addition, there will have to be a speed-up in implementation of electricity generation or transmission projects in Lesotho, Swaziland, and Mozambique. Assistance will be needed to absorb migrant workers expelled from South Africa. There will have to be industrial development projects to allow the neighbouring states to make some of the things they now import from South Africa. Finally, there must be help to reorient trade; this means both a revolving fund to encourage intra-SADCC trade, and some assistance in developing independent import/export capabilities. Considerable international assistance would be needed on transport. At least one of the railways to Zimbabwe, and one to Malawi, needs to be upgraded, at a cost of perhaps $500m.

Meanwhile, assistance is needed to diversify the region's sources of imports. It is not surprising that South Africa is prepared to fight to protect the regional market: it sells more to the seven neighbours, taken together, than to any one of its main trading partners (US, UK, Japan and West Germany). By contrast, it seems strange that so little has been done by Western countries to try to win the region away from South African supply. The region's purchases from South Africa are more than South Africa buys from any one of the main four Western nations: in other words, the SADCC states are already a large enough market to be considered in the same league as South Africa itself. Likewise, investment in the mining sector would develop alternative sources of the minerals which allow South Africa to claim such a privileged position in the Western world.

Even in their everyday policy, aid agencies have an important role, because they are putting more than $1bn per year into the eight countries in this study. Much more attention could be paid to buying products from within SADCC, both as an alternative to buying from South Africa, and as an alternative to buying from Europe. Aid agencies suffer from the same problem as other buyers in the region — it *is* more convenient to buy from South Africa, with its telephones and colour catalogues. As a result, aid agencies in Mozambique, for example, often do not even know what is available in neighbouring Zimbabwe or Malawi. These habits have been broken in a few cases — for example, vehicles for relief work in Mozambique have been imported in kit form and assembled in Zimbabwe. This lowers the foreign exchange cost and helps local economies. Too often, however, aid agencies salve their conscience by turning to dummy companies in Swaziland and Botswana, and buy their South African goods there — at 15% extra.

Aid agencies could do much more; one of the most useful investments would be to make a concerted effort to find out what products can be made regionally, and to provide the raw materials and if necessary some of the finance to get it done. This will set a useful precedent which the countries themselves could follow, and it will develop habits which will be needed if sanctions are imposed.

The second kind of assistance required is aid to resist South African pressure. Under some circumstances, this could well include a Berlin-style airlift for Lesotho; the publicity associated with such an airlift would be particularly useful in building support. In reality, it seems unlikely that South Africa would totally isolate Lesotho, but would apply pressure step by step as in 1985/86. This would require early and highly public action to break any counter-sanctions imposed by South Africa.

Several aid donors, including Norway, Sweden, Italy, and the Netherlands, have used aid money to replace war-damaged facilities in Mozambique and Angola. This should be encouraged, again with maximum publicity.

Nevertheless, this would not be enough in the face of the kind of destabilisation experienced by the region to date. The extra development money is likely to be wasted without the one kind of assistance no-one likes to talk about — military assistance. Unless ordinary people can feel secure, destabilisation will continue to lower morale, foster political instability, and accelerate economic decline. The armed forces of the region need to be better trained and better equipped, for example with anti-aircraft missiles. It would be essential to have outside help to protect fuel and transport facilities. For the West, there is clearly a political problem about providing help to Angola and Mozambique, especially when the United States is financing UNITA. Britain is already giving Zimbabwe some military aid for its actions in Mozambique and training Mozambican officers in

Zimbabwe. It might be politically more acceptable for Britain (and perhaps the US and France) to aid Zimbabwe to guard the railway to Maputo.

The backers of the region cannot shy away from this. During the 1983 famine in Mozambique, aid donors tried to maintain a 'neutral' position, and were unwilling even to send food aid into contested areas with a strong MNR presence. But famine was being used by the MNR and its South African backers as a tactic of the war. Not to send food aid was to undermine the Mozambique government's position and so in effect to take sides in the war. Neutrality is not an option in southern Africa today.

The cost

It is hard to put specific costs to cushioning the region from destabilisation. Professor Reginald Green has estimated that in the event of sanctions 'the initial support for neighbouring states might well require $750-1000 million plus $250-500 million a year thereafter.'[6] The estimates in Appendix 2 are somewhat higher, but in the same range.

The sums required are large, but two comparisons need to be made. Firstly, many of these projects are needed anyway for long-term regional economic development. Upgrading the transport routes, for example, is already SADCC's highest priority. Secondly, the costs of South African sabotage and destabilisation are now around $4500m per year. If Western action was comprehensive and effective, the process of political change in South Africa could be quick. The cost of withstanding sanctions should be seen as an investment in ending destabilisation. It would be a worthwhile investment both in breaking South Africa's economic dominance of the region, and in finally ending apartheid.

There is a war going on

There is a war going on for the control of southern Africa. Will white South Africa become a regional power, with the right to hegemony, or will the majority-ruled states win the right to self-determination? White South Africa is determined to defend apartheid by fighting the war beyond the borders of South Africa. At best, the neighbouring countries would be turned into vassals who pour wealth into South Africa and who meekly oppose sanctions. At worst, they would be plunged into chaos to create a cordon of instability.

The West has persistently avoided taking sides in the conflict. But that position is becoming ever more tenuous. More than 100,000 dead and $10,000m in damage is not a good advertisement for constructive engagement. Now the United States seems to have taken sides. Its assistance to UNITA in Angola has caused the greatest alarm in the region. Botswana has traditionally been a good friend of the United States, yet the Vice-President of Botswana, speaking for SADCC at the February 1986 Annual Conference, said that these moves 'run counter to American professions of friendship and co-operation with the independent states of southern Africa. This now places the United States clearly in league with South Africa in fomenting instability in this region.'

Military and economic help is essential for the region. Those who help must recognise that there is a war going on, and side with the people of southern Africa.

Appendix 1.
The Cost of Destabilisation
MEMORANDUM PRESENTED BY SADCC TO THE
1985 SUMMIT OF THE ORGANISATION OF AFRICAN
UNITY

1. South African aggression and destabilisation has cost its neighbours in excess
    of $10 billion in the five years since the founding of SADCC. This is more
    than:
    all the foreign aid received by the SADCC states during this five year-
    period; or
    one-third of all SADCC exports in the past five years.

2. It must, however, be remembered that even before 1980 the countries of the
    region incurred massive costs as a result of South African and Rhodesian
    aggression. The following calculations do not, for instance, include the costs
    of South African aggression against Angola during 1975-79, nor the costs to
    Mozambique and Zambia of imposing internationally agreed sanctions
    against Rhodesia. These earlier costs are at least comparable to those dealt
    with in this analysis.

3. This paper attempts to quantify some of the costs to the independent states of
    southern Africa (Angola, Botswana, Lesotho, Malawi, Mozambique,
    Swaziland, Tanzania, Zambia and Zimbabwe) of South Africa's campaign of
    military and economic destabilisation against them in the five years since the
    founding of SADCC in 1980. It is estimated that the approximate costs, in
    millions of US dollars, of South African destabilisation during this period are:

Direct war damage	1610
Extra defence expenditure	3060
Higher transport and energy costs	970
Lost exports and tourism	230
Smuggling	190
Refugees	660
Reduced production	800
Lost economic growth	2000
Boycotts and embargoes	260
Trading arrangements	340
Total	10120

These items are discussed in the following paragraphs. More detailed
calculations are available from the SADCC Secretariat.

THE COST OF DESTABILISATION

4. *Direct War Damage*
    The most obvious impact of destabilisation relates to the direct consequences of South African military actions — its invasions of Angola, Botswana, Mozambique and Lesotho; its clandestine commando raids on bridges and oil terminals; and its support for puppet anti-government groups.
      Direct war damage includes major attacks, like those which caused $80m damages to the Thornhill air base in Zimbabwe, $24m to the oil refinery in Luanda and $20m to the oil storage depot in Beira. In reality, however, most of the damage is not caused by single large explosions, but by the hundreds of houses, schools, lorries, and so on which have been destroyed. Of particular significance is the enormous damage which has been done to the region's transport system: railway lines sabotaged, bridges destroyed, locomotives and wagons damaged, etc. The estimated total cost of such direct war damage is $1610m, most of which relates to Angola and Mozambique.

5. *Extra Military Expenditure*
    Stepped-up South African aggression, particularly since 1980, has forced the SADCC states into ever higher military budgets for larger and better equipped armies as well as expanded people's militias. These armies must be fed, clothed, housed and transported — all of which uses up resources which are desperately needed for the development of the countries concerned. It is impossible to know what 'normal' defence budgets would have been if there were no threat from South Africa, but SADCC estimates that destabilisation has forced its member states to spend an extra $3060m on defence.

6. *Higher Transport and Energy Costs*
    The region's railway network has been a particular target, especially for the puppet rebel groups. This is because South Africa understands that Angola and Mozambique have the natural ports for most SADCC cargo, and thus the only way to keep cargo flowing through its ports is by disrupting competing railways. Thus landlocked states, particularly Malawi, Zambia and Zimbabwe, have had to pay higher transport costs, while Angola and Mozambique have lost revenue. Finally, sabotage of power lines and oil installations by puppet groups and South African commandos has forced Angola, Malawi, Mozambique and Zimbabwe to use more expensive fuel or pay extra to have it transported. The combined amount for higher transport and energy costs and lost transport revenue is $970m.

7. *Lost Exports and Tourism*
    Several SADCC states have lost vital foreign exchange earnings, particularly because the breakdown of transport links disrupted the export flows of coal, iron and steel, sugar, etc. The raid on the Luanda oil refinery meant lost oil exports for Angola. Raids have prevented the production of crops and cement for export in Mozambique. Tourism, an important foreign exchange earner, has been adversely affected by destabilisation. The total prejudice to SADCC states in lost exports and tourism to date is at least $230m.

8. *Smuggling*
    Perhaps surprisingly, smuggling by bandit groups has cost Angola and Mozambique $190m. Diamonds, semi-precious stones, ivory from more than

10,000 elephants and timber are smuggled and sold through South African firms.

9. *Refugees*

The war has created tens of thousands of refugees. It is sometimes difficult to distinguish between drought and war refugees but in some areas South African and bandit group activities have effectively cut off relief to drought victims, thus creating a famine. So drought victims became war refugees. The cost is difficult to estimate accurately but SADCC puts the figure at $660m.

10. *Reduced Production*

Destabilisation has undermined SADCC economies, most seriously the economies of Mozambique and Angola. In addition to lost exports, there has been a serious fall in agricultural and industrial production for local consumption. Numerous development projects have been delayed. Based purely on what could reasonably be expected to have been produced without the war, SADCC estimates the value of lost production at $800m.

11. *Lost Economic Growth*

Money spent on higher military budgets and repairing damage should have been more productively employed on development projects. Unquestionably, factories have not been built and capital goods not purchased because of the conflicts. This lack of investment has significantly slowed growth in what are still very poor countries. If the money referred to in paragraphs 4 and 5 above had been productively invested, it is conservatively estimated that it would have increased domestic production in the region by more than $2000m during this five-year period alone. Clearly this loss continues into the future.

A POLICY OF ECONOMIC AGGRESSION

12. South Africa not only attacks its neighbours militarily; it also destabilises them economically. A key reason for the founding of SADCC was to reduce the region's dependence on South Africa. For its part, the apartheid state is wielding its economic power to keep its neighbours weak and dependent, while at the same time trying to strengthen its economic hold.

13. *Boycotts and Embargoes*

Because of frequent disruption caused to the railways in Angola and Mozambique by South African proxies, most SADCC cargo still passes through South Africa. Pretoria can, therefore, cut the flow of goods at any time it wishes to apply additional pressure on its neighbours. It has done this to all the neighbouring states. Conversely, Maputo is the natural port for the South African Transvaal, but with the founding of SADCC the apartheid state boycotted Maputo (at extra expense to itself, but costing Mozambique considerable revenue). The cost of such boycotts and embargoes has been estimated at $260m.

14. *Trading Arrangements*

A number of member states have special trading arrangements with South Africa. Although the countries concerned gain substantial revenue from such arrangements, they do so at a high cost because of, for instance, higher prices of fuel and a loss of industry. It has been estimated that, on balance, such arrangements have cost at least US$340m during the past five years. Furthermore, South Africa is increasingly using such arrangements for political purposes, particularly to force member states to recognise the bantustans. It is further feared that withdrawal from such arrangements could bring blockades and increased destabilisation.

15. *South African Penetration of the Region*

There is a wide range of other effects of economic destabilisation which simply cannot be quantified. South African companies in the neighbouring states engage in transfer pricing and other improper practices to take goods and money from the SADCC states. They also block the development of independent SADCC industry and trade routes. For example, South African domination of forwarding has kept cargo flowing through South Africa even after the line to Beira was reopened. South African boards of directors have blocked the expansion plans of local managers in subsidiary companies operating in SADCC states.

16. *Undermining Investment in the SADCC Region*

One of the objectives of South African destabilisation has been to undermine confidence in the ability of the SADCC member states to manage their own affairs effectively. South Africa points to the situation in neighbouring states as evidence that they are incompetent. A massive programme of disinformation has been mounted by the South African government, both in the region and internationally, to foment unrest and to distort people's perception of what is happening in southern Africa. Too often multinational companies believe the South African interpretation of events and, even when they do not, the South African-induced disruption makes them reluctant to invest or to expand their activities. It is, however, impossible to quantify the damaging effect that such psychological factors have on the development of the region. Clearly, however, South African action makes the SADCC region seem a less attractive and less stable environment for investment.

SADCC COOPERATION

17. *Towards Reduced Dependence*

Many of SADCC's programmes are specifically designed to reduce the region's dependence on South Africa and, as far as is practicable, to insulate its member states from the repercussions of South African instability. A Southern African Transport and Communications Commission (SATCC) has been established in Maputo to coordinate the rehabilitation and efficient operation of the region's transport network so that the natural trade routes can be used thus avoiding excessive and expensive dependence on South

African railways and ports. Telecommunications infrastructure is rapidly being upgraded so that SADCC member states can communicate with each other more efficiently and without going through South Africa. In respect of energy, national electricity grids are to be inter-connected so that power can flow between countries. Furthermore, a detailed feasibility study is in hand to determine how best the region might become self-sufficient in the supply of oil products. Programmes are being developed in mining and industry to reduce dependence. Work is also underway to establish a food security system which will increase regional self-reliance.

Thus the SADCC states are working closely together both to meet the challenge of destabilisation and to enhance regional economic development in spite of the adverse conditions obtaining in southern Africa.

18. *A Task to be Shared*
Although many of SADCC's strategically important projects are under implementation, many others are still at the level of studies. SADCC requires a massive inflow of technical, managerial and financial resources if its programmes are to be implemented expeditiously. The region looks to the rest of Africa, and to the international community as a whole, to express clearly their solidarity with and support for SADCC in its efforts to reduce dependence and to mobilise the additional resources urgently needed if the region's objectives are to be met.

CONCLUSION

19. South Africa's aggressive activities constitute a growing threat to peace which cannot be confined to this region or even this continent; it is an international problem. South Africa has, however, been recognised for decades as a problem of particular concern for African states, but in recent years the international debate has concentrated on the issues of South Africa's illegal occupation of Namibia and her domestic racist policies. Without detracting from the importance of these issues, this paper seeks to draw attention to the heavy cost being borne by OAU member states neighbouring South Africa and to suggest that this aspect of the struggle should be given equal prominence in international debates. There should be a continuing effort to expose the irrationality and hypocrisy of Western financial and technical resources being used to shore up a regime which is substantially engaged in destroying economies which these same Western interests are helping to develop.

20. The demand for sanctions must be viewed in the context both of destabilisation and of Western support for the apartheid regime. Those opposed to sanctions argue that they will hurt the neighbouring states. Undoubtedly this is true. But if it accelerated the ending of apartheid, it would be well worth the additional cost. And those who are concerned about the negative effects of sanctions on the neighbouring states should provide assistance to these states to minimise that impact.

More important, however, destabilisation is directly linked to sanctions.

The very existence of SADCC threatens South Africa's economic stranglehold on the region. If SADCC states were free to use the most convenient and cheapest ports and railways, and free to buy fuel and other goods on the world market, their dependence on South Africa would be sharply reduced. Then sanctions would not hurt the neighbouring states so much. So South Africa destabilises its neighbours to keep them dependent so that they will be harmed by sanctions. South Africa's capacity to sustain its destabilisation is buttressed by support from the same Western states who point to the harm sanctions would do.

21. SADCC's figures can only be estimates at best — the organisation does not keep a score card of destruction. But in making its estimates SADCC has erred on the side of caution, listing only those things which can be sensibly quantified. Thus $10,000m — an astromical sum for a region of nine developing countries, some of which are least developed and landlocked, — is surely an underestimate. And SADCC has only costed bricks and mortar, steel and machinery. There is no price for blood, no cost that can be assigned to the thousands who have died as a result of actions instigated and supported by apartheid.

Author's note

From SADCC figures it is possible to estimate the annual costs of destabilisation for 1980-1984 and to extrapolate to find the likely cost for 1985 and 1986:

	SADCC					*extrapolation*	
	1980	*1981*	*1982*	*1983*	*1984*	*1985*	*1986*
Annual cost ($m)	681	1395	1872	2801	3291	4000	4680
Cumulative total ($bn)	—	2.1	3.9	6.7	10.0	14.0	18.7

Appendix 2.
The effect on neighbouring states of sanctions against South Africa

Assessing the potential effect of sanctions requires some judgement of how rapidly they are applied, and if the neighbouring states also apply them. Clearly a sudden border closure, as in the case of Rhodesia, would have the most impact on South Africa, but would also be most disruptive to the neighbours. More likely, however, are phased or step-by-step sanctions which would give both South Africa and the neighbouring states time to adjust. Almost certainly the international community would exempt Lesotho from a UN decision to impose sanctions on South Africa. It would be important for neighbours to ensure that they do not become sanctions-busting conduits.

Assuming limited or step-by-step sanctions, applied first by the north and only later by the neighbours, and with Lesotho exempt and no South African retaliation, the neighbouring states would in some ways gain from sanctions. This is because sanctions would push them along the road of delinking on which they set out when they established SADCC. In addition to the obvious benefits of delinking, sanctions would also have these implications:

● *Import/export ban.* Seven of the neighbouring states import substantial quantities of goods from South Africa. Sanctions would reduce this in two ways. Obviously, if the neighbours joined an international boycott of South African goods, these items would have to be imported from elsewhere. A really tight ban by outside states on exports to South Africa would have the same effect — the neighbouring states would be unable to buy from South Africa goods which the apartheid state itself could not buy, such as oil. South African goods dependent on banned raw materials or other inputs would also become unavailable. The major loss would be the disruption and the restructuring required to import from the world market. For Botswana, Lesotho and Swaziland this would be significant; if sanctions were really tight, they would probably have to leave the customs union (which would be no bad thing — see Chapter 9). The other states in the region already import substantial quantities of goods from all over the world, and replacing South African goods would be much less difficult.

There would be three important gains. First, after the necessary restructuring, the neighbouring states would import directly from the world market, without South Africa as intermediary, and thus on average at a lower price. Second, transnationals would be forced to set up separate regional offices within SADCC and stop selling to the region from South Africa. Third, it could provide a useful fillip to intra-SADCC trade. However, assistance would be required, probably in the form of money for a revolving fund to

271

encourage regional trade; help might also be needed to assist Botswana, Lesotho and Swaziland to set up some kind of buying agency to look for other sources for goods now bought from South Africa.

There are two other losses worth noting. First, Swaziland and Zimbabwe both sell manufactured goods to South Africa, and that market would be lost if there were a total trade ban. Second, if bans on buying South African goods cut mineral sales sufficiently, there would be a loss of jobs for migrant miners. Other migrant workers, especially those working illegally, are also vulnerable.

● *Service limitation.* This would cause much less damage to SADCC now than it would have a few years ago. All SADCC states now have, or will soon have, international airports and ground stations for satellite telecommunications. They are no longer dependent on South Africa, and much less intra-regional air traffic and telecommunication goes through Johannesburg. If the embargo reached the stage of totally stopping the use of South African ports and railways, and if the region had had time to prepare, the region would gain both from lower cost transport for the inland states and increased revenues for the coastal states. If tourism were banned, however, there could be a small loss of revenue to several states.

● *Loan and investment restrictions.* Initially this harms those countries which use the rand as currency or are closely linked to it; they would be forced to delink their currencies. Otherwise they can gain, if some of the investment which would have gone to South Africa goes to the neighbouring states instead, and lose if a (useful) TNC decides to pull out of southern Africa altogether.

Retaliation by South Africa

The preceding rosy picture assumes that South Africa does not retaliate. That is highly unlikely, and government ministers have threatened to cut transport links and to expel migrant workers. In an important paper on the issue, G.M.E. Leistner, the head of the Africa Institute in Pretoria, warns that 'if sanctions were to disrupt South Africa's transport system' it would feel 'constrained to reassess its own transport needs vis-a-vis those of neighbouring countries', and would act in a way which 'would inevitably affect them quite seriously'. And he goes on to cite the 1981 withdrawal of locomotives and transport embargoes against Zimbabwe as an example of what might happen.[1] South Africa has also threatened to cut off food, fuel, and other exports to the neighbours — and has done so during the past five years.

The more obvious forms of retaliatory sanctions against the neighbours are less easy to impose than to threaten, however. The mining houses themselves want to keep the skilled Basotho labour, and would resist any South African government retaliatory attempt to expel all migrants suddenly. But the total migrant numbers could be cut back rapidly. As for trade and transport, South Africa needs the SADCC states as a market. It seems unlikely to cut off this lucrative market voluntarily, merely as retaliation (nor would the business community allow it to).

Several more minor forms of retaliation are available. For example, South Africa could eliminate the small amount of cargo passing through Maputo port, and if Swaziland participated in sanctions Pretoria could cut off traffic passing over the new rail link.

Finally, it could cut off electricity supplies to Swaziland, Lesotho, Gaborone, and Maputo. Botswana is already building alternative power supplies and

Lesotho could accelerate its Oxbow project. There is a new power line from the Massingir dam to Maputo, but that dam draws much of its water from a river rising in South Africa so it is unclear how much power it could guarantee. Mozambique could build a new line to serve Maputo and Swaziland from the Cahora Bassa dam, at the same time cancelling the contract to supply South Africa. Nevertheless, restructuring electricity supply would require substantial capital investment, which would have to come from foreign assistance. The Cahora Bassa power line would cost perhaps $100m, and a Lesotho hydro-electricity scheme would cost a similar amount.

Military and sabotage action against neighbouring states would be a much more important and dangerous response. This would probably take four forms:

● Pretoria would step up support for anti-government groups in all neighbouring states which support sanctions.

● Oil would be a major military target. In the past five years South Africa has sabotaged supplies in or for Mozambique, Zimbabwe, Angola, Malawi, and Lesotho, and blocked independent supplies to Lesotho and Botswana; such action should be expected again. Botswana, Lesotho and Swaziland obtain all their fuel from South Africa, which would try its utmost to ensure that they were unable to import oil independently. In his paper, Leistner points to 'South Africa's key role in channelling fuel and other petroleum products to neighbouring countries'. And he notes that 'the frequent acts of sabotage against the Beira-Mutare pipeline as well as the railway line from Beira to Harare are constant reminders of the vulnerability of Zimbabwe and the other landlocked countries.'[2] However, the Beira pipeline has functioned for three consecutive years now, and Botswana could also be supplied from the Zambian refinery.

● South Africa might send in troops to guarantee its continued access to Lesotho water, Cahora Bassa electricity, and the railway through Swaziland.

● There would definitely be military action aimed at preventing neighbouring states from imposing sanctions. Transport would be the main issue as it has been in the past five years. Swaziland, Botswana, Zambia, Zimbabwe, and Malawi all have adequate rail access to Angolan, Mozambican, and Tanzanian ports, under 'normal' circumstances. Only one cargo would create problems: Botswana and Zimbabwe use special port facilities to keep their beef frozen, and these do not exist in Mozambican ports (although they could be built, probably in less than a year). Some new bulk facilities might be needed, especially for Zimbabwe's maize exports.

The problem, of course, will be South African sabotage, as at present. At the time of writing, only the Tazara is secure. The Zimbabwe-Beira line is open only because of Zimbabwe soldiers. The Swaziland-Maputo and Malawi-Nacala lines are subject to attack, while the Malawi-Beira, Zimbabwe-Maputo and Benguela (Zambia-Lobito) lines are all closed. To end the use of South Africa and handle all present external trade, one of the Malawi lines must be kept in use and either Zimbabwe-Maputo or Benguela must be reopened. The Zimbabwe-Maputo line would be the best, because it could serve both Zimbabwe and Zambia (Maputo is actually closer to the copperbelt than Lobito). However, for 400 km this line runs through semi-desert and parallel to the South African border, in some cases within 50 km of the Kruger Park. This makes it extremely easy to sabotage; keeping it open would require a large increase in troops. South Africa might intervene openly, rather than clandestinely, on the grounds that the reopening of the Maputo line threatened its 'vital national interests'. The 1000 km of Benguela railway in Angola would be even harder to defend militarily, and part of the line passes through Zaire, which imposes a possible political constraint.

The other choice would be to upgrade the Tazara and Zimbabwe-Beira lines to handle all of the region's cargo. This would not be the preferred option, because Maputo is a better port than either Dar or Beira and the lines do not now have the capacity, so more work would be required. But they would be more defensible. It is clear, however, that whatever choice was followed would require substantial financial assistance to upgrade port and railway facilities. At a minimum it would take $300m to rehabilitate the frequently sabotaged Zimbabwe-Maputo line, to provide essential port facilities for transferred cargo, and to purchase new locomotives and rolling stock. For example, Mozambique has to replace or repair more than 100 locomotives damaged or destroyed by the MNR. This would be simply to satisfy demand; more money would be needed later to increase efficiency. If it were necessary to send cargo via Dar and Beira, the initial cost would probably be pushed up to $500m because of the need to improve both ports and upgrade the two railways, both of which pass through difficult mountainous terrain. The Nacala, Dar and Beira Port Corridor programmes of SADCC, which have in practice had top priority since 1985, would provide enough upgrading and rehabilitation to meet the basic trade requirements of all the states except Lesotho (assuming Swaziland and southern Mozambique could still use Maputo).

Retaliation and counter-sanctions would not be imposed simply by the South African government; business would also play a role, as it has in the past (for example when sanctions were imposed on Mozambique in 1980). Small and medium capital would probably resist calls for retaliation, as would SATS, because they would not want to lose important markets.

Anglo American is the key non-government body. Through its membership on the Chamber of Mines, it would play an important role in any decision to expel migrant miners and would probably oppose it. Anglo is central to the economies of Botswana and Zimbabwe. How would the relationship of these two states to Anglo be affected by sanctions? Anglo might be pressured into pulling out of Zimbabwe, but would surely want to keep control of Botswana's diamonds.

One question relates to South African-owned off-shore companies, like Anglo's Minorco and Barlow's Astra. If there were very wide-ranging sanctions, would the region's states refuse to deal with such firms? Conversely, if South Africa imposed counter-sanctions, would such off-shore subsidiaries ignore them? Indeed, would Anglo transfer all its regional companies to them? If there were some doubt, would South African troops take control of the Botswana diamond mines, as they occupied the Ruacana hydro-electric scheme in Angola?

How countries would be hit

Because it is so hard to predict the course of sanctions and reaction, it may be useful to look at the most extreme case: total closure of the South African border. This could come about through the imposition of sanctions by most of the world or by partial sanctions followed by South Africa's pulling up the drawbridge. On a country-by-country basis, the possible results would be:

Lesotho: This is the hostage state, totally surrounded by South Africa and dependent on it for food, fuel, and income. It is the only state which cannot survive in isolation, and it would be essential to make some exception to sanctions regulations for Lesotho. The question really is how tightly South Africa would isolate Lesotho. For example, would it transport sealed containers of food, fuel, and other supplies? Even without sanctions, South Africa has already refused to transport oil and arms to Lesotho. Tanzania's President Julius Nyerere noted that 'An airlift took goods into West Berlin when it was under siege; if the Front Line states are to join in this boycott, something similar may be necessary for Lesotho.'[3] In addition to the cost of the airlift itself, at least $200m per year would be needed to replace lost mine wages and customs union revenues, if these were cut off. Some of this money could be spent on local development projects to increase self-sufficiency, such as the $75m Oxbow scheme to provide electricity and irrigation water.

Botswana and Swaziland: So long as the SADCC rail links are available, these two reasonably stable economies could ride out sanctions, though at a heavy cost. Membership of the Customs Union with South Africa means that most trade is with South Africa, so the reorientation would cause substantial temporary disruption. Loss of migrant labour jobs would exacerbate unemployment problems. South Africa could disrupt water supplies to both states. Swaziland's electricity from South Africa is potentially the most serious problem. Swaziland would lose exports, but some can go elsewhere within the region. South African military intervention is possible at the Botswana diamond mines, to control the Swazi railway (which links the eastern Transvaal to Richards Bay), and to attack fuel supplies to both states.

Mozambique: The loss of more than US$100m per year from migrant labour and South African cargo passing through Maputo could be partly offset by increased earnings from other transit traffic. Electricity shortages in Maputo are inevitable. Stepped up South African sabotage and military action would be the most serious problem, as Mozambican ports and railways are key to regional survival against South African retaliation.

Zimbabwe: Some manufactured exports, particularly clothing, would be lost. There would be significant disruption in trade patterns, but no long term trouble if Mozambican ports are open. Problems would be created if Anglo pulled out quickly, though this is unlikely.

Zambia: There was little trade with South Africa in the mid-1970s and it is still not large, so a cutback would only cause minor dislocations *provided* foreign exchange and credit was available for alternative supplies.

Malawi: Some migrant labour would be lost. The disruption in trade patterns and loss of South African consumer goods would not be serious if Malawi had good access to a port. At present, sabotage of rail routes to the sea has made it nearly as much a hostage state as Lesotho, but sanctions and counter-sanctions might force Malawi to stop aiding MNR, which would improve its own security and transport position.

Angola: No extra effect, except perhaps increased fighting over the Benguela railway.

Support

Thus the final question is what support must be given to the SADCC states in the event that sanctions are imposed. In part, this depends on how South Africa responds, but the following seems necessary:

Lesotho: At worst Lesotho would need $200m per year, and an airlift.

Dislocation help: Reorienting trade patterns will be time-consuming and expensive in the short run, albeit profitable in the long run. Foreign aid will be needed to establish a revolving import credit fund, to replace South African credits, though Botswana, Swaziland and Zimbabwe would presumably be able to obtain normal commercial credit from the new suppliers. This would require up to US$600m to provide 180 day credit. Help may be needed to establish some sort of regional import-export agency or import-export enterprises in the BLS states. Temporary assistance, perhaps in the form of agricultural development projects, will be needed to absorb 150,000 expelled migrant workers from Mozambique, Botswana, Swaziland, and Malawi (Lesotho is dealt with above).

Infrastructure: Urgent help will be needed to upgrade and extend railway and port facilities and electricity lines. This might have to be done much more quickly than such aid is normally dispensed, and between $300m and $800m would be needed (dependent on the extent of harassment and retaliation).

Military: Mozambique will need military help to protect vital railway and power lines. Botswana may need help to protect fuel supplies and diamond mines. Angola and Zimbabwe might also require assistance. This is the most serious need, and is the one donor states will steer farthest away from.

Statistical Annex

SUMMARY

Table 1. Dependence on South Africa
(all figures 1982, except + = 1981)

	Imports		Trans-port	Energy from RSA		Labour
	% from RSA	*rank of RSA*	*imp/exp via RSA*	*Elec-tricity*	*Oil*	*% of formal sector workers in RSA*
Customs union countries:						
Bot.	84%+	1	most	21%	all	30%
Les.	97%+	1	all	100%	all	>50%
Swa.	83%	1	half	77%	all	15%
Non-customs union countries						
Zimb.	32%	1	half	1%	63%	1%
Zambia	14%	1	half	—	little	—
Malawi	36%	1	one-third	—	half	4%
Moz.	8%	2	—	28%+	little	5%

Role of RSA firms in the economy
Customs union countries:
Botswana: Anglo operates mines. South African firms dominate rest of economy.
Lesotho: South African firms control virtually the entire economy.
Swaziland: South African firms control mining and non-farm industries, share agriculture and timber with UK firms.

Non-customs union countries:
Zimbabwe: South African firms control 26% of firms, particularly mining, agriculture, and manufacturing.
Zambia: Anglo important in mining, engineering, and other sectors.
Malawi: Little direct South African control, except shipping, fertiliser, insurance.
Mozambique: Little direct control except shipping agencies.
Angola: Anglo ran diamond mine.

Table 2 — Regional payments deficit with South Africa
(US$m, all figures 1982 unless noted)

By countries, including visible trade, tourism, Customs Union revenue, and migrant labour remittances[1]

230	Swaziland
40	Lesotho
0	Mozambique
0	Angola
180	Zimbabwe (1983)
480	Botswana (1981)
130	Malawi (1980)
130	Zambia

1190

Other

230	ports and railways[2]
100	insurance and other services[3]

330

TOTAL = US$1520m

Notes
1. Country totals are taken from the tables for each country, summarised in Table 3. In general the most recent year for which nearly complete data is available has been used. Thus the numbers are not strictly comparable. Furthermore, there have been significant changes in recent years, caused by the dramatic collapse in the value of the rand, partly cancelled out by rising mine wages and customs union payments. Nevertheless, the estimate of $1.5 billion must be roughly correct for the years covered by the study.
2. Ports and railways. SATS earned at least US$250m from the neighbouring states in 1982 (probably more — see *AED* 19 Dec 82), while it paid US$20m for use of Maputo port and the associated railways in 1982.
3. Services. Zimbabwe estimates that it paid US$45m to South Africa for reinsurance. Other countries must spend similar amounts. In addition there are other services like consultants. Finally some people from the neighbouring states go to South Africa for holidays and business trips, and their expenditure is not accounted for anywhere in these tables. Thus US$100m seems a modest estimate.

Table 3 — Detailed payments breakdown
(US$m, not including transport and invisibles)

	Customs Union	Migrant Labour	Tourism	Exports	Imports	TOTAL
	Income from South Africa				*Income to S. Africa*	
Customs union countries						
Bot	121	21	1	65	684	−476
Les	77	356	12	20	506	− 41
Swa	104	9	5	122	466	−226
Customs union totals						
	302	386	18	207	1656	−743
Non-customs union countries						
Zimbabwe		8	6	189	382	−179
Malawi		16	1	8	152	−127
Zambia		—	2	3	135	−130
Mozambique		61	—	4	67	− 2
Non-customs union totals						
		85	9	204	736	−438

Notes

Years as in Table 2. Note slight differences from figures reported by South African sources, particularly of mine wage remittances.

Revenue from South African tourists in neighbouring states is included, while expenditure by SADCC tourists in South Africa is not.

Mozambique also earns money ($20m in 1982, not included in this table) from South African traffic through Maputo port, and thus is the only country in the region to have a balance of payments surplus with South Africa; it does not, however, earn money from the Cahora Bassa dam.

Table 4. Port and railway traffic — 1982 (m tonnes)

SADCC countries through SADCC ports

Via Mozambique

Mozambique	2.5
Zimbabwe	1.1
Swaziland	0.7
Malawi	0.7

Via Tanzania

Zambia	0.8
Tanzania	1.1

Via Angola

Angola	0.4

	TOTAL	7.3

South Africa through SADCC ports
Via Mozambique	2.2

SADCC and Zaire to and through South Africa

Botswana	0.4
Lesotho	0.4
Swaziland	0.4
Zaire	0.4
Zambia	0.4
Zimbabwe	1.9
TOTAL	3.9

Trade between SADCC member states
TOTAL	0.6

Summary of international traffic

	8 countries in this study		SADCC		6 inland states	
Through SADCC ports	6.2	60%	7.3	64%	3.3	45%
To or through RSA	3.5	34%	3.5	31%	3.5	47%
Between SADCC states	0.6	6%	0.6	5%	0.6	8%
TOTAL	10.3		11.4		7.4	

Sources
For Mozambique traffic, Joseph Hanlon, *The Revolution Under Fire*, Zed, London, 1984.
For South African traffic, Gavin Maasdorp, *Transport Policies and Economic Development*, Economic Research Unit of the University of Natal, Durban, 1984.
For other data, SADCC and estimates.
Note: data excludes overland trade between SADCC states and other African states.

SUMMARY

Table 5. South African trade 1984

	EXPORTS		IMPORTS	
	Total (Rm)	*To Africa[1]*	*Total (Rm)*	*From Africa*
Fruit, grain and vegetables	480	14%	996	4%
Other agricultural products	833	11%	801 ·	8%
Gold[2]	11,684	—	—	—
Diamonds and precious metals	2,387	. . .	129	38%
Other minerals and mineral products	5,515	4%	1,721	5%
Chemicals	672	33%	1,785	7%
Textiles	762	5%	1,037	9%
Machinery	309	41%	6,397	. . .
Transport equipment	169	24%	2,653	. . .
Other manufactured	808	12%	2,980	1%
Other	1,776	. . .	3,254	. . .
Total	25,395	4%	21,717	2%

Notes
1. This excludes Botswana, Lesotho, Namibia and Swaziland, and so understates the full African shares substantially in some categories.
2. This figure is net gold output.
. . . means less than 1%.

Source: South Africa, *Monthly Abstract of Trade Statistics*, December 1984.

ANGOLA

A. Basic Data

Population: 8.4 million (est)
Area: 1,246,700 square kilometres
Per capita income: GNP per capita, 1984 US$302
Rate of exchange: Kwanza (Kw) per unit of foreign currency

	1979	1981	1983	1984	1985
US$	29.9	28.4	30.2	30.2	30.2
UK£	68.0	54.1	46.7	40.9	39.0

(The Kwanza was fixed in terms of the dollar in 1985 at Kw 30.214 = $1)

B. Foreign Trade

	1973	1979	1982
Imports from			
W. Europe	70%	56%	62%
Comecon	—	16%	7%
America	11%	16%	20%
Other	19%*	10%	9%

(*of which 6% from South Africa)

	1973	1979	1982
Exports to			
W. Europe	44%	29%	43%
Comecon	—	7%	2%
America	40%	56%	54%
Other	11%	5%	—

Main export products

	1979	1982	1983
Petroleum & derivatives	74%	87%	89%
Coffee	14%	6%	5%
Diamonds	11%	7%	5%

C. Other South African Links

Customs union revenue: not relevant
Migrant labour: none
Tourism: none
Fuel: none
Transit trade: none
Other links: Ruacana/Calueque hydroelectricity scheme sometimes sends power to South Africa and always to Namibia.

D. Foreign Ownership/Control of Economy

Unless noted, the Angolan state has a majority interest.

Oil

Production — Gulf, Texaco (both US), Petrofina (Belgium)
Prospecting — above + Mobil, Cities Service, Marathon (all US), Petrobras (Brazil), Agip (Italy), Total, Elf-Aquitane (both France), Hispanoil (Spain), BP (UK), Diminex (FRG).
Refining: Petrofina (Belgium)

Mining

Diamonds — De Beers (Anglo) 1.7% + management, sales; Société Générale de Belgique 17.4%.
Iron — Voest-Alpine (Austria)
Phosphates — Bulgareomina (Bulgaria), Energoprojekt (Yugoslavia).

Transport

Benguela Railway — Société Générale 90%
Forwarding — AMI (SG)

Import-export

Tradeangol — 2/3 government, 1/3 foreign incl. Chief Fernandez (Nigeria)

BOTSWANA

A. Basic Data

Population: 1.07 million (1985 est)
Area: 582,000 square kilometres
Per capita income:

	1980/81	1981/82	1982/83
GDP, factor cost (Pula)	P793	P694	P886
GNP (US dollars)			$900

Sources: 1, 7.

Rate of Exchange:
Pula (P) per unit of foreign currency

	1979	1981	1983	1984	1985
Rand	.96	.96	1.00	.90	.89
US$	.77	.85	1.08	1.21	1.75
UK£	1.75	1.65	1.67	1.64	2.26

B. Foreign Trade
(P million)

	1974	1981	1983	1984
Imports	125	665	807	899
of which				
Common Customs Area*	94 (75%)	580	667	702 (78%)
Other Africa	17 (14%)	42	59	79 (9%)
UK	4 (3%)	8	10	28 (3%)
Exports	82	331	692	858
of which				
Common Customs Area*	31 (38%)	55	57	75 (9%)
Other Africa	3 (4%)	35	64	34 (4%)
UK	35 (43%)	22	30	18 (2%)
Other Europe	3 (4%)	138	487	650 (76%)
North & South America	8 (10%)	80	52	70 (8%)

*RSA, Lesotho, Swaziland.

Main export products				
Diamonds	30	134	462	617
Meat and meat products	32	60	79	62
Copper/nickel	8	79	65	68
Textiles	2	16	32	40

Source: 1.

C. Other South African Links

Customs union revenue

	1975/76	1979/80	1981/82	1983/84	1985/86B
SACU revenue (Pm)	25	80	104	157	(154)
SACU as % of govt rev	29%	38%	32%	31%	(23%)

Sources: 2, 3. B = budget.

Migrant labour

	1977	1979	1981	1983	1984
Migrant miners in RSA (000)	25	20	21	19	19
Migrant non-miners in RSA (000)	. . .	. . .	21	. . .	. . .
Total migrants in RSA (000)[a]	. . .	. . .	42	. . .	. . .
Tot mig as % of wage labour force	. . .	. . .	30%	. . .	. . .
Total migrants in RSA (000)[b]	44	32	29	26	26
Remittances (Pm)	19	15	18	. . .	. . .

Sources: (a) 1; (b) 6.

Tourism

	1980	1981	1982	1983	1984
RSA arrivals (000)	203	150	190	189	225
% of total arrivals	77%	82%	64%	61%	69%
Spending by RSA visitors (Pm)	13	16	12	18	33

Source: 1.

Fuel: Electricity imports from South Africa

		Actual		Estimated	
	1980/81	1981/82	1982/83	1985	1990
GWh from RSA	0	27	101	227	90
% of total	0	6%	21%	31%	10%
Cost (Pm)	0	1	4	. . .	. . .

Sources: Actual: 4, Accounting year April to March. Estimated: 5.

Transit traffic

On Botswana railway, between RSA and Zimbabwe, Zambia, Zaire

	1972	1980	1982	1983	1984
Transit % of total tonne-km	86%	85%	78%	81%	79%
Estimated revenue (Pm)	9	35	42	44	. . .

Source: 1.

Other links
   Contractors and suppliers for development projects
   Most food from RSA
   All oil products

D. Economic Balance with South Africa

(Pm)	1981
Income	
Customs Unions	103
Migrant labour	18
Tourism	1
Exports to RSA	55
Expenditure	
Imports from RSA	−582
Total deficit with RSA	−405

E. Foreign Ownership/Control in Economy

Mining
   Diamonds — De Beers (Anglo American — RSA)
   Coal — Anglo-American
   Copper-nickel — Anglo American + Amax (US)
   proposed soda ash — BP (UK)

Agribusiness
   Botswana Meat Commission (parastatal) controls meat processing but half of cattle are produced by non-Botswana firms and individuals. The largest ranch is South African and other major ranches are owned by CDC and South Africans.

Other manufacturing
   Brewery — South African Breweries (Anglo)
   smaller firms — RSA, Zimbabwe, local

Other
   Construction — Of three largest firms, one is RSA and two are UK
   Freight & forwarding — Renfreight (Old Mutual)
   Wholesale & retail — RSA plus some UK & local
   Hotels — RSA, UK, local
   Banking — Barclays, Standard (UK)
   Insurance — RSA plus some UK

Sources
1. *Statistical Bulletin*, Central Statistics Department, Gaborone.
2. *Annual Report*, Bank of Botswana, Gaborone.
3. *Financial Statements, Tables and Estimates*, Government of Botswana, Gaborone, 1985.
4. *Annual Report*, Botswana Power Corporation, Gaborone.
5. *Energy sector report*, distributed at the SADCC conference, 2-3 Feb 1984, Lusaka.
6. South Africa *Yearbooks*, quoted in Alan Whiteside, *Past Trends and Future Prospects for Labour Migration to South Africa*, SAIIA, Johannesburg 1985.
7. The World Bank, *Toward Sustained Development in Sub-Saharan Africa*, Washington 1984.

LESOTHO

A. Basic Data

Population: 1.5 million (1985 est)
Area: 30,444 square kilometres
Per capita income

	1981/82	*1982/83*	*1983/84*
GDP	254	273	300
GNP (US dollars)	. . .	510	. . .

Sources: 1, 2, 7, 8.

Rate of exchange
(Maloti per unit of foreign currency)

	1979	*1981*	*1983*	*1984*	*1985*
Rand	1	1	1	1	1
US$	.84	.88	1.09	1.50	1.92
UK£	1.81	1.72	1.68	1.96	2.52

B. Foreign Trade

(Mm)	*1979*	*1981*	*1982*	*1983*	*1984*
Imports	304	439	522	622	690
of which from RSA	296 (97%)	427	. . .	. . .	. . .
Exports	38	43	40	25	40
of which to RSA	13 (34%)	20	. . .	. . .	. . .
Main export products					
diamonds	21	18	15		
wool	4	4	5		
mohair	4	3	3		
umbrellas	. . .	. . .	3		
clothing & footwear	. . .	. . .	3		

C. Other South African Links

Customs union revenue

	81/82	*82/83*	*83/84*	*84/85*
SACU revenue (Mm)	71	77	110	(152)
% of total revenue	64%	57%	65%	(66%)

Sources: 2, 3.

Migrant labour:

	1972	*1977**	*1979*	*1981*	*1983*	*1984*
Total numbers (000)	131	174	. . .	150	146	138
Migrant miners in RSA (000)	99	130	124	124	115	. . .
Remittances — cash (M m)	6	28	38	63	178	. . .
Remittances — earnings (M m)	. . .	. . .	179	255	416	. . .
Remittances — earnings (% of GNP)	. . .	. . .	40%	43%	. . .	. . .

In 1979 there were a total of 157,000 Basotho employed outside Lesotho in mining and other sectors, compared to only 71,000 salaried workers employed inside Lesotho. Thus migrants were 69% of the salaried work force and migrant miners 54% of the total salaried workforce.

In 1979 there were 145,000 men working inside Lesotho, both for a salary and self-employed, compared to 148,000 men working outside. So 51% work outside the country.

Sources: 1, 2, 3, 4, 6.

Tourism

	1981
RSA tourists (000)	123
% of total	97%

Source: 1.

Fuel: All supplies, including electricity, from South Africa.
Transit traffic: none.
Other links
    All transport via South Africa.
    Proposed sale of water to South Africa.

D. Economic balance with South Africa

(Mm)	1981	1982 (est)
Income		
Customs union	71	77
Migrant labour	255	356
Tourism (ext)	12	12
Exports to RSA	20	20
Expenditure		
Imports from RSA	−427	−506
Total deficit with RSA	−69	−41

Source: 4, 5

E. Foreign ownership/control of economy

South African firms dominate all sectors.

Sources
1. *Annual Statistical Bulletin 1982*, Bureau of Statistics, Maseru.
2. *Annual Report 1983*, Central Bank of Lesotho, Maseru.
3. *Quarterly Review*, June 1984, Central Bank of Lesotho, Maseru.
4. *Notes on migrant labour*
    Cash remittances are actual remittances and deferred pay withheld from wages by the mining houses and sent to Lesotho.
    Earnings remittances are the Central Bank of Lesotho estimate of all earnings transferred to families in Lesotho including cash remittances.
    1977 was the year with the maximum number of miners in South Africa.
5. There are no tourist expenditure statistics, so as with Swaziland assume each tourist spends M100.
6. South Africa *Yearbooks*.
7. IMF, *International Financial Statistics*, Jan 1986.
8. IBRD, *Toward Sustained Development in Sub-Saharan Africa*, Washington 1984.

MALAWI

A. Basic Data

Population: 7 million (1985 est)
Area: 95,586 square kilometres (plus 23,000 sq km of Lake Malawi/Nyassa)
Per capita income

	1982	1983	1984	1985
GNP, (Kwacha) factor cost	170	192	230	248
GNP, (US dollars)	210	. . .	. . .	. . .

Source: 1, 7

Rate of exchance:
Kwacha (K) per unit of foreign currency (mid year)

	1979	1981	1983	1984	1985
Rand	.97	1.04	1.04	.91	.93
US$	.82	.91	1.13	1.37	1.78
UK£	1.76	1.78	1.74	1.79	2.34

B. Foreign Trade
(Kwacha m)

	1974	1979	1981	1983	1984
Imports	158	325	313	364	382
of which					
RSA	37 (23%)	135	103	141 (39%)	. . .
UK	36 (23%)	61	44	49 (13%)	. . .
Exports	90	176	232	265	437
of which					
RSA	4 (4%)	9	12	22 (8%)	. . .
UK	33 (37%)	74	55	73 (28%)	. . .
Main export products					
Tobacco	39	99	99	137	230
Tea	17	31	31	56	113
Sugar	9	57	57	27	29

Sources: 2, 3.

C. Other South African links

Customs union revenue: not relevant

Migrant labour:

	1973	1976	1979	1980	1981	1984
Migrant miners in RSA (000)[a]	123	—	18	11	13	. . .
% of Malawi wage labour force	36%	—	5%	3%	4%	. . .
Migrants in RSA (000)[b]	140	13	36	32	31	29
Remittances (Km)	19	3	. . .	14	. . .	. . .

Sources: (a) 2, 3; (b) 6

Tourism

	1979	1980
RSA tourists	2841	2499
% of total	38%	39%
Amount spent (K)	540,000	500,000

Sources: 2, 4.

Fuel sources:

(Km)	1978	1980
Coal		
South Africa	1 (56%)	2 (63%)
Mozambique	1 (32%)	1 (36%)
Oil products		
South Africa	31 (93%)	37 (70%)
Iran	1 (3%)	3 (5%)
Bahrein	—	5 (9%)
France	—	2 (4%)

Source: 5

Transit traffic: none

Other links:

Most transport via RSA due to closure of normal routes to sea.
South African consultants and managers are increasingly important.
Aid and credits: 1969-71 — Nacala railway and Lilongwe
                 1980-82 — Lilongwe grain silos, wheat, development aid

---

D. Economic Balance with South Africa

(Km)	1980
Income	
Migrant labour	14
Tourism	1
Exports to RSA	7
Expenditure	
Imports from RSA	−132
Total deficit with RSA	−110

E. Foreign Ownership/Control in Economy

Press Holdings (owned by President Banda) and Admarc (the government marketing board) dominate the economy.
South African firms are important in:
Freight and Forwarding — Renfreight (Old Mutual)
Specialised fertiliser — Optichem (Triomf — RSA)
Insurance — Old Mutual
Construction — Murray & Roberts (Sanlam).
Lonrho is the main British firm, active in agribusiness & textiles.
Standard Bank manages the largest local bank.
Other firms include Unilever, African Lakes, Imperial, Gallaher.

Sources
1. *Financial and Economic Review*, Reserve Bank of Malawi, Lilongwe.
2. *Malawi Statistical Yearbook 1981*, National Statistical Office, Zomba.
3. *Monthly Statistical Bulletin*, National Statistical Office, Zomba.
4. *Malawi Tourism Report 1979 and 1980*, National Statistical Office, Zomba.
5. *Annual Statement of External Trade 1980*, National Statistical Office, Zomba.
6. South Africa *Yearbooks*.
7. World Bank, *Toward Sustained Development in Sub-Saharan Africa*, Washington, 1984.

MOZAMBIQUE

A. Basic Data

Population: 14 million (1985 est.)
Land area: 786,380 square kilometres
Per capita income:

	1980	1981	1982	1983	1984
GDP, factor cost (Meticais)	5894	5935	6039	5221	5548

Source: 8.

Rate of exchange:
Meticais (Mt) per unit of foreign currency

	1979	1981	1983	1984	1985
Rand	38	42	37	28	22
US$	32	37	40	42	43
UK£	71	67	61	57	56

B. Foreign Trade

(US$m)	1973	1979	1982	1984
Imports	422	580	831	545
of which from				
East Germany	—	55	80 (10%)	4%
South Africa	86 (20%)	83	67 (8%)	12%
France	35 (8%)	24	65 (8%)	6%
Portugal	81 (19%)	27	51 (6%)	8%
West Germany	57 (13%)	28	30 (4%)	4%
USSR	—	5	36 (4%)	19%
Exports	205	260	228	97
of which to				
USA	28 (14%)	61	36 (16%)	14%
East Germany	—	21	21 (11%)	12%
Spain	—	5	18 (8%)	9%
Tanzania	—	1	14 (6%)	...
South Africa	19 (10%)	12	4 (2%)	...
Main export products				
Cashew nuts	40	54	44	15
Refined oil	11	40	38	5
Prawns	5	24	38	29
Tea	9	13	26	11
Cotton	45	24	17	8
Sugar	22	36	10	6
Tyres	—	—	7	—

Sources: 1; 8 (for 1984).

C. Other South African links

Customs Union revenue: not relevant

Migrant labour

	1975	1977	1981	1982	1983	1984
Migrant miners in RSA (000):						
Moz. govt figures	118	41	41	45	40	45
Total migrants in RSA (RSA figures)	151	68	59	52	61	60
Migrants as % of wage labour force						
(using govt figures)	12%	5%	5%	5%	. . .	. . .
Remittances (US$m)	. . .	30	60	61	. . .	. . .

Sources: 1, 2, 4, 8

Tourism: none since independence

Fuel: Electricity

	1980	1981	1982	1983	1984
Imports from RSA:					
Cost (US$m)	1	5	8	9	9
GWh	70	240	. . .	. . .	. . .
% of total consump	9%	28%	. . .	. . .	. . .
Exports to RSA:					
GWh	. . .	4213	. . .	. . .	. . .

Sources: 3, 6, 7, 8.

Transit traffic:

	1973	1975	1979	1980	1981	1982	1983
RSA Traffic (m tonnes)	6.2	4.4	4.0	3.5	3.0	2.2	1.5
Earnings (US$m est.)	. . .	. . .	40	40	30	20	15

Source: estimated from 1.

Other links
Several important rivers rise in South Africa, which has at various time cut off water and caused floods

D. Economic Balance with South Africa

(US$m)	1979	1982
Income		
Migrant labour	40	61
Port & railway	48	20
Exports	12	4
Expenditure		
Imports from RSA	−83	−67
Total surplus with RSA	17	18

E. *Foreign Ownership/Control in Economy*

(Entreposto and João Ferreira dos Santos are the two largest local private firms. Both have Portuguese links.)

Freight forwarding

Renfreight (Rennies, Manica): Old Mutual (RSA) via Safmarine, Anglo

AMI Mozambique: AMI (Société Générale de Belgique) 57%, Interquimica 16%, Anfrena-Mocargo-Enacomo 27%.

Industry

Mabor tyre: Mabor (Portugal) 9.5%, General Tire (US) 3.5%, Mozambique 87%

Textáfrica textiles: Portuguese private (also owns 43% of Texmoque)

Têxtil do Pungué: Quimigal (Portugal) 63%

Cicomo sisal: Quimigal 53%

Socajú cashew processing: Portuguese state maj, Quimigal

Carmoc cartons: Barlow Rand (RSA)

Metal Box: Metal Box (UK).

Energy

Hidroeléctrica de Cahora Bassa: Portuguese state 13.5%, Portuguese banks 17.1%, Portuguese private 41.4%, Mozambican state 18.3%

Oil pipeline: Lonrho 33%, Entreposto 17%, govt 50%.

Agriculture

Agroindustrial de Lonrho-Moçambique: Lonrho 50%, govt 50%.

Entreposto, Madal (Norway), Somofar (Algeria) and private Portuguese firms have farms.

Romanian state in joint venture to produce cotton.

Banking

All banks state except Banco Standard Totta: Banco Totta e Açores 40%, Standard (UK) 30%, Standard (RSA) 5%, Anglo 5%, Mozambique state & private 20%.

Other

Lonrho to take over several hotels and a gold mine.

Firms from more than 12 countries (East & West) are prospecting for oil, gas, coal, and other minerals; the USSR is assisting with production of tantalite and East Germany with coal.

Sources

1. Joseph Hanlon, *Mozambique: The Revolution Under Fire*, Zed, London, (2nd edition with revised tables) 1985.
2. *Economic Report*, National Planning Commission, Maputo, Jan 1984.
3. *Complemento à Informação Económica*, National Planning Commission, Maputo,
4. *South Africa Yearbooks*, Pretoria.
5. World Bank, *Toward Sustained Development in Sub-Saharan Africa*, Washington 1984.
6. *Energy*, report at the SADCC annual conference, Lusaka, 2/3 Feb 1984.
7. Note that Mozambique earns nothing from Cahora Bassa electricity exports, with the money going to Portugal, so electricity exports are not included in the foreign trade table. Electricity imports, however, are included in the foreign trade table.
8. National Planning Commission, *Informação Estatística 1975-84*.

SWAZILAND

A. Basic Data

Population: 630,000 (1985 est)
Area: 17,364 square kilometres
Per capita income

	1979	1981	1982
GDP, factor cost (Emalangeni)	. . .	E.766	E.775
GNP (US dollars)	. . .	. . .	$940

Sources: 1, 7, 9.

Rate of Exchange
(Emalangeni per unit of foreign currency)

	1979	1981	1983	1984	1985
Rand	1	1	1	1	1
US$	.84	.88	1.09	1.50	1.92
UK£	1.81	1.72	1.69	1.96	2.52

B. Foreign Trade

(Em)	1979	1981	1982	1983	1984
Imports	366	519	563	609	637
of which					
from RSA	344 (91%)	433	466 (83%)	. . .	. . .
Exports	197	318	321	313	357
of which					
to RSA	45 (23%)	108	122 (38%)	**	. . .
to UK	52 (26%)	62	44 (14%)	. . .	. . .

Main export products

	1979	1981	1982	1983	1984
Sugar	69	124	105	122	132
Wood pulp	28	51	46	44	69
Chemicals	10	36	55	40	39
Canned fruit	9	13	18	22	29
Citrus	9	9	16	14	21
Asbestos	18	18	15	17	18
Electronic equipment	4	12	16	7	4

**note: exports to RSA fell sharply in 1984, because of closures of fertilizer and electronics factories.

Sources: 3 and 8.

C. Other South African Links

Customs Union revenue:

	79/80	81/82	82/83	83/84B	84/85B
Revenue (Em)	74	63	118	121	130
% of tot govt rev	59%	48%	67%	67%	63%

B = Budget

Source: 2.

Migrant labour

	1979	1981	1982	1983	1984
Migrant miners in RSA (000)[a]	13	11	14	. . .	. . .
% of Swazi wage labour force	15%	12%	15%	. . .	. . .
Total migrants in RSA[b]	13	13	14	17	17
Remittances (Em)	5	9	9	. . .	. . .

Sources: (a) 3, 4; (b) 6.

Tourism

	1975	1979	1981	1983
RSA tourists (000)	83	59	46	47
% of total	63%	61%	55%	59%

Source: 5.

Fuel: Electricity

	1977	1979	1981	1982
% of total consumption imported from RSA	45%	61%	62%	77%

Source: 3.

Note: 1982 Swazi hydroelectricity production down owing to drought.

Transit traffic: New rail link from Transvaal to Richards Bay.
Other links: Rivers rise, and are dammed, in South Africa.

D. *Economic Balance with South Africa*

(Em)	1981	1982
Income		
Customs union	66	104
Migrant labour	9	9
Tourism (est)	5	5
Exports to RSA	108	122
Expenditure		
Imports from RSA	−433	−466
Total deficit with RSA	−245	−226

Note: Customs payments are for the year ending 31 March, so for this table they have been assigned proportionately to calendar years. There are no figures for tourist expenditure, except Source 3 gives expenditure on hotel rooms at E40 per person, so assume each tourist spends roughly E100.

E. *Foreign Ownership/Control in Economy*
The Swazi Nation has large stakes in most major enterprises, but effective control usually remains with the foreign partner.

Sugar
    Umbombo Ranches: Lonrho 60%, Tibiyo 40%
    Mhlume: CDC 50%, Tibiyo 50%
    Royal Swazi (Simunye): Tibiyo 32.5%, Swazi govt 32.5%, Nigeria govt 10%, Tate & Lyle 8.7% (+ management contract), DEG 5%, Coca Cola 4.2%, Mitsui 3.8%, CDC 2.5%, IFC 1%.

Timber
    Usutu Pulp: CDC 50%, Courtaulds 50%
    Peak Timber: Anglo-American 100%
    Shiselweni Forestry: CDC 100%

Mining
    Havelock Asbestos: Gencor 60%, Tibiyo 40%
    Mpaka Colliery: Trans-Natal Coal (Gencor) 100%
    Diamonds: Trans Hex (RSA)

SWAKI (SWAziland KIrsh Industries): 50% Kirsh (Sanlam), 50% NIDCS controls:
    Swaziland Milling
    new cotton spinning mill: also NIDCS, CDC, IFC
    Swaziland Farm Chemicals
    Swazi Plaza (shopping precinct, Mbabane): also NIDCS
    Simunye Plaza (shopping precinct): Swaki 25%, Tibiyo 25%, NIDCS 25%, Royal Swazi Sugar 25%.
    Metro: Swaki 50%, NIDCS 50%.
    Mtimane Forest
    Swaziland Warehouse.
    Tracar (holds franchises for Mercedes, Nissan, Massey-Ferguson, BMW).

Banking and Insurance
    Barclays: Swazi govt 40%.

Standard: Swazi govt 40%.

Bank of Credit and Commerce International: Tibiyo 45%.

Swazi Royal Insurance Co: Swazi govt 52%, South African Eagle, Commercial Union

Other

Swaziland Fruit Canners: Zululand Fruit Producers 90%, Swazi govt 8%, CDC 2%.

Neopac: Barlow Rand 80%, CDC 10%, Swazi govt 10%.

Swaziland Brewers: SAB (Anglo-American) 60%, Tibiyo 40%.

Swazi Spa Holdings: Sun International (Old Mutual) 50%, Tibiyo 37.5%, public 12.5%.

Swazi Chemical Industries: Hanhill 100%.

Swazi United Transport: British Electric Traction 60%, Tibiyo 40%.

Interfood Swaziland: Tibiyo 40%, Interfood Deutschland 26%, Trade & Technology Transfers (Belgium) 25%.

Langa Brick: Tibiyo 51%, London Brick 17.5%, CDC 12.5%, Roberts Construction 7%.

Cotona Ginnery: Tongaat (RSA).

Swazi Pine: National Savings & Finance Corp (RSA) 100%.

Roberts Construction: Tibiyo 50%, Murray & Roberts (Sanlam) 50%.

Wholesale, retail, distribution

mainly RSA

Road transport

mainly RSA

For detail, see text.

Sources
1. *The National Accounts of Swaziland* 1976-82, Central Statistical Office, Mbabane.
2. Ministry of Finance, 1985.
3. *Annual Statistical Bulletin* 1982, Central Statistical Office, Mbabane.
4. *Economic Review* 1978-81, Prime Minister's Office, Mbabane.
5. Central Statistical Office.
6. South Africa *Yearbooks*.
7. IMF, *International Financial Statistics*, Jan 1986.
8. *Quarterly Review*, Central Bank of Swaziland.
9. IBRD.

ZAMBIA

A. Basic Data

Population: 6.6 million (1985 est)
Land area: 752,614 square kilometres
Per capita income

	1977	1980	1982	1984
GDP (current prices), Kwacha	382	539	594	737
(1977 prices), Kwacha	382	351	340	310
GNP (US dollars)	...	...	640	...

Source: 1, 7.

Rate of exchange:
Zambian Kwacha (K) per unit of foreign currency

	1979	1981	1983	1984	1985
Rand	.94	1.03	1.05	1.30	1.20
US$	.80	.89	1.15	1.76	2.36
UK£	1.71	1.73	1.77	2.37	3.04

B. Foreign Trade

	1970	1975	1979	1980	1982	1984
Imports (Km)	340	598	594	877	930	1108
of which %						
RSA	17%	7%	11%	15%	14%	...
UK	24%	20%	29%	22%	13%	...
USA	10%	12%	9%	7%	10%	...
Zimbabwe	6%	—	—	...	5%	...
Exports (Km)	710	518	1090	1023	950	1188
of which %						
RSA	1%	—	—	1%	—	...
UK	22%	22%	13%	14%	7%	...
rest EEC	32%	39%	32%	...	...	...
Japan	23%	17%	18%	17%	21%	...

Main export products (Km)

	1970	1975	1979	1980	1982	1984
Copper	681 (96%)	472	...	872	...	1031 (87%)
Cobalt	6 (1%)	7	...	87	...	20 (2%)
Zinc	11 (2%)	20	...	20	...	52 (5%)

Sources: 1, 2, 3.

C. Other South African Links

Customs Union revenue: not relevant.

Migrant labour

	1977	1981	1984
Total migrants in RSA (000)	0.6	0.7	1.2

Source: 5.

Tourism:

	1981	1982	1983	1984
RSA visitors	4311	3786	3610	4051
% of total	3%	3%	3%	3%
Amount spent (Km)	2	2	2	2

Sources: 1, 4.

Fuel: Occasional imports of diesel fuel from South Africa.
Transit traffic: Some traffic between Zaire and South Africa.
Use of South African ports:

Route	Proportion of foreign trade (by weight)				
	1980	1981	1982	1983	1984
Dar es Salaam	53%	55%	56%	49%	47%
Zimbabwe/RSA/Mozambique*	42%	40%	40%	46%	45%
Angola/Zaire	3%	2%	2%	3%	3%

(* = not normally disaggregated by route, but relatively little via Mozambique — in 1981 it was 34% via RSA and 6% via Mozambique)

Sources: 3, 6.

Other links: some grain from South Africa.

D. Economic Balance with South Africa

(Km)	1981	1982
Income		
Exports	5	3
Tourism	2	2
Expenditure		
Imports	−139	−135
Total deficit with RSA	−132	−130

E. Foreign Ownership/Control in Economy

Zimco and Indeco are state holding companies.
The largest local private company is Andrew Sardinis' Chibote Group, in which Lonrho's Henrich's Syndicate also has an interest.

Mining
ZCCM (main copper mining company): Anglo 27.3%, Sardinis 6.9%, Zimco 60.3%

Engineering companies
Boart, Diacarb, Deep Drilling, African Wire Ropes, Scaw: all majority or 100% Anglo
Turnpan: Lonrho
Metal Fabricators (Zamefa): Phelps Dodge 20%, Anglo 19%, Continental Ore 10%, Sardinis, Indeco 51%
Karironda: Covilink 30.5%, Cobar 15%, Indeco 54%
South Wales Electric: Hawker Siddeley
Mitchell Cotts (Zambia): Mitchell Cotts (UK)
others controlled by ZCCM or private individuals

Other industry
  Dunlop tyres: Dunlop 77%, Indeco 23%
  Chilanga Cement: CDC 27%, Anglo 12%, Indeco 60%
  African Match: Lonrho
  Livingstone Motor: Fiat 20%, Intersomer 10%, Indeco 70%
  Star Motors, Central African Motors, Commercial Motors, etc — distributors of most
    makes of cars, trucks, and tractors: Lonrho
  National Milling: Anglo 13%, Spillers (UK) 13%, Indeco 51%
  TAP Building Products: Turner & Newall (UK)
Beer, alcohol, and soft drinks
  Zambia Breweries: Anglo 45%, Indeco 55%
  National Breweries: Lonrho 49%, Indeco 51%
  Duncan Gilby & Matheson: Duncan Gilby & Matheson 33%, Anglo 25%, Indeco 42%
  Zambia Bottlers: Lonrho
Freight and forwarding
  Renfreight (Manica Freight): Old Mutual via Safmarine
  AMI: Société Générale de Belgique
  Leopold Walford: British & Commonwealth Shipping
Hotels
  Ridgeway: Anglo 30%
  Lusaka Hotel: Lonrho
  Zambia Hotels: Intercontinental Hotels 20%, Zimco 80%
Energy
  Tanzam pipeline: 33% Tanzania govt, 67% Zambia govt
  Agip Zambia: Agip (Italy) 50%, Zimco 50%
  Indeni refinery: Agip 50%, Zimco 50%
  Zamlube oil recycling: Anglo, Shell, BP, Zimco
Banking
  Barclays
  Standard
  Zambia National Commercial Bank: govt
Agriculture
  Zambia Sugar: Tate & Lyle 11% (+ management contract), Anglo 4%, Indeco 78%
  Kalengwa Farm: Lonrho
  Arbor Acres: Booker McConnell (UK)
  Mpongwe Development: IFC, CDC, Rembrandt (via Edesa), Zimco 51%

Sources
1. *Monthly Digest of Statistics*, Central Statistical Office, Lusaka.
2. *Annual Statement of External Trade — 1979*, Central Statistical Office, Lusaka; plus
   additional data provided by CSO.
3. *Report for the year ending 31 Dec 1983*, Bank of Zambia, Lusaka.
4. *Annual Report*, Zambia National Tourist Board, Lusaka (no direct information on
   RSA tourists).
5. South Africa *Yearbooks*, Pretoria.
6. Southern African Transport & Communications Commission, Main report, presented
   at SADCC annual conference, Maseru, 27 Jan 1983.
7. IBRD.

ZIMBABWE

A. Basic Data

Population: 8.2 million (1985 est)
Land area: 391,109 square kilometres
Per capita income

	1981	1982	1983	1984
GDP, factor cost	Z$550	Z$610	Z$656	Z$714
GNP, (US dollars)	. . .	US$850	. . .	. . .

Sources: 1, 5, 6.

Rate of exchange:
Z$ per unit of foreign currency (mid year)

	1979	1981	1983	1984	1985
Rand	.80	.79	.89	.88	.79
US$	.68	.76	.99	1.19	1.56
UK£	1.47	1.37	1.53	1.61	2.00

B. Foreign Trade

(Z$m)	1981	1982	1983	1984
Imports	1018	1082	1062	1201
of which				
RSA non-oil	280 (28%)	239	260	232 (19%)
UK	102 (10%)	162	122	143 (12%)
USA	74 (7%)	104	100	112 (9%)
Exports	888	807	1026	1271
of which				
RSA	192 (22%)	138	187	232 (15%)
UK	62 (7%)	77	118	163 (13%)

Main export products				
Tobacco	224	195	233	287
Ferro-chrome	80	77	116	155
Asbestos	76	61	69	74
Nickel	47	45	68	63
Iron & Steel	43	42	43	50
Cotton	61	53	75	117
Sugar	55	52	52	56
Maize	35	40	41	0
Manufactured	47	31	29	52

Export totals do not include gold sales, which were:

76	141	104	160

Source: 1.

C. Other South African Links

Customs Union revenue: not relevant.

Migrant labour:

	1977	1981	1983	1984
Total migrants in RSA (000)	38	17	8	7
of which miners	26	5	. . .	. . .
Migrants as % of employees	4%	2%	. . .	. . .
Remittances (Rm)	. . .	31	9	. . .

Source: 3.

Tourism

	1982	1983
RSA visitors	62,006	53,131
% of total	24%	27%
Amount spent (Z$m)	7.2	6.1

Source: 2.

Fuel: Some petroleum products from or through South Africa.
Transit traffic: Railways handle traffic between South Africa and both Zaire and Zambia.
Use of South African ports:
(% of tonnes of National Railways of Zimbabwe cargo)

	1980	1981	1982	1983 (Jan-Jun)
Via Mozambique	1%	46%	53%	43%
Via South Africa	99%	54%	47%	57%

Source: 4.

D. Economic Balance with South Africa

(Z$m)	1983
Income	
Migrant labour	8
Tourism	6
Exports to RSA	187
Expenditure	
Imports from RSA	−378
Total deficit with RSA	−177

E. Foreign Ownership/Control of Economy (by Colin Stoneman)

South African firms own about one third of publicly-quoted companies.

Control of capital in Zimbabwe's leading productive sectors (% of assets)

	Agriculture	Manufacturing	Mining	Distribution	Transport	Finance	Overall*
Domestic	55	45	15*	65	65	25	48
RSA	35	25	45	15	15	—*	24
Delta Corp*	—	3	—	10	—	—	2
British	10	22	30	10	20	65	21
Other For.	—	5	10	—	—	10	3
	100	100	100	100	100	100	
(GDP share)	14	29	6	15	7	5	76

(* = see notes below)

This is an estimate of *control* of capital, so that minority interests have been ignored unless they represent a measure of control. No official statistics are collected on ownership of investment; the present estimates derive from a number of sources, partly quantitative, partly impressionistic. The capital employed by the main firms in each sub-sector was found or estimated, and the country of controlling interest was identified. In the case of manufacturing and mining, sub-sectors were assessed. Because of the interpenetration of British and South African capital, and also because many firms are involved across two or more sub-sectors, considerable elements of judgement as to distribution are necessarily involved.

Four firms need special mention. *Delta Corporation* (see text) is the largest single company in Zimbabwe. At the time of writing it is still controlled by South African Breweries; however, negotiations are proceeding which could result in substantial government participation, although control may not be relinquished. *Wankie Colliery* is majority owned by the government but managed by Anglo American, so it has been included in RSA-controlled; if it is treated as local, the domestic share of mining rises to 25% and the South African share falls to 35%. Thus, depending on the assignment of Wankie and Delta, South African control of productive capital can range from 23% to 26%. Two major investors are not directly reflected in this table, namely the South African-controlled *Old Mutual* and the British *Electra Investments*, each accounting for some Z$300m which spans a wide range of companies. But neither company, in general, seeks or achieves a position of control, normally holding below 10% of the total equity of any company. (A possible exception where a degree of influence may be involved is in the case of TA, where Old Mutual is the largest single shareholder with 14.8%.) Thus it is possible that our percentages of foreign *control* may be somewhat lower than the foreign percentage of *total investment*. Two factors will reduce that difference, however: a high proportion of Old Mutual and Electra investments are in companies that are in any case under South Africa or British control, while we have similarly ignored minority Zimbabwean holdings in foreign controlled companies.

In the *finance* sector, the lack of South African control is recent and in some ways still nominal. Barclays and Standard Bank are both British but until recently, at least, the Zimbabwean subsidiaries were treated as off-shoots of the much larger South African operations. The purely South African-owned Nedbank was nationalised (as Zimbank) after independence.

The *overall* figure is for productive investment. We have excluded the 'other' category, both from the table and in compiling the overall figure. 'Other' comprises electricity & water, real estate, public administration, and services. 'Other' is 90% domestic (because of the large government share), and 5% RSA and 5% UK, both largely real estate.

Sources
1. *Quarterly Digest of Statistics*, Central Statistical Office, Harare.
2. *Monthly Migration and Tourist Statistics*, Central Statistical Office, Harare.
3. South African *Yearbooks*, Pretoria.
4. Charles N. Hova, *Zimbabwe Energy Accounting Project Working Paper*, Harare, 1984.
5. IMF, *International Financial Statistics*, Jan 1986.
6. IBRD.

References

REFERENCES FOR CHAPTER 1

1. *Observer*, London, 13 Oct 1985.
2. As many journalists pointed out in reporting the reasons for the 1986 coup in Lesotho.
3. Figures in this paragraph relate to 1982, the most recent year for which statistics were available. See Statistical Annex, Tables 2 and 3.
4. There is ample evidence of the South African role there, for example in Catholic Institute for International Relations, *Namibia in the 1980s*, London, new edition 1986, or International Defence and Aid Fund, *Namibia — the Facts*, London, new edition 1986.
5. A point made in various studies of Namibia by Professor Reginald Herbold Green, especially Peter Manning and R.H. Green, *Namibia: South Africa's 'Total Strategy' for Domination and Exploitation*, in David Martin and Phyllis Johnson (ed), forthcoming, Zimbabwe Publishing House; and Caroline Allison and R.H. Green, *Political Economy and Structural Change: Namibia at Independence*, Discussion Paper 212, Institute of Development Studies, University of Sussex 1986.

REFERENCES FOR CHAPTER 2

1. Orchestrated and conceived by BOSS (Bureau of State Security), and involving secret diplomatic contacts, detente was an attempt to win a few allies within the Organisation of African Unity (OAU) without changing apartheid. Its successes included Prime Minister Vorster's visits to Ivory Coast in September 1974 and Liberia in February 1975, plus his August 1975 Victoria Falls talks with Kenneth Kaunda. But in April 1975 the OAU council of ministers adopted the Dar es Salaam declaration, saying that 'any talk of detente with the apartheid regime is such nonsense that it should be treated with the contempt it deserves'. Once South Africa invaded Angola, no African state would disagree with the OAU view.
2. *South Africa in the 1980s* (CIIR, London, 3rd Edition, 1986) is a good overall guide to South Africa itself. *The Struggle for South Africa*, by Rob Davies, Dan O'Meara, and Sipho Dlamini (Zed, London, 1984), which was produced at the Centre of African Studies of Eduardo Mondlane University in Maputo, is also particularly useful.
3. The concept of the total strategy is drawn from the writing of the French general, André Beaufre, and is based on an analysis of counter-insurgency in Algeria, Indo-China, and elsewhere. Useful sources on the total strategy and on the militarisation of the government are: Davies and O'Meara, 'Total Strategy in Southern Africa', *Journal of Southern African Studies*, Apr 1985; Richard Leonard, *South Africa at War*, Lawrence Hill, Westport (Conn. USA), 1983; Kenneth Grundy, *The Rise of the South African Security Establishment*, South Africa Institute of International Affairs, Johannesburg, 1983; Deon Geldenhuys, *The Diplomacy of Isolation*, Macmillan, Johannesburg, 1984 (hereafter

Geldenhuys 1984); and Philip Frankel, *Pretoria's Praetorians*, Cambridge University Press, Cambridge (UK), 1984 (hereafter Frankel).
4. Position Paper, Vol 6 No 1, Southern African Forum, Johannesburg, 1983.
5. Commentary 'Soviet destabilisation of southern Africa', Johannesburg radio in English, 15 Jun 1985.
6. Dirk and Johanna de Villiers, *PW*, Tafelberg-Uitgewers, Cape Town, 1984.
7. Frankel.
8. Frankel gives the following figures (except 1984/85 — government estimate):

Financial year	Budget (Rm)	% of GNP	% of state expenditure
1960/61	44	1 %	6.6%
1966/67	255	...	...
1979/80	1857	5 %	14.3%
1984/85	3755	4 %	14.8%

But the official figures exclude a number of key military-related expenditures, which have probably been rising faster than the official budget. On the other hand, rapid inflation means that the real increase is less than the annual cash increase.
9. In particular Pik Botha to the Swiss-South African Association in Zurich, 7 Mar 1979, and P.W. Botha at the Carlton Conference, Johannesburg, 22 Nov 1979.
10. Geldenhuys 1984, pp 161-3.

REFERENCES FOR CHAPTER 3

1. *Observer*, London, 13 Mar 1983.

2. The fourth target was the Johannesburg office of Fluor, a major Sasol contractor, but those bombs were found and defused. Richard Leonard, *South Africa at War*, Lawrence Hill, Westport (Conn USA), 1983.
3. The quote comes from an article on the SASOL Commando unit in the SADF magazine *Paratus* (Aug 1979). 'The importance of the task of the Sasol Commando in defending these two key points cannot be over-emphasised', it said, referring to the Sasol plant itself and the adjoining Natref refinery, both of which were successfully attacked on 1 June.
4. See my more detailed account of this organisation — J. Hanlon, *SADCC: Progress, Projects & Prospects*, Economist Intelligence Unit Special Report 182, London, Jan 1985. The South Africans like to dismiss SADCC as a 'counter-constellation'. In fact, the centrality of Zimbabwe to the region, and the economic rearrangement that would take place once the war there ended, was clear to all. The Front Line states saw the need for an economic arm, and began planning SADCC in 1978; the first formal meeting was in Arusha, Tanzania, in July 1979, and included the then five Front Line states, plus representatives of 18 potential donors, including the UN, EEC, Commonwealth, various development banks, the US, UK and Scandinavian countries.
5. SWAPO, ANC, and PAC representatives are invited to some SADCC meetings, and SADCC has made clear that it hopes Namibia will join after it becomes independent. It remains unclear what relationship SADCC would have with a majority-ruled South Africa; some SADCC leaders have said it would be welcome to join, yet the restructuring SADCC is trying to carry out will be equally essential to prevent a majority-ruled South Africa from dominating the other states in the region. Attempts were made by several European countries to press SADCC to include Zaire, but this was rejected, in part because of Zaire's close links with South Africa.
6. The full title is 'Southern Africa: Toward Economic Liberation, A Declaration by the Governments of Independent States of Southern Africa made at Lusaka on the 1st of April 1980.'
7. As a journalist I worked for five years in Mozambique, travelling all over the country, and I never found any indication of the existence of ANC bases. South African intelligence

on Mozambique is very good, and I am sure that if there had been ANC bases there, they would have been found and attacked, instead of houses which the South Africans called bases but which were not.

8. *Financial Times*, London, 3 Sep 1981.
9. Chester Crocker, *Foreign Affairs*, Winter 1980/81.
10. *Guardian*, London, 20 Jul 1984.
11. 'Worldnet' press conference with Chester Crocker, 26 Sep 1985.
12. Richard Leonard, *South Africa at War*, Lawrence Hill, Westport, (Conn USA) 1983.
13. 'Worldnet' press conference, 26 Sep 1985.
14. *Economist*, London, Mar 1985.
15. *New African*, London Aug 1981.
16. *Star*, Johannesburg, 20 May 1981.
17. In an interview with Donald Trelford, editor of the *Observer*, London, 13 Oct 1985.
18. 'Worldnet' press conference, 26 Sep 1985.
19. Chester Crocker, *Freedom at Issue*, Nov-Dec 1980.
20. Speech to a conference of editorial writers, 23 Jun 1983.
21. At the first SADCC annual conference, in Maputo in 1980, West German diplomats stressed to journalists that they wanted to fund regional transport projects, but would try to organise their own international coordinating body to bypass SADCC. They even defined the region differently, including Zaire and excluding Tanzania. This effort failed, and West Germany eventually fell into line and accepted the region and priorities as defined by SADCC.

REFERENCES FOR CHAPTER 4

1. Under the terms of the agreement, either party could give one year's notice of termination, which South Africa did. Nearly a year later, days before it was due to expire, South Africa revoked the termination, and the agreement still continues. (See Chapters 14-15).
2. Deon Geldenhuys is a prolific writer. His most important works are probably: 'Some Strategic Implications of Regional Economic Relations for the Republic of South Africa', *ISSUP Strategic Review*, Pretoria, Jan 1981 (hereafter Geldenhuys 1981); *Destabilisation Controversy in Southern Africa*, S A Forum Position Paper, Johannesburg, Sept 1982 (the source of the quotes here, and hereafter Geldenhuys 1982); and *The Diplomacy of Isolation*, Macmillan, Johannesburg, 1984 (hereafter Geldenhuys 1984). Geldenhuys is close to at least some of the National Party strategists and ideologists. As well as doing research for them, his writing accords with their thinking on regional issues, and he articulates *verligte* policy on regional issues better than any other academic. It is suggested that Geldenhuys may be seen as a future Henry Kissinger or Chester Crocker of South Africa — the academic who first studies government policy but then graduates to create it.
3. Geldenhuys' argument for supporting dissidents is remarkably disingenuous. He describes them all as 'significant domestic political opposition'. For example, he claims that 'given the repressive nature of the Frelimo regime, opposition was bound to find extra-constitutional expression, the main vehicle being the MNR' — without pointing out that Rhodesia had created the MNR from nothing, and South Africa had rebuilt it after it was beaten in 1980.
4. Geldenhuys 1981.
5. Geldenhuys 1984.
6. The three not used were:
    Devaluation as a way to promote exports in the face of sanctions, which would have 'severe effects' on the three countries with currencies closely tied to the rand. Geldenhuys himself admitted that 'for South Africa, this is hardly an appropriate or necessary measure'. But it happened anyway, without South Africa intending, with the collapse of the rand in 1984/85.

Curtailing official South African aid. (Unused as South Africa gives so little aid). Increased aid also suggested as 'an incentive lever'.

Ignoring Law of the Sea requirements to give sea-bed and fishing access to land-locked states. (Never applicable.)

7. One possible explanation for the apparently counter-productive act of the MNR in cutting the line between South Africa and Cahora Bassa is that the SADF wanted the line out of action to forestall arguments against destabilisation which took into account cutting the line as possible retaliation.

8. Loubser cannot have been pleased with the boycott of Maputo port either, as after Mozambican independence South African Railways had spent R70m electrifying the line to the border. But this boycott continued.

9. *Star*, Johannesburg, 22-24 Mar 1983.

10. *Financial Mail*, Johannesburg, 25 Feb 1983.

11. Published in *ISSUP Strategic Review*, Pretoria, Aug 1983.

12. *Sunday Times*, London 10 Oct 1982.

13. US sources claim that it was only their efforts that stopped South Africa from overthrowing Machel. If so, it would be one of the few successes of constructive engagement, but only in the most convoluted way — the idea of overthrowing Frelimo only seemed possible in the first place because of the licence granted by constructive engagement. It may be more propaganda than reality, but at the time there was serious discussion of the possibility. In late 1982 embassies in Harare were spreading the rumour that Machel would be overthrown soon. This apparently affected Mozambique-Zimbabwe negotiations; there seemed no point in signing agreements with a government that trusted Western advisers claimed was to be overthrown. This is a good example of how false rumours can be used to sabotage SADCC.

14. It was not only over Mozambique. The US ambassador gave a speech which was described as 'a veiled warning to South Africa to deliver the goods or forfeit constructive engagement'. Ambassador Nickel stressed the need for better links with Zimbabwe, and continued: 'to those in this country who take exception to Mr Mugabe's public utterances, we would give the friendly advice to pay at least as much attention to what Mr Mugabe does'. The suggestion was rejected by South African officials as 'diplomatically impolite'(*Star*, Johannesburg, 5 Mar 1983).

15. *Star*, Johannesburg, 23 Mar 1983.

REFERENCES FOR CHAPTER 5

1. *Economist*, London, 30 Mar 1985.

2. Dirk & Johanna de Villiers, *PW*, Tafelberg-Uitgewers, Cape Town, 1984 (hereafter *PW*).

3. Harry Oppenheimer was a lone dissenter, but his successor at Anglo, Gavin Relly, backed it.

4. *Guardian*, London, 20 Jul 1984. The number of 'armed incidents' attributed to the ANC by South Africa during 1985 was twice the 1984 figure.

5. *Sunday Times*, Johannesburg, 18 Mar 1984.

6. *Sunday Times*, Johannesburg, 13 May 1984.

7. But Deon Geldenhuys made clear just what South Africa's 'vital interests' were. 'The safeguarding of the Republic's national security becomes synonymous with the preservation of the political status quo: apartheid and security are two sides of the same coin.' (*Leadership SA*, vol 3 No 2, 2nd quarter 1984).

8. *PW*.

9. Mozambican diplomats reported that tourism was a South African obsession. But this is an economic lever — see Chapter 4 — and it would also provide something concrete to white voters who really do want to return to the famous Mozambican beaches. In the end, only the Cahora Bassa commission produced concrete results; although there was talk of

South Africa setting up new tourist facilities, only Lonrho actually signed on the dotted line.

10. Roger Parsons, Assocom chief executive, quoted in the *Cape Times*, Cape Town, 25 Apr 1984.

11. *Citizen*, 19 Mar 1984.

12. *Optima* (Anglo house magazine), Johannesburg, 13 Jul 1984.

13. Robert Davies, 'South African Strategy Towards Mozambique in the Post-Nkomati Period', *Scandinavian Institute of African Studies Research Report* no 73, Uppsala (Sweden), Sep 1985.

14. *Sunday Tribune*, Durban, 12 Aug 1984.

15. *Citizen*, 27 Apr 1984.

16. Two Anglo companies also entered serious negotiations, but these were still unconcluded more than a year later: AECI was interested in ammonia production and Premier Milling proposed to compound animal feeds in Mozambique. Anglo itself kept a substantial distance from links with Mozambique; at the Nkomati signing, Harry Oppenheimer commented that 'it is a bit early to talk of economic involvement in Mozambique'. (*Citizen*, 19 Mar 1984).

17. Americo Magaia, president of the Mozambican Chamber of Commerce, quoted in *Notícias*, Maputo, 10 Jul 1984.

18. *Hansard*, col. 6204, 10 May 1984.

19. *Citizen*, 7 June 1984.

20. Speech to the South African Institute for International Affairs, 31 Aug 1984.

21. *Rand Daily Mail*, Johannesburg, 4 Oct 1984.

22. Dennis Austin, *South Africa 1984*, Chatham House Papers 26, Routledge & Kegan Paul, London, 1985.

REFERENCES FOR CHAPTER 6

1. *Daily Telegraph*, London, 25 Jun 1985.

2. *Economist*, London, 30 Mar 1985.

3. *Documentos da Gorongosa*, Ministry of Information, Maputo, 1985.

4. Robert Davies, 'South African Strategy Towards Mozambique in the Post-Nkomati Period', *Scandinavian Institute of African Studies Research Report* No. 73, Uppsala (Sweden), Sept 1985 (hereafter Davies 1985). Much the best analysis published so far.

5. Herwig Rudolph, *Africa Institute of South Africa Bulletin*, vol 24 no 2, 1984.

6. According to the diary, 'Pick Botha responded to him [Crocker] that he previously held the same view, but that now the situation is different.' Throughout the diaries Pik Botha is always referred to as 'Pick'.

7. Technically it was a statement by South Africa, made in the presence of the MNR and Mozambican delegations. It said that Samora Machel was 'acknowledged' as President of Mozambique, that there *should* be an end to the fighting, that South Africa should play a role in implementing the declaration, and that there should be a commission to implement the declaration. The agreement is curious and seems very much like a minimal agreement reached simply for the sake of reaching some kind of accord. Although it says there should be an end to the fighting, it is not a cease-fire and establishes no way to reach one. It does involve two concessions, one by each side. On the Mozambican side, it was a major concession to talk for the first time to the MNR (rather than only to their South African masters). On the South African side, the recognition of Machel was clearly meant to end talk of overthrowing him (and thus may also have been pointed at some elements in the South African military).

8. Britain has played a small and quiet role to help Mozambique. It put diplomatic pressure on both Swaziland and Malawi not to support the MNR, and provided equipment to the Zimbabwean army for use against the MNR in Mozambique. Finally, some Mozambican soldiers are to be trained in Zimbabwe by British officers.

9. This was also the official Frelimo line. Some Mozambicans did believe it. It remains unclear if the top Frelimo leadership were convinced, or if they chose to accept a convenient fiction as a way of keeping talks open and not causing a diplomatic breach.
10. This is the MNR's report of events, but, from other evidence, this division seems likely. But it is also possible that the South Africans were magnifying the divisions for external consumption — to the MNR as an excuse for not giving them more support, and to Frelimo as an excuse for not having cut it off.
11. Jenkins in *Economist*, 30 Mar 1985; Deon Geldenhuys, *The Diplomacy of Isolation*, Macmillan, Johannesburg, 1984 (hereafter Geldenhuys 1984).
12. Davies 1985.
13. Mozambican sources claim there were really four parties in the negotiations leading up to the 3 October 1984 Pretoria declaration: Mozambique, the MNR, the South African Foreign Ministry, and South African Military Intelligence (which seemed to be acting entirely independently of the Foreign Ministry).
14. 'Worldnet' press conference, 26 Sept 1985.
15. *Economist*, London, 30 Mar 1985. According to Angolan Politburo member Pedro van Dunem, Cuban troops will act only if the SADF goes north of the 14th parallel, roughly 350km north of the Namibian border (press briefing, Harare, 31 Jan 1986).
16. *Rand Daily Mail*, Johannesburg, 16 Aug 1984.
17. *Financial Mail*, Johannesburg, 26 Oct 1984.
18. *Leadership SA*, vol 3 no 2 (2nd quarter 1984).
19. Stanley Uys, *Guardian*, London, 25 Sept 1985.
20. SABC Johannesburg home service in English, 12 Dec 1984; *Guardian*, London, 7 Oct 1985.
21. *Guardian*, London, 25 Sept 1985.
22. After Botha criticised the meeting a few days before it was to be held, the Afrikaner businessmen, including Anton Rupert of Rembrandt, withdrew. So the delegation was Anglo-dominated. The four with Anglo links were: Relly; Anglo executive director Zac de Beer; Tony Bloom, chairman of Anglo-owned Premier Milling; and Tertius Myburgh, editor of the Anglo-controlled *Sunday Tribune*. The other three were: Peter de L. Sorour, director of the South Africa Foundation; Hugh Murray, editor of *Leadership SA*; and Harold Pakendorf, editor of *Die Vaderland*.
23. *Guardian*, London, 25 Sept 1985.
24. This led Stanley Uys to point out that it had been 16 years from Sharpeville to Soweto, and then eight years from Soweto to Sharpeville II. 'Will the timespace between Sharpeville 1984 and the next black uprising be four years?' (*Guardian*, 5 Sept 1985).
25. Howard Preece (deputy editor of *Finance Week*), *Guardian*, London, 10 Sept 1985. CIIR, *Update 3*, June 1985.
26. There was, however, also pressure for reforms inside that would expand the market. The chairman of South African Breweries (by then acquired by Anglo) noted that 'there can be no doubt that the future of this consumer goods company lies in black spending'. He warned that 'the politics and economics of this country are totally interwoven'. And he also commented that 'there is no way we are ever going to manage our business with white skills alone'. *Financial Times*, London, 2 Oct 1984.
27. *Financial Mail*, Johannesburg, 26 Oct 1984. In 1984, the US-based Citibank and the British based Hill Samuel became leaders in efforts to expand South African export through barter and counter-trade. For example, after Nkomati, Hill Samuel set up a R30m credit line for exports to Mozambique, to be paid in Mozambican exports to South Africa.
28. *Financial Mail*, Johannesburg, 30 Nov 1984.
29. 'Worldnet' press conference, 26 Sept 1985.
30. *Guardian*, London 7 Oct 1985.

REFERENCES FOR CHAPTER 7

1. G.M.E. Leistner, background paper prepared for an Africa Institute (Pretoria)

conference *Southern Africa: the challenge of the 80s*, Aug 1981; Chairman's Report to the Africa Institute AGM, 17 Aug 1983; G.M.E. Leistner, *Africa Institute Bulletin*, 1985 no 5 (15 Apr 1985).

2. Deon Geldenhuys, *The Diplomacy of Isolation*, Macmillan, Johannesburg, 1984, p 42.

3. Philip H. Frankel, *Pretoria's Praetorians*, Cambridge University Press, Cambridge (UK), 1984, p 59.

4. In 1983, Africa accounted for only 4% of South Africa's non-customs union exports, but 24% of exports if minerals and gems are excluded, and in three key areas it was 47% of machinery, 46% of plastics, and 39% of chemicals. (G.M.E. Leistner, *Africa Institute Bulletin*, Pretoria, 1985 no 5.) Most of those will be to Zambia, Zimbabwe, and Malawi. If exports to the three customs union partners (Botswana, Lesotho, and Swaziland) are included, it is likely that SADCC members account for more than half of South African exports in those three sectors.

5. Extrapolated from calculations done by Earl McFarland, a consultant to the Botswana Ministry of Finance, and published in M.A. Oommen, *Botswana's Economy Since Independence*, Tata McGraw Hill, New Delhi, 1983. (See also Chapter 9)

6. The rapid collapse of the rand in 1985 changed this somewhat, because it suddenly made many South African goods much cheaper than competing goods priced in dollars. This advantage will largely disappear as high inflation and the higher costs of imported fuel and imputs work their way through the economy. Nevertheless, if the rand stays below US$0.40 then some goods remain competively priced which were not before.

7. Deon Geldenhuys, 'Some Strategic Implications of Regional Economic Relationships', *ISSUP Strategic Review*, Pretoria, Jan 1981.

REFERENCES FOR CHAPTER 8

1. Robin McGregor, *Who Owns Whom 1983; Star*, Johannesburg, 10 Aug 1983. In *The Struggle for South Africa* (Zed, London 1984), the co-authors calculate the percentage of total assets of non-state corporations (a somewhat larger pool of assets than stock exchange listed firms) controlled by these firms, and find: Anglo 25.9%, Sanlam 16.8%, Barlow 5.6%, Volkskas 4.8%, Old Mutual 4.5%, Anglovaal 2.5%, and Rembrandt 1.4%. However it is counted, a few monopoly groups clearly control the South African economy.

2. A detailed account of Anglo American is given in Duncan Innes, *Anglo*, Raven, Johannesburg, 1984.

3. Premier's head, Tony Bloom, has been an outspoken advocate of better relations with the neighbouring states, as part of his attempts to push up the company's exports into the region.

4. SAB is the only brewer in South Africa and controls the country's largest retail chain, OK Bazaars, and a smaller retail chain, Edgar's. It also controls brewing in Botswana, Lesotho, Swaziland, and Zimbabwe. SAB controls one of the two major hotel groups, Southern Sun.

5. *Economist*, London, 16 Jul 1983.

6. It also has the Holiday Inn in Harare and is proposing investments in Mozambique. Southern Sun (SAB-Anglo) controls hotels inside South Africa and in Zimbabwe. The two groups are halves of an empire set up by Sol Kerzner, which was divided when Kerzner chose not to follow SAB into Anglo control. A similar deal had happened in 1982, when Barlow Rand feared that Anglo would use its large stake to take control of the group. A complex swap was done, in which Barlow took over two Old Mutual-controlled food companies, Tiger Oats and Imperial Cold Store, and Old Mutual gained a 24% share of Barlow. Old Mutual could control Barlow, but so far has treated it simply as an investment. Barlow is a diversified mining, engineering, manufacturing, packaging, and food company.

7. *Africa Economic Digest*, London, 4 Jul 1980.

8. Two other foreign companies with important regional roles should be mentioned. The

British RTZ is best known for the Rössing uranium mine in Namibia. It also has mining and industrial interests in South Africa and Zimbabwe. Anglo has a small holding in RTZ. The other is the Société Générale de Belgique, which is associated with Anglo in the diamond business and elsewhere, such as the Wankie Colliery in Zimbabwe. Société Générale now controls the Benguela Railway and its Tractionel subsidiary is active as a consultant, for example to SADCC on energy.

9. *Africa Economic Digest*, London, 17 Dec 1982.

10. Nacala and Dar es Salaam are served by the east African conferences, while Maputo and Beira are treated as part of South Africa by most international shipping lines. Notable exceptions are the Indian and Soviet shipping lines, which do not call at South African ports.

11. *Financial Mail*, 27 Jul 1984.

12. *Rand Daily Mail*, Johannesburg, 21 Oct 1984.

13. *African Business*, London, Dec 1985.

14. Lesotho has virtually no exports of goods. Its major export is of labour to South Africa, so that its 'export earnings' (remittances from those labourers) are primarily in rands.

15. *Africa Economic Digest*, London, 2 Nov 1985.

16. *African Business*, London, Jun 1980, Feb 1982, & Jul 1982.

17. *Sunday Tribune*, Durban, 29 Apr 1984.

18. Paper presented at Apartheid and Southern Africa conference, Amsterdam, 12 Sept 1985.

19. The *Botswana Examiner* (Gaborone, 12 Nov 1982) estimated that Botswana paid Pula 17m extra over three years, roughly $6m per year extra, equivalent to $12m per year for all three BLS states.

20. The Southern African Customs Union revenue-sharing formula double-counts fuel to the detriment of the BLS states. (See footnote 2 of Chapter 9.) Oil is imported into SACU while petroleum products carry excise duties, so that petrol is included *twice* in the denominator, once in I and once in D. (Excise revenues on petrol are included in the total revenue — and indeed make up the largest item — as well as in D.) But as all refining is done in South Africa, the petrol consumed in the BLS states occurs in the numerator only in i. This double counting in the denominator was not serious when the SACU formula was first derived, but oil price rises in 1973 and 1979 mean that oil imports now exceed $4000m per year, and petroleum products now represent nearly half of I + D. The rising cost of fuel consumed inside South Africa depresses the revenue share of BLS states. Actual oil import statistics for SACU are secret, but it seems likely that if the import value of crude oil were counted only once instead of twice in I + D, it would raise BLS revenue by at least 15%.

21. *Africa Confidential*, London, 30 Mar 1983; Shipping Research Bureau.

22. *Africa Confidential*, 30 Mar 1983.

23. This was apparently opposed by the Anglo-owned mines.

24. Ruth First, *Black Gold*, Harvester, Brighton (UK), 1983.

25. Alan Whiteside, *Past Trends and Further Prospects for Labour Migration to South Africa*, Occasional Paper, South African Institute of International Affairs, Johannesburg, Nov 1985. (Hereafter Whiteside)

26. G.M.E. Leistner, *Africa Institute of South Africa Bulletin*, Pretoria, 15 Apr 1985. (Hereafter Leistner)

27. Whiteside gives this estimate, while Leistner comments that 'the frequently heard estimate of "over one million workers" seems excessive in light of official control measures'.

REFERENCES FOR CHAPTER 9

1. However, it is not a common market like the EEC, because there is no free movement of people.

2. The 1969 formula for a particular country, say Botswana, is:

$$\text{Revenue share} = \text{total revenue} \times 1.42 \times \frac{i + d}{I + D}$$

where:
i = value of goods imported into Botswana
I = value of goods imported into SACU
d = value of excise dutiable goods produced *and* consumed in Botswana
D = value of excise dutiable goods produced and consumed in SACU and where:
1) all values are for two years before, and
2) all duties paid are included in the value

Excise dutiable goods include petrol, wine, beer and spirits, and excise duties on them are a significant part of the calculation.
For 1978/9 (in million rand):

Components of I + D		*Components of total revenue*	
Imported goods	8158	Customs	371
Sales duty goods	920	Customs surcharge	359
Excise goods:		Sales duty	117
Beverages	765	Excise duty	˹1396
Tobacco products	262		
Oil products	2097	Total	2246
Other	695		
Total	12898		

Sales duty was later eliminated; customs surcharge varies considerably from year to year.
The BLS states complained that revenue under this system varied too much, so the formula was revised slightly in 1977 to include a stabilisation formula which ensures that revenue share is between 17% and 23% of i+d.
3. Derek Hudson 'Botswana's Membership of the SACU', in *Papers on the Economy of Botswana* (ed. Charles Harvey), Heinemann, London, 1981. Hudson is Director of Research of the Bank of Botswana, and his paper makes the case for staying in the SACU.
4. Possibly 0.42 is a compromise between 1/3 and 1/2.
5. 'Estimate of Duty Content of Botswana's Importers', paper submitted to the 6 May 1981 meeting of the SACU study group on the revenue sharing formula. To compute value before duty of South African produced goods, it simply deflated the price by the import duty.
6. Gavin Maasdorp, *Journal of Contemporary African Studies*, Oct 1982.
7. The government requires that motor manufacturers use at least two-thirds local car parts, even if cheaper ones are available abroad. Jacqueline Matthews, 'South Africa's Trade Relations', *International Affairs Bulletin*, (2A) Vol. 4, 1980.
8. Kenneth Grundy, 'The Rise of the South African Security Establishment', *Bradlow Paper* No. 1, South African Institute of International Affairs, Braamfontein, 1983.
9. Trucks & transport supplement, *Financial Mail*, Johannesburg, 19 Oct 1984.
10. J. G. Gray & S. G. Hoohlo, 'The Direct Duty Content of Lesotho's Imports', *Ford Research Project* Paper FRP/1 1978. It was based on 1977 prices of 42 commodities for which comparable prices were available. They represented 29% of Lesotho's total imports.
11. Measured in terms of value added — that is, real local gain after subtracting imported raw materials, etc. John Gray, 'Final Report' (FRP 15) of the Ford Research Project,

Maseru, August 1979.

12. There are two key assumptions involved in the actual calculation: first that each R1 increase in South African exports leads to an eventual increase of R2 in GDP (it is suggested that this is low, and that a factor of 3 or more might be more appropriate), and second that imports of services from South Africa average 28% of imports of goods. (Earl L. McFarland Jr in *Botswana's Economy Since Independence*, ed. M. A. Oommen, Tata McGraw-Hill, New Delhi, 1983.)

13. C.F. Scheepers, *Finance & Trade Review*, Dec 1979. G.M. Leistner, the director of the pro-government Africa Institute, noted that 'Experience everywhere has shown that the free movement of commodities and production factors tends to widen rather than narrow the discrepancies between highly and little developed regions in a common market.' Leistner added that 'The less developed areas generally tend to stagnate or even regress economically.' ('Closer union in southern Africa', paper presented at a symposium at the University of the North, Pietersburg, 4 May 1979).

14. C.M. Rogerson in *The Geography of MNCs* ed. Michael Taylor & Nigel Thrift, Croom Helm, London 1982.

15. Gavin Maasdorp, *Journal of Contemporary African Studies*, Oct 1982.

16. *Business in Swaziland*, Mbabane, Jan 1983.

17. BLS would prefer tariffs that would earn more money for the SACU.

18. J. Hanlon, 'SADCC', *Economist Intelligence Unit Report* 182, London 1984.

19. C.M. Rogerson, *South African Geographical Journal*, Sept 1978.

20. 'Reducing Dependence', report submitted to the Commonwealth Secretariat, London, Jan 1979.

21. Hunso Kizillyali, *Revenue Sharing Formula of the SACU*, Finance Ministry, Maseru, August 1980.

22. *Financial Mail*, Johannesburg, 11 May 1984.

23. *Sunday Times*, Johannesburg, 29 July 1984.

24. Bernard Decaux, *The Industrial Sector in Lesotho*, World Bank, 7 Mar 1980. The study looked at 1977 as a test case, and concluded that it would have gained R36m in local value added from the enlarged domestic market. The costs from lost SACU revenue and industrial inefficiencies were R20m to R29m, depending on assumptions, leading to a profit to Lesotho of between R7m and R16m from withdrawal. Thus Lesotho could gain an increase in GDP of between 4% and 10% by leaving SACU. Decaux considers three cases. In the 'optimistic' one, industries which shift to Lesotho are as efficient as they were in South Africa while there is no loss of exports to South Africa. This produces the R16m gain. In the 'intermediate' one, which seems most realistic to me, output of industries which shift costs an extra 10% while some exports are lost. This produces a R7m gain. The 'pessimistic' or worst possible case assumes the new firms produce at 50% extra cost and Lesotho loses all its exports. This produces a huge loss (R39m) but is not a credible picture.

25. John Gray, *Final Report* (FRP 15) of the Ford Research Project, Maseru, August 1979.

26. Botswana keeps some of its reserves in South Africa even though it is not a member of the rand zone.

27. P.A. Lane, 'Policy Implications of Issuing an Independent Currency,' FRP/14, Maseru, Aug 1979.

REFERENCES FOR CHAPTER 10

1. *The Times* of Swaziland, Mbabane, 30 Jan 1985.

2. There were some extraordinary features about the incident. Mozambique denied that the raid had even occurred. And even as reported, it was clearly not an 'ambush' — it was a shot from an unknown sniper which caused no damage and hurt no one. Previous more damaging raids provoked no response, but this time Swaziland Railways Board chief

executive officer Danie Slabbert announced that he was suspending operations through Mozambique. Slabbert, like several other Swazi rail officials, comes from SATS (South African Transport Services). The 'ambush' was timed to send a reminder to the SADCC meeting, and Slabbert's action may have been intended to remind Swaziland that its best interests lay with SATS.

3. The prepared text was released to SADCC officials the week before the meeting, and was as anodyne as such opening speeches usually are (*Africa Confidential*, London, 13 Mar 1985). Quotes are from the text of the English translation of Prince Bhekimpi's impromptu speech distributed to the press the following day. This section was then deleted from the text given to SADCC for publication in the formal record of the conference (*SADCC-1985*, Gaborone 1986).

4. *Business in Swaziland*, Mbabane, Dec 1984.

5. 1985 population. The Gambia has less area and Djibouti has fewer people.

6. In 1975 the King decided that Tibiyo had enough capital and could continue without further mineral royalties, so a second fund, Tisuka TakaNgwane, was established to use mining royalties. Tisuka concentrates on property and housing, and is becoming an important patronage base and source of accumulation for a royalist landlord group. Two government (as distinct from Swazi Nation) development agencies were set up in 1970 and 1971: the Small Enterprise Development company (SEDCO) and the National Industrial Development Corporation of Swaziland (NIDCS).

7. Robert Davies et al, *The Kingdom of Swaziland: A Political, Economic, and Social Profile*, Centre of African Studies, Eduardo Mondlane University, Maputo, 1984.

8. For example, in 1981 Swaziland allowed the CIA to establish a radio listening facility in Mbabane aimed mainly at Mozambique. (*Guardian*, New York, 7 Apr 1982).

9. His death interrupted that weaving, suddenly freezing his steady movement in one particular position. Thus it is impossible to say what shifts the King had planned to follow his agreeing to the non-aggression pact with South Africa, and if he had intended implementation of it to be linked to implementation of the land deal (see below).

10. KaNgwane is one of South Africa's newly created rural slums. It has an area of only 3700 square kilometres (less than one-quarter that of Swaziland) but removals in the 1970s pushed its population up from 120,000 to over 350,000 (more than half that of Swaziland). Conditions are severely overcrowded, and it was in KaNgwane that the 1980 regional cholera epidemic first gained hold.

11. G.H. Pirie, *Aspects of the Political Economy of Railways in Southern Africa*, Environmental Studies Occasional Paper 24, Department of Geography, University of the Witwatersrand, Johannesburg, 1982.

12. J.G.H. Loubser (SAR General Manager), 'Transport Diplomacy', lecture to the Institute of Strategic Studies, Pretoria, 26 Sept 1979. Note that in 1982 the South African government formed SATS which runs South African Railways, South African Airways, harbours, and lorry and bus services; SATS is the largest South African state corporation.

13. *A Guide for Investors in Swaziland*, National Industrial Development Corporation of Swaziland, Mbabane, no date (probably 1981).

14. According to Western diplomatic sources.

15. Loubser.

16. Although the Swazi parliament passed legislation authorising the government to raise a loan for the railway from an agency in France.

17. South Africa's attitude on water is openly criticised in Swaziland's *Fourth National Development Plan 1983/4-1987/88*. In mid-1984 plans were announced for a dam on the Komati River (*Observer*, Matsapa, 23 Aug 1984; SABC Johannesburg home service in English, 7 Sept 1984). The dam would be in Swaziland but the lake behind it would stretch into South Africa. Both countries would draw water from the lake. The Komati flows back into South Africa and then into Mozambique, but so much water is already taken out by South Africa that it is often dry at the border (at the point where Mozambique and South Africa signed the Nkomati Accord). The reports do not indicate if Mozambique agreed to allow further water to be taken from the river.

18. G.M.E Leistner, *South Africa's Development Aid to African States*, Occasional Paper No 28, Africa Institute, Pretoria, 1970.

19. *Africa*, London, Feb 1982.

20. *Swazi Observer*, Matsapa, 4 Mar 1985.

21. *Africa Now*, London, Feb 1985.

22. *Swazi News*, Mbabane, 7 Apr 1984. The border closures took the form of extensive searches of cars, with advance newspaper warning (for example in the *Star*, Johannesburg, 16 Apr 1984) that delays of up to 'a day' could be expected by visitors going to Swaziland. The government could be expected to take notice, because of a similar much publicised border closure of Lesotho the previous year.

23. One is said to have been Major Craig Williamson, the long-time South African secret agent who infiltrated the International University Exchange Fund (IUEF). Before being exposed in 1979, he had had regular contacts with the ANC, and was reported to have been seen in the Tavern Hotel in Mbabane. He has become an important figure in South African raids into neighbouring states. For example, Williamson briefed the press after the 14 June 1985 raid on Gaborone, Botswana (see Chapter 17).

24. *New Statesman*, London, 11 May 1984.

25. J. Daniel, *South Africa and a BLS State*, paper presented at Uppsala, 10 Apr 1985.

26. J. Hanlon, *Mozambique — The Revolution Under Fire*, Zed, London 1984.

27. Mozambique's Foreign Minister Joaquim Chissano commented that 'South Africa pushes groups into Swaziland, then suddenly becomes friendly and tells us the MNR is operating from Swaziland.' (Press briefing in London, 25 Jul 1985).

28. *Swazi Observer*, Matsapa, 24 Apr 1984; *Times of Swaziland*, Mbabane, 30 Apr 1984.

29. *Swazi Observer*, Matsapa, 18 May 1984.

30. *Swazi Observer* and *Times of Swaziland*, 28 Feb 1985.

31. Metro and the Swazi firm Swaki are owned by Kirsh Industries, which was started, in Swaziland, by Natie Kirsh. Sanlam now controls Kirsh Industries through its 49.9% holding in a parent company, Sanki.

32. *Business in Swaziland*, Mbabane, Mar 1984.

33. *Fourth National Development Plan 1983/84-1987/88*, Mbabane, 1985.

34. King Sobhuza II turned down an offer from De Beers in the 1970s. After his death, a lease was granted to Trans-Hex without the knowledge of the Swazi government's adviser on minerals and with few details ever being made available even inside government. Swaziland does not have a contract with De Beers, but the first diamonds were sold to it.

35. *S.A. Digest*, Pretoria, 14 May 1982.

36. *Africa Economic Digest*, London, 8 Jul 1983.

37. *Business in Swaziland*, Mbabane, Mar 1983 and Dec 1984.

38. See ownership list in Statistical Annex.

39. *Times of Swaziland*, Mbabane, 1 Jun 1983.

40. Of professional and managerial technical workers, 48% in the private sector and 12% in the public sector are non-Swazi; of the non-Swazis, 35% are British and 25% South African. Of administrative and managerial personnel, 43% in the private sector and 7% in the public sector are non-Swazi; of the non-Swazis, 43% are British and 32% South African. As there are relatively few South Africans in the public sector (except the railways), this means South Africans dominate the private sector.

41. *Times of Swaziland*, Mbabane, 10 Dec 1981.

42. The National Industrial Development Corporation of Swaziland in its Investment Brief (undated but being distributed in 1981) points out that 'products made in Swaziland can enter South Africa' without duty. 'On the other hand, goods produced in Swaziland are fully acceptable in other African countries which might not be willing to admit imports from other parts of this region' — clearly 'other parts' means South Africa. Finally, 'EEC, USA, and Canadian markets are also open to goods made in Swaziland, with preferential tariff concessions.'

43. Tinned pineapples and pinewood furniture enter the EEC duty free, whereas the same products from South Africa would pay a 20% tax on entry. Swaziland has guaranteed

access to the EEC for 120,000 tonnes of sugar and 3363 tonnes of beef where they are sold at roughly double the normal world price (*Courier*, EEC — Brussels, Sept-Oct 1984). Swaziland also has privileged access to the US for roughly 40,000 tonnes of sugar (the actual amount varies each year).

44. *Business in Swaziland*, Mbabane, Mar 1984; interview by Joseph Hanlon with the South African trade mission head, Sam Sterban, 29 Jan 1985.

45. *African Business*, London, Jul 1982.

46. *Swazi Observer*, Matsapa, 14 Dec 1984. Copperland opened in 1978 with 40 workers and in 1982 cut back to 20 (who still operate) when it opened a new plant in Ciskei. Swaziland Knitting (25 workers) moved to a bantustan in 1983. Swazi Scene, an Edesa owned clothing maker, closed in 1984 putting 160 out of work because it could not compete with subsidised prices of bantustan firms, and because a new South African imposed import duty raised the price of woollen materials. The Solara TV factory was taken over by a South African competitor, who ended TV production and moved non-TV production to a bantustan in 1984. At its peak, Solara employed 550 workers (see Chapter 9).

47. The following year, however, Kirsh did decide to go ahead with a smaller CDC/ADB funded cotton spinning mill in Swaziland, which will provide 400 jobs (*Business in Swaziland*, Mbabane, Mar 1983 and Dec 1984).

48. *Africa Confidential*, London, 7 May 1980.

49. *Africa Economic Digest*, London, 10 Apr 1981.

50. *Times of Swaziland*, Mbabane, 10 Aug 1983 and 22 Apr 1985.

51. *Economic Review 1978-81*, Prime Minister's Office, Mbabane, Feb 1982.

52. Swazi government sources interviewed by Joseph Hanlon, Apr 1982.

53. *Africa Economic Digest*, London, 13 Nov 1981.

54. *African Business*, London, Jan 1982.

55. This was much longer than necessary on health grounds — if, indeed, there ever was a public health justification.

56. *Economic Review 1978-81*. Prime Minister's Office, Mbabane, Feb 1982.

57. Millard W. Arnold, *CSIS Africa Notes* No. 30, Washington DC, 13 Jul 1984.

58. Reportedly with the aid of the South African police, which is not surprising — South Africa is happy to make a former opponent beholden.

59. One of the four Swazi firms named later by the ombudsman as being involved in the scandal is Liberty Investments (*Times of Swaziland*, 28 Feb 1985). One of the shareholders of Liberty is Prince Mfanasibili (*Rand Daily Mail*, Johannesburg, 16 Jun 1984, and *Swaziland Register of Companies*).

60. The internecine battles are much too complex to record here, but are well chronicled in the annual *Africa Contemporary Record* from 1983. Also *Drum*, Johannesburg, May 1984.

61. *Star*, Johannesburg, 18 Jun 1984.

62. Once South Africa had gained its security agreement, it lost interest in the land deal, and was probably looking for an excuse to cancel it. But just a month before a top level Swazi delegation had been in South Africa for further talks on the land deal, and it is significant that South Africa did not formally jettison the deal until after its two allies were sacked. (*Guardian*, London, 11 and 20 Jun 1984).

63. *Swazi Observer*, Matsapa, 28 Feb 1985. Foreign Minister Mhambi Mnisi on Mbabane Radio home service, 18 Oct 1984.

64. Interview with Joseph Hanlon, 29 Jan 1985.

65. For example, in his radio interview 18 Oct 1984, Mnisi stressed that Swaziland cannot afford economic sanctions against South Africa, and Swaziland's rapprochement with Mrs Thatcher over the sanctions issue at the 1985 Commonwealth Heads of Government meeting was widely reported in Britain. Nevertheless Swaziland did support SADCC's calls for sanctions at its annual conference in January 1986.

66. *Star Weekly*, Johannesburg, 4 Mar 1985.

REFERENCES FOR CHAPTER 11

1. It is the only country in the world entirely above 1,400 metres (4,600 ft) in altitude, although other countries have higher mountains.
2. The people of Lesotho are called 'Basotho' (singular 'Mosotho').
3. G.M.E. Leistner, 'Lesotho and South Africa', *Africa Institute of South Africa Bulletin*, Vol 23 No 16, Pretoria, 20 Sept 1983. Information Minister Desmond Sixishe confirmed this in a February 1985 interview with this author, adding, 'We could not have won in 1965 on an anti-South African programme — we had no infrastructure and no friends.'
4. Jonathan had the personal humiliation of being defeated in his own constituency, and had to win a by-election three months later before he could become Prime Minister.
5. G.M.E. Leistner, 'South Africa's Development Aid to African States', *Africa Institute Occasional Papers* No 28, Pretoria, 1970.
6. Particularly G.M.E. Leistner, director of the Africa Institute. In addition, the brutal behaviour of the police Stock Theft Unit, set up with South African assistance, lost the BNP support in the key mountain constituencies. For a Lesotho (but not BCP) account, see B.M. Khaketla, *Lesotho 1970*, Hurst, London 1971.
7. In 1984, in briefings to the press, South Africa finally admitted its role in the 1970 coup. (*Observer*, London, 8 April 1984; *Times*, London, 23 April 1984; *Africa Contemporary Record* 1983-84, Holmes & Meier, New York).
8. D. Hirschmann, 'Southern African Voting Patterns in the United Nations General Assembly, 1971 and 1972', *SA Institute of International Affairs*, Johannesburg, Aug 1973.
9. Interview, Feb 1985. (All other Sixishe reference in this chapter also come from here.) Particulars of some of Roach's earlier activities are given in Khaketla, op.cit.
10. Some LLA men had been trained in Libya under the umbrella of the PAC, apparently without the knowledge of the Libyan government. In December 1979 Mokhehle said he had broken with the PAC because of PAC attempts to 'press gang' his men into their guerrilla forces.
11. Two economic issues were also discussed. It was agreed that talks would resume on the Highland Water Scheme to supply water to South Africa; the talks had been suspended by Lesotho after the 1976 Soweto uprising. And it was agreed that South African farmers would plough 20,000 ha of Lesotho's best farmland, just over the South African border — a project which was later abandoned.
12. *Star*, Johannesburg, 23 Nov 1982.
13. Including Edgar Motuba, editor of the Protestant church paper, *Leselinyana la Lesotho*, and Odilon Seheri, formerly private secretary of the king.
14. Splits also occurred over South Africa links and BCP support for UNITA. *Vanguard*, Roma (Lesotho), Dec 1980.
15. Relations with the Pan Africanist Congress (PAC) remain tense, however, because of its historic links with the BCP.
16. Patrick Laurence (of the *Rand Daily Mail*), *Guardian*, London, 2 Oct 1981.
17. *Star*, Johannesburg, 4 Dec 1981; Prime Minister Jonathan's statement to Parliament 11 April 1983 (published as *Destabilisation*, Prime Minister's Press Office, Maseru, 1983).
18. *The Courier*, EEC, Brussels, Jul-Aug 1984; *Africa Econ. Digest*, London, 5 Oct 1984.
19. Extensively covered in the press, for example *New African*, London, Sept 1983. Evaristus Sekhonyana (foreign minister at the time) argued to me that the South African foreign ministry did not have control over the border closures, and that in one case he had negotiated a reopening with Pik Botha, but that Botha was unable to get the gates opened for two weeks.
20. Interview, Feb 1985 (as are all other quotes from Sekhonyana, unless indicated).
21. For example, an SABC News Commentary (7 Jul 1983) said that 'governments alive to the implications will no doubt react appropriately.' Two weeks later (20 July 1983), another SABC commentary warned that Lesotho and Zimbabwe were becoming bases of 'Soviet imperialism'.

22. G.M.E. Leistner, *Africa Institute of South Africa Bulletin*, Vol 23 No 16, 20 Sept 1983.

23. *Rand Daily Mail*, Johannesburg, 10 Feb 1984; *Star*, Johannesburg, 23 Feb 1984; *Observer*, London, 8 Apr 1984.

24. *Sunday Tribune*, Durban, 1 Apr 1984. An election was scheduled in September 1985. It was boycotted by opposition parties, however, and no voting took place.

25. From at least 1980, the BCP had been allowed to recruit in the mines — just as the BNP had been 15 years before.

26. Statement in the UN Security Council, 16 Dec 1982.

27. 11 Apr 1983.

28. *International Herald Tribune*, Paris, 2 Feb 1983; *New African*, London, Feb 1983.

29. The opposition parties always stress their anti-communism and their view that the Jonathan government was 'completely communist-inspired and run' (Statement by the Leaders of the Lesotho Opposition Parties, Maseru, 6 Nov 1985.)

30. Each candidate had to pay a deposit of M1,000 — a large sum — and bring 500 supporters (not signatures, but actual people) to the constituency centre on nomination day. Voting lists were not made available so it was impossible for the opposition to know if its supporters were registered. In any case, opposition supporters were reluctant to show themselves because of intimidation by armed BNP youth, and because jobs and food aid increasingly depended on membership of the BNP. (See, for example, *The Comet*, Maseru, 15 Feb 86, which had a headline: 'Party membership cards no longer the key to better things'.)

31. Intimidation at the National University of Lesotho became so serious that students staged a three week strike in October 1985 to demand that the Youth League be expelled from the campus. Some armed BNP students had been suspended and ordered to leave the campus, but with BNP Youth League approval they simply refused. The Youth League also retaliated by issuing and attempting to implement 'deportation orders' on some South African student leaders of the strike.

32. In an interview with the South African Press Association (14 Jan 1986) Pik Botha said he had provided proof during his visit that ANC 'terrorists' were trained in Lesotho: 'I even gave him room numbers where South Africans have been receiving crash training over weekends.' He also objected to programmes about the liberation movements on Radio Lesotho (*Lesotho Elections and the South African Connection*, Press Office of the Prime Minister, Sept 1985.)

33. While flying over South Africa, the Zambian Airways plane was apparently intercepted by air force jets and ordered to circle until further instructions were given. None were, presumably with the intention that as the plane ran out of fuel it would be forced to land inside South Africa; instead, the pilot eventually returned to Lesotho. The incident was never explained, and the 150 were flown out on four Air Lesotho flights, the last leaving shortly before the 20 December raid.

34. The raid was set up by an agent who served as an ANC driver. The six ANC members were at his house for a meeting, and he invited them to stay on for a party, inviting three Basotho women as cover. The agent left the party, supposedly to search for petrol, and never returned. The gunmen arrived, killing four ANC people and three Basotho; the other two (an ANC man and his schoolteacher wife) had already left, but they were tracked down to their house and murdered.

35. *The Kairos Document: Challenge to the Church* (published in Britain by CIIR and the British Council of Churches) is a trenchant statement by 150 South African theologians first published in September 1985. Among other things, it says that revolution in South Africa is inevitable, and describes the god of the South African state as the antichrist.

36. *Guardian* (London) 13 Jan 1986; Radio Maseru 15 Jan 1986; and many other reports.

37. *Guardian* (London) 21 Jan 1986.

38. *Times*, London, 21 Jan 1986; BBC Africa Service, 25 Jan 1986, 0515 GMT.

39. Including some PAC and some ANC members no longer in Lesotho, as well as some of those killed on 20 December.

40. Some reports suggest that the plot was launched by colonels and Maj-Gen Lekhanya was only brought in later.

41. The North Koreans training the Youth League were expelled soon after the coup, but the North Korean mission remains.

42. Interview with Planning Minister Dr Michael Sefali in Harare, 30 Jan 1986.

43. One mark of South African displeasure is that Ntsu Mokhehle rejected the new government and its amnesty offer and said the LLA would fight on. In a statement dated 23 Jan 1986 he said many people considered the King 'a worse character than Leabua Jonathan'.

44. Interviewed by Joseph Hanlon, 20 Feb 1986.

45. C.D. Mofeli argued that if Lesotho can have a Soviet embassy, there was no reason not to have a South African one.

46. Mofeli even added, 'We are not convinced that South Africa is destabilising Lesotho; we have no evidence that South Africa is destabilising. We have no evidence that South Africa helps the LLA.'

47. Colin Murray, *Families Divided*, Cambridge 1981; Paul Spray, *A Tentative Economic History of Lesotho*, mimeo, IDS, University of Sussex, 1976.

48. The average wage of gold miners in South Africa rose from R221 in 1971 to R1,103 in 1976, which was equivalent to R667 in 1971 rands (James Cobbe, 'The Changing Nature of Dependence', paper at the (US) African Studies Association, 4 Nov 1982). Until then, wages had risen very little since the early part of the century (Ruth First, *Black Gold*, Harvester, Brighton (UK), 1983).

49. B. Decaux, *The Industrial Sector in Lesotho*, World Bank, Washington, Mar 1980.

50. Paul Wellings, *Development by invitation?* University of Natal.

51. *Newsletter*, Lesotho National Development Corporation, Maseru, 2nd Quarter 1984.

52. Bernard Dixon, *The Industrial Sector in Lesotho*, World Bank, Washington, 7 May 1980.

53. *Dry Ports Report — Lesotho*, United Nations Conference on Trade and Development, New York, 1 Feb 1984.

54. Often there is LNDC participation. In a few cases LNDC owns 100%.

55. Interview, Feb 1985. There are exceptions, including a Hong Kong clothing company, an Italian shoe firm, and two European firms which moved to Lesotho from Zimbabwe after independence there. The Italian shoe company wants to sell to South Africa without producing there, Monyake said, and the Hong Kong clothing company is taking advantage of Lesotho's unfilled clothing quota in the US.

56. LNDC owns a majority (51%); other partners are South African Breweries (39%) and Commonwealth Development Corporation (10%).

57. James Cobbe, op.cit.

58. Interview, Feb 1985.

59. D.A. Etheredge, talk at St Gallen, Switzerland, 18 May 1981, published as *Occasional Paper* 3 by the Southern African Forum, June 1981. A parallel but much smaller involvement was the De Beers woodlot project in Lesotho, designed as a pilot soil conservation and fuel wood effort.

60. *Financial Mail*, Johannesburg, 29 Mar 1985.

61. Botswana is the highest. Aid to Lesotho averaged $96m per year in 1980-83, about $70 per person per year, according to the EEC.

62. James Cobbe, op.cit.

63. Sam Montsi, interview Feb 1985.

64. One government minister I interviewed went much further, claiming that the US knew in advance about the 9 December 1982 raid, and pulled its embassy staff out of the city that night. He also alleged that the US had been helping to whip up anti-government feeling and support for opposition parties. Both the USA and UK objected when Lesotho allowed the opening of eastern bloc embassies in Maseru, he noted, and Britain actually dropped its proposed £2m support for a road project.

65. *The Comet*, Maseru, 15 Feb 1986.

REFERENCES FOR CHAPTER 12

1. The author was a correspondent in Mozambique 1979-84, and is the author of *Mozambique: The Revolution Under Fire* (Zed, London 1984) which goes into many of these issues in much more depth. Most otherwise unreferenced material comes from that book; statistics come from the updated 1985 edition. Mozambique published few statistics, but when it had to reschedule debts its creditors demanded more data. Thus two limited circulation documents provide more details: *Economic Report*, National Planning Commission, Maputo, Jan 1984 (hereafter Economic Report) and *Complemento à Informação Económica*. National Planning Commission, Maputo, May 1984 (hereafter *Complemento*).
2. Initially Malawi was reached by a ferry across the Zambezi River, but a 3800-metre long bridge was built in 1935. A line from Lourenco Marques reached the Swazi border early in the century, but was only extended into and across Swaziland in 1964 by Anglo-American to serve its iron mine.
3. The United Nations estimated that imposing sanctions cost Mozambique between US$450m and US$550m (*Economic & Social Council report* E/5812, 30 April 1976).
4. Ruth First, *Black Gold*, Harvester, Brighton (UK), 1983.
5. The numbers actually rose in 1975, as Mozambicans temporarily replaced Malawian miners held back by President Banda, but then they were cut back sharply in 1976.
6. Rennies and Manica Freight Services, now merged into Renfreight.
7. A unique 1400-km direct current power line links the dam to South Africa. The dam was built by a consortium headed by an Anglo company, LTA. (Duncan Innes, *Anglo American and the rise of modern South Africa*, Raven, 1984). Under the contract, South Africa received 1470 MW (megawatts) and Mozambique 150 MW (some of which would be supplied to Maputo via the Escom grid). Escom was to pay R3 per MWh, dropping to R1.75 after 15 years. Faced with the massive losses on the dam by the Portuguese government, the accord was renegotiated and in 1979 Escom agreed to pay R5 in rand — still some of the cheapest power in the world (*Complemento*).
8. In 1984 Sweden actually had to issue a specific instruction that its aid money could not be spent in South Africa. Other aid agencies are not so careful; Unicef ordered US$350,000 worth of pipe from South Africa in 1984, despite protests from its own staff in Maputo that it was cheaper to buy that type of pipe in Europe. Nor was there any policy against selling to South Africa; despite the oil embargo the Maputo refinery sold heavy fuel oil to South Africa until 1981.
9. South Africa had always paid Portugal part of miners' wages in gold, but when the free market price diverged from the official price, South Africa continued to use the official price. This was probably intended as a subsidy to Portugal to help pay for the war against Frelimo, and only became significant in 1972 when the free market gold price began to rise substantially. By independence in 1975 gold was over $150 per ounce compared to the official price of $42.22, but the price fell slowly to a low the following year of $104. Then it began rising rapidly and was over $175 when the special arrangement with Mozambique ended. It was surprising that South Africa allowed the system to continue for so long. Independent Mozambique probably earned US$300m by selling this gold on the free market.
10. The Southern African Transport and Communications Commission (SATCC) is the only independently constituted subsection of SADCC.
11. During 1982 and 1983, Mozambican port and government officials vociferously denied that this was occurring. But data appeared in *Economic Report* and *Complemento*. Indeed, a curious aspect of compiling this whole book is how reluctant officials sometimes are to admit they are under South African pressure.
12. *Africa Economic Digest*, London, 28 Aug 1981.
13. Alves Gomes in *Tempo*, Maputo, 5 Sep 1982. The story has also been reported from South African sources, notably Eschel Rhoodie.
14. The one exception was the bombing of an ANC house in the border town of Namaacha

in February 1979; two people were killed.

15. *Observer*, London, 20 Feb 1983.

16. The railway bridge was repaired and reopened on 17 December but it was 16 July 1982 before a Bailey bridge was put up over the river for the road.

17. *AIM Information Bulletin*, Maputo, May 1985.

18. Now part of Renfreight, following Old Mutual's purchase of Safmarine.

19. For example, Gordon Winter, *Inside Boss*, Penguin, London, 1981, and Deon Geldenhuys, *The Diplomacy of Isolation*, Macmillan, Johannesburg, 1984.

20. According to captured MNR documents, the idea was actually suggested by the South Africans to demonstrate that the MNR was independent of them. It proved somewhat counterproductive, causing power shortages in South Africa in the cold winter of 1981. In any case, Frelimo saw little point in sending in troops to restore the power line, because Mozambique earned no money from the electricity (although with the line cut it did have to pay up to US$8m per year to import power for Maputo). Consequently the line has been down more than it was in use after 1981.

21. According to Constantino Reis, an Olympic runner who defected to the MNR and then back to Frelimo, Dlhakama had not wanted to attack the Malawi railway but had been forced to do so by the South Africans. (AIM [Mozambique Information Agency], Maputo, Dec 1984)

22. Radio Mozambique, quoted by AIM, 28 May 1985.

23. *Economic Report*.

24. These villages should not be confused with the 'communal villages' Frelimo set up to speed development, and which were usually voluntary and popular and thus became targets of MNR attacks.

25. *Financial Mail*, Johannesburg, 15 Feb and 10 May 1985.

26. *New Statesman*, London, 3 Feb 1984.

27. *African Business*, London, Sept 1984.

28. By mid-1985 Mozambique still had not reached agreement with the IMF to allow new credits. But several actions apparently linked to the appeals to the IMF and western creditors will increase dependence on South Africa. One was the decision to allow exporters to keep some of the foreign exchange; considering the lack of importing expertise of most firms, this will usually be spent through agents in South Africa. Another was the inclusion in the foreign investment code of a proposal for free trade zones, said to have been mainly aimed at attracting South African firms to manufacture goods in Mozambique for export to countries which ban South African goods.

29. The ANC was allowed to maintain a ten-member diplomatic mission (vetted by South Africa); also ANC members actually employed by the government remained. Others were allowed to stay if they accepted a non-political refugee status under the UNHCR; few did, as this implied giving up their positions as ANC militants, and more than 200 people, including women and children, left Mozambique.

30. Three serious proposals for South African investments were discussed which remain possibilities. They are: purchase by AECI (Anglo/ICI) of ammonia made from natural gas at Pande, development by Sun International (Old Mutual) of a tourist complex at Bilene, and development of irrigated farmland near the border by various Transvaal farmers. All three areas have a strong MNR presence, and Frelimo seems to have intentionally pointed would-be South African investors in that direction in the hope that if they had a vested interest they would encourage their government to stop supporting the MNR. Similar arguments were partly behind a push to attract US and British investment.

31. Joseph Hanlon, *SADCC*, Economist Intelligence Unit Special Report No. 182, London Jan 1984.

32. *Financial Mail*, 15 Nov 1985. In addition, the South African subsidiary of the German firm Krupp tried to organise a complex deal in which Swiss banks lent money to South Africa for use in Mozambique, but this fell through. (*Africa Economic Digest*, London, 15 & 29 Mar 1985)

33. The tariff was raised 50% to R7.5 per MWh, with a premium of R3.5 per MWh if

regular supply is maintained. Mozambique would, for the first time, get some money out of the dam — 28.57% of the premium, which could reach R10m per year (worth substantially less with the collapse of the rand). In addition Mozambique's share of power is increased from 150 to 200 MW. But this remains academic at the time of writing as the flow of power has never been restored for very long.

34. Statement issued by the SACBC at a conference in Hammanskraal, South Africa, 28 Sept 1984.

35. Foreign Minister Joaquim Chissano, speaking at a briefing in London 25 Jul 1985. He added that 'if we do not restore life in these areas, then the bandits can still recruit' — an important admission from a high Frelimo official that the MNR does sometimes 'recruit' and does not simply kidnap all its new members.

36. *Casa Banana* is Portuguese for 'Banana House'. It was recaptured by the MNR in February 1986.

37. *Documentos da Gorongosa*, Ministry of Information, Maputo, 1985.

38. *Africa Contemporary Record* 1983-84, Africana, London.

39. But its voice has not been totally stilled. A senior defence force officer told the Federated Chambers of Commerce that despite Nkomati, the MNR had to be taken into account because 60% to 80% of the Mozambican people supported it and not Frelimo. (SABC Johannesburg home service in English 17 Oct 1984)

40. The closest the South Africans were able to come was agreement in April 1985 to set up a joint monitoring centre on the border near Komatipoort. (*Guardian*, London, 25 Apr 1985)

41. For example, *O Jornal*, Lisbon, 24 Feb 1984.

42. *Leadership SA*, 2nd Quarter 1984.

43. *South African Press Association* (in English), 25 Apr 1985.

44. Press conference in Maputo, 30 Sep 1985.

45. *Weekly Mail*, Johannesburg, 14 Jun 1985.

46. SAPA (South African Press Association), 18 Sep 1985; various newspapers, 20 Sep 1985.

47. Defence Minister Magnus Malan argued that Mozambique had given tacit approval to continued contact with the MNR if this could bring about peace talks (SAPA, 18 Sep 1985). And in briefings to journalists it was claimed that Mozambique had secretly authorised Nel's visits. Top Mozambican officials strongly deny this. Security Minister Sergio Vieira said Mozambique had not even known about the visits and would not have given permission for such a violation of Nkomati (press conference in Maputo, 30 Sep 1985). Foreign Minister Joaquim Chissano also denied the South African claim (press briefing in London, 27 Sep 1985).

48. *News Review*, Mozambique Information Office, London, 3 May 1985.

REFERENCES FOR CHAPTER 13

1. The best overall book on post-independence Angola is Michael Wolfers & Jane Bergerol, *Angola in the Front Line*, Zed, London, 1983. (Hereafter Wolfers/Bergerol)

2. A discussion as brief as this is necessarily very superficial. More details are available in Wolfers/Bergerol; John Stockwell, *In Search of Enemies*, W.W. Norton, New York, 1978 (hereafter Stockwell); and W.G. Clarence-Smith, Class Structure and Class Struggles in Angola in the 1970s, *Journal of Southern African Studies*, vol.7, 1980.

3. In a memorandum to the Portuguese general Luz Cunha dated 26 September 1972, Savimbi talked of the MPLA as 'the common enemy' and 'the main obstacle to peace'. He continued that 'we shall never make the mistake of taking up arms against the authorities' but instead will use them against the MPLA, in 'joint efforts' of UNITA and Portuguese military. (Aquino de Bragança, 'Savimbi: Estudo Sobre a Contra-revolução', *Estudos Mocambicanos* 2, Centro de Estudos Africanos, Universidade Eduardo Mondlane,

Maputo, 1981; *Afrique-Asie*, Paris, 3-21 Jul 1974.)

4. But there was a major CIA presence in the Zairian capital Kinshasa (the CIA had helped put Mobutu in power in 1965), and the FNLA received some CIA help from the early 1960s. This was stepped up substantially in 1973; at the same time the Zaire police began arresting Angolan refugees and taking them to FNLA training camps. At that stage, the CIA did not support UNITA because of its Chinese connections.

5. Stockwell.

6. This line was particularly pushed by Secretary of State Henry Kissinger, who overruled objections even within the US government. The US consul general in Luanda argued that the MPLA was best qualified to run Angola and that its leaders seriously wanted a peaceful relationship with the US. The Assistant Secretary of State for African Affairs argued that the US should support a diplomatic solution and that the US was backing the wrong side; he resigned in protest at the Kissinger policy. The two US multinational corporations most involved with Angola, Gulf Oil and Boeing Aircraft, backed the MPLA. Even the CIA's allies were not happy; in September 1975 Savimbi sent out feelers to the MPLA looking for a negotiated solution, but the CIA forced him to stop. And the CIA station chief in Luanda (the operation was being run from the larger CIA station in Kinshasa) went to Washington to argue that the MPLA was not hostile to the US and should be supported (Stockwell).

7. The MPLA had aimed its anti-aircraft guns down the road to Kifangondo. The first Cubans brought with them 'Stalin organs' (40-pod mobile 122mm rocket launchers), which were also aimed down the road. The MPLA waited until the column was in sight, then opened fire. Stockwell reported that the column 'broke and fled in panic, scattering across the valley in aimless flight, abandoning weapons, vehicles, and wounded comrades alike'.

8. P.W. Botha admits that as Defence Minister he sent a 26-man team to help the FNLA shell Luanda, and that it had to be rescued by the frigate President Steyn, according to his biography *PW*, by Dirk and Johanna de Villiers.

9. It had been designed, along with the Cahora Bassa project in Mozambique, to link South Africa more closely to the Portuguese colonies. South Africa had already invested R600m on this scheme, which involved a series of dams on the Cunene River. The two most significant are Ruacana, which is actually on the Namibia border and involves a dam and power station, and Calueque, about 65 km upstream and totally inside Angola. The latter dam is smaller and has a reservoir and pumping station intended to regulate the flow at Ruacana and to provide irrigation water to northern Namibia. The turbines in the Ruacana Dam are on the Namibian side of the border, but the sluice gates are on the Angola side. (*Windhoek Observer*, 18 Apr 1985). Without control of the sluice gates in the Ruacana dam itself, and at Calueque, the turbines can only run on a seasonal basis. In 1979 a South African helicopter pilot, Jacques Migotte, flew to Calueque to close the gates. (*Windhoek Advertiser*, 10 Feb 1982). From then until the South African withdrawal in April 1985, power was generated with amounts varying on a seasonal basis. With the opening of a new power line to South Africa, Ruacana allowed Namibia in 1982 to become a net exporter of electricity to South Africa. This did not continue into 1983, however, because of the low level of the Cunene River caused by the regional drought. (*Windhoek Observer*, 13 Aug 1983).

10. Clark was defeated in the 1978 election. South Africa was behind the defeat, according to Eschel Rhoodie who helped organise South Africa's secret information war. Rhoodie claims that the South African Information Department provided $250,000 to aid the campaign of Clark's right-wing opponent; other sources report that South African funds were used to support a mass door-to-door distribution of right-wing pamphlets by anti-abortionists opposed to Clark. (Richard Leonard, *South Africa at War*, Lawrence Hill, Westport, Conn USA, 1983).

11. *White Paper on Acts of Aggression by the Racist South African Regime against The People's Republic of Angola*, published by the Angolan government in 1983 and reprinted by the UN Security Council, 7 Dec 1983.

12. *Africa*, London, Sept 1980.

13. There were also two major raids on Namibian refugees, a paratroop assault on the Kassinga refugee camp in which 612 Namibian refugees were killed, and a bombing raid on a refugee school at Boma in which 198 people were killed.

14. In the north activity continued at first, and there were continued forays into Angola. But in 1977 and 1978 Zairian exiles in Angola and Zambia launched two unsuccessful uprisings in Zaire's southern Shaba province. Mobutu realised the need to control the border with Angola, which led to a temporary agreement between Zaire and Angola, and thus calm in the north as well.

15. For example, *West Africa*, London, 18 Aug 1980.

16. *Transport and Communications*, report for the SADCC conference in Blantyre, 19 Nov 1981.

17. Raids were detailed in the press at the time, and are chronicled in *Africa Contemporary Record*. An official record is given in the Angolan *White Paper* (up to mid-1982), *Angola Information Bulletin* (1982-84), and *Angop Newsbulletin* (1985).

18. In his 1982 New Year message.

19. *New African*, London, Nov 1981.

20. *Times*, London, 15 Mar 1982.

21. *Rand Daily Mail*, Johannesburg, 22 Jan 1983; *Star*, Johannesburg, 22 Nov 1984.

22. *Times*, London, 6 Jan 1984.

23. It is impossible to know the actual numbers involved; many people have been resettled and are no longer internal refugees, while others are in inaccessible areas. United Nations agencies and non-government organisations tend to use the round figures of 600,000 internal refugees and 100,000 foreign refugees (South African and Namibian) in Angola.

24. SABC Johannesburg home service, 15 Apr 1985; *Times*, London, 18 Apr 1985.

25. *Star*, Johannesburg, 1 Sept 1981.

26. *New African*, London, Jan 1982.

27. *Guardian*, London, 29 Jan & 2 Feb 1981.

28. *Africa Confidential*, London, 14 Apr & 25 Aug 1982; *Economist Development Report*, London, Jul 1984. UNITA has a more secure rear base at Jamba on the Namibia border, which is where most journalists are taken to meet Savimbi.

29. *Times*, London, 5 Sept 1983.

30. Press Conference 24 Aug 1983, text in *Angola Information Bulletin*, London, 23 Sept 1983.

31. For example Savimbi's biographer, Fred Bridgland, and a BBC Panorama journalist in February 1983 — *Star*, Johannesburg, 18 & 19 Mar 1983.

32. *Daily Telegraph*, London, 25 Jun 1985.

33. *Angop Newsbulletin*, London, 13 Jun 1985. Malanje is 800km from Namibia, so the planes may have flown from an intermediate base in Moxico province or even in Zaire.

34. *Financial Times*, London, 19 Sept 1984; *Times*, London, 20 Sept 1984; and *Guardian*, London, 24 Sept 1984.

35. *Weekly Mail*, Johannesburg, 11 Oct 1985.

36. *Guardian*, London, 21 Sept 1984 and *Times*, London, 23 Sept 1984.

37. Angop, London, Document No. 2, 14 Jun 1985.

38. Based at Longebaan on Saldanha Bay, 100km north of Cape Town.

39. The raid on the ships in Luanda harbour was attributed at the time to the 4th Reconnaissance Commando. (*Observer*, London, 5 Aug 1984.) At about the time of the Cabinda raid, two frogmen in the Reconnaissance Commando were given decorations for successful sabotage with limpet mines of 'waterside targets' in 1980 and 1981. This is assumed to be the Lobito oil tanks and Luanda oil refinery. (*SA Report*, Excomm (RSA), 7 Jun 1985).

40. Du Toit explained that the plan was to put two limpet mines on each tank, at roughly 1.5m above ground level. Although he did not make the point explicitly, this is exactly the same method used to destroy the fuel tanks in Beira, Mozambique, on 9 December 1982.

41. For example, by the Angolan ambassador to France in 1981 and the US magazine

Newsweek in October 1983. (*New African*, London, May 1981; *International Herald Tribune*, Paris, 8 Oct 1983.)

42. *International Herald Tribune*, Paris, 7 Jun 1985.

43. Though UNITA still claims Zambian support. *Africa Confidential*, London, 13 Feb 1985.

44. *Daily Telegraph*, London, 16 May 1984; *Africa Confidential*, 25 Aug 1982 & 13 Feb 1985; see also Chapter 8.

45. *Africa Confidential*, 4 Jan 1984.

46. *Observer*, London, 23 Jan 1983.

47. For example a 60 tonne consignment arrived in Zaire in May 1983, according to the *Times*, London, 5 Sept 1983.

48. *New African*, London, Feb & Oct 1982.

49. *Guardian*, London, 19 Oct 1984.

50. *Guardian*, London, 18 Oct 1984.

51. Angop, London, Document No. 4, 19 Jul 1985.

52. Interview with the *Washington Post*, 10 Oct 1984 — text published in *Angola Information Bulletin*, London, 31 Oct 1984.

53. The South African army admitted that in August 1985 an army medic, Lance Corporal Fidler, had been killed while serving with UNITA, and that he was part of a larger team. (*Guardian*, London, 18 Sept 1985).

54. *Africa*, London, Sept 1980.

55. *Guardian*, London 19 Oct 1984.

56. *Star*, Johannesburg, 18 Mar 1983; *African Business*, London, Aug 1983 & Jul 1984.

57. *Times*, London, 17 Sept 1984.

58. Gervase Clarence-Smith and Richard Moorsom, 'Underdevelopment and Class Formation in Ovamboland, 1844-1917', in Robin Palmer and Neil Parsons, ed., *The Roots of Rural Poverty in Central and Southern Africa*, Heinemann, London, 1977.

59. *African Business*, London, Feb 1983; see also Chapter 17 on a Frama plane shot down in Botswana.

60. *Sunday Tribune*, Durban, 15 & 22 Apr 1984.

61. The Angolan government has the remaining 10%, while Anglo retains a small interest in Tanganyika Concessions.

62. See, for example, G. Lanning & M. Mueller, *Africa Undermined*, Penguin, London, 1979.

63. *Financial Times*, 30 Dec 1985.

64. Bruxelles Lambert also owns 23% of the Angolan Eka brewery.

65. *International Herald Tribune*, 30 and 31 Jan 1986.

66. *Times*, 31 Jan 1986, *International Herald Tribune* 31 Jan 1986.

67. *New York Times*, 3 Dec 1985

68. *Financial Times*, 31 Jan 1986.

69. *Washington Post*, 1 Dec 1985.

REFERENCES FOR CHAPTER 14

1. Names have changed regularly, and some arbitrary choices have been made for the sake of simplicity. The name 'Zimbabwe' has been used for the post-independence period as well as anything (like geography) that is permanent; 'Rhodesia' is used for the colonial and UDI period through the end of 1979, covering times when the country was called 'Southern Rhodesia' and 'Zimbabwe-Rhodesia'. Current names and spellings are used for towns and cities, even if the change was recent. (The capital Harare was previously known as Salisbury.) We have called the two main parties simply ZANU and ZAPU, both before and after independence. Technically they are now 'ZANU-PF', as the name ZANU was registered by a splinter group, and 'PF(ZAPU)'. ZANU was the Zimbabwe African National Union and its guerrilla army was ZANLA; ZAPU was the Zimbabwe African

People's Union and its guerrilla army was ZIPRA; their joint structure was the Patriotic Front.

2. One white security man now working for the Zimbabwe government commented to us: 'We all did something to support the old government, and against ZANU. But the new government needs our professionalism.'

3. The two white CIO men were later acquitted of the spying charges on the grounds that their confessions had been obtained forcibly. One of the men admitted in court that during the period just before and during the election he had been part of the CIO 'dirty tricks desk' for action against ZANU and ZAPU and had taken part in rocket attacks and planting evidence. Security Minister Emmerson Munangagwa said later that 'immediately after their arrest, South Africa approached us through their trade mission in Harare and admitted the spies were their men.' Pretoria unsuccessfully tried to include them in a complex prisoner exchange in which they returned more than 100 Angolan soldiers and a Soviet citizen to Angola (*Times*, London, 12 Feb 1983).

4. South African reconnaissance aircraft had been detected over the air base six weeks before the raid.

5. Broadcasts of 14 and 18 Oct 1984.

6. In an interview soon after his capture he said he had been in Messina, just over the border from Beit Bridge, looking for work, when he was picked up. In court he said he was kidnapped in Zimbabwe and taken to South Africa. The former story seems more likely, as the South Africans are known to pick up illegal immigrants and try to integrate them into dissident groups.

7. *Chronicle*, Bulawayo, 15 Mar and 17 Oct 1984. There are a number of other such cases.

8. However, it is necessary to point out that some stories must be viewed with caution. For example, substantial publicity was given to the case of Spar Mapula and Watson Sibanda, who were presented to press conferences in September 1983. They told the press that they had murdered eight people, attacked an army base and had several battles with the security forces, having been sent back to Zimbabwe by the South Africans after military training. But when Mapula and Sibanda were brought to trial two months later they were charged only with undergoing military training and possessing arms. Ministry of Information, *A Chronicle of Dissidency in Zimbabwe* (Harare, Aug 1984); *Chronicle*, Bulawayo, 8 Oct and 8 Dec 1983.

9. No one disputed that arms had been hidden on Nitram farms, but Dabengwa and Masuku denied ordering weapons to be hidden as part of a plan to overthrow the government. The trial ran from 2 Feb to 27 April 1983. Of the seven men tried, only one was convicted. Nitram accountant Misheck Velapi was found guilty of helping to transport the arms, and given a three year sentence. Masuku became gravely ill and was released from prison in March 1986. Dabengwa remains in prison.

10. AFP, Harare, 9 Jun, 9 Aug and 11 Oct 1982.

11. The tourists were returning from a visit to Victoria Falls when they were captured 80 km from Bulawayo. The ransom note demanded the release of Dabengwa and Masuku and the return of ZAPU properties. The badly spelled note was written in block lettering on lined paper. It noted: 'Robert Mugabe diseted from ZAPU in 1963 & he is a true disident.' (sic) It also said, curiously: 'If these freedom fighters are not realesed, we blast these kids.' (sic) This has led to suspicions that the dissidents had written the note in advance, and had intended to capture a party of schoolchildren also returning from Victoria Falls and only kidnapped the tourists by mistake.

12. *Moto*, Harare, Mar 1983.

13. *A Chronicle of Dissidency in Zimbabwe*, Ministry of Information, Harare, Aug 1984; *Guardian*, London, 11 May 1984.

14. Weapons supplied to ZIPRA before independence and still in use by dissidents (perhaps after having been hidden) still display the manufacturer's identification marks and serial numbers. Some weapons discovered in various raids have the original numbers removed, sometimes with new numbers added; this means they are unlikely to be weapons from ZIPRA caches, but supplied from outside. South Africa is the obvious source. Some

RPK light machine guns found in the Hillary Vincent caches had numbers ANC 3011, ANC 3014, etc, while a dissident killed in a raid in March 1984 was using an RPK numbered ANC 3002 and thus assumed also to have been supplied by South Africa. Folding butt AK 47s in the Vincent caches had numbers including ZAN 2169, while identical guns found in a cache at Maitengwe in Zimbabwe in September 1983 were from the same series, with numbers ZAN 2149, ZAN 2154, and ZAN 2162.

15. At independence some ANC cadres came into assembly points in Zimbabwe with ZIPRA, particularly Gwaai River Mine. In July 1980 South Africa objected. In May 1981 the Police Minister, Louis Le Grange, was referring specifically to Gwaai when he warned that South Africa would hit ANC targets in Zimbabwe just as it had in Maputo on 30 January 1981. *Financial Times*, London, 5 Jul 1980; SABC English for Abroad, 9 May 1981; *Rand Daily Mail*, Johannesburg, 10 May 1981.

16. In fact Joshua Nkomo has been a member of parliament continuously since independence.

17. *Times*, London 1 Sep 1984.

18. 'Accomplices' were told in court that no charges would be brought against them if they gave acceptable evidence which incidentally incriminated them.

REFERENCES FOR CHAPTER 15

1. *Africa Economic Digest*, London, 11 Jul 1980.

2. This was procedurally correct, as the agreement allowed either side to terminate it after giving one year's notice.

3. R.C. Riddell, *Zimbabwe's manufactured exports and the ending of the trade agreement with South Africa*, CZI, Harare, Dec 1981.

4. Richard Hall & Hugh Peyman, *The Great Uhuru Railway*, Gollancz, London, 1976.

5. Depending on the commodity and the source or destination in Zimbabwe. Also see below for more detailed rates.

6. J.A.C. Girdlestone, *Trade and Investment in Zimbabwe — Vol 1 — Trade*, Whitsun Foundation, Harare, 1983. As a percentage of total imports and exports, excluding those to and through Zambia and excluding gold; by value for 1953 and by volume thereafter. Note that the Zimbabwe Energy Accounting Project gave much higher figures for use of Mozambique routes in 1981. All observers agree, however, that traffic through Mozambique rose to more than half the total in 1982, then fell below half in 1983.

7. *Sunday Express*, 13 Sept 1981.

8. This process was covered in detail in the press at the time; the London weekly *Africa Economic Digest* provided regular reports.

9. During the year to 30 June 1981, NRZ handled a record 13.1m tonnes of cargo (This includes operations in Botswana. *Quarterly Digest of Statistics*). The problem was that an estimated 15m tonnes were on offer, and the rest could not be transported.

10. South African Transport Services (SATS) was formed in April 1982 and includes SA Railways (SAR), SA Airways (SAA), harbours, pipelines, and road transport. It is the largest parastatal in South Africa.

11. Interview, Dec 1984.

12. *Citizen*, Johannesburg, 2 Sept 1981.

13. Six went to Zambia Railways and 10 to Botswana for use by NRZ there, which would be of more benefit to Zambia and Zaire whose transit traffic was also being disrupted by the South African actions. But soon SAR lent 10 to NRZ for use in Zimbabwe itself.

14. *Herald*, Harare, 2 Oct 1981; press reports in South Africa and Zimbabwe at the time put the cost as high as Z$7m per week.

15. In the end, most of the delayed exports were moved. The delay to sugar, however, proved expensive as sugar prices were falling rapidly during 1981 and 1982; probably the delayed sugar earned Z$10m less in 1982 than it would have if it had been exported promptly in 1981. There were other costs, too, particularly in agriculture, industry, and

transport due to the fuel shortages but these are impossible to quantify.

16.   For example, *Sunday Express*, Johannesburg, 22 Nov 1981, and *Citizen*, Johannesburg, 8 Jan 1982.

17.   *African Economic Digest*, London, 9 Oct 1981.

18.   Again for example the *Sunday Express*, Johannesburg, 13 Sept 1981.

19.   *Argus*, Cape Town, 25 Sept 1981.

20.   The MNR is described in much more detail in Chapter 12.

21.   The commandos probably came up the coast in a large boat, and then up the Pungue River in a smaller inflatable boat. Raids of this sort were carried out in Angola, where a member of the Reconnaissance Commandos was caught and described his exploits (See Chapter 13). The raid was also timed to hit trains carrying North Korean arms from Beira to Zimbabwe for the Korean trained Fifth Brigade; none of the trains was on the bridge at the time, but transport of some arms was delayed.

22.   Before UDI, Rhodesia built a refinery at Feruka, just over the border, and crude oil was sent up the pipeline. After being idle for 15 years, it was not worth the cost of rehabilitation, so diesel and petrol were pumped up the pipe. Other refined products, particularly aviation fuel, could not be pumped up the pipeline in that way. Following modifications, however, aviation fuel was also put through the pipeline, starting in 1985. The entire monthly fuel demand can be pumped in only 10 days, allowing ample time to repair MNR damage.

23.   *Financial Times*, London, 4 Aug 1982.

24.   The line in South Africa went to Beit Bridge but was not linked to the Rhodesia Railways system until October 1974. Rail tankers from Lourenço Marques (Maputo) were sent to Beit Bridge for unloading into a depot there from 1965 until 1974.

25.   *Star Weekly*, Johannesburg, 18 Dec 1982.

26.   Interview with Rex Chiwara, Dec 1984. Chiwara was NRZ Assistant General Manager for Operations at the time, and participated in the Johannesburg negotiations.

27.   The line was still closed at the end of 1985.

28.   Rates vary considerably according to distance, type of cargo, and the nature of the contract, but it is not unusual for the rail cost for goods to Durban to be double or triple the rate to Beira or Maputo. This can make the difference between profit and loss. For example, Zisco exports 80% of its steel production, at prices of only around Z$100 per tonne. (*Industrial Review*, CZI, Harare, Sept 1984.) So an extra $30 per tonne for rail freight hurts.

29.   Interview Dec 1984. This is not unreasonable; Zimbabwe imports and exports over 3m tonnes per year, which at Z$30 per tonne would be Z$90m extra.

30.   Chiwara interview.

31.   *Africa Economic Digest*, London, 14 Aug & 18 Sept 1981.

32.   Rennies was owned by the Hong Kong-based Jardine Matheson. In November 1981 the Zimbabwe government allowed the merger in Zimbabwe of Rennies and Grinaker, the latter owned by Anglovaal of South Africa, which strengthened the South African link. Then in 1984 Old Mutual of South Africa took over both Rennies and Safmarine. Both were political sales: Jardine Matheson was disinvesting, while the South African government was denationalising in an effort to curry favour with the business community. The two purchases gave Old Mutual a dominant position in the shipping and tourist industry, and it created a new company, Safren (Safmarine and Rennies Holdings). Within Safren is Renfreight, a merger of Rennies and Manica Freight Services to create a new regional freight forwarding agency. It will have 90% of the forwarding business in South Africa and is the only operator of container depots there. Thus it will totally dominate freight forwarding in Zimbabwe. Anglo retains 25% of Renfreight, but Safmarine will run the new company. The UK-based British and Commonwealth Shipping holds a minority 10% of Safren. (*Financial Mail*, Johannesburg, 10 Aug & 7 Sept 1984.)

33.   The East African conferences serve Nacala, the northernmost Mozambican port.

34.   And for Zimarine (Zimbabwe Marine), the Zimbabwe subsidiary of Safmarine.

35. Joseph Hanlon, SADCC: *Progress Projects & Prospects*, Economist Intelligence Unit, London, Jan 1984.
36. US$1500m was spent on SAECS containerisation, according to the *Financial Mail*, 27 Jul 1984.
37. *Africa Economic Digest*, London, 10 Apr 1981.
38. Reflecting local sensibilities, SAECS is sometimes called the Souther*n* Africa Europe Container Service in Zimbabwean publicity (for example by Zimarine) but the more normal form is retained elsewhere.
39. The shipping agents make a great deal of the issue of speed, and stress that Durban is much faster than Maputo or Beira. This is true, but for most products it is not very important. What is needed is predictability, reliability, and lower cost.
40. The two were convicted of the lesser offences of knowing in advance about the raid, and Hamilton of possessing weapons and of 'acts amounting to terrorism'. Fox and Hamilton are now serving sentences of 8 and 20 years, respectively. The week before the oil tank raid, employees of Manica were warned to fill their cars with petrol because a shortage was imminent. This tipped off the Mozambican authorities. The lesser charge was used because the government was unwilling to present evidence that would have brought convictions of Portuguese and British nationals of capital offences at a time it was trying to improve relations with both countries. There was strong evidence of Hamilton's role in the tanks raid; evidence of his role in the bridge attack is only circumstantial, but the author spoke with him shortly after that raid and found him surprisingly knowledgeable of the structural details of the bridge and of the damage done. Hamilton had been working with shipping agencies in Beira since the beginning of sanctions, and it is widely suspected that he may have been a British security agent then.

REFERENCES FOR CHAPTER 16

1. There were a few exceptions, notably Lonrho in its early days. But even Lonrho now holds its mining interests through South Africa.
2. Ian Smith's Unilateral Declaration of Independence in 1965, followed by British sanctions in 1965 and 1966 and UN sanctions in 1967.
3. J.A.C. Girdlestone, *Trade and Investment in Zimbabwe* — Vol 1 (Trade), Whitsun Foundation, Harare, 1983.
4. Considering SITC sections 6-9, only one-third goes to South Africa; however eliminating unworked copper, nickel, and ferrochrome, as well as various simple shapes of steel (which are not 'manufactured goods' in the commonly understood sense), raises the share to three-quarters. If attention is restricted to SITC sections 8 and 9, South Africa's share of exports is over 80%.
5. Even TA is one-quarter South African, with Old Mutual holding 14.8% and RAL (Anglo) holding 10%. Note that not all big companies are listed on the stock exchange. Ranking depends on which criteria are used. In general, these eight appear on all top ten lists, especially in terms of sales and assets, but in varying orders.
6. The holdings are usually by several different nominee companies in the Anglo Group, particularly Security Nominees and RAL Nominees. But Anglo plays a dominant role in management, in contrast to Old Mutual (see below) or Electra Investments (an old UK firm) which both have substantial holdings in the economy, but almost entirely as financial investments rarely exceeding 15% of the total equity.
7. The producers of fertilisers in Zimbabwe are Zimphos (phosphate mining and production) and Sable (nitrogen). ZFC is a fertiliser and pesticide distributor, with 55% of the market. Anglo controls Zimphos and is influential in Sable and ZFC, in the following way: Anglo controls AECI in South Africa (with the participation of ICI UK) which controls Chemplex in Zimbabwe. Chemplex owns Zimphos and 50% of Fertiliser Holdings (28% Norsk Hydro of Norway and 22% TA). FH owns ZFC and holds 42% of Sable; TA also holds 42% directly and British Oxygen most of the balance. Norsk bought its share from Fisons (UK) in 1984. (*Herald*, Harare, 4 Oct 1984).

8. It does not control Blue Ribbon, which is 51% owned by TA (see below). The position of National Foods is unclear; *Africa Economic Digest* (29 Jul 1983, 27 Jan 1984) says Anglo controls National, while the Harare business weekly, the *Financial Gazette*, says it does not (30 Nov 1984). Barlow Rand (RSA) and Dalgety (UK) also have significant holdings in National, but less than Anglo.

9. Zisco is the only integrated steel works in black Africa, and before 1985 was held 57.8% by the government (49.7% directly and the rest through Lancashire Steel), Messina (RSA) 13.7%, Anglo (RSA) 12.7%, Stewart & Lloyds 8%, and Tanks (Société Générale de Belgique) 3.7%. (*Financial Gazette*, Harare, 9 Mar 1984). During 1985 the government financed a rehabilitation programme through a major share issue, most of which it acquired. Anglo's share was thus diluted to 2.45%.

10. The Malaysian state owned Guthrie group has 18.3% of Hunyani.

11. In 1983 it held 60.4% of all life insurance company assets in Zimbabwe, received 65.1% of revenue, and made 71.7% of disbursements. (Report of the Registrar of Insurance Societies for 1983, Ministry of Finance, Harare, Nov 1984.)

12. For example the financial manager I interviewed in 1981 is now in Cape Town.

13. As no equity transfer is involved, this is primarily a matter of restoring rights to Zimbabwean policyholders. However both the Old Mutual Investment Corporation and the Old Mutual Fire and General Insurance Company Ltd are wholly-owned subsidiaries of Old Mutual (South Africa), which will retain control of these two (smaller) institutions.

14. For example, it is the largest shareholder in TA Holdings, with 14.8%. Electra Investments of Britain is the main rival among institutional investors. Anglo, and probably Lonrho, have larger total investments (direct and indirect).

15. Bulawayo Holiday Inn (100%), Harare Holiday Inn (50%), and Montclair (50%). The Harare hotel opened in 1983; it is a joint venture with the government, which owns the other half, and there is a joint management agreement. Rennie-Grinaker used blocked funds for its share; Holiday Inns in the United States receives a franchise fee of 3% of room revenue. It was not intended to set up a joint venture with a South African company, and at the time of the agreement in 1981 Rennie-Grinaker was controlled by Jardine Mathieson of Hong Kong.

16. S. Cronje et al, *Lonrho: Portrait of a Multinational*, Penguin, London, 1976.

17. The exact position is confusing. *Africa Economic Digest* (London, 12 Oct 1984), reported that UDC was taken over by Edesa, which is Swiss registered, but connected to Rembrandt in South Africa, which seems confirmed by the name change. But in Zimbabwe the renamed Edesa Holdings lists all shares being held by UDT International (UK), with no mention of Edesa.

18. Anglo's relationship to the government can hardly be considered warm, although it may be improving. A good example is Wankie Colliery. Its then chairman, Sir Keith Acutt, greeted independence with a complaint about the 'unexpected national holidays' which cut production. Then Wankie resorted to what the press called unexpected 'confrontation tactics', including efforts to delay foreign loans, in an attempt to force the government to raise the price of coal in 1981 (*African Business*, London, Aug 1981).

19. Anglo Zimbabwe has 11.4% directly and another 11.6% through nominee companies. Union Minière (Société Générale de Belgique) which has close links with Anglo but has only 3% of the shares also appoints a director.

20. *Africa Economic Digest*, 10 Apr & 1 May 1981.

21. Indeed, despite SAB's apparent desire to get out of Zimbabwe, Delta continued to tighten its stranglehold on the lucrative retail trade. In 1984 it bought out Banet & Harris and Bon Marché, and kept the Springmaster Furniture shops while selling the production side. A further concentration of the retail trade in South African hands would not normally have been allowed, and the government would not have permitted SAB to simply buy Bon Marché. So SAB only bought the stock of Bon Marché and took over the leases on the shops, while allowing Bon Marché to continue as an independent shell company with no assets.

22. *Sunday Mail*, Harare, 28 Oct and 4 Nov 1984.

23. Another example is Delta chairman J.D. Carter citing the company's 'commitment to its thousands of employees to playing an ever-increasing role in the development and progress of Zimbabwe'. Noteworthy was his stress on commitment to employees, by implication rather than shareholders. *Financial Gazette*, Harare, 17 Apr 1985.

24. In 1983/4 profits were falling and Delta chairman John Carter painted a grim picture. Suddenly there was a turnaround, and profits to 31 March 1985 were Z$21m — triple those of the previous year, and well above the forecasts of even four months earlier; as a resu!t the share price increased tenfold between January and August 1985. *Africa Economic Digest*, London, 6 Jul 1984, 30 Nov 1984, 1 Jun 1985.

25. There have been rumours for some time that because of the size of Delta, a third party would also be involved — probably Lonrho.

26. It is, however, not necessarily sufficient to replace a South African company with a European one. We looked at L.H. Marthinusen (Zimbabwe), which is owned by GEC (UK). Previously it reported to L.H. Marthinusen (RSA), then to the parent GEC (RSA), which is connected to the Barlow Rand group. It now reports directly to GEC (UK), yet this seems not to have changed the informal day to day relations with LHM and GEC in South Africa. Indeed, it has a formal licensing agreement with LHM (RSA) for which it pays Z$10,000 per year. Nor has LHM (Zimbabwe) done anything to raise its regional profile, so that Mozambique and other SADCC states still buy from LHM (RSA).

27. The only other rival, Cape Gate, developed through rolling billets bought from Zisco; it joined Haggie in supporting the final coup.

28. *Star*, Johannesburg, 7 May 1984.

29. The Risco chairman at the time was Carey-Smith of Anglo.

30. One such was a Voest-Alpine contract for a US$45m slab caster for the Iscor Vanderbijl Park plant (*Metal Bulletin*, London, 21 Dec 1984). It is also pointed out that in general, South Africa is a much more important market for Austria, accounting for eight times as much in exports as Zimbabwe (*Africa Economic Digest*, 21 Sept 1984).

31. Compare the parallel situation in 1985, when Zisco's rise of 20% was immediately followed by permission for Lancashire to raise its rod prices by 47%.

32. It seemed particularly strange to many observers at the time that Kuhn was asking Lancashire to trust Haggie, when at that same time Haggie was asking for a new 25% duty on Zimbabwean steel that would have affected Zisco even more than Lancashire. (Zisco exports more than 80% of its production.)

33. *Industrial Review*, Harare, Jul 1984; *African Business*, London, Sept 1984.

34. *Financial Gazette*, Harare, 2 Aug 1985. Ironically, in view of Kuhn's role in Lancashire's downfall, Zisco's own exports to South Africa are equally affected.

35. Only the Wankie Colliery Company still uses the colonial spelling; the town and power station use the more accurate spelling of the local word, Hwange.

36. A special coal price agreement guarantees the owners of the mine a profit based on capital employed, so expanding the colliery was the only way to increase mining profit. Another important source of profit, however, comes from interest to banks, and Wankie's owners were closely associated with arranging finance. Société Générale arranged the biggest Euroloan (US$55m) for the power station, while Anglo's RAL Merchant Bank organised the Z$35m local financing for the colliery expansion. Standard and Barclays were also involved.

37. Construction actually started in 1975, and some civil works were completed, but the project was halted because sanctions prevented the import of key equipment. In January 1980, after the Lancaster House agreement but even before formal independence, the Electricity Supply Commission resumed work. In fact, the project has four components, of which three are under way or completed:

	Power	Cost	Construction	
	MW	Z$m	start	finish
Stage I	480	450	1980	1986
Stage II Phase 1	400	400	1983	?
Stage II Phase 2	400	400 (est)	not yet approved	
Wankie Colliery expansion		120	1980	1982
Estimated total cost		1370		

38. *Africa Economic Digest*, London, 22 Jan & 5 Nov 1982. It predicted that demand would increase by half between 1980 and 1985, which would have been an incredible rate of expansion even in the best of times; in fact, in 1983 consumption was identical to what it had been in 1980.

39. Abel Mkandawire, chairman of the Energy Council of Zambia, protested publicly (*Herald*, Harare, 20 Oct 1982) while Mozambican government officials and even some Zimbabwean officials made their views known privately.

40. Indeed, Anglo often put pressure on Zimbabwe during the talks over the partial nationalisation of the Wankie Colliery (at one point even leading the IFC to threaten withdrawal of a loan if the government did not come to heel). *African Business*, London, Aug 1981.

41. *Herald*, Harare, 15 Dec 1984.

42. *Sunday Mail*, Harare, 6 Jan 1985.

43. *Herald*, Harare, 23 Jan 1985.

44. *Financial Mail*, Johannesburg, 26 Oct 1984.

45. *Herald*, Harare, 29 Nov 1984.

46. Duncan Clarke, *Money and Finance in Zimbabwe*, Whitsun Foundation, Harare, Oct 1983.

47. Indeed, when the government took over a majority from Nedbank in 1981 it accepted the unusual condition of keeping the management and policies unaltered for two years. Ann Seidman, *A Development Strategy for Zimbabwe*, University of Zimbabwe Economics Department, 1982.

48. There seems no evidence of serious displeasure by a South African firm even when there has been nationalisation. The government has tended to pay above the odds, for example paying nearly four times the stock market valuation for Messina's controlling share of the MTD copper mine. (*Africa Economic Digest*, 28 Sept 1984.) So if there is discontent, it is that the government has refused some offers to sell.

49. In January 1985 the government registered a new Zimbabwe Milling Corporation, but it remained a shell company and nothing was done with it.

50. *Herald* Business Editor Linda Loxton billed the Abercal takeover as 'the first move by the private sector to cut links with South Africa and ensure local ownership'. (*Herald*, Harare, 6 Jun 1985) In fact it was not the first, and in any case was motivated more by commercial considerations; a high proportion of its exports (particularly castings and files and rasps made by Temper Tools) will still go to South Africa. Soon afterward Apex announced the takeover of Supersonic Radio, which was US-owned (ITT); Supersonic mainly exports to South Africa, increasing Apex's links south of the Limpopo.

51. It also has a clearing bank, which allows imports from member countries to be set against exports to them, subject to periodic settlement in hard currency. So long as trade remains regionally balanced, this has the effect of allowing imports partly in soft local currency. This has started out somewhat erratically, however.

52. Doris Jansen, *Zimbabwe Government Policy and the Manufacturing Sector*, Apr 1983.

53. Initially, the IMF appeared to encourage profligacy: during 1980 it indicated, first, that Zimbabwe was 'underborrowed' by Third World standards, and thus should take large loans for rehabilitation and development projects. Second, it advised that Zimbabwe should dismantle the exchange control system built by UDI Rhodesia and allow rapid

repatriation of profits in order to attract new foreign investment. Inevitably this created a virtual haemorrhage of foreign exchange; dividends poured out at the rate of at least Z$80m per year, but new investment totalled only Z$8m a year. As a result the impact of the South African squeeze was much worse, because Zimbabwe was dependent on those exports to pay for the foreign exchange leaving the country.
54. Taking into account that under EEC rules, bids from developing countries are allowed to be 15% higher.

REFERENCES FOR CHAPTER 17

1. Frequently mentioned by Botswana officials, for example the High Commissioner in London, S.A. Mpuchane, in a talk in London on 17 Jul 1985.
2. *Botswana Daily News*, Gaborone, 15 Jan 1981, 29 Apr 1981, 4 Aug 1981, and 4 Jan 1982.
3. *Botswana Daily News*, Gaborone, 14 Apr 1982, 7 Sept 1983, 7 Oct 1983; *Examiner*, Gaborone, 22 Apr 1983.
4. The proposal was formalised in 1982, and would involve a joint venture of BP and the government. Soda ash is heavily used in the manufacture of steel, paper, chrome, and detergents. The project would produce 200,000 tonnes per year of common salt (NaCl), 300,000 of soda ash (Na$_2$CO$_3$), and probably potash for SADCC fertilser project.
5. Interview with Vice President Peter Mmusi, 31 Jan 1985.
6. *Africa Economic Digest*, London, 21 Sept 1984.
7. Sales to South Africa dropped from 37% of the total in 1982 to 32% in 1983 (of roughly the same number of cattle in both years). *Africa Economic Digest*, 31 Aug 1984.
8. *Star*, Johannesburg, 20 Aug 1984; *Botswana Daily News*, 4 Sept 1984.
9. Many articles in the *Botswana Daily News*, *Sowetan*, and *Star*.
10. The people of Botswana are called 'Batswana' (singular 'Motswana') and the majority language is Setswana.
11. *Times*, London, 16 and 18 Dec 1982.
12. *New York Times*, 13 Apr 1982; *Botswana Daily News*, 22 Dec 1982.
13. *Botswana Daily News*, 2 Mar 1982. Despite Botswana government and OAU protests, Lengene was never returned; two men said to be 'South African Police agents' were sentenced to four years in jail.
14. *Botswana Daily News*, 28 Jul 1982 and 15 Jul 1983.
15. *Star*, Johannesburg, 28 Nov 1983.
16. *Star*, Johannesburg, 11 and 12 May 1984; *Financial Mail*, Johannesburg, 23 Mar 1984.
17. Talk given at the Africa Centre, London 17 Jul 1985.
18. In South Africa after the raid, the press was briefed by security policeman Major Craig Williamson (South African Press Association, 20 Jun 1985). Williamson was also involved in raids on the ANC in Swaziland (see Chapter 10) and was a former undercover agent within European anti-apartheid bodies.
19. *Guardian*, Gaborone, 21 June 1985.
20. *Daily News*, Gaborone, 19 Jun 1985; *Guardian*, Gaborone, 21 Jun 1985.
21. South African Press Association, 6 Jan 1986.
22. *Sunday Times*, Johannesburg, 25 Jan 1986.
23. *Africa Economic Digest*, London, 17 Dec 1982.
24. *Botswana Daily News*, 7 Sept 1984.
25. *Botswana Daily News*, 13 Nov 1984.
26. Botswana's economy is unusually well studied. Three books and three reports are important: Charles Harvey, *Papers on the Economy of Botswana*, Heinemann, London, 1981 (hereafter Harvey); M.A. Oommen et al, *Botswana's Economy Since Independence*, Tata McGraw Hill, New Delhi, 1983 (hereafter Oommen); Christopher Colclough and Stephen McCarthy, *The Political Economy of Botswana*, Oxford University Press, Oxford, 1980 (hereafter Colclough); E. Brian Egner and Isobel Appiah-Endresen, *The Potential for Resource-based Industrial Development — Botswana*,

UNIDO (IS.274), 31 Dec 1981 (hereafter Egner); Jan Isaksen, 'Macro-Economic Management', *Scandinavian Institute of Africa Studies Research Report* 59 (hereafter Isaksen); Bertil Oden, 'The Macro-Economic Position of Botswana', *Scandinavian Institute of African Studies Research Report* 60, Uppsala (hereafter Oden).

27. There are other costs to the government. It has foregone royalties, and as the Permanent Secretary in the Ministry of Mineral Resources has noted, government officials found themselves 'devoting huge amounts of time to preparations for negotiations, travel, and to briefings of officials. At times, the Ministry of Mineral Resources and Water Affairs was practically paralysed due to the absence of key people away on negotiations.' Another cost was that Botswana raised P55 million in aid loans for a power station, dam, town, roads and railway links (loans for the most part guaranteed by the private investors in the mine) — but they have had considerable value to the rest of the economy. S.R. Lewis, 'The Impact of the Shashe Project on Botswana's Economy', in Harvey; C.M. Tibone, in Oomen.

28. Pieces of the project have changed hands a number of times and split control was one of the problems. It is now owned 15% by the government, 25.5% by Anglo, and 25.5% by the US firm AMAX.

29. See for example, Government of Botswana, *National Development Plan 1979-85*, Gaborone, 1980, paras 8.26 and 8.49.

30. *Botswana Daily News*, 24 Jan 1984.

31. Egner. For beef generally, see M. Hubbard, *Agricultural Exports and Economic Growth: a Study of Botswana's Beef*, KPI, London, 1986, and P. R. Spray, *Botswana as a Beef Exporter*, National Institute of Development and Research, Gaborone, 1981.

32. S. Ettinger, 'South Africa's Weight Restrictions on Cattle Export from Botswana 1914-1941', *Botswana Notes and Records* 1972.

33. Bank of Botswana and Ministry of Commerce figures. Egner gives the ownership of registered industrial enterprises (that is, those with more than 10 employees), in 1980, as:

Foreign-owned	
South African	15
Other	40
Mixed Botswana/foreign	
With South Africa	9
With other	13
Wholly Botswana	11
TOTAL	88

Note that these include a portion of the manufacturing sector of the Selebi-Pikwe mining complex, and do not include wholesale/retail. Nevertheless, taking into account the relatively larger size of South African firms and the dominance of the abattoir in the locally owned firms, it is probably safe to assume that half of non-mining and non-cattle business is South African controlled.

34. *Financial Times*, 16 Nov 1983.

35. These problems are much discussed in the works cited in footnote 26. For the general problems of oil (or diamond) dependent states, see Dudley Seers, *The Life Cycle of a Petroleum Economy*, IDS (Sussex) Discussion Paper 139, 1978.

36. Several analysts concluded that in the later 1970s Botswana could have invested P100m of the surplus money in development and that this would have created over 33,000 jobs (Isaksen). See also Jones, in Harvey, calling for a 'laughably small' subsidy to arable farming. On the financial surplus, see *Annual Report 1982*, Bank of Botswana, Gaborone: reserves were over P300m, enough to finance seven months' worth of imports.

37. Egner

38. Egner. The banks had over P70m in surplus money, ie over the legally required liquidity.

39. Egner

40. See various papers by Charles Harvey, eg 'Botswana's Monetary Independence — Real or Imagined?', *IDS Bulletin*, 11, 4, Sussex 1980.

41. Interview with E.D. Bell, chief executive of Botswana Power Corporation (BPC), Mar 1984. It was not a total victory, however, because the World Bank negotiated a contract in which the electricity tariff for Selebi-Phikwe was based on an 8% return on the historic cost of the power station. This means that BPC is now being paid a rate well below that normal for electricity in southern Africa; the main beneficiary of this low rate is Anglo, while BPC earns nothing toward investment in future power developments.

42. Escom insisted on a 10-year contract, which means that BPC must pay a standing charge for five years after Morupule comes on stream.

43. In Morupule's case, those parts of the project funded by Arab funds excluded South African contractors, but other donors such as the World Bank expected open international tendering, including South Africa, for their sections.

44. Harvey, in Harvey, op cit.

45. Interviews with government officials, Mar 1984.

46. *Financial Mail*, 12 Apr 1985.

REFERENCES FOR CHAPTER 18

1. John Hooper, *The Politics of Patronage*, MA thesis submitted to the Centre for Southern African Studies, University of York, September 1984. This is an excellent discussion of how Banda uses the medieval court system to prevent anyone from becoming too powerful.

2. It is notable that virtually anyone billed as a 'successor' to Banda has retired from the political scene. For example, Dick Matenje became MCP secretary general and was billed as 'number two'. It was he who signed the initial SADCC agreement for Malawi in Lusaka on 1 April 1980. He was apparently killed in a highly suspicious car crash in May 1983, along with the popular minister of the Central Region and new Press chairman, Aaron Gadama. Speaking in the Central Region several months later, Banda noted that some people were saying they had been friends of Gadama. He had no friends, Banda said, and 'those who call themselves friends of Gadama and try to cause confusion among the people of the Central Region will hear from me'. (A third minister and a former minister were killed at the same time. There were no public funerals or other indication of public mourning, as might have been expected if they were really killed in a crash. It is widely believed they were assassinated, perhaps after an abortive coup while trying to escape to Mozambique. See for example *New Africa*, Jul 1983).

3. The last issue is typified by his announcement in August that he was naming Jorge Jardim as Malawi's Honorary Consul in Beira. Jardim was close to the Portuguese dictator Salazar, and this was more than the level of cooperation required by geographical necessity. Jardim established the Press oil distribution company (Oilcom) and became chairman of the Commercial Bank of Malawi; he helped to set up the Young Pioneers and worked with Malawi in his anti-Frelimo efforts both before and after Mozambican independence.

4. All three embassies share the same building in Lilongwe, which is thus sometimes dubbed 'Pariah House'.

5. G.M.E. Leistner, *South Africa's Development Aid for African States*, Africa Institute, Pretoria, 1970.

6. As recently as 1980, the *Daily Times* (Blantyre, 5 Dec 1980), in an editorial praising South Africa, said that South Africa had provided 'the financing of the new capital city', when in fact South Africa provided only about 10% of the total cost.

7. Only Lonrho has expanded significantly, largely reinvesting locally generated finance. Lonrho's Tiny Rowland has personal links with Banda, as with many African leaders, and he has been allowed to expand into areas including tobacco farming and vehicle and agricultural machinery distribution normally reserved for Press. Lonrho has also

participated in the expansion of sugar production and in a new ethanol plant; started at the time of rising world sugar prices and a larger US quota, the new plantation has proved totally unprofitable. Finally, Lonrho owns and has expanded David Whitehead, the main textile producer in Malawi, and produces Chibuku traditional beer.

8. Jonathan Kydd, personal communication and 'Malawi — An Alternative Pattern of Development', a paper presented at a conference at the Centre of African Studies, University of Edinburgh, 24-25 May 1985.

9. Until the merger of Rennie and Manica to form Renfreight, there were two agencies, Manica (which was the larger) and AMI-Rennie-Press (which was operated by Rennie). Following the Renfreight merger, the Belgian AMI is now independently represented.

10. Oil imports make this drop seem somewhat more precipitous than it was. Malawi imported all its oil from South Africa. When the revolution in Iran cut that supply to South Africa, Pretoria in turn cut back on Malawi, forcing it to import some petroleum products from the world market starting in 1980. Nevertheless, South Africa's share of non-oil imports also fell significantly.

11. There was one exception. The World Bank forced Malawi to close down the Capital City Development Corporation, which had remained a South African sinecure.

12. *Sunday Times*, Johannesburg, 13 Sep 1981.

13. *Daily Times*, Blantyre, 18 Feb 1983.

14. Three donors — the United States, Britain, and West Germany — objected vociferously to this criticism of South Africa during the closed discussion of the communiqué. After a lengthy objection by the United States, the head of the World Bank delegation ran from the other side of the room and was clearly heard to ask the US delegate what he should do. After that consultation, the World Bank also opposed the reference. The SADCC members, however, decided not to accept these objections on the grounds that the communique came from the chairman and not donors. (I was present at the conference as a journalist for the BBC and the *Guardian*.)

15. Data presented at a workshop in Lilongwe, 13 Feb 1984.

16. *Financial Times*, London, 16 Apr 1985.

17. It is perhaps notable that a substantial portion of recent South African aid to Malawi has been in SADCC areas — fisheries, for which Malawi has responsibility in SADCC, and transport and communications, which are the general SADCC priority.

18. *Financial Mail*, Johannesburg, 15 Oct 1982.

19. *Financial Mail*, Johannesburg, 15 Oct 1982.

20. This link is particularly ironic, because it was the refusal to build such a link that partly provoked the initial 'cabinet crisis'.

REFERENCES FOR CHAPTER 19

1. That white coach was in the news nine years later on the border between Mozambique and South Africa when it was used for the signing of the Nkomati Accord. (*Star*, Johannesburg, 13 Mar 1984)

2. The first meeting had been supported by Front Line and liberation movement leaders; Mozambique actually had a representative at it. The second meeting was generally opposed by Front Line leaders, and was publicly criticised by Nyerere and Mugabe. Botswana was not happy either, and allowed the meeting on its border so long as it was made clear that it was not 'hosting' the meeting. The reason was obvious from the headline in the (London) *Observer*: 'Botha has a PR windfall'. The meeting improved Botha's image and seemed to support the US policy of constructive engagement (*Times*, London, 30 Apr 1982; *Observer*, London, 2 May 1982).

3. *New African*, London, Feb 1983; *Africa Economic Digest*, London, 28 Sep 1984. In 1976 Mushala was nearly caught when security forces overran his camp, but he escaped. It seems likely that as one concession of the Victoria Falls Bridge meeting, South Africa turned in its own stooge. There is no indication as to whether or not South Africa

supported Mushala after 1976.

4. *Africa News*, Durham NC (US), 27 Apr 1981.

5. There were accusations in Zambia that South Africa was involved in the unsuccessful 16 October 1980 coup attempt, but no evidence has ever emerged to support this.

6. A railway to Tanzania was included in Kaunda's UNIP party manifesto in 1962.

7. To save too many name changes in a few paragraphs: 'Zambia' also refers to northern Rhodesia, both before and after independence; 'Tanzania' also refers to Tanganyika; 'Rhodesia' is used for the colonial period for what was called at various times 'Rhodesia', 'Southern Rhodesia', and 'Zimbabwe-Rhodesia, while 'Zimbabwe' is used for the post-independence period.

8. Richard Hall and Hugh Peyman, *The Great Uhuru Railway*, Victor Gollancz, London, 1976.

9. Paper presented at a UN sponsored conference in Blantyre, 3-6 May 1982, and published as UNCTAD/LDC/62, 1 Dec 1983.

10. *CZI Industrial Review*, Harare, Aug 1984.

11. Deon Geldenhuys, *The Diplomacy of Isolation*, Macmillan, Johannesburg, 1984.

12. *New African*, London, Jun and Aug 1979.

13. *Financial Times*, London, 2 Mar 1980; *Africa Economic Digest*, London, 1 May 1981 & 29 Oct 1982.

14. In 1984 the US firm AMAX sold its share to Andrew Sardanis, the Greek-born millionaire who was chief government negotiator with the mining companies in 1969 and then was the first chairman of the new state holding company, Mindeco (Mining Development Company). Thus ZCCM is now owned by government (60.3%), Anglo (27.3%), Sardanis (6.9%), and US and UK private shareholders (5.8%). (*African Business*, London, Sept 1984).

Anglo came out of the nationalisations very well, because it gained a massive profit while keeping effective control of the mines. Indeed, it probably gained more from the nationalisation than it would have if it had continued to own the mines. Full compensation for the 1969 nationalisation and 1973 contract termination was paid in US dollars without any restriction placed on repatriation. With this money Anglo established Minorco in the tax-haven of Bermuda. Minorco invested heavily in North and South America, and on its base of Zambian money became a major foreign investor in the United States in the early 1980s. (Duncan Innes, *Anglo American and the rise of modern South Africa*, Raven, Johannesburg, 1984; Anthony Martin, *Minding Their Own Business*, Penguin, London, 1972).

15. For example, only one operating division had a Zambian head until ZCCM finally named a second one in 1985. (*Africa Economic Digest*, London, 12 Apr 1985).

16. Interviews in the copperbelt in 1984 by Taffere Tesfachaw of the Institute of Development Studies, University of Sussex, UK.

17. Although Anglo's main interests are in mining, it is also active in other sectors of the economy: National Milling (13%, Indeco 51%), Zambia Breweries (25%, Indeco 55%), Duncan Gilby & Matheson (25%, DG&M 33%, Indeco 42%), Chilanga Cement (12%, CDC 27%, Indeco 51%), and Ridgeway Hotel (30%). It has also reinvested some blocked profits in agriculture, including Zambia Sugar (4%, Tate & Lyle 11%, Indeco 51%). Indeco is the government's Industrial Development Corporation (From information complied by Gilbert Mudenda and Neva Seidman Makgetla of the University of Zambia).

18. Half of this was direct foreign exchange (generally known as forex in Zambia) costs of ZCCM and the other half was forex costs of ZCCM's suppliers and agents. Copper represents nearly all forex earnings, and Zambia spends 20% of its forex on fuel (some of which goes to the copper mines and is thus included in the 64%). Zambia is also supposed to allocate up to 40% of its forex just to pay debts. So fuel plus the mines plus debt repayments is supposed to be over 100%, without taking account of any other imports. Thus it is hardly surprising that falling copper prices have forced Zambia to turn to the IMF often and reschedule its debts.

19. Zambia's economic difficulties have been much studied. See, for example, *Basic*

Needs in an Economy Under Pressure, International Labour Office, Addis Adaba, 1981; *Africa Economic Digest*, Special Report on Zambia, May 1985; Ben Turok (ed), *Development in Zambia*, Zed, London 1979.

20. The IMF has strengthened South African links in another way as well. Under IMF pressure, companies which make new exports are allowed to keep half of their earnings outside the country, either to buy raw materials (or luxury goods, no doubt) or to pay off part of the 'pipeline' of not yet repatriated profits. This has given South African (particularly Anglo) companies even more freedom to buy (and resort to transfer pricing) without government control. And it has led firms to export local products such as beef and vegetables by air at a huge loss in order to earn forex; some transnationals are going into farming intending to export at a loss as a way of transferring money abroad. This will surely lead to an overall forex loss to Zambia, because of the high import content of fuel, fertiliser, and other inputs bought with local currency.

21 *Africa Economic Digest*, London, 15 Jun 1985.

22. *Daily Mail*, Lusaka, 29 Dec 1983.

23. Recommendations of the UNIP 3rd National Convention, Lusaka, 23-25 Jul 1984.

24. The existence of the elite may also be part of the reason why Zambia has followed this economic path.

25. 1974 Household Budget Survey showed that the top 5% of the population enjoyed 35% of the national income, the same as the bottom 80%. A 1983 survey (still unpublished) showed that the top 5% had 50% of the national income.

26. Various authors have written about this, notably Neva Seidman Makgetla at the University of Zambia (unfortunately largely in unpublished papers) and Marcia Burdette, (*Journal of Southern African Studies*, Apr 1984 — which provides a much deeper class analysis and also has a good set of further references).

REFERENCES FOR CHAPTER 20

1. A Swazi radio broadcast on 6 Feb 1986 said: 'Prince Bhekimpi (the Swazi Prime Minister) said the Kingdom of Swaziland has hailed the step taken by South Africa's State President, Mr P.W. Botha, towards reducing racial discrimination in South Africa. Prince Bhekimpi said Swaziland is happy that President Botha will form a council comprising all tribes in South Africa, and pass laws will be changed and all South African citizens will carry one identity pass with effect from July this year. He said President Botha should continue in his present state of reducing apartheid and amend where possible so that even complainants could be satisfied.'

2. *Times*, 18 Dec 1985.

REFERENCES FOR CHAPTER 21

1. The figure is based on an extrapolation from the SADCC calculation; see Appendix 1.

2. President Samora Machel reportedly gave a Bulgarian official a particularly harsh dressing-down when it was discovered that South Africa was buying arms from Bulgaria to give to the MNR. Hence also the significance of the 1986 US decision to supply UNITA with Stingray missiles.

3. *Economist*, London, 30 Mar 1985.

4. See for example, Catholic Institute for International Relations, *Comment: Sanctions against South Africa*, London 1985.

5. *Guardian*, London, 17 Aug 1985.

6. Reginald Green, *Economic Sanctions against South Africa*, paper prepared for the UNA/AAM seminar on the Front Line states, Sheffield, 29 Feb 1984.

REFERENCES FOR APPENDIX 2

1. G.M.E. Leistner, *Sanctions Against South Africa*, Africa Institute of South Africa Bulletin, Pretoria, 15 Apr 1985 (hereafter *Sanctions*).
2. *Sanctions*. To make the point even clearer, Leistner then footnotes an article in the *Economist* (London, 16 Mar 1983), specifically citing page 23 on which writer Simon Jenkins points out that it was South African commandos (and not the MNR) who blew up the oil depot in December 1982, and that when this had been done, Pretoria cut off Zimbabwe's other fuel sources as well.
3. Opening statement at the SADCC summit, Arusha, 9 Aug 1985.

Index